All Rivers
Run to the Sea

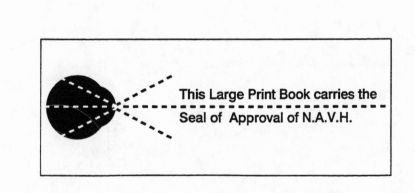

This Large Print Book carries the
Seal of Approval of N.A.V.H.

All Rivers Run to the Sea

Memoirs

ELIE WIESEL

Thorndike Press • Thorndike, Maine

Photo Credits: Page 4, top, Attar Photographers
                  Page 5, bottom, Eliahu Attar
                  Page 7, Photo Abramovitz
                  Page 8, Photographed by Yona Zaloscer

Thorndike Large Print ® Basic Series.

The tree indicium is a trademark of Thorndike Press.

The text of this Large Print edition is unabridged.
Other aspects of the book may vary from the original edition.

Set in 16 pt. News Plantin by Warren Doersam.

Printed in the United States on permanent paper.

Library of Congress Cataloging in Publication Data

Wiesel, Elie, 1928–
    [Tous les fleuves vont à la mer. English]
    All rivers run to the sea : memoirs / Elie Wiesel.
        p.   cm.
    ISBN 0-7862-0673-X (lg. print : hc)
    1. Wiesel, Elie, 1928–   — Biography.   2. Authors,
French — 20th century — Biography.   3. Jewish authors
— Biography.
    4. Holocaust, Jewish (1939–1945) — Personal narratives.
    5. Holocaust survivors — Biography.   6. Large type books.
    I. Title.
    [PQ2683.I32Z52313   1996]
    813'.54—dc20   96-2649
    [B]

What profit hath a man of all his labor which he taketh under the sun? One generation passeth away, and another generation cometh; but the earth abideth forever. The sun also riseth, and the sun goeth down, and hasteth to his place where he arose. The wind goeth toward the south, and turneth about unto the north; it whirleth about continually, and the wind returneth again according to his circuits. All rivers run to the sea; yet the sea is not full; unto the place from whence the rivers come, thither they return again. All things are full of labor; man cannot utter it: the eye is not satisfied with seeing, nor the ear filled with hearing.

ECCLESIASTES

Contents

For almost thirty years, Marion Wiesel has been the first to read and edit the English versions of my books (when not translating them herself), including this volume of memoirs.

I owe her more than gratitude.

E.W.

Childhood

Last night I saw my father in a dream. His unshaven face was the same as ever, its expression frozen, but his clothing changed from moment to moment — from his Shabbat suit to the striped rags of the damned and back again. Where had he come from? From what landscape had he escaped? Who sent him? I can't recall if I asked. All I remember is how sad he looked, and how resigned. I could see by the way his lips were moving that he wanted to tell me something, but no sound came. Then all at once, in my sleep — or was it in his? — I suddenly doubted my own senses. Was this really my father? I was no longer sure.

In dreams all certainties are blurred and dimmed. Dawn and dusk, reality and fantasy, merge. And yet it was my father who appeared to me last night. Bearing a message? Or was it a warning? I awoke drenched with sweat, my heart pounding. A terrifying idea crossed my mind; that he had come for me.

I never really knew my father. It hurts to admit that, but it would hurt him even more if I deluded myself. The truth is I knew little of the man I loved most in the world, the man whose merest glance could stir me. What was the secret of his inner life? What was he thinking as he stared in silence at some far-off, invisible point in space? Why did he conceal his cares and disappointments from me? Because I was too young, or because he thought me incapable (or worse) of comprehending them?

I wonder whether other sons face this same problem. Do they know their fathers as someone other than the authoritarian, omniscient figure who leaves in the morning and returns in the evening, bringing bread and wine to the table?

As a child and adolescent I saw him rarely. Carelessly dressed, often preoccupied but always friendly, he spent the week in his little grocery store — where he enjoyed chatting with customers as much as selling them things — and at the community offices where he quietly worked to assist prisoners and refugees threatened with expulsion.

Sighet was a typical shtetl, a sanctuary for Jews, in this case since 1640, when, according to historians, refugees began arriving from Ukraine, fleeing the pogroms and persecutions of the reign of Bogdan Khmelnitski. Still, in 1690 the local populace demanded that the authorities expel all Jewish inhabitants from the region. The authorities resisted; even then there must have been men like my father to protect our community.

Shabbat (the Sabbath) was the only day I spent with him. In Sighet, Shabbat began on Friday afternoon. Shops closed well before sundown, stragglers and latecomers having been admonished by rabbinical emissaries and inspectors: "Let's go, it's late, time to close up! Shabbat is coming!" And woe to him who disobeyed. After the ritual bath we would walk to services, dressed for the occasion. Sometimes my father would take my hand, as though to protect me, as we passed the nearby police station or the central prison on the main square. I liked it when he did that, and I like to remember it now. I felt reassured, content. Bound to me, he belonged to me. We formed a bloc. But if a fellow worshipper joined us, my suddenly useless hand was returned to me. Did my father have any idea how much that hurt? I felt abandoned, even rejected, and after that it was never the same.

I would have loved to have had a real conversation with my father, heart to heart, to have spoken to him openly of things serious and frivolous. But no — at that age everything seems serious. I would have liked to have told him of my nighttime anguish, and of my fear of the dead who, I was sure, left their tombs at midnight to pray in the great synagogue — and heaven help the passerby who failed to heed their call to come and recite the customary blessings before the reading of the Torah. I would have told my father about my poverty-stricken friends and classmates, whose hunger made me feel guilty. I thought of myself as rich and unworthy, naïvely ascribing great virtue to poverty. Deep down, I was jealous of the poor. To paraphrase the great Yiddish humorist Sholem Aleichem, I would have given anything for a tiny taste of misery. Yes, I would have loved to have discussed all this with my father. Sometimes I even envied Isaac, who was alone with his father when they climbed Mount Moriah. God alone could have known then that there would come a time when he and I would walk together toward a solitude and an altar of another dimension, and that, unlike in the Bible story, only the son would come back, leaving his father behind with the shadows.

I admired him, feared him, and loved him intensely. He, in turn, genuinely loved all people — the weak, the needy, even the madmen. He enjoyed listening to them as they laughed, sang, wept, and chattered with birds they alone could see. Beggars were drawn to him, and he never failed to invite them to share our Shabbat meal. "The Talmud seeks to convince us that poverty is the lot of the Jews," one of them once said to him. "But how is that possible? Poverty is ugly; it begets ugliness." And my father nodded as if to say, You who are poor know better than the Talmud what poverty is.

If only I could recapture my father's wisdom, my mother's serenity, my little sister's

14

innocent grace. If only I could recapture the rage of the resistance fighter, the suffering of the mystic dreamer, the solitude of the orphan in a sealed cattle car, the death of each and every one of them. If only I could step out of myself and merge with them.

If only I could hold my memory open, drive it beyond the horizon, keep it alive even after my death.

I know it isn't possible. But what of it? In my dreams the impossible is not a Jewish concept.

My father enjoyed considerable renown in the community. To this day old men stop me on a street in Brooklyn, or on the Rue des Rosiers in Paris, and ask, "Aren't you the son of Reb Shloime Wiesel?" And I feel proud, delighted to be known as his son, for it means I come from somewhere and that while I am but a branch, the trunk is sturdy, and the treetop stirs the clouds.

My father was famous for his intelligence, his perspicacity, and his kindness. People turned to him for advice. Patient and tolerant, he would see anyone, for any reason, listening with the same attentiveness to rich and poor, friend or stranger. His views mattered, his advice was invariably followed. I was not surprised that he was so sought after, but I never understood fully why he had time for everyone but me. Why did he seem so lost in thought when I spoke

15

to him? Why were his answers so brief? How I wish he had told me of his own childhood, of his studies and experiences. How had *he* behaved at *heder* (elementary Hebrew school)? Had he been dutiful or headstrong? Who had been his friends? What games had they played? What about his father, whose name I bear? My paternal grandmother talked of him often, and always with a smile. But that wasn't the same.

I can see Grandma Nissel now, with her pale, thin face, framed by the black scarf she never seemed to take off. And her eyes, I remember her eyes. When she gazed at me, she must have seen another Eliezer. To smile at me was to smile at him.

Friday was our special time. I would stop and see her on the way home from *heder*. "Eliezer, my boy, come, I'm waiting for you!" she would call out from her window. She would give me fresh buns from the oven and sit and watch fondly, her hands folded, happy and at peace, a glimmer in her blue-gray eyes, as I washed and recited the appropriate prayer. It was as though she wanted to say something, to ask me something, but never quite managed it. She was probably like that with her husband too: humble, respectful, always ready to receive his words as an offering. Strangely, her silence never troubled me. I would look at her as I ate and, fifteen minutes later, I would get up. "I have to go home and get ready, Grandma. Shabbat will be here any minute now." But then, when I was already at the door, she would call me back. "Tell me what you learned this week." It was part of the ritual. I would share a Bible story or, later, an insight of the Midrash (commentary on the Bible text). Once, I remember, I made her laugh. I was a little boy and had just learned that Moses fled out of Egypt. "Grandma," I exclaimed, "I have great news for you. Moses is alive! Wicked Pharaoh couldn't kill him. He's going to get married, our Master Moses, and you know to whom? To Zipporah, the daughter of a priest called Jethro . . ."

Grandma Nissel lived alone in her widow's house, just a few steps from ours, though she certainly could have moved in with us. We adored her, our only grandmother, and she knew it.

On market days she helped out at the store. I can see her now, sitting motionless at the till, her lips sealed, giving change to peasants in vests and striped skirts of garish colors. But in the evening she went home to her own house, not wanting to be a burden. Maybe she was trying not to show favoritism toward any of her children. My father was the oldest, but she was just as close to my Uncle Mendel, who had a modest grocery store on the other side of town. I also had two aunts in Czechoslovakia: Aunt Idiss in Slotvino and Aunt Giza (whom we considered the more beautiful, since she used to bring us presents) in Ungvár. Aunt Giza survived deportation. When I saw her again in Israel in 1950, she wept with happiness, and with misery. She had lost her husband and children, but after the liberation rediscovered a childhood friend she had once loved and who had loved her. He, too, had lost his children and their mother in Birkenau. Ironically, years earlier their families had blocked their marriage. Now there was no opposition; the families were gone. Married at last, they seemed happy enough. Did they, in some illogical way, feel guilty? As for me, I am dogged by a feeling of remorse when I think of them. They gave me some money to buy and bring something back to Tel Aviv from Paris, but I never saw them again. They died before I was able to send what they had asked for. I had been too slow.

Grandma Nissel's other two daughters lived in Sighet. Zlati, the youngest, was chronically despondent because people called her an old maid behind her back. She married late, you see — at twenty-one. I remember her husband, Nahman-Elye, as a distant, haughty man who paid no attention to those he considered beneath him, and these were many. They had two young daughters.

"Do me a big favor, will you, Grandma?" I asked during one of our weekly meetings, a Friday in June, between the holidays of Pesach and Shavuot. Zeide the melamed had let us out of *heder* earlier than usual, and I had time to kill.

"Ask me for the secrets of the forest and I

shall lay them at your feet," she said, her voice soft and tender. "Ask me for the world and its riches and they're yours."

I had never heard her speak so many words at once.

"No," I stammered, embarrassed. "All I want is for you to tell me about Grandpa."

Her face darkened.

"Why?"

"Just because. I mean, since I'm named after him . . ."

She was silent for a long moment, her eyes wandering in the distance. Was she praying, or remembering how it was when she was young and beautiful? She still seemed beautiful to me.

"Your grandfather, my boy, your grandfather . . . How can I explain it? . . . He loved God and His Torah. He never lived apart from or outside God, apart from or outside the holy Torah. From morning to night, even at the store, his nose was buried in the holy books. I sometimes wonder if he even noticed me."

There was no rancor or complaint in her voice. On the contrary, she seemed proud and happy to have been married to such a pious man.

"But what about you, Grandma? Did you notice him?"

"Constantly. I would watch to be sure he was well and lacked for nothing, to make sure his shirt wasn't torn or his caftan didn't need mending. When he smiled his light brightened my darkness. When he sang, the whole world an-

19

swered him. Shabbat with him was paradise. The house and garden were bathed in an indescribable heavenly purity and I could hear angels singing with us, in his honor. I wonder if I was worthy of it. But I felt elevated, yes, elevated to the divine throne."

I knew that Grandpa Eliezer had been killed in World War I not far from our city, in a savage battle. A stretcher-bearer, he was trying to help a wounded man. He died for the Fatherland, for the glory of His Majesty the Emperor Franz Josef.

"When they told me," my grandmother said, "I learned what catastrophe meant, and I knew my mourning would never end."

Motionless, her hands still folded, she began to weep in silence, tears flowing down her cheeks and disappearing into the knot in her scarf. I felt stupid and clumsy. I didn't know what to say to make her stop. I stared at her, transfixed.

"Remember, little one," she finally whispered. "Remember the name you bear. Try not to dishonor it."

Many years later, when I returned to my town, I went to the cemetery in search of my grandfather's grave. The stone, overgrown with weeds, loomed over its neighbors, but it was hard to decipher the inscription. An emotion I had never felt before took hold of me. I saw Grandma Nissel again, and her words echoed in my memory. I recited a psalm and began to talk to the man whose presence had sanctified a small piece of the universe. "It's me, Grandpa, Eliezer ben Shlomo ben Eliezer, your grandson. I would like to say Kaddish for your soul's salvation, but there's no minyan. I'm alone. But I would like to tell you of the man who bears your name, that you might judge whether he is worthy of it. And since you're with Grandma Nissel again, say hello to her for me. Tell her I remember our Friday visits. I remember her smiles and her silences."

And I began to weep, as she once had, like a desperately hungry child who would always remain hungry. Mute tears flowed down my face, onto my chin, my neck, my chest. I did nothing to stop them.

A moment later I went on. "If Grandma had a grave, I would go to the ends of the earth to visit it. But as you know, she doesn't. Did you know she expected that? Did you know, Grandpa, that Grandma Nissel was the only one in the family, almost the only one in the whole community, who guessed it all? She knew she would never come home. She left this wretched town in her funeral dress. Yes, she wore her shroud under her black dress. She alone was ready. In the train, she alone was silent. Am I worthy of her silence, Grandpa?"

The child within me refuses to let go of his grandparents, as the man I am refuses to be separated from his father. My companion, my judge, or simply my guide, he never leaves me.

21

It is to him I turn at times of doubt. I fear his verdict, I seek his approval. His encouragement is essential to me, and his reproaches hurt. How often have I changed course solely in order not to disappoint him?

I was hardly a model child. I complained easily. My concentration wandered. I spent too much time daydreaming with my friends instead of studying. I didn't eat enough and my parents worried constantly about how thin I was, and how pale. Lavish sums were spent dragging me from doctor to doctor, city to city, to treat my migraines. (It was thanks to my illnesses that I discovered Satu-Mare and Budapest. Had my parents been richer, I would have been taken around the world.)

For the most part I was not too bad a pupil. My tutors liked me. I learned my lessons, did my homework. Perhaps they thought me spoiled. My illnesses kept me home for days on end, but for my teachers that was no excuse. The body may be ill, but that should not prevent the mind from pursuing its quest to come nearer to God.

The truth is, it was not illness that kept me in bed, at least not at first. I stayed in bed because I didn't feel like leaving the familiar walls of my room, or the windows from which I could survey the life of the street and gaze upon our garden and especially my mother. Smile all you want, Dr. Freud, but I was attached to my mother, maybe too attached. When she left me to help out at the store, I would tremble under my blanket. When she was away, however briefly, I felt rejected, exiled, imperiled. I search my mind for my earliest memory, and I see a little boy sitting on his bed, calling for his mother. At the age of three, four, or five, I felt unhappy and harassed by my classmates at *heder*. I would count the minutes that separated me from my mother. I didn't understand why she couldn't spend all morning and afternoon with me. Had she been present, I would have learned the Hebrew alphabet and the Pentateuch — the first five books in the Scriptures — in no time flat and vanquished all the enemies of Israel. My dream was never to leave her. I would cling to her skirts even when she went to the ritual baths. I would sit on the stairs, hold my breath, and wait for her. "How come I can't go in?" I would ask. "Because it's forbidden," she replied. "Why?" I persisted. "It says so in the Torah." That stopped me. The Torah demanded silence and a kind of sacred respect. All prohibitions came from the Torah.

With time, however, study became a true adventure for me. My first teacher, the Batizer Rebbe, a sweet old man with a snow-white beard that devoured his face, pointed to the twenty-two holy letters of the Hebrew alphabet and said, "Here, children, are the beginning and the end of all things. Thousands upon thousands of works have been written and will be written

23

with these letters. Look at them and study them with love, for they will be your links to life. And to eternity."

When I read the first word aloud — *Breshit,* "in the beginning" — I felt transported into an enchanted universe. An intense joy gripped me when I came to understand the first verse. "It was with the twenty-two letters of the *aleph-beth* that God created the world," said the teacher, who on reflection was probably not so old. "Take care of them and they will take care of you. They will go with you everywhere. They will make you laugh and cry. Or rather, they will cry when you cry and laugh when you laugh, and if you are worthy of it, they will allow you into hidden sanctuaries where all becomes . . ." All becomes what? Dust? Truth? Life? It was a sentence he never finished.

There was something terrifying and fascinating about reading ancient texts, something that filled me with awe. Without moving I could ramble through worlds visible and invisible. I was in two places at once, a thousand places at once. I was with Adam at the beginning, barely awakened to a world streaming with light; with Moses in Sinai under a flaming sky. I seized upon a phrase, a word, and distances vanished.

Yet reading isolated me. My classmates were no longer beside me. I no longer saw or heard them, for I was elsewhere, in far-off kingdoms ruled by the word alone. Even my mother remained behind, as if on the far side of a river.

To rediscover her at home was always a joy, but how could I ease that wrenching feeling that preceded my return? I found a solution: take her with me. All I needed was determination and imagination. When I went to see Adam, Eve wore my mother's sensitive face. When I followed Moses in the desert, his sister Miriam became my mother. Now nothing could separate us. Even at *heder*, I had only to open a book and I would see her. Only when I paused, when there was no book before me, did I feel alone and abandoned.

Once, however, we made each other suffer. But the suffering came neither from her nor from me, but from Rabbi Israel of Wizhnitz when he came to Sighet.

I was eight years old. As usual, my mother took me with her to seek the Rabbi's blessing: good health for her family, success and respect for the head of the family, good husbands for her daughters, fear of God for her son. A large crowd thronged the antechamber, spilling out into the corridor and onto the street. As the daughter of Reb Dodye, my mother did not have to wait on line. She herself, not the secretary, wrote out her request to the Rabbi, who talked with her about countless family matters as I stood holding my mother's hand, not understanding everything they said, focused as I was on the beaming face of this rabbi, whose *ahavat Israel* (love for Israel, and therefore for every being in Israel) was legendary. I was cap-

25

tivated by his eyes, his eyebrows, his beard. Suddenly the Rabbi told me to approach. He put me on his lap and asked me tenderly about my studies. I answered his easy questions as best I could, stammering, almost incoherent. At which point the Rabbi asked my mother to leave us alone. "Good," the Rabbi said when she closed the door behind her. "Now we can speak calmly." About everything: the sidra of the week (a portion of the Torah read on Shabbat), the Rashi commentary, the chapter of a Talmudic tractate I was studying at the time. We were alone a few minutes. Or was it a few hours? At last he kissed me on the forehead and told me to wait outside. "Tell your mother to come back," he said. When she reemerged from talking with him, what seemed like days later, I froze. I tried to run to her, but my legs would not obey. She was a changed woman. Violent sobs shook her body. People stared at her in commiseration. The Rabbi must have said terrible things to her, terrifying, painful things — about me. I must have shamed her with my bad behavior, or by giving wrong answers to the Rabbi's questions. "Why are you crying?" I asked. She refused to answer. I repeated my question again and again, but in vain. I tried the next day too, and the day after that, to no avail. All I got were those same tears. I persisted stubbornly, desperate to know what evil I might have done to cause such sorrow. It went on for weeks, until finally I gave up, exhausted.

By then she had stopped crying.

One day, some twenty-five years later, I got an urgent phone call from a distant relative who told me my cousin Anshel Feig was gravely ill. He needed an operation, but had refused to sign the consent form until he could see me. Fearing the worst, I jumped in a cab. Anshel had owned a fish market on Amsterdam Avenue near Eighty-sixth Street, close to where I lived. Whenever I had seen him, he was modest and happy. A kipa on his head. He spoke in Manhattan just as he had in Sighet: in song.

"Thank you for coming," Anshel said. "I need you. I need your blessing."

"Are you out of your mind?" I asked, trying to hide my concern. "You want *me* to bless *you?* Your standing up above is surely a lot stronger than mine."

Anshel, in fact, had retained his old Hasidic fervor, carefully observing all the commandments of the Torah, going to synagogue morning and evening, whereas I . . . But he insisted. "What are you waiting for?" his doctor — the relative who had called me — whispered in my ear. "His life is at stake."

So I took the patient's hand and gave him my blessing, the same one I had received when I was sick as a child: May everything turn out for good, may God bring a swift and total cure.

A few days later I went to visit Anshel. The operation had been a success and I could now speak to him freely. I asked him why he had insisted on receiving my blessing. He did not seem surprised by the question.

"Do you remember the last time the Rabbi of Wizhnitz visited Sighet?" he asked.

"Like yesterday," I replied. "How could I forget?" The painful image of my mother's sobbing surged back. "It's funny," I told Anshel, "but I never found out why she came away from the Rabbi in tears."

"I know why," Anshel said with the hint of a smile.

"You know?" I jumped. Stunned, I felt like grabbing him by the shoulders and shaking him, even if it sent him back to the O.R. "You knew all along and you never told me?"

His eyes clouded, and he spoke as if in a dream. "I was one of the people waiting in the antechamber to see the Rabbi, but when I saw your mother crying I left to see her home. You were walking ahead of us and that was when she swore me to secrecy and told me what Rabbi Israel of Wizhnitz, may his memory protect us, had said to her. He said: 'Sarah, know that your son will become a *gadol b'Israel*, a great man in Israel, but neither you nor I will live to see the day. That's why I'm telling you now.' And now you know why she cried."

I stared at him. Neither of us spoke until finally he sighed deeply and said, "That's why I wanted your blessing. If the Rabbi of Wizhnitz had such faith in you, your blessing must mean something in heaven."

As for me, the only blessing that meant anything was my mother's. Away from her I felt lost, surrounded by enemies. In my child's imagination, my first teacher viewed me with scorn. To please him I had to work infinitely harder. There was another melamed who wore a heavy coat winter and summer. I was troubled by his cold and indifferent air, and tried to win him over by redoubling my efforts to explain a page of the Talmud. I was convinced that my classmates detested me, and I decided to mollify them with bribery. At first I shared my buttered bread, fruit, and snacks, and later I let them divide it all among themselves while I stood apart and watched. They would laugh and devour my treats without so much as thanking me, as though I didn't exist. I should have been bolder, devised other ways of asserting myself, but years went by before I dared. Until my bar mitzvah, whenever I received a present, I gave it away to my classmates. Sometimes — though it shames me to recall it — I even dipped into the till at the store, not out of generosity but out of insecurity. I feared exclusion and isolation, but as much as I yearned to be part of the group, to be like the others and with the others, I always remained apart. My mother was my sole ally and support. She alone understood me. Yet I never gave *her* a present.

At the time we had a lodger. The only thing I remember about him is that he did magic tricks for us in the evening. He claimed to be an expert hypnotist and said he could predict the future. Whenever I hid something, he would find it immediately. I told myself that when I grew up, I would be like him, I would have his powers. No one replaced him when he moved out, but the house was always full. One or another yeshiva student took his meals with us every day. On Shabbat there was always a guest, usually a stranger, sometimes a beggar. Often it was Moshe the drunkard. In my stories I call him Moshe the madman, but he was mad only in summer. The rest of the year he acted normal, by which I mean, like a normal madman. He spent most of his time at the House of Study, helping the beadle sweep up and keep the stove burning. He would study only when there was no one else around. When he came to our house, he would sing the zemirot (Shabbat songs) for my father's benefit. I remember how his beautiful voice brought out the power in every word, every syllable. Eyes closed, he seemed in ecstasy. He sang in summer too only faster.

One evening I ran into him at the well while I was fetching water for the kitchen. "Did I scare you?" he asked when I gave a start. No, I said, it was the well that scared me. It was said a woman once drowned in it, and I was afraid of hauling up her body. I expected him to laugh, but instead he fell silent and leaned over to stare down toward the bottom. "Don't worry," he said hoarsely. "If she's there, I'll find out and take care of it. You don't have to be afraid anymore."

I was convinced we were well off. How else could we have entertained so many visitors and fed so many beggars? How else could I have been so generous with my classmates?

In fact, we were far from rich; comfortable at best. When we bought cherries, we got ten each. When there was corn, it was one ear per person. Three apricots or a piece of watermelon or cantaloupe on a summer's evening was a rare treat. When I think back on it now, a sense of remorse comes over me. My parents worked hard for the daily bread that I gave away to my *heder* classmates.

Many years after leaving my town I returned for a day and a night. When I saw our house and the homes of the other Jews on my street and the neighboring blocks, I realized my misperception. Even seemingly well-off Jews lived on the edge of poverty. I recalled my parents interminable family discussions on autumn nights. Should we buy a new stove for the dining room or a winter coat for my little sister Tsipouka?

But this never stopped them from feeding anyone who was hungry or from hiring the best tutor in the region for me. "You can never give too much to the needy or study too much," my father used to say. One day a week — I think it was Wednesday, market day — our servant, Maria, whom we considered a member of the family, would put a huge cauldron of bean soup in the yard for beggars roaming from village to village. "How can I tell which ones are really hungry?" she asked. "Don't try," my father said. "I'd rather feed someone whose pockets are full than send someone away on an empty stomach." Maria had no way of knowing — nor did I — that my father often had to borrow money to make it to the end of the month. My mother never complained.

I am trying to remember if my parents ever quarreled or bickered, if there was ever any tension between them. If so, I have no memory of it. I want to believe that they loved each other, and that nothing ever clouded that love. That may be too idealized a memory, but I cling to it nevertheless. In fact, years later an old Hasid in New York, Reb Itzikl Fuchs, told me there had been some gossip when they married, because my father had fallen in love with my mother. You weren't supposed to marry for love. Good Jewish families called in the community matchmaker instead. But one day my father saw a beautiful young girl in a carriage and was so struck by her that he ran after her, calling out, "Who are you?"

Of course, she did not deign to reply, but that evening the driver gave him the answer. The girl was the younger daughter of Reb Dodye Feig, of the village of Bichkev. The following year they were married, and they had four children, three girls and a boy. I was the third, after Hilda and Bea. Tsiporah was the youngest. The Romanian authorities would not allow certain Jewish names, so her birth certificate lists her as Judith. We nicknamed her Tsipouka. There were times when I quarreled with my older sisters, but never with her. We all loved her madly. My father treated her with a special tenderness, always had time for her. He would play with her, make her laugh, take her wherever she wanted to go. He would hold her on his lap and tell her stories. He pampered her, spoiled her, as did we. Perhaps we sensed that time was short, that we had to shower her with all the love and all the joys and favors of which she would soon be deprived.

"Memoirs?" people ask. "What's the hurry? Why don't you wait awhile?" It puzzles me. Wait for what? And for how long? I fail to see what age has to do with memory. I am sixty-six years old, and I belong to a generation obsessed by a thirst to retain and transmit everything. For no other has the commandment *Zachor* — "Remember!" — had such meaning.

You have plenty of time, people tell me. Time for what — to let oblivion wipe out the victims' final traces? To explore the planet, witnessing its degradation?

To write your memoirs is to draw up a balance sheet of your life so far. Am I ready for a final reckoning? Memory, after all, may well prove voracious and intrusive. Remembering means to

33

shine a merciless light on faces and events, to say "No" to the sands that bury words and to forgetfulness and death. Is that not too ambitious?

It's been years since I was young. But I would love to rediscover, to recapture, if not the anguish and exaltation that I once felt, then at least the road leading to them. Like everyone else, I have sought and sometimes found. Like everyone else, I have loved and ceased to love. I have done good things and bad, laughed out loud and cried in silence.

Some urge caution on me, insisting on the need for perspective. So be it. I will not tell all in a single breath. I will stop in the middle. In Jerusalem, on the day . . . But that can wait.

I am also told that to write your memoirs is to make a commitment, to conclude a special pact with the reader. It implies a promise, a willingness to reveal all, to hide nothing. People ask, Are you capable of that? Are you ready to talk about the women you have loved for a year or a night, the people who have helped or denigrated you, the grandiose projects and petty schemes, the true friendships and the ones that burst like soap bubbles, the fruitful adventures and the disappointments, the children dead of starvation and old men blinded by pain? You have yourself written that some experiences are incommunicable, that some events cannot be conveyed in words. How do you intend to surmount that contradiction? How can you hope to transmit truths that you yourself have said lie beyond human understanding and always will? It was said of Rabbi Mendel of Kotzk that he remained silent even when speaking. Is there a language that contains another silence, one shaped and deepened by the word?

And yet. Those are my two favorite words, applicable to every situation, be it happy or bleak. The sun is rising? And yet it will set. A night of anguish? And yet it too, will pass. The important thing is to shun resignation, to refuse to wallow in sterile fatalism. That great pessimist King Solomon put it well: "The days come and the days go; one generation passeth away, and another generation cometh; but the earth abideth forever. The sun also riseth, and the sun goeth down. . . . What has been will be. . . ." Must we stop time, then, and the sun? Yes, sometimes we must try, even if it is for nothing. Sometimes we must try *because* it is for nothing. Precisely because death awaits us in the end, we must live fully. Precisely because an event seems devoid of meaning, we must give it one. Precisely because the future eludes us, we must create it.

I mean to recount not the story of my life, but my stories. Through them you may perhaps understand the rest a little better. Some see their work as a commentary on their life; for others it is the other way around. I count myself among the latter. Consider this account, then, as a kind of commentary.

Moreover, I must warn you that certain events will be omitted, especially those episodes that might embarrass friends and, of course, those that might damage the Jewish people. Call it prudence or cowardice, whatever you like. No witness is capable of recounting everything from start to finish anyway. God alone knows the whole story.

To paraphrase a Talmudic saying, I hope the last page will bring me greater certainty than the first.

Do we write because we are happy or because we're not? A legend of the Midrash says that King Solomon wore a ring with the power to make him happy when he was sad and sad when he was happy. Why would he want to be sad when he was lucky enough to know happiness? Solomon was a Jew and a writer, which is to say, never content. Is the story meant to make us laugh or cry? To cry is to sow, said the Maharal of Prague; to laugh is to reap.

And to write is to sow and to reap at the same time.

Yes, last night I saw my father in a dream. The landscape around him was changing, but he was not. He looked at me strangely; I don't know why or for how long. Was he waiting for me to speak to him, to tell him I was happy to see him again? But I wasn't. Now, I wasn't unhappy. I was . . . I don't

know what I was. I don't know what I felt.
I know that I looked at him and he looked
at me, but that our eyes never met.

Did he beckon to me? Did he want to take
me to a place where only memory remained
alive? To our dead town?

Like all children, I had my share of rebellion
against this or that teacher or classmate, and
even against my parents. Sometimes I felt they
didn't understand me, that they judged me
wrongly or were unfair. A single stern look or
harsh word and I wanted to flee, far beyond
the rivers and valleys, preferably to my grandfather's, or to the Holy Land. Don't laugh, I
really thought it was possible. All you had to
do was climb the mountain and look for the
secret door to the special corridor that led to
Galilee. There, far from my family, all my anger
would vanish. But I wasn't old enough. It was
easier to sulk in silence. Fortunately these storms
did not last long.

World events had little direct effect on me
at the time. I was too young. I remember only
feeble echoes of Franklin Delano Roosevelt's
victory in the American presidential elections,
the Reichstag fire, the first Stalinist purges, social and political convulsions in Spain, the war
in Ethiopia, the death of the League of Nations:
there was talk of all these things at the synagogue, and my father would discuss them with
visitors at night, but they felt very far away.

The local situation, on the other hand, did scare me. When the anti-Semitic Iron Guard raised its head, we lowered ours. Slogans would sprout on the walls: "Jews to Palestine!" Thugs, their faces twisted with hate, would assault Jews in the street, tearing at their beards and side curls. The Kuzists, as they called themselves, were the Romanian version of Nazis. Savages thirsting for Jewish blood, they would launch pogroms on the slightest pretext. "Don't go to *heder* today," my worried father would say. My sisters often didn't go to school. On those days the store was bolted shut, and regular customers were escorted in through the living room. At the slightest warning we rushed to the cellar, though I had no idea why. Were the thugs afraid of the dark? We couldn't rely on the police, who not only failed to protect us from these murderers but helped them. We lived in terror. Our enemies were capable of anything, including accusing us of ritual murders.

I remember a sad song my mother used to sing to me, a popular song about a Hungarian village. In it a Jew recounts his grief: Accused of cutting the throat of a Christian child for ritual purposes, he cries out, "Cursed be our enemies who claim the Jews need blood to practice their religion."

In general, I accepted outbreaks of anti-Jewish hatred as endemic to our condition. If they beat us on Christmas Eve or threatened us at Easter, it would pass soon enough. If drunks insulted us, cursing us for having "profaned the Host," "poisoned the wells," or "killed the Lord," it was only natural, to be expected. I faced these ordeals without astonishment, almost without sorrow, as though telling myself, it's their problem, not ours.

But during the darkest times, I would ask myself simple, perhaps simplistic questions: Why do they hate us? Why do they persecute us? What did we do to arouse such cruelty? I would discuss it with my teachers, and even more often with my friends.

My teachers' response was to have us read and reread the Bible, the prophets, and martyrological literature. Jewish history, flooded by suffering but anchored in defiance, describes a permanent conflict between us and the others. Ever since Abraham, we have been on one side and the rest of the world on the other. Hence the animosity. "Abraham, the first of the patriarchs, was a better Jew than you," said one of my tutors, a tense and agitated man with eyes that burned with rage. "He was a thousand times better than all of us, but the Midrash tells us that he was cast into a burning furnace. So how do you expect to breeze through life without a scratch? Daniel was wiser than you and more pious, yet he was condemned to die in a lion's den. And you dream of living your life without suffering? The children of Jerusalem were massacred by the soldiers of General Nebuzaradan, and you complain?" Later Kalman, my Kabalist Master, had me recite aloud the litanies and chronicles of the afflictions of Jewish communities dispersed during the Crusades and ensuing pogroms. The communities of Blois and Mainz, York and Reims, all perished by sword and fire for refusing to renounce their faith. And he would conclude by quoting the Talmud: "Better to be among the victims than among the killers."

I thrived on these stories, proud of these Jews whose fidelity to the Covenant made them both vulnerable and immortal. I felt drawn to the prisoners of the Inquisition. Each of them recalled Isaac, though no angel intervened to extinguish the flames that were to consume them. I was haunted by their ordeal. Would I have had the strength to endure? I dreamed of Rabbi Hanina ben Tradyon, the Talmudic sage condemned by the Romans to die slowly on the pyre because he had taught the law in the public square. How had he and his disciples and theirs managed not to yield? I thought of my own ancestor Rabbi Yom-Tov Lipmann, author of the *Tossafot Yom-Tov*, who was imprisoned in Prague and Vienna during the Thirty Years' War. Would I, too, be able to remain Jewish under my jailers' eyes? I liked to invoke the memory of another ancestor, the Sh'la Hakadosh: at the supreme moment would he come to help me follow him without fear or shame?

Today, half a century later, these questions remain open. My people's survival leaves me perplexed even now, just as the undying hatred for it continues to preoccupy me.

Guided by my teachers, I hoped to find the answer in books. I read assiduously, perhaps too assiduously. Hence my disdain — surely a failing — for sports. Football, skiing, tennis: none of them was for me. Certain rich young Jews of assimilated families engaged in these sports, but I didn't even know how to swim. For relaxation I played chess, and sometimes cards on Christmas Eve, when even ultra-orthodox Jews played cards rather than show themselves on the street. Other evenings I spent with friends among the Hasidim, who always found some occasion for celebration. On Saturday afternoons in spring I would go for walks in the Malompark or along the banks of the Tisza and Iza, our town's two rivers. One summer evening I followed a crowd to the main square and spent hours watching an acrobat perform on two enormous stilts, his head touching the roofs. Another time I saw a tightrope walker. I still remember the crowd's cry of fright when he fell. "That's human life," someone remarked, "a tightrope." A Jewish theater troupe from Vilna, I think, came to put on several performances. I don't remember which plays. Once my mother took me to the movies to see a Yiddish film about Jewish settlements in Palestine, or was it Birobidzhan? Boys and girls were shown working in the fields, laughing and singing. Another time a Hungarian film, *Girl of the*

Night, was shown. I remember the face and the name of the star, the beautiful Karády Katalyn, from a poster. But I never saw the film. After all, a good Jewish boy, religious to boot, did not waste his time — and lose his soul — watching women doing God-knows-what.

From the pedagogical point of view, of course, my parents were making a mistake. Though I hadn't seen the film, the actress occupied my thoughts. Considerable efforts were required to drive her out, especially at night, just before I went to sleep. And she was not alone. Despite (or because of) the prohibitions, there were times when my glance roamed where it shouldn't have, in the direction of a young female neighbor or a beautiful stranger passing through the neighborhood. This troubled me, and I punished myself. Satan was leading me astray, casting a spell over me. He wanted to make me his slave, his prey; he was trying to capture my soul and poison it. How could I defend myself? I remember a judge's daughter, a lovely, haughty blonde with long silky hair who would walk past our house at a measured pace. I didn't know why, but she made my heart pound. To purify my spirit I resorted to prayer, a common and sometimes effective device. At least it took time. There were psalms in the morning, psalms in the afternoon, and psalms in the evening. At the time of my bar mitzvah I went to the ritual baths every morning before services. Thirteen immersions, corresponding to the numerical value of Ehad, God is one, or twenty-six immersions because the Tetragrammaton adds up to twenty-six. I prayed with fervor, convinced that with a bit of *kavanah,* of concentration, I would vanquish the temptations of evil, along with evil itself. Just a bit more inner discipline and my prayers would rise to seventh heaven, leaving the judge's daughter and all the others behind.

I sometimes envied one or another friend not because he was better dressed or more often praised by our teachers, but because he prayed with greater devotion.

Would that I could open my soul to prayer and aspire to purity today as I did in those days.

I see my father, I dream I see him. Sometimes I see only him. He seems worried, somber. Is he looking for a little Jewish boy like any other, in a little Jewish town like so many others, a Jewish adolescent in search of redemption? He is looking for me: Eliezer, son of Shlomo. I see him at the store. Across the street from us lives the Rebbe of Borsha, Reb Pinhas Hager. On our right the Slotvener Rebbe holds court for his elated faithful. On our left is the home of Reb Shloimele Heller, a rabbinical judge known for his levelheadedness.

It seems funny, I know. This little town has so many rabbis, each drawing his own followers. You might think Sighet was one enormous synagogue, that God's service was all we cared about, that material considerations were of no concern. But you'd be wrong. We had our share of thieves and informers. There was "Yankel the horse thief" and "Berl the fink."

Of course, we all awaited the Messiah. It would all work out in the end. A little patience. If the inhabitants of my town were optimists, it was because they had little choice. What would become of a Jew who resigned himself to pessimism? Can you imagine a pessimistic Messiah?

The Messiah. My poor mother never ceased to demand and await His coming. He was never far from her mind. At night, as she rocked me to sleep, she would sing of her deep conviction that nothing bad would happen to her child, since the Messiah would come in time to protect him. Anti-Semites? Doomed, reduced to impotence. His merest stirring would scare them off. Military service? "Fear not my child. There will be no more armies." My mother believed this with all her soul. The Jewish people would soon be delivered, never again sending their children to be killed for European emperors and kings. I don't know whether the Savior was awaited anywhere else with as much fervor and love as in Sighet. But I do know that every Jewish child in shtetls everywhere lived the same hope.

Yet each town and hamlet has its own personality, its own character and mentality, color and temperament. With just one glance I can tell the difference between Krechnev, where my

Uncle Israel, the grocer, lived, and Bichkev, where Grandfather Dodye had his little farm.

But let us linger a moment in Sighet, the region's capital, which wasn't much of a capital. It did, however, have a penchant for changing — its name, its nationality, and thus its allegiance. When my father was born, it was a proud part of the Austro-Hungarian Empire and called itself Máramarossziget. When I first saw the light of day, it proudly bore the name of Sighetul Marmaţiei and belonged to the Kingdom of Greater Romania. When I left it, it was Máramarossziget again, a Hungarian city of noisy patriotism. Today its capital is Bucharest once more, but Budapest demands its return in the name of God-knows-what.

I will never forget having to learn the Hungarian national anthem overnight, the Romanian royal hymn having been tossed aside like a dirty old sock. Now we shouted "God save Hungary!" with the same enthusiasm with which we had earlier cried "Long live the king!"

At home, of course, Yiddish predominated. But we also spoke German, Romanian, and Hungarian. At the store you might also hear Ruthenian, Ukrainian, and Russian. You had to be a born polyglot to communicate with the peasants, though often just a few words would suffice: hello, yes, no. Most of our customers could get along in Yiddish. Maria, our servant, spoke it fluently, with nearly no accent and with great conviction. She knew our customs, mores, and laws. Sighet, after all, was pretty much a Jewish town, and all our Christian neighbors knew that a Jew could not light a fire on Saturday, eat leavened bread during Passover, or touch impure meat. The opposite was not the case: I knew nothing of the Christian religion, which inspired in me no curiosity, only fear. I would cross the street when I passed the church on my way to the synagogue or the House of Study. Was it the incense, liturgical processions, and icons that frightened me, or the crowd, whom I imagined filled with hate for the people of Israel? Perhaps I subconsciously recalled traumatizing stories about Jewish children kidnapped by monks and forced to convert.

Yet I did have Christian friends — well, maybe not friends, but classmates. I can still see them playing in the schoolyard among themselves. Some came to the store to buy a kilo of sugar or flour. They smiled at me then, but at school they pretended not to know me. On Christmas Eve they wore masks with horns and carried whips, taking part in the hunt for Jews. No, not all of them. I remember one pallid, timid boy, an excellent pupil. When his comrades let us feel their hatred, Pishta would wink at me, as if encouraging me to hold on. Later, when the ghetto was created, he helped me carry our radio to a friend of my father's.

Outside *heder*, I was always terrified by exams, but I got good grades in elementary school, partly because I did my homework and learned my history and geography lessons by heart, but perhaps also because my teachers, including a gruff man named Muresan, were eager to please my parents. They were our, shall we say, special customers, and in exchange I was their pet pupil in class. They were kind enough to look the other way when I was absent, which was often, since I was less concerned with secular studies than with holy books. I was no more interested in the patriotic slaughters of Hungarians and Romanians than I was in legends about the birth of Remus and Romulus or Attila's military exploits. Passing exams was no problem: I simply crammed for a month. During that time I did nothing else, neglecting the Talmud while begging its forgiveness and pledging to return as soon as exams were over, a promise I always kept. Within a week I had forgotten everything secular.

Then there was the violin. My instructor was an officer of the gendarmerie. I would go to his quarters twice a week, a bottle of *tzuika* in hand. He drank, I played. When the bottle was empty I would stop.

In high school I continued to learn, only to forget. My parents enrolled me as a special student in Jewish high schools, first in Debrecen and later in Nagyvárad. My mother's dream was for her son to become a *doktor rabiener*, a rabbi with a doctorate. Private tutors in Latin, algebra, and physics drilled me for a month before I set out to meet the big-city professors. My sister

Bea went with me. I can see her now wearing her beret, leaving me at the gate, smiling and confident, as if to say, I'm here, you'll be all right. It was an image that came back to me years later in a Montreal hospital, where Bea, ravaged by cancer, knew she was dying, and I knew she knew. I held her hand and smiled as if to say, I'm here, you'll be all right.

Hilda and Bea attended the girls' high school in Sighet. One of their problems was to avoid being forced to write on Shabbat. Generally my father worked that out through a method tried and true: he bribed the principal. My little sister Tsipouka was too young to go to school, so she learned alone at home. I loved to watch her bending over a book, serious and intent — with her golden hair she was as beautiful as an angel. I would hold my breath so as not to disturb her. What I felt for her I will never feel for anyone else.

I remember the night she was born. My father sent me to fetch Dr. Fisch, who stayed alone with my mother while Maria and Grandma Nissel came and went, lugging tubs of boiling water. At one point my grandmother told me to knock on the Borsher Rebbe's window. "But he's sleeping, Grandma," I protested. "Then wake him up," she said. "Ask him to intercede for your mother in heaven." Naturally, I obeyed. The Rebbe wasn't sleeping. His lighted window was open, and he seemed to be waiting for me. "Come in," he said, and then, "Let's go downstairs to the Beit Hamidrash." So we went to the House of Study and Prayer. There he opened the Holy Ark, stood before the sacred scrolls, and invited me to recite a psalm with him. "It is impossible that a child like you and an old man like me would not be heard in heaven." Verse upon verse, we recited the appropriate psalm. "Another," said the Rebbe, frowning. I obeyed. After the third psalm he fell silent and I went home. Through the closed door I could hear my grandmother begging my mother: "Don't hold back! Cry! Shout! You have to shout when it hurts, and I know it hurts."

I went back to the Rebbe. "It's not working," I told him. "My mother won't shout."

"Very well," he said. "Let's open the prayer book." He found something that spoke to my mother's condition and recited a verse which I repeated after him. Suddenly we heard a piercing cry from across the street. The Rebbe leaned over to kiss the book. "You see?" he said. "Our people have just been enriched by a new child. May God bless it."

My little sister was a blessing. But . . . No, no buts. Not yet. Everything in its time. My little sister did have a few years of happiness, as did I.

A few years later it was my mother's turn to rush to the Borsher Rebbe. I had come down with a terrible case of appendicitis, and the doctor felt that I urgently needed surgery. He advised us to leave that very day for Satu-Mare

49

and the Jewish hospital there. "But it's Shabbat!" my parents cried. The doctor shrugged. "You have no choice." Desperate, my mother ran across the street to consult the Rebbe, who told her, of course, that the law permitted violation of the Seventh Day when a life was at stake.

Of my hospital stay I remember mainly the ether I had to inhale (if there is a smell that epitomizes hell, it is not sulfur but ether) and the nurse. I know that if there is an angel on high who attends the sick, it is Raphael, but in my case it was a marvelous young woman, beautiful and kind. I was very young but could easily have fallen in love with her. I remember her lovely face, her dark eyes, her gentle fingers. When she smiled at me, that alone eased my pain. I especially liked the way she helped me sit up to drink. Her chest would brush my head as she leaned over me, arousing my body in heretofore unknown ways.

It shames me to admit that I was sorry to leave the hospital after only a week.

I was ten in 1938, the year of Munich, Daladier and Chamberlain, Léon Blum's "cowardly relief," and Churchill's prophetic wrath. The first refugees began arriving from Czechoslovakia, that small country so devoted to democracy, the country of Masaryk and Beneš, of tolerance and liberty, the envy of Central and Eastern Europe.

Among the refugees were disillusioned soldiers and resigned civilians betrayed by the grandiloquent promises of their Franco-British allies. Toward what lands were these exiles headed? They had little to say and asked for nothing. I don't even know if they spent the night in Sighet. It all came back to me in 1968, the year of the West's second betrayal of Czechoslovakia. If Václav Havel inspired such support throughout the world in 1989 and 1990, I want to believe it was due in part to the "civilized world's" feeling of guilt toward his nation.

Tragedy loomed, but life went on. I paid little attention to the outside world. I was growing up, maturing, learning more difficult and obscure texts. Hitler's howling failed to penetrate my consciousness. The Nuremberg laws, the Olympic Games, the assassination of Von Rath, Kristallnacht? Hadrian and the Inquisition had done worse. We hoped that the Third Reich would crumble of its own weight, that the great powers of Europe would hold the line, that Hitler and his acolytes would founder. We hoped there would be no war.

But there was. It broke out on a Friday in the month of Elul, when we were all preparing for the High Holidays. In the morning the blowing of the shofar called upon sinners to repent. During Elul, they say, even the fish tremble in the waters. In a corner of the Beit Hamidrash my father and his friends, draped in their prayer shawls and wearing their phylacteries, talked about the latest news. Their excited voices rose, and their elders hissed at them to be quiet: "Ssh, we're praying here!" To this day I can still hear that "Ssh," and I know so well what it meant: What an idea to chatter and fret when Jews are addressing the King of the Universe. What an idea for peoples and their armies to slaughter one another over a few scraps of land or a few slogans while God was listening to His faithful.

The discussion was halted and the service continued, concluding, as usual, with the prayer for the dead, the Kaddish. Cannon fire could already be heard in the distance. The dying had begun, and the first orphans were learning to bear their grief. Yet my own existence was not disturbed unduly. That Friday I received my usual braided bread from my grandmother. I went to the ritual baths to purify myself for the approach of the Queen of Shabbat. I put on a white shirt, my best suit, and prepared myself for the peace of the seventh day of Creation, which the passions of men must not disturb.

Nothing exceptional occurred that Shabbat. At the morning service I heard that a famous preacher was in town and would deliver a sermon that afternoon. He was so thin you could hardly see him. How could such a tiny man have such a deep, resonant voice? I expected him to talk about current events, but he had other priorities. Using an intonation customary among Lithuanian preachers, he described the fierce, implacable punishment that awaited the wicked, those guilty of sexual transgressions and depravities I was too young to understand. They said he was so nearsighted as to be almost blind, but he seemed to know his way around hell as though he had lived there from birth.

We were at war, but I did not feel threatened. For me life went on as before. I had to prepare myself for the Jewish New Year, not an easy task. Salvation requires sincerity: cheating is forbidden. On the Day of Judgment an incorruptible celestial tribunal will decide who shall live and who shall die, who shall perish by the sword, who by fire, and who by thirst.

My grandfather came to spend the High Holidays with us. I gave him my bed and slept on a bench, delighted to gain on two fronts: The discomfort would help me expiate my sins while also making my grandfather happy. I remember that he wept more than usual during the arduous Rosh Hashana service, especially during the last part, the Musaf. Perhaps he sensed what I was too young to imagine: that this war, once unleashed, would sweep away thousands upon thousands of destinies in its torrent.

We knew something of what was happening beyond the borders. The Hungarian and Yiddish newspapers offered vague reports, but we knew things were bad. These were trying times for Jews in German-occupied territories. That was only to be expected. Hitler had made no secret of his criminal intentions toward our people, and we knew very well that hatred backed by power always meant catastrophe. And Hitler's hatred of the Jews was so visceral and his power so absolute that we had to expect the worst. But we could not anticipate the horror of reality. From Polish refugees passing through our town, all bearing bad news, we heard tales of the German army's invincibility and brutality. We were told of arbitrary arrests, systematic humiliation, collective persecution, and even of pogroms and massacres. And yet.

The truth is that, in spite of everything we knew about Nazi Germany, we had an inexplicable confidence in German culture and humanism. We kept telling ourselves that this was, after all, a civilized people, that we must not give credence to exaggerated rumors about its army's behavior.

Yes, that's what many of the Jews in our town thought, including my mother. We all fell into the trap history had set for us. During World War I the German army had rescued Jews who, under Russian occupation, had been beaten, ridiculed, and oppressed by savage Cossacks whose mentality and traditions were steeped in anti-Semitism. When they left, our region enjoyed a spell of calm. The German officers had been courteous and helpful, unlike the Cossacks. Lulled by memories of the Germans of that era, the Jews refused to believe that their sons could be inhuman. In this the Jews were not alone.

Neville Chamberlain reacted in much the same way.

One of the consequences of the Phony War (1939–40), was that Stalin and Hitler redrew the borders of Poland, Hungary, and Romania. The Soviet Union came closer to Sighet, and about a dozen young Jews took the opportunity to slip across the frontier to help build the workers' paradise. Their Communist "brothers" imprisoned them immediately upon arrival and dispatched them to that empire of oppression that would later be called the Gulag. Leizer Bash and his young fiancée, both distant relatives of my father, spent more than ten years there. I learned of their experience in Canada in 1954. Arrested just after setting foot on Soviet soil, they were accused of spying for the bourgeois fascists. They were sentenced, sent from prison to prison and camp to camp, and finally wound up in Siberia. In his suffering Leizer discovered in himself a vocation as a Yiddish writer. His works are eyewitness accounts of life in the Gulag ten years before Solzhenitsyn.

Another consequence was the German invasion of the Netherlands, Belgium, and Luxembourg. Jews nevertheless were optimistic. The beginning of the real war, we felt, would mean the end of Hitler's Germany.

A third consequence was that Sighet became Máramarossziget again. The population joyfully greeted the first "motorized" units of the Hungarian army: troops on bicycles. My mother, too, was pleased with our change of nationality. For her it was a kind of return to her childhood for which thanks were due to God.

Yet there were many harbingers of evil. Though no one was yet talking of liquidation or extermination, news of massacres in Poland began to filter through. And that should have been enough to awaken us. In 1941 more than a thousand "foreign" Jews — those unable to document their Hungarian citizenship — were expelled from Hungarian territory to Polish Galicia. I remember going to the station to say goodbye. Everybody was there. We thought we would see them again someday, but only one managed to escape, and that was Moshe the beadle. Dazed, madness in his eyes, he told a hair-raising story: Those expelled (they were not yet called deportees) had been slaughtered and buried naked in ditches near Kolomyya, Stanislav, and Kamenets-Podolski. He talked on and on about the brutality of the killers, the agony of dying children, and the death of old people, but no one believed him. The Germans are human beings, people said, even if the Nazis aren't. The more convincing Moshe the beadle tried to be, the less seriously he was taken. He has suffered too much, people said, so much that he doesn't know what he's saying. Then he would lose his temper. "Listen to me!" he would shout. "I'm telling the truth, I swear it! On my life I swear it, and on yours! If I'm lying, how come I'm alone? Where is my wife and our children? What about the others, your former neighbors? Where are they? I'm telling you, they killed them. If you don't believe me, you're crazy." Poor guy, everyone said. Raving mad. Which only made him angrier: "You're irresponsible, I'm telling you! What happened to us will happen to you. If you want to look away, go ahead! But if I'm lying, why do I say Kaddish morning and night? And why do you say, 'Amen'?" That much was true. He recited the prayer for the dead ten times in the morning and ten times in the evening, attending every service, rushing from synagogue to synagogue seeking a minyan so he could say another Kaddish, and yet another. But the people were deaf to his pleas. I liked him and often kept him company, but I, too, could not bring myself to believe him. I listened, staring into his feverish face as he described his torment, but my mind resisted. Galicia is not exactly the end of the world, I told myself. It's only a few hours from here. If what he's saying were true, we would have heard.

Besides which, my mother was not entirely wrong. Her optimism was understandable. Things had been relatively quiet for the Jews since Admiral Horthy had taken power in Hungary. He had influential Jewish friends, some of whom had converted. The most outrageous forms of collective harassment ceased, and expulsions to Galicia were suspended. Though allied to Germany, Hungary treated its own Jews as it saw fit. Apart from the *numerus clausus* in the university and the major academies, the Jews had little cause for complaint. The vociferous insults of the Nyilas fascists were troubling, but no more than that, for they were not in power. Exempted from military service, young Jewish males were drafted into the Munkaszolgálat, a kind of auxiliary force that accompanied the troops as quartermasters, digging antitank trenches in summer and cutting wood in winter. They did not complain unduly, nor did their families. Synagogues and Jewish elementary and secondary schools were packed and yeshivas flourished, as did Jewish commerce. Sports clubs, cultural centers, and Zionist organizations conducted their activities openly and legally: there were field trips, seminars, public debates.

Still, Regent Horthy was anything but a democrat. He tolerated no opposition. His police persecuted and tortured Communists — especially Jewish Communists — and terrorized their families. There was talk of this in the Houses of Study. I didn't know it at the time. I only found out long after the war, when I was researching my book *The Testament*.

I am still fascinated by the phenomenon of religious Jews opting for communism. How could a Jew imbued with Moses and Isaiah adopt the theories — or the faith — of Marx and Stalin? In the course of my research I was stunned to discover that there were such people, among them some prestigious names, even in my small town. Strange as it may sound, these students of the Talmud gathered by night in a darkened Beit Midrash to analyze the works of Lenin and Engels with the same fervor they showed in the daytime when poring over the teachings of Maimonides.

I believe that even my mother, pious as she was, felt the attraction of the Communist ideal. I remember a laughing, mustached man who would visit her at the store when things were slow. They would talk in low voices. After the war I found out he was an underground Communist activist. Perhaps it was under his influence that at one point she abandoned the broadcasts of Radio London for those of Radio Moscow.

The fall of Paris, German victories in North Africa, the Japanese bombing of Pearl Harbor — there was talk of all this, of course, and previously unknown names became current: Tobruk, El Alamein, Voronezh, Stalingrad. But the war itself seemed distant and unreal, almost mythical, coming home to us only when Italian troops passed through the city on their way to the front (strumming mandolins) or on their way back (silent, their heads hanging). It forced its way into our consciousness indirectly, when Polish refugees arrived. Assigned by the community to look after them, my father listened to their testimony and moved heaven and earth to get them money and false papers and to prevent the gendarmes from expelling them.

Once someone came to tell my father that a young woman had been seen being escorted by two gendarmes. He seemed to hesitate for a moment. Should he get up in the middle of the Shabbat meal? We quickly recited the customary blessings, and my father left. A few hours later he was back. "This is serious," he said, looking gloomy. "More serious than usual. She told the investigating officer everything. Her flight from a ghetto in Galicia, the murder of her parents. She should have kept silent."

These officers, thank God, could be bribed with money and a few bottles of *pàlinka,* their underlings with a single bottle and a bit of small change. When the laws got stricter, my father had a new idea. Having discovered that anyone apprehended with foreign currency would immediately be transferred to the counterespionage bureau in Budapest, he arranged to supply refugees with a few U.S. dollars, Swiss francs, or pounds sterling, which prevented them from being sent back to Poland. In Budapest there was an underground network to help them, and almost all survived. One, however, was arrested in a raid, taken to the police station, and tortured. In his confession he named the person who had helped him.

I will never forget my father's arrest, nor the look on his face after his release: all the things he never said could be read in his eyes. He spent weeks in prison, first in Sighet, then in Debrecen, and was released, thanks to his friends in Budapest, who managed to buy off either the prosecutor or the judge himself. Bea, the most resourceful of the family, took the train to bring him home. When he saw us waiting at the station, a sad, disenchanted smile I had never seen before flickered across his face. He seemed to have aged. Day after day I watched him. Had he been beaten, tortured? What had they done to him to give his face that grayish color, those lines of exhaustion and resignation? I didn't dare ask, yet I yearned to know. "I know," Bea told me years later. I begged her to share the secret with me, but she refused, simply repeating, "I know, I know." She was already gravely ill, and I didn't insist. I could have asked him myself in the camp, where we shared our grief and fear, but I was too shy even to mention his imprisonment. I told myself it wasn't the time or the place. I was wrong.

Why is it that my town still enchants me so? Is it because in my memory it is entangled with my childhood? In all my novels it serves as background and vantage point. In my fantasy I still see myself in it.

I often re-create my town, so like and yet so different from all others, refusing to accept that it ever changed. I stroll through it alongside my characters, who act as scouts, guides, and guardian angels. With their help, evil remains hidden and time suspended. I wrote *The Town Beyond the Wall* in 1961, before my return to Sighet. I wrote it because at the time that was the only way to bring it back to life.

Even when I tell Biblical, Talmudic, or Hasidic tales, it is from my town that they take flight. It is in the gardens of Sighet that the Sages compose the Talmud, in the flickering light of its candles that they weave legends for the Midrash, along its rivers that exiles hang their harps and weep when they remember Zion. It is in the darkness of its forests that Rabbi Itzhak Lurie and his disciples dream of ultimate redemption. That's how it is, and there is nothing I can do about it: I left Sighet, but it refuses to leave me.

The closer I come to my native town, the farther away I am. The better I know it, the more I strive to discover it. For I do not know it well. I thought I did, but I was wrong. It had a secret life I never suspected. I never knew, for instance, that respected members of the community engaged in smuggling and illegal currency trading. Nor that there was a bordello in Sighet. According to stories I heard from Sighet's inhabitants after the war, a few of the Jewish working girls spoke a highly literary Yiddish. One in particular liked to discuss religion with her customers. So yes, I freely admit that many things escaped my notice. Yet I loved to look and listen. I was interested in everything. A Hasidic quarrel? I was determined to learn the reasons, ramifications, and stakes. A young Jewish woman converted to marry a Hungarian officer? I worried about the tragedy of her shame-struck parents. Everything aroused my curiosity: a beggar who might be a *tzaddik,* a just man, in disguise; an abandoned wife scouring the province for the hundred rabbinical signatures that would allow her to remarry; a rich trader gone bankrupt; a novelist whose book described the turmoil in heaven when the Angel of Death went on strike; an apostate excommunicated by the community. Not only the people but also the trees, the birds, the clouds interested me. And I was taken most of all with the visionaries. Moshe the madman, whose laugh haunted my dreams; Kalman the Kabalist, whose veiled glance darkened mine; Schmukler the prince; my friend Itzu, with whom I studied the siddur — prayer book — of Rabbi Jacob Emden; my friend Yerahmiel, with whom I learned modern Hebrew — of course, I remember them all. Just as I remember the silent beggar who put his finger to his lips to show me how much he distrusted speech. And the family of five — or was it seven? — dwarfs, whom people came from far and wide to see; all of them survived Mengele's selections and tortures in Birkenau.

My bar mitzvah was celebrated by the Rebbe of Borsha, across the street from our house. Called to the Torah, I recited the appropriate blessings and silently read a passage of the Prophets. After the service the faithful were invited to a Kiddush. I can see myself now, as Rebbe Haim-Meir'l, successor to old Rebbe Pinhas, helped me strap the phylacteries onto my left arm and forehead for the first time, as the Bible tells us to do. And here I was a responsible adult, a full-fledged member of the community of Israel.

A new life began for me. I was now so obsessed with God that I forgot His creation. Was it Ernest Renan who wrote that the Greeks had reason, the Romans power, and the Jews the sense of God? I sought God everywhere, tracking Him especially to holy places as though He were hidden there. Was Giordano Bruno right when he said that light is God's shadow? I sought Him everywhere, the better to love Him, to enjoy His gifts, to share His suffering in our exile: in the chapels of tailors and of shoemakers, in the great synagogue of the rich, and in the Houses of Study where the poor gathered.

In Sighet they used to say that everyone had his own synagogue, even atheists. We young people created the Tiferet Bachurim, a rather gloomy room in the "Talmud Torah" building. I was elected *gabbai,* or president, perhaps because my father provided wood to fuel the stove all winter. We were delighted to have a place of our own to celebrate the holidays, recite psalms, study the sacred texts, and pray among ourselves. Like the adults, we now followed the disquieting developments of the war. Yiddele Feldman, grandson of the rabbinical judge, was our skilled strategist of the Russian front. He had hidden a large map covered with colored arrows inside a Talmudic folio, and we would lean anxiously over his shoulder to listen to his account of German victories in Ukraine and in White Russia. Sucking pensively on a pencil, he would describe the situation: tanks, armored vehicles, infantry, air support, troop movements. Yiddele was a budding general. "The German advance is like lightning," he said, "a fearsome, unstoppable tactic. The Red Army won't be able to halt the invader. Not yet. Later it will, but by then it'll be too late. We'll have to find other ways to escape catastrophe." What other ways? Leave for Palestine? Kalman the Kabalist advised his disciples to meditate, to pray in deeper contemplation. The divine response lay in the human quest for mystery.

Why not in the occult? Kalman was inclined to oppose "practicing the Kabala" as such, for he was concerned exclusively with messianic enlightenment. But that didn't stop me from trying. I began reading Hebrew, Aramaic, and Hungarian works on the irrational in all its diversity. Astrology, magic, morphology, hypnotism, graphology, parapsychology, alchemy. In short, I became entranced by what lay beyond reality. With a little luck, I thought, I would learn how to turn dust into gold, danger into security, harmless gestures into acts of war against war. I was fascinated by the mystical experiences, or alleged mystical experiences, recounted in these books yellowed by the centuries. Could Satan really be driven beyond the mountains by mixing vinegar with the blood of a ritually slaughtered rooster while uttering magic formulas? Could the repetition of certain "names" at certain times repel the forces of evil, bring down planes, drive back tanks, vanquish and humiliate the horsemen of Death? Fifty years later I can reveal the truth: It doesn't work, and I say that from experience. Countless times I tried to thwart Hitler, visiting myriad evils and maladies upon him.

And I will confess another failure as well — one that will not surprise anyone — in a domain in which my competence is found wanting even now: financial investments. I had read in some work on occult sciences that you could make your savings grow by burying money after invoking the protection of a heavenly spirit with special expertise in the field. I decided to risk a meager fifteen pengös. Every morning I would dig up my investment just to check, and one day it was gone. I discontinued these unprofitable practices.

To make my father happy I agreed to sing in the choir of the great synagogue, under the direction of Akiva Cohen. It was thanks to what he taught me that I was later able to lead a chorus in the O.S.E. — the children's rescue society — orphanage in France. One night, in

66

the late seventies, during an address at a university in Connecticut, I mentioned my musical debut and the name of my first choir director, paying homage to his abilities. "That's me!" someone in the audience exclaimed. He was then the cantor in a local synagogue.

I saw Cohen only rarely, for music lessons and before the High Holidays, but I met with my master of mysticism every evening. Under his vigilant eye three of us decided to venture into the Pardes, the orchard of forbidden knowledge. We began our quest for the absolute by fasting on Mondays and Thursdays. We would stay at the House of Study until midnight, poring over the *Sefer Yetzirah* (which is attributed to Rabbi Yehuda Hechasid) and the writings of Rabbi Hayyim Vital, favorite disciple of the founder of Lurianic mysticism. I was insatiable, captivated by the dazzling theories of creation: the shattering of the vessels, the emanations of first light, the scattered sparks. How could the purity of the beginning be recovered? How to liberate the Lord, prisoner of Himself and of our own actions? How to join the first breath to the last, to master the source and that which overflows it? For an adolescent thirsting for knowledge and dreams, there is nothing more romantic and alluring than the Kabala. Within its gates, higher than heaven, prayer and meditation are driven to their limits and allow apprehension of the mystery of human power as manifested in good and evil alike. Sitting on the floor, we would recite the litanies attributed to Rachel and Leah. Cautiously, the master guided us toward the propitious moment at which, through the pronouncing of occult formulas, it was given to man to hasten events and to advance the coming of the Messiah. "This is the only way," our master said. "To save our people, we must save all humanity."

Of course, it was dangerous. We knew the tragic story of Rabbi Joseph della Reina, disciple of Ari Hakadosh and friend of a mysterious old man, Natala Natali of Safed, and of an "Italian madman." This poor and daring young dreamer had set about to realize man's most sublime dream. Having triumphed over countless dangers on land and sea, he very nearly succeeded. Satan was disarmed, bound hand and foot, reduced to impotence, humiliated. Another instant and humanity would have entered the light and joy of truth. But at that last moment the Rabbi made a mistake, allowing himself to be moved by Satan, who broke his chains, whereupon the whole edifice crumbled, and man's hope was extinguished anew. If Rabbi Joseph della Reina had failed, how ought we to proceed? Would we be able to avoid the same pitfalls? We told ourselves that if we, too, failed, we would begin anew. After all, the Besht, punished for having attempted the same experiment (being deprived of his gifts, his knowledge, and even his memory), nevertheless refused to abandon hope. And were we not all his disciples?

Having heard talk of our adventure, childish in more ways than one, my father took me aside one Saturday afternoon to question me. I replied not in words but with a nod: Yes, the rumors were true. "Aren't you a little young to be exploring — or, worse, practicing — the Kabala?" he asked. I shook my head no. Had I not been bar-mitzvahed? Had I not given proof of my maturity? He wanted to know more of my extracurricular activities, but since my two classmates and I had taken a vow of silence throughout Shabbat, I was unable to satisfy his curiosity. This made my father angry. "I order you, *bigzerat ha'av*, in my capacity as father, to answer me." Now I had no choice but to reveal our project to him. Inveterate rationalist that he was, he made a bargain with me: "You can do all you want with the Kabala, provided it does not stop you from studying what really counts: the Talmud and its commentaries on the one hand, modern Hebrew on the other." Modern Hebrew? I protested. What for? But my father insisted: modern Hebrew, and modern Hebrew literature. He showed me some poems and stories by David Frishman, Hayyim Nahman Bialik, Saul Tchernichowsky, and Zalman Shneur. Some of them were so obviously infused with eroticism that they made me blush. Did my father really want me to study these? He did. But weren't these authors heretics? In his eyes ignorance was worse than heresy.

In town our trio was looked upon askance.

Parents warned their children: "Those fools are hurtling to their own destruction. Keep away from them." Everyone knew that mysticism was dangerous to anyone unworthy of receiving its teachings. Eschatology was a forbidden domain, a minefield. One did not trifle with the fundamental mysteries of Creation and annihilation with impunity. That was to risk madness, heresy, or death, like the sages who penetrated the legendary orchard. It was easy to see why. The human brain is incapable of absorbing too powerful a light, just as the heart cannot contain too deep an emotion. There are limits that must not be transgressed. How could a weak, vulnerable mortal contemplate forcing the hand of God? Countless legends over the centuries recounted the traps and perils that threatened all who dared attempt it. "Yes, my children," our master remarked, "the danger exists. Satan, not yet disarmed, will seek to sabotage our undertaking. But the stakes are worth the grief."

Six months went by, and we suffered our first defeat: Yiddele, the oldest of the three of us, fell ill, losing the power of speech and his will to live. Stretched out on his bed from dawn to night, he stared vacantly, unreachable and lethargic. Rebbes were called in, psalms recited; prayers were said at the graves of the just, and special prayers during Shabbat services. Doctors were consulted in our small town and in the great cities of the region. My friend remained mute, his condition unchanged. Strings were pulled, and a renowned psychiatrist arrived from Budapest to spend an entire day at the young patient's bedside. The next day he visited schools and synagogues and questioned parents, neighbors, and friends, myself among them. Sworn to secrecy as I was, I said nothing that might damage our project. No, I had seen nothing suspicious, nothing bizarre, in my friend. He was not subject to fits of madness. He suffered no turmoil. The psychiatrist questioned my other friend, the second of our trio, but received no further enlightenment. Perplexed, he decided to call in a Swedish colleague, the famous Dr. Olivecrona. So it was, that one fine day our little Transylvanian backwater was honored by a visit from the great Swede. He strolled through town with a contemplative air, looking straight ahead but scrutinizing everyone who crossed his path before finally being escorted to the patient. Olivecrona examined him, tested his reflexes, questioned his parents, summoned his friends — and departed disappointed.

The following Shabbat my father spoke to me again. "I hope you've learned your lesson."

"What lesson is that, Father?"

"Stop this senseless business."

"I can't, Father."

"Why not?"

"We're not doing anything wrong. We're deepening a teaching that is part of our heritage. Where is the sin in that?"

My father's face darkened. "I understand,"

he said. "But be reasonable. Promise me you'll be careful."

I breathed a sigh of relief. It had been a narrow escape. My friend Sruli and I resumed our work, still guided by our master. Ascetic exercises, feverish incantatory litanies, descent into the torments of the abyss in the hope of reascending toward dizzying heights. By night, beyond the howling of dogs, we heard the now faint, now heavy tread of the approaching Messiah. A little more effort and salvation would be at hand. One last burst of spiritual energy, of daring imagination, and the enemy of our people, the enemy of all peoples, would be brought to his knees.

But once again an alert Satan foiled our plan. My second friend fell ill, with symptoms similar to the first. Today I know the technical terms: aphasia and ataxia. Once again the city was abuzz. Funds were collected to bring in doctors from neighboring cities, psychiatrists from Kolozsvár, neurologists from Budapest. Olivecrona put in another appearance. This time he stayed for a week, asking questions, analyzing, rummaging in the mysteries of my friends' unbalanced brains. Once again he left without answers.

Forty years later I was dining with my wife, Marion, and several psychiatrists who introduced us to a Swedish woman who turned out to be Olivecrona's daughter. I asked her whether the name Sighet meant anything to her.

"Sighet," she murmured. "Yes, wait a minute. My father made a trip there during the war, I forget why." I reminded her of our childish adventure and she smiled. "Yes, I remember now. My father was completely baffled. You could have spared him quite a few sleepless nights."

After Olivecrona's departure my father made no secret of his mounting concern. "You have to bow to the evidence now. Your friends have been struck by an illness that looks very much like a curse. Stop before it's too late." I tried to argue. "Have confidence in me, Father. I'm cautious, and I'll be seven times more so." Did my mother know of all this? Until then she had said nothing to me. But that night she stared at me with a pained expression and said, "You look pale. I'm afraid you're getting sick." I reassured her. As God was my witness, I felt fine.

I feel fine, I told her whenever I noticed her anxiety. Have faith in me. She need not have worried. My friends' illnesses had undoubtedly been smoldering for a long time. Anyway, I was all right. She, too, begged me to be careful.

I promised her I would be, but I knew it was a promise I wouldn't keep. In fact, I was prepared to confront far greater perils, for my friends' illness had convinced me of the importance of our mission. If Satan struck at us so hard, it was because we were hindering him. We therefore had to press on, going all the way.

Now as I recount this episode of my adolescence, I realize how naïve I was. I really believed that a few prayers and Kabalistic formulas could halt the hangman and save his victims. My friends believed it too. Was it because they came to understand their mistake that they slid into madness?

Alone with my master, I found him confident and full of ardor. "The Messiah will come," he told me. "You'll see, Eliezer, in the end He will come. It's enough for a single being to want it, to want it sincerely and completely, and the universe will be saved." That very evening we set to work again.

April 1943. It was the middle of Passover. My mother, busy in the kitchen, commented on a report she had just read in a newspaper. The Warsaw ghetto had rebelled, and the German army was conducting reprisals. The ghetto was in flames. "Why did our young Jews do that?" she mused. "Why couldn't they have just waited calmly for the war to end?" That was the word she used — calmly.

My poor mother.

Years later I would learn the truth about the uprising, one of the most noble and admirable of Jewish history, the first civilian insurrection in occupied Europe. It lasted as long as the French army held out against the German invasion in 1940. The Jewish combatants knew they had no chance of winning, or even of surviving. Their battle was lost in advance. But they were determined to salvage what they called Jewish honor. On the first night of the revolt the insurgents congratulated themselves, embracing before the bodies of the first dead German soldiers. The hangmen were mortal after all. Mordechai Anielewicz, commander in chief of the Jewish Resistance, wrote: "The ghetto has risen. . . . It is the most beautiful day of my life." But his aide, Antek Zuckerman, sent into the Aryan zone to purchase weapons, faced a wall of incomprehension and indifference. The ghetto burned, and on the other side lovers came to gaze upon the spectacle. Czesław Miłosz drew inspiration from this for his moving poem "Campo di Fiori." "We were betrayed," wrote Anielewicz before committing suicide in the underground shelters of Mila 18. In London, Artur Zygelbojm, a leader of the Zionist Bund and a member of the Polish parliament-in-exile, killed himself in an effort to arouse the conscience of humanity. But no one took notice of the poor man's "gesture."

The days passed quickly in my little town. We were getting ready for the next holiday, Shavuot, which commemorates the revelation at Sinai. "Thou shalt not kill," the Lord ordered man on that day.

But men would be killers, as I would soon enough discover.

We didn't take any vacation in 1943. Usually we went to Fantana, a mountain village near

Borsha, where my father would join us for Shabbat. I loved that monthlong "change of scene." Sometimes I played chess with my father's friends. I often lost, but was delighted to be playing with adults, since it meant I was being taken seriously. In the afternoon I would take long walks by myself. But one day, as I left the village, I noticed a man and a woman lying on the grass. They were laughing. I recognized them and averted my eyes. A saying of the Besht came to my mind: If you see someone committing a sin in secret, it is a bad omen for you as well; you should not have been there, and should not have seen.

Perhaps we took no vacation that year because of money problems, or because the news was becoming more troubling. Everyone knew that the Warsaw ghetto had been destroyed, but we were completely unaware of the Final Solution. Other families set out for the countryside, but I was happy to stay home. My master needed me. Jewish history needed our dreams, our dreams of children gone mad. On the night of Tisha b'Av, after the service in which the Lamentations of Jeremiah are recited, I went to my master's and we stayed up all night, repeating passionate verses laden with mystery. I felt a terrible force pulling at me, dragging me down one precipice, then another. Near four in the morning I thought I saw a being with a hidden face chained to an enormous dead tree. As in the tale of Rabbi Joseph della Reina, a thousand dogs were baying, spitting flames, but the being remained motionless, his head supporting the heavens. "It's him!" I cried. "Master, look! It's him! Let's free him!"

"Careful," he answered. "Be careful, for . . ."

I awoke drenched in sweat, delirious, unable to tell dream from reality, not knowing who or where I was. My master sat on the floor in apparent despair, his body racked by sobs, hitting his head against a wall. At that moment I felt madness lurking, menacing us both, but I was determined to continue our quest at any cost. Even today I remain convinced that if the Germans hadn't entered Sighet the following spring, I would have suffered the same fate as my two unfortunate comrades and would have awakened in the depths of the abyss. Thus it was the killers who "saved" me. Woe unto me, it is to them that I owe the fact that I was spared. Olivecrona did not make a third visit, and the Messiah did not come.

Anything but a good little boy, I was subject to phobias, outbursts of anger and jealousy, frivolous envy, and childish rebellion. If two friends seemed too close to each other, it would keep me awake at night. If one of the faithful looked at me askance in the House of Study, I wished I were buried alive. Meanwhile, the demon of eroticism visited me often. When Hilda and Bea had their girlfriends over to the house, I became too tongue-tied to answer their questions. And then of course there was the judge's daughter: pretty, blond, her hair spilling shamelessly over her shoulders. I would wait for her to walk by in midafternoon, my cheeks flushed, breath halting, and even that made me feel guilty. One night I saw her close-up — smiling, beckoning me toward something I couldn't yet manage to name — and I awoke in hell.

The time has come to take a last look at one of the villages near Sighet. It was called Bichkev (in Yiddish), Bocskó (in Hungarian), and Bochkoi (in Romanian), and it was there that my maternal grandfather, Reb Dovid (Dodye) Feig, lived until . . . But no, let us not yet speak of his death. First I need to see him alive.

And how alive he was, my grandfather, alive and magnificent. Yes, I know, most grandchildren adore their grandfathers. But mine was truly special. If that makes you smile, so be it, for it is with a smile that I recall him. He allowed me — obliged me — to love life, to assume it as a Jew, to celebrate it for the Jewish people. A devout follower of the Rabbi of Wizhnitz, he was the embodiment of Hasidic creative force and fervor. His father, Getzl, a man who loved to go into the forest at night to play his violin under a tree, with God his only audience, lived to be ninety-four. My grandfather surely would have reached that age too . . .

A burly man with broad, powerful shoulders,

Reb Dodye Feig knew how to work the land, impose respect on tavern drunks, and break recalcitrant horses. But he was also a man of broad knowledge, respected in the village and the surrounding hamlets. He was a notable. When a rebbe of the Wizhnitz dynasty came to visit, he would stay at Reb Dodye Feig's.

A cultured and erudite man, an avid reader of the Bible and of the Rashi and Ramban commentaries, and especially of the work of Rabbi Hayyim ben Attar, my grandfather was fascinated with the Midrash, with the works of the Musar — a movement founded in Lithuania to foster the teaching of Jewish values and ethics — and with Hasidic literature. He maintained a perfect balance between his quest for the sacred and the exigencies of daily life. He was a whole being.

Visiting him was a festival for the heart and mind. I would lose sleep preparing myself physically and mentally, and in his presence I felt purified, uplifted, and secure. At his house no one looked at me askance, and no one judged me. I was free and at ease. Everything belonged to me, and I was given everything. The sun's rays playing in the branches of the fruit trees, the river that carried my secrets to the next village, the blue, gray, and purple carpet of sky stretching to the horizon — nature seemed to exist only for my grandfather to tell me of its eternal beauty.

He was a marvelous singer, with a warm, melodious voice that could conjure worlds near and far. He knew the songs of the Wizhnitz court, those sung on the eve of Shabbat and those murmured at dusk the next day, at the hour of its departure. He knew the romantic, mystical songs the Rebbe of Kalev sang in Hungarian, and the nostalgic tunes of Romanian shepherds, slow and thundering *doinas* that were calls to glorious dreams and the love of broken hearts. When he stopped to catch his breath, I would beg him for more, and with an ever more gleeful smile he would recall a new song attributed to this or that *tzaddik*. Once he stopped in the middle of a *niggun*. Eyes closed, he seemed asleep. Afraid of waking him, I didn't budge. But he wasn't sleeping. "I'm dreaming," he said. "I've never sung so much. Thanks to you, I think I can rise to *Haikhal Haneggina*, the celestial sanctuary where words become song."

He told stories too. Stories of miracle-makers, of unhappy princes and just men in disguise. It is to him I owe everything I have written on Hasidic literature. The enchanting tales of Rebbe Nahman of Bratslav, the parables of the Rebbe of Kotzk, the sayings of the Rebbe of Rizhin, and the witticisms of the Rebbe of Ropshitz: he knew them all, and he taught me to savor them. Suddenly I would find myself on the boat that carried Rebbe Nahman to the Holy Land. I followed the Rizhiner into exile, waited at the Kotzker's door to glimpse him in his terrible isolation. I saw them all, and saw myself before them. I felt exhilarated, inspired, and enriched from moment to moment, from tale to tale. "I'll never forget these stories," I told him, and he answered, "That's why I'm telling them to you. So they won't be forgotten."

For the High Holidays he would come into town to attend the service of Rebbe Pinhas, the Rebbe of Borsha. He would always stay with us. Since my father prayed at the Great Synagogue, I would accompany my grandfather to the Hasidic Beit Midrash across the street. As a privileged guest, he would stand near the Rebbe, and so would I. During those special prayers that are recited with fear and trembling, he would draw me under his talit to protect and comfort me. I would feel his heavy hand on my head and follow the words that soared to the highest spheres, interceding on my behalf and on the people of Israel's.

We used to have an open house on Rosh Hashana. After the reading of the Torah and before the particularly solemn service of Musaf, the Borsher Rebbe's faithful were invited to have a glass of tea in our yard. The children acted as waiters. For my grandfather it was a moment of pride: he would watch us and bless us with his eyes. Then we would stay with him for the second half of the service.

Later, dressed in his caftan and his wide-brimmed fur hat, the yellowed *Makhzor* under his arm, a prince among princes, he would sing all the way back to our house. "Happy New

Year!" he would call out joyfully. And he exuded so much confidence, so much grace and love, that I knew the year would be good. Yes, even 1943. And yet. That was his last Rosh Hashana.

In April 1944 my parents invited him and his wife to live with us. "Let's stay together," they proposed. There was already talk of a ghetto in Sighet. "Let's be in it together," they said. But he refused. He preferred to stay with his three sons, Israel, Chaim-Mordechai, and Ezra, and their children. I don't know what his last weeks and days were like. I have been told they were all forced into the ghetto of a nearby city and that their transport was attached to the third convoy out of Sighet.

I try to picture him in the ghetto, and to picture myself at his side. How did he express the joy, the Hasidic joy, he drew from Creation and its Creator? I try to picture him in the sealed cattle car. How did he say his prayers? To whom did he entrust his testament? I try to imagine him walking with the sick and the old toward the fiery site from which there was no return, and . . . No, I don't want to imagine that. I cannot. It would be indecent. A man's encounter with death must remain private. I prefer to avert my eyes, or to close them, and thus to remember him full of spirit, ecstatic, preparing to chant the songs of Judgment Day. "Grandpa," I ask him, "what is the Sanctuary of Song like?" And he answers: "The Sanctuary blazes and illuminates; its flame warms the most frigid hearts."

I had four uncles on my mother's side: Chaim-Mordechai was the most dynamic and resourceful, Ezra the most timid, Israel the most authoritarian, Moshe-Itzik the most romantic.

Chaim-Mordechai, a tall, slim redhead with sharp eyes and a melodious voice, charmed me with the moral fables of the Maggid of Dubno. Here is one: A woman has just died, leaving a husband and a little boy too young to comprehend his tragic fate. He doesn't know that he is now an orphan, doesn't cry during the funeral, and plays with the black cloth draped over his dead mother's coffin. "Now, isn't that what so many Jews are doing today?" my uncle asked. "They ought to be in mourning, but instead they're having fun."

Ezra, poor Ezra, was the neediest. Reserved and withdrawn, a sad smile fluttering on his lips, he was always murmuring inaudibly, probably praying, perhaps begging pardon for bothering someone, though he never disturbed anyone at all.

Israel, the oldest, came to Sighet only rarely. To see him we had to go to his house, in the village of Krechnev, where he owned a tiny grocery store. Wearing his patched caftan, the Book of Psalms always within reach, he served his customers, peasants who lived in the neighboring small towns.

Moshe-Itzik had tuberculosis. When you talked to him, you wanted God to take pity on him. But I admired him. He walked with a nervous, rapid gait, and always seemed to be leaving soon after he had arrived. He traveled constantly, though in search of whom or what I don't know. When asked, he would shrug. I loved to see him smile. His was the smile of a man unafraid of distance or of death. We were afraid for him, yet he outlived his brothers and sisters. Perhaps he was so familiar with the prospect of death that the enemy had no hold on him. I found him in Israel in the early fifties. Spry and ambitious, he was beginning to travel in Europe again. Then one day I received a letter from a lawyer in Berlin: My uncle had recently died there and had left me his estate of about a hundred dollars. I can see him now, hovering eternally between two fits of coughing, two absences. I would have liked to have known his story better.

My cousins' stories, the few who survived, are more or less similar to my own. On my father's side there were Leizer, Yanku, Velvel, Reshka, Aigyu; on my mother's Voïcsi, Dvora, Leibi, Shiku, Sruli, Eli. Some live in Belgium, others in California. One female cousin settled in Buenos Aires, another in São Paulo, but most abandoned the Diaspora for the Land of Israel. Among my cousins and their children you will find doctors, rabbis, diamond merchants, teachers, businessmen, scribes. I keep up with them through Hilda. The husband of one cousin died in Argentina after having both legs amputated. Another's went mad during the Gulf War.

I often think of those who did not survive — the youngest, the smallest. I remember their visits to our house, and mine to theirs. During holidays we would sit under the trees and trade long-forgotten secrets.

Even more often I think of my friends of those days: Itzu Junger, Haimi Kahan, Itzu Goldblatt, Moshe Sharf, Hershi Farkas. For me friendship has always been a necessity, an obsession. Later I would come to love Epicurus, the Greek philosopher who posited friendship as an ethic.

Friendship or death, the Talmud says. Without friends, existence is empty, sterile, pointless. Friendship is even more important in a man's life than love. Love may drive one to kill, friendship never. Cain killed Abel because Abel was only his brother, whereas he should also have been his friend. David shines in history not only because of his territorial conquests but because of the true friendship, noble and indestructible, that bound him to Jonathan. A man capable of such friendship could only be exceptional.

The Hasidic movement owes its success to its emphasis on friendship among the faithful as well as to fidelity to the master. Friendship is indispensable, essential. The Hasid comes to the rabbi's court not simply to see him, hear him, and spend Shabbat under his roof, but also to meet with friends who come for the very same reasons. He feels an attachment to each and every one of them, through what Hasidic literature calls "the root of the soul." Together they form a community whose members are equal before God, as before the rebbe. Granted, there are more poor than rich among them, and more are unhappy than fulfilled. But it is incumbent upon the rich to aid those in need, as it is incumbent upon the poor to accept without envy those more fortunate than they. In Brooklyn as in Paris, Hasidic solidarity is real. Whoever is in need, his friends come to his aid. A refugee arriving out of nowhere is immediately taken in, given food and lodging, a loan and a network of support.

To praise God the famous Rebbe Pinhas of Koretz said: God is not only the Father of our people, the King of the Universe, and the Judge of all men. He is also their friend.

As a child I needed friendship more than tenderness to progress, reflect, dream, share, and breathe. The slightest dispute with a friend gave me a sleepless night as I lay wondering whether I would ever again know the excitement of a nighttime walk, of discussions about happiness, humanity's future, and the meaning of life. Disappointment in this domain caused me greater pain than a failure in school.

Shortly before my twelfth birthday I began to feel more sure of myself. I no longer sought to "bribe" my friends. Our bonds were strengthened by our common projects. A thousand memories tie me to them.

I would have loved to have deserved the friendship of young Dovid'l, grandson of the legendary Reb Shaye Weiss. A precocious Talmudist, he seemed destined for a dazzling future. Unfortunately, he was even more studious than I. In our community he was the child prodigy, impossible to tear away from his books. We became friends much later, when he was professor of Talmud at the Jewish Theological Seminary in New York and I was professor of Jewish studies at City College.

Yerahmiel Mermelstein, the son of a melon merchant, had his whole career set out for him. An ardent Zionist, he was indefatigable in his efforts to "convert" us to the ideas of Theodor Herzl. On Saturday afternoons, when we were supposed to be at the synagogue, he insisted on treating us to socioeconomic disquisitions on Palestine. He decided to learn modern Hebrew and argued that we should all follow suit. But the poor boy got nowhere. None of us was tempted until my father persuaded us to learn it. My father found us a teacher and Yerahmiel managed to come up with a grammar — the only one in town — which he loaned to me. I learned it by heart, as though it were a chapter of the tractate of *Sanhedrin*.

When I first went to Israel, in 1949, my father and Yerahmiel were both in my thoughts. It was thanks to their obsession with modern Hebrew that I was able to become the Paris correspondent for an Israeli newspaper. I asked myself, over and over again, why I, more than Yerahmiel, deserved to know the country and speak the language for which he had fought so ardently in our little, far-off town.

I remember Itzu Junger — serious yet cheerful, thin and agile. His parents were rich, or so I supposed. They lived in a big, "luxurious" house with many rooms, near the great synagogue. I went often to their garden. Always pleasant and generous, Itzu may well have suffered from the same insecurity as I did: he was desperate to bond with his friends. For a year we had the same tutor. About ten of us would study together in a room set aside for us in Itzu's spacious house. Sometimes we studied late into the evening, and then we would spend the night. This was a welcome diversion, for I detested routine.

A change of tutors separated us, but we continued to see each other at services, on Shabbat afternoon, and on holidays. Then came the tempest that separated us.

We ran into each other in Israel, where he loaned me his room, a windowless cell in a Tel Aviv suburb. I gave it back to him a few nights later, afraid I would suffocate there. I saw him again in Brooklyn in the early fifties, during my first visit to the United States. We went for long walks in Williamsburg, exchanging plans and memories. After that we corresponded regularly. He must have been sick already, but he didn't know it yet, or at least there was no mention of it in his letters. He died of cancer of the liver. But nobody told me. I thought he wasn't writing back to me because he was too busy, so I kept on writing for some time. Two or three years later I was in New York again and tried to get in touch, but his number had been disconnected. I called his sister in Brooklyn, and she burst into tears. I had been writing to a dead man.

As for Haimi, he died of a heart attack one Shabbat afternoon in 1989, at his home in Monsey, New York. We had seen each other again in Israel in 1949. I was giving classes in a children's home, and a technician came to do some electrical work. He looked familiar. "You! An electrician?" He had learned the trade in the concentration camp. As a child Haimi had been a jack-of-all-trades who would willingly repair a leaky fountain pen, a broken lock, or an electrical short. His father, Reb Nokhum-Hersh, was the chief rabbi's private tutor. It was to him that we turned for explanations of obscure Talmudic passages.

Haimi had uncommon physical strength. I felt safe when we went out together at night, for the thugs of our town feared him. Yet I never saw him fight or become violent. On the contrary, he was so good-natured as to seem somewhat phlegmatic. His older brother, Leibl, short and thickset, with herculean strength, was crushed by a tree in the camp. Haimi saw it happen.

89

Haimi went from a displaced persons camp in occupied Germany to Palestine, illegally of course. He passed through a detention camp in Cyprus, served in the Israeli army, and eventually went on to a new life in the United States. In Sighet he had been pious, and he became infinitely more so in America, where he grew an impressive beard. He worked as a jeweler on Forty-seventh Street, New York's street of diamond merchants. On Shabbat he wore a *shtreimel,* a widebrimmed fur hat, like his father in the old days. Close to the Rebbe of Sighet, as his father had been, Haimi apparently fell under the influence of Satmar, whose followers are known for their extreme hostility to Israel, Zionism, and any Jew less pious than themselves. In their eyes, I was doubly heretical: a lover of Israel and a liberal in matters of religious observance. Belonging as we did to two different, even opposing worlds, Haimi and I stopped seeing each other.

A few days before his sudden death, he asked Itzu Goldblatt, a fellow goldsmith, to get him a tape of my speech to the Bundestag. Why that particular speech? Perhaps because, for symbolic reasons, I had begun it with a few words in Yiddish. Haimi did not live to hear it.

In the old days Itzu Goldblatt and I tried to outdo each other in everything: piety, devotion, and even — don't laugh — modesty. Each of us wanted to be closer to heaven than the other.

Who would be the first to see the Prophet Elijah in his dreams? I told him mine and he told me his, and together we consulted the appropriate manual to decipher them. How could we ensure that we merited the ascension of our souls? Where Itzu recited the prayer of Shmoneh Esreh in ten minutes, I took thirty. Where he took an hour to absorb a passage of *Etz-Hahaim* (The Tree of Life), I took three. If I immersed myself in the ritual bath twenty-six times before the morning service, he was satisfied only with forty-seven. It was the same with secular studies. Where I learned Latin and modern Hebrew, he discovered English. In fact, it was Itzu who gave me my very first English lessons, and his English would be as useful to him as my modern Hebrew was to me. Interned in a camp in Cyprus with thousands of clandestine immigrants expelled from Palestine by the British, he held an important post in the camp administration. He probably could have pursued a university career, but I, with my two left hands, could never have succeeded as a goldsmith.

Then there was Moshe-Haim, the cantor's son. And Hershi whose sister drowned in the Iza a few days before Tisha b'Av; and Moishi, the precocious businessman; and Chaim-Hersh, with his mischievous eyes and lovely baritone voice. I remember the defeated air of the Selishter Rebbe's two sons. I should have shown them greater warmth.

I stress the role of friendship and its place in my life as an essential component of everything I do. I can work only in an atmosphere of understanding — in other words, of friendship. As a journalist I enjoyed the friendship of my employers; as a teacher I sought the friendship of colleagues. A single suspicious look could cause a sleepless night, one cold word and I became full of self-doubt. I often felt inferior to others and always to my image of myself — or to their image of me. I therefore had to redeem myself. As a child I gave away candy; as an adult I was always ready to do favors: translations, advice, recommendations, intercessions, prefaces. I needed not so much to please as to feel useful and loved. Sometimes I made promises I knew I couldn't keep. I know I shouldn't have, but it eased my solitude to know that someone expected something of me, that I was sharing in someone else's possible happiness.

The charge would later be made that I am often unfair to my female characters, failing to accord them sufficient scope or depth. Perhaps it's true. My male characters are better realized. Is that because my relations with them have to do with the theme of friendship? Surely I was wrong to conceive of friendship only among men. I have written several novels — among them *The Town Beyond the Wall* — solely to celebrate friendship. I love the character of

Pedro because he evolves in a world illuminated by friendship.

In *The Gates of the Forest* I wrote:

What is a friend? More than a brother, more than a father: a traveling companion with whom we rebuild the route and strive to conquer the impossible even if only to sacrifice it later. Friendship stamps a life as deeply as — more deeply than — love. Love can degenerate into obsession, but friendship never means anything but sharing. It is with friends that we share the awakening of desire, the birth of a vision or a fear. It is to friends that we communicate our anguish at the setting of the sun or the lack of order and justice: is the soul immortal, and if so, why does fear sap our strength? If God exists, how can we lay claim to freedom since He is its origin and its end? And what, exactly, is death? The mere closing of a parenthesis? And life? Among philosophers such questions often ring false, but raised among friends during adolescence they trigger a change of being: the glance begins to burn, the everyday gesture strives to reach beyond itself. What is a friend? The person who first makes you aware of your own solitude and his, and helps you escape it so that you, in turn, may help him. It is thanks to him that you can fall silent without shame, and unburden yourself without loss of face.

In the camp I thought of my childhood friends and of all those who had formed part of my inner landscape. Sadly, we did not stay together. They left with the first transports and I a week later, with the last. In the camp there were no friends to remind me of my childhood. In the camp I had no more childhood. I had only my father, my best friend, my only friend.

Darkness

March 19, 1944. Cursed be that day, Jeremiah and Job would have said, a day of malediction, of punishment and grief. Why was it born? Who sired it? Why was it marked by a star of ashes? From that day on, the shadows, din, and flames of enemy destiny would rule the rhythm of our existence. To paraphrase the Bible: By night we yearned for dawn; at dawn we prayed that night might come. From that day on I was like a man who feels blindness overtaking him: I looked and stared, desperate to retain it all.

I remember I was at services. It was a Sunday. We had just joyfully celebrated Purim. At the House of Study we were still talking about the traditional play the children had put on at the home of the Borsher Rebbe. We paid no attention to the vagabond who stood near the door and refused to laugh. The Rebbe of Krechnev played the violin longer and in a tone more heartrending than usual. Why did tears stream down his face into his bushy beard?

Suddenly a man burst in, interrupting the service: "Have you heard the news? No? Are you deaf? Stupid? Don't you know what's going on?

You sit here praying while . . ."

"While what?" we asked. He took a deep breath and shouted, "While the Angel of Death stands at the city gates!" Like Kierkegaard's clown, he cried "Fire!" and his audience thought he was joking or raving mad. Hands were waved in disdain: let him get out and let us continue our prayers in peace. But then we heard a voice behind him. "He's right. I heard it on the radio: The Germans have crossed the border. They're occupying the country."

A heavy silence fell over the congregation. People looked at one another. "What does it mean?" someone asked. Someone else replied, "Just that the front is getting closer." "And the war will soon be over," an optimist added. The madman, Moshe the Beadle, said nothing more. His gaze lingered on those who had spoken. Then he shrugged and walked to the door, hesitated, then left, hands in his pockets, his disgust apparent. Someone called us to order. "What about the Aleinu, the final prayer?" We had forgotten the prayer without which orphans could not say Kaddish. We recited it and absently listened to the Kaddish.

Back home I found the family gathered around the radio. I wanted to announce the news, to tell them of Moshe's outburst, but I was told to keep still. "Ssh," my little sister said, finger to her lips, her face uncharacteristically grave. The table was set for breakfast, but no one had eaten. "The Germans . . ."

Bea whispered. "I know," I said. My father frowned in concentration, as if trying to foresee the future or thwart fate. If they were afraid, they didn't show it. I don't know what I felt, but it wasn't fear. Curiosity, perhaps? I sensed that this was a crucial moment, that a new chapter in history was opening. Soon we would hear its roar as it changed humanity. The distant monster would finally show his savage, howling, bloodstained snout. At last we would cease to live on the sidelines. Spectators no more, we would be actors, with no further need of emissaries to tell us what was going on.

"This does not augur well," my father said as he turned off the radio. "Yes," my mother replied, "but we've seen bad omens before. Come. Breakfast is waiting and the customers will be here soon." The store was closed on Sunday, but our neighbors knew they could come in through the kitchen. I hurriedly downed some steaming coffee and a slice of buttered bread, then went to tell my grandmother. "The Germans are coming. Yes, the Germans. They'll be here soon." My grandmother's face collapsed. "May the Lord have mercy on my children," she murmured, wringing her slender hands. "I think . . . I think I should go to the cemetery . . . meditate at your grandfather's grave." I left her and ran to "my" House of Study.

My friends were there, and we talked things over. Everyone agreed that the German occupation would be bad for the Jews, but that was as far as our imagination went. After all, the Red Army was so near, just across the mountains. Yerahmiel, the ardent Zionist, suggested we take the opportunity to escape to Palestine. "Let's go, right now! Take advantage of the fact that the Germans aren't here yet." Someone reminded him that there was a war on. "Exactly," he retorted. And how were we supposed to get across the border? "Never mind, we could do it if we wanted to." Everyone but me was skeptical. I was secretly convinced that we would soon meet again in the Holy Land, and that the Messiah himself would lead us there. The war was the climactic battle between Gog and Magog — "the torments of redemption," it's called. The enemy now preparing to invade us would be vanquished, and his defeat would mark the Savior's triumph. "You and your mystical hallucinations," my friends said.

I slipped out and went to visit my two sick comrades, but they still refused to recognize me. Granted, they were not about to betray our secret, but why did they hide from me? Why did they pretend not to see me, or not to know me? Alone in the shadows with each of them, I whispered that our adventure was about to bear fruit. Another few days, another few weeks, and God Himself would slay the Angel of Death. Did they hear me? They smiled, or was it only an illusion? Perhaps they resented me for not following them into madness.

It was a feverish day, but everyone went about

his own business. One customer came to buy salt, another sugar. My mother and older sisters worked all day without a break. Tsipouka played hoops in the yard with a playmate. My father went in search of news, but the other leaders of the community knew no more than he did. Their Christian friends did not answer calls. My father ran from one to another, but no one was home. As for me, I plunged back into contemplation and the Midrash.

No one in Sighet suspected that our fate was already sealed. In Berlin we had been condemned, but we didn't know it. We didn't know that a man called Adolf Eichmann was already in Budapest weaving his black web, at the head of an elite, efficient detachment of thirty-five SS men, planning the operation that would crown his career; or that all the necessary means for "dealing with" us were already at hand in a place called Birkenau.

In my dreams my father always looks at me with a distant air, and I never know whether he sees me. Does he speak to me? I do not hear him.

I ask him about his life and about his death. About the wandering souls he has sent to brighten my path with their evanescent light.

Why does he say nothing? What does he seek to teach me with his silence?

Suddenly shadows loom around him. I beg them not to separate me from him. Far from him I cannot live, even after his death.

Don't get separated, don't get separated, my mother kept saying, before our separation.

Don't allow us to be separated again, don't, I say to my father, who does not answer. What must I do to make the dead agree at last to speak in my dreams?

The Third Reich was already doomed. The Germans themselves knew it. Hitler had just issued an order drafting young boys and old men. The siege of Leningrad had been lifted in January. The Allies had come ashore on the beaches of Anzio. The advancing Red Army was very near, the Normandy landing not far off. Berlin needed every soldier, every train. Nevertheless, the deportation of the Hungarian Jews was given priority over military convoys. Hitler was determined to keep the promise he had made to his people. To the very last day, with his very last weapons, he would strike inexorably at the last Jewish survivors of his empire. Washington knew it, and so did London. Stockholm knew it, and so did Berne and the Vatican.

But we, in our little town, did not.

The next day my father was visited by a Polish Jewish refugee for whom he had obtained a residency permit two or three years earlier. The refugee was a so-called assimilated intellectual who lived on the fringes of the community. He had been an engineer in Cracow or a lawyer in Warsaw. He was not without resources and had rented a "luxurious" apartment overlooking Sighet's main square. He had a very blond wife whose jaded air, it must be admitted, was quite becoming. She spoke only Polish, occasionally condescending to throw in a few words of "refined" German. Their only son was my age. At my mother's request I kept him company from time to time. He knew no one with whom he could share his reading and his games. I remember him well: a puffy yet sensual face, an evasive glance. How was I to communicate with him? He spoke Polish using a lot of body language in a vain effort to make himself understood. Fortunately, he liked chess, so twice a week I did my good deed by playing with him in his room, winning and losing in silence. In time, to his mother's open displeasure, I taught him a few phrases of Yiddish. Was that why I had to stop visiting?

His parents lived strangely apart from the community. They didn't go to synagogue, even on the High Holidays. Were they accepted in non-Jewish circles? I didn't think so. Actually, I had stopped thinking about them entirely. I had problems of my own.

And suddenly the man was at our house. What could he possibly want? My father explained it to us later: he had come to confide his anguish. If — if? — the Germans arrived, he and his family would surely be among the first to be arrested. What to do? Where could they find shelter? Budapest was out: the Germans were already there. Maybe they should convert. After all, he wasn't a believer anyway.

He was the only one to ask these questions. In general, our Jews preferred to wait and see.

Rumors reached us from big cities and small villages: The Nyilas were taking advantage of the German presence to unleash their fury against the Jews, their favorite prey — beards torn out, students thrown from moving trains, women humiliated, children persecuted. Nothing was too low for these bastards. Never mind, my father said, it will pass. Everything passes, even the thirst for Jewish blood. If the local fascists decided to flaunt their "patriotism" by targeting the Jews, so be it. That too would pass. Eventually they would tire of it. Besides, we knew these Nyilas. They were our neighbors, our customers. Their bark was worse than their bite. But what about the shattered windows, the holy books profaned, the old men whipped in the streets? All right, we would have to redouble our vigilance, pray in softer voices, stay inside more. Anyway, we soon had little choice. The government in Budapest issued decrees designed to limit the visibility and activities of the Jews. Stores were closed, and we were forbidden to go out except at certain hours. Jewish state employees were fired. Jews no longer had the right to walk in municipal parks or go to the movies or take the bus, tram, or train. However (thank God), they could still breathe the mountain air and warm themselves in the spring sun. The important thing was that even this abnormal life be normal. The important thing was that there be no pogroms.

The synagogues were still open. People were getting ready for Passover. Several of us gathered at the house of our neighbor, the Rebbe of Slotveno. The special oven in which the unleavened bread, the matzoh, would be cooked was ready. I loved it when the Rebbe, his beard quivering, eyes closed in ecstasy, cried, "A matzoh in the oven, another matzoh in the oven!" In fact, he was always ecstatic, this rebbe. If he could pray, study, eat, and visit the ritual baths, his soul would dance and sing his love of the Lord. Anything that brought Jews closer to heaven sanctified them. The Rebbe of Slotveno even called matzoh holy. Then suddenly someone came running: "They're here, they're here!" The Rebbe froze, a plate of matzoh dough in his hand. The messenger left, and several men followed him. At first I stayed alone with the motionless Rebbe, but finally curiosity got the better of me and I rushed out to the street. Yes, the Germans were here, in their tanks, jeeps, and motorcycles, wearing black uniforms, black to strike fear, walking straight ahead, looking neither right nor left. I watched for just a few seconds, for when I went back in I found the Rebbe just as I had left him. "Rebbe," I said, "I'm sorry, I shouldn't have . . ." He roused himself, put the dough in the oven, and called out his battle cry once more: "A matzoh in the oven, a holy matzoh for holy Passover." He sighed. "Where are the others?" he asked. "Outside. They went to look. The Germans are here." He lowered his head, then lifted it. "The Germans are here, you say? You say so because you see them? Well, let me ask you this: Do you see the blessed Creator? No, you don't, but He is here, whereas they will disappear. Do they think they can upset our work just like that, with impunity? That they can offend the Creator by preventing us from fulfilling His law? In a few days we shall welcome Passover, and that is all that matters. Have you forgotten the meaning of Passover? Our enemies are swallowed up; the people of Israel survive." I helped him prepare another matzoh. When the others came back, I went home. My parents, sisters, and several visitors were standing at the windows looking out at the vehicles rolling in from Bichkev, heading for the main square and the adjacent streets.

A page had been turned. The German occupation of Hungary was now a physical presence. But to everyone's astonishment, the officers of the Third Reich behaved quite correctly. There was little to complain about. The maids in requisitioned apartments (those of Jews and others) found that the officers made their own beds. They bowed politely to the mistress of the house and offered children candy. We were baffled. What about the rumors of atrocities, of the savagery of Nazism? Exaggerations.

Propaganda. "It's just like World War I," the older people said. "We've been fed lies. The people of Goethe and Schiller cannot sink to barbarism." No one warned us that we would pay dearly for the smiles and hand-kissing of the German officers, that their courtesy was part of the plan conceived by Eichmann and his specialists. Their psychological action against our people proved effective. Their aim was to lull us into a false sense of security. Our confidence and credulity was their weapon. Accustomed as we were to resignation, we told ourselves that since the enemy was cheerful and polite, there was no cause for alarm.

Anyway, it was Passover, festival of hope and remembrance. On the eve of the holiday a decree was issued closing the synagogues. My friends and I sadly took our leave of our own Beit Hamidrash. I glanced one last time at the walls, entrusting to them the holy scrolls and the volumes of the Talmud. Would we see them again? What a question! Of course we would, after all this was over. Otherwise we would have had to bury them in the cemetery, in accordance with tradition. In fact, I felt a sudden urge to go to the cemetery, to plead with the dead to intercede on our behalf. I didn't, though I don't remember why. Perhaps because there were more urgent tasks, like trying to decide where we would pray during the holiday. If the synagogues were closed, we would gather in private homes. My father and I went to services at the house of the Borsher Rebbe. We recited the Hallel, the song of gratitude, a group of psalms thanking God for His kindness to His people. Our hearts were heavy, but we sang just the same, albeit softly. We shook hands all around and left, wishing one another a happy holiday.

Back home the table was set: a white tablecloth, six candles, gleaming silver. My grandmother, in her holiday dress, was even more thoughtful than usual, as was little Tsipouka. My father made no effort to conceal his distress: "This is the first time in a long while that we've had no guest at our table." Usually we found guests in the Houses of Study and Prayer, but they were now closed. My father, however, did not give up. "Wait for me," he said, and disappeared. A good hour went by. We were just beginning to fear the worst when the door opened and my father came in with our guest: little Moishele, Moshe the beadle, his eyes gleaming strangely and full of pain. I had not seen him in weeks. Where had he been hiding? My father happily showed him to his place, on my right. Our guest didn't say a word during the first part of the Seder service. Did he read the Haggadah, or follow the narration? My father took Tsipouka on his lap and announced: "This is the bread of our affliction. . . . Our ancestors ate it in the land of Egypt." Why did our guest's smile seem half-ironic, half-desperate? I asked the first of the four ritual questions. "Why is this night different from all other nights?" Here again, our guest seemed both amused and exasperated. My father replied: ". . . Because once we were slaves, under Pharaoh in Egypt . . ." I glanced at the man sitting next to me. No doubt about it, he was laughing, but it was a joyless laughter. Suddenly I thought: What if he was the Prophet Elijah disguised as a beadle? Wasn't this the night Elijah was supposed to visit all Jewish homes, the night we remember and drink four cups of wine in honor of our deliverance? In the middle of the meal Moishele began talking in a soft, feverish voice. "Reb Shloime," he said, "I thank you for inviting me. Everyone else forgot me. They're afraid of me. You alone were not afraid. So I have a present for you. I would like to tell you what is in store for you. I owe you that."

Around the table all eyes hung on his parched lips. My little sister, lovely and sweet, lovely and heartbreakingly grave, sitting quietly on my father's lap, put her hand over her eyes as if to shield herself from a painful sight. My father stroked her hair, reassuring her. "Not now," he said to Moshe the beadle. "Your stories are sad, and the law forbids sadness on the night of Passover." "But this is important," Moshe insisted, "very important. You don't know what's in store for you, but I do. Why won't you listen to me, Reb Shloime? This concerns your future, the future of all of you." "Not now, Reb Moishe," my father repeated, "not now. Some other time." We finished the meal in silence. We recited grace. As we were about to rise to open the door, glasses in hand, to greet the Prophet Elijah, our guest disappeared.

This was my last Passover, my last holiday, at home. Its sadness would weigh upon all those to come.

Let us linger for a moment with Moishele, or Moshe, as I call him in my books. Perhaps he plays such a central role in the world of my novels because he represents the first survivor. Sometimes he is confused — or I confuse him — with Moshe the drunkard or Moshe the madman. But Moshe the beadle is different, for he lived our destiny before any of us. Messenger of the dead, he shouted his testimony from the rooftops and delivered it in silence, but either way no one would listen. People turned their backs so as not to see his eyes, as though fearing to glimpse a truth that held his past and our future in its steely grip. People tried, in vain, to make him doubt his own reason and his own memory, to accept that he had survived for nothing — indeed, to regret having survived.

On the seventh day of Passover, which symbolizes our ancestors' miraculous crossing of the Red Sea, a series of nefarious decrees was issued. Events now moved rapidly. The town crier, a hunchback carrying a drum that was too big for him, imperturbably announced these decrees. By order of the military command all stores

110

and offices belonging to Jews were closed. No Jew was allowed to go out, except in the late afternoon to buy food. There was a sudden frenzy of shopping. Though we no longer had the right to sell anything, the store's shelves were soon emptied. It mattered little whether customers paid or not. My father simply gave them what they needed. My sisters and I pitched in. Even little Tsipouka, her hair carefully combed, helped out. If the police caught us, God would not forsake us. Who could tell what tomorrow might bring? Then there were three days of curfew. Fortunately, everyone was well provisioned. There was nothing more to fear.

The yellow star? That scarcely bothered me. It made me feel more intimately bound to the Jews of the Middle Ages who wore the *rouelle* in the ghettos of Italy. I felt I was living — not learning, but living — an incandescent chapter of history, one that later generations would study. No, I was not afraid of the yellow star. All Jewish families were cutting up bits of yellow cloth. A wretched market sprang up; there were stars of every possible style. Those worn by the rich were bright, those of the poor faded. Strange as it may seem, I wore mine with newfound pride. Some passersby stared at me derisively, while others averted their eyes. That was their business. But the posters that suddenly appeared on the walls were something else. They were signed by the German military governor, and their message was clear: Whoever opposed the new order would be shot. Shot? I didn't believe it, couldn't believe it, but my legs trembled.

Special units of the army and the notorious Gendarmerie began raiding Jewish homes. There were inspections, searches, threats. You had to turn in your jewelry, silver, foreign currency, precious stones, objects of value. My father tried to make light of it. "They're going to be disappointed. The only thing they'll find in most Jewish homes is poverty. I hope they confiscate that too." But even poor families had silver candlesticks or Kiddush cups for Shabbat, so they left the least valuable objects in sight and hid the others in cellars and attics. It was reported that anyone who resisted was beaten by soldiers, though not at our house. A lieutenant and two gendarmes drew up the list. They went through the living quarters and the store, searching cupboards, opening drawers, throwing books on the floor. But my poor mother was impressed nonetheless. "Did you notice?" she asked. "The lieutenant saluted on the way in and the way out?" Maybe she was trying to be funny. One way or the other, the gendarmes got what they wanted: the poor Jews of my town became poorer still.

It would be hard to exaggerate the malice of the Hungarian gendarmes. Ordered to implement the Eichmann plan, they did so with a zeal and brutality that will forever remain the dishonor of the Hungarian army and nation. Were they all anti-Semites or members of the fascist Nyilas party? Why were they so cruel, so sadistic? They beat women and children, trampled on old people and the sick. The announcement that a ghetto was to be created came almost as a relief. At least we would be among Jews, with our families.

Once again I felt as though I were reliving a page of medieval Jewish history. We would now live as our ancestors had in Italy and Spain, and later in Germany and Poland, and we would not be alone, for their presence would protect us. I pictured myself within the walls of Frankfurt or Venice, Lublin or Carpentras, listening to masters from beyond the grave who explained that these gloomy little alleyways led to the light of discovery. We must not give way to pessimism. In search of certainty, I rushed to the shelf where my mother kept her German books. There I consulted her pride and joy: the *Jewish Encyclopedia*. I looked up "ghetto" and was surprised to find that in ancient times the Jewish quarters were created by the Jews themselves, out of fear of alien influences. Such was the case for the communities of Rome, Antioch, and Alexandria. Only later were ghettos imposed on them, under various names: Judería in Spain and Portugal, Rue des Juifs in France. In 1288 King Alfonso III ordered the Jews of Saragossa to live apart from the Christians. In 1480 the Catholic monarchs Ferdinand and Isabella issued a similar order. In 1555 Pope Paul IV drove the Jews from his cities, except those who lived

113

in the ghettos. In Mainz in 1662 the Great Elector Jean-Philippe deprived the Jews of the right to live outside the walls of their quarter. But the ghetto, however deprivational, could be spiritually rewarding. It helped to preserve the culture and tradition that constitute the Jewish heritage. After all, in 1652 my own ancestor, Rabbi Yom-Tov Lipmann-Heller, rejoiced in having helped to build the walls ringing the Jewish quarter of Leopoldstadt.

The truth is that some Jews in Sighet could have escaped the ghetto. It was a mild spring, and they had only to flee to the mountains until the ordeal was over. Maria — our old housekeeper, wonderful Maria who had worked for us since I was born — begged us to follow her to her home. She offered us her cabin in a remote hamlet. There would be room for all six of us, and Grandma Nissel as well. Seven in one cabin? Yes, she swore it, as Christ was her witness. She would take care of us, she would handle everything. We said no, politely but firmly. We did so because we still didn't know what was in store for us.

It was April 1944, just a few weeks before the Allied landing in Normandy, but the Jews of Sighet had not been informed of the ramifications of the Final Solution. The free world, including Jewish leaders in America and Palestine, had known since 1942, but we knew nothing. Why didn't they warn us? Though this in no way attenuates the guilt of the killers and

114

their accomplices, it is impossible not to feel indignation at the passivity of our brothers and sisters in America and Palestine. How many of our people would have escaped the enemy if Roosevelt, Churchill, Ben-Gurion, Weizmann, and the leading lights of world Jewry had issued radio appeals: "Hungarian Jews, don't let yourselves be locked into ghettos, don't get into the cattle cars! Flee, hide in the caves, take refuge in the woods!" Had we been told that the road from the ghettos led to the railroad stations, and that the trains' destination was Auschwitz, had we been told what Auschwitz meant, many Sighet Jews would have chosen to go underground — and thereby would have survived.

This question has haunted me ever since the war: Why did the Jews of the free world act as they did? Hadn't our people survived persecution and exile throughout the centuries because of its spirit of solidarity? Driven from their land after the defeat of Judea, the Jews found a haven among their brothers in Rome and Cyprus. Expelled from Spain, they were welcomed by their fellow Jews in Turkey and the Netherlands. When one community suffered, the others supported it, throughout the Diaspora. Why was it different this time?

In my first essay on the Eichmann trial, published in *Commentary*, I suggested that, before condemning the criminals and their accomplices, we confess our own shortcomings. Free Jews did not do all they could to save the Jews of

115

Europe. The Palmach in Palestine could have sent emissaries to Poland and Hungary to train Jews for combat, or at least to inform them. It did not.

This article drew the wrath of Golda Meir, then Israeli minister of foreign affairs. "You forget," she replied, "that the world was at war, that Palestine was under a British mandate. How could our boys have reached occupied Europe?" Usually I didn't dare argue with her. I respected her and was careful not to irritate her. But this time I decided to answer: "Every boy or girl who risked his or her life going from ghetto to ghetto or community to community to maintain contact among persecuted Jews ran a greater risk than your emissaries. Yet they accepted this risk, while your men were ordered to remain in Palestine."

"You're forgetting the paratroopers," Golda said. "They were ready to go, as soon as the British army gave its green light."

"Exactly," I replied. "The paratroopers. Their courage and heroism are laudable. But by the time they arrived in Budapest, there were almost no Jews left to save in the provinces."

This is an observation that applies equally well to Raoul Wallenberg, to whom we will be eternally grateful. He risked life and liberty, abandoning the security of his home in Sweden for the Hungarian capital, where he saved thousands of Jews. But for the Jews of the provinces, it was too late.

For us it was too late, in every sense. Sacrificed, abandoned, and betrayed, delivered to the invader and left to face him alone, we were ignored by everyone but the enemy. He alone paid attention to us. And when he drove us to the ghetto, we went.

I see images of exodus and uprooting, reminiscent of a past buried in memory; ravaged, dazed, disoriented faces. Everything changed overnight. A few words uttered by a man in a uniform, and the order of Creation collapsed. Everything was dismantled: ties were severed, words were emptied of their meaning. Homes became unrecognizable; my house was no longer my own. Everything a family had managed to accumulate in a lifetime had to be left behind. Utensils, clothing, pots and pans, books, and furniture: it was all too heavy, too burdensome, to be carried to the small room or cellar to which the family would be assigned in the ghetto. There were wrenching scenes: an old Hasid, Reb Feivish, pushing a child's carriage before him. He is alone, weeping. A young boy offers help. Reb Feivish tries to thank him, but his voice is choked by sobs. The chief rabbi and his family had to move. So did the Borsher Rebbe, and Reb Shloime Heller, the rabbinical judge, and the leaders of the community. It was exile within exile, incessant comings and goings, as though the city had become a whirling carousel. My head was spinning too. I wanted to

117

be everywhere at once, to see it all, absorb it all, give everyone a hand. For we were among the lucky ones: since our house was within the designated quarter, we didn't have to move, but only had to rearrange the rooms, keeping the largest one and giving the others to relatives. The Reichs moved in with us, and I gave their daughters Hebrew lessons. I searched in vain for my Kabalist master. I was told he was in the smaller ghetto, across town. I wanted to believe he was in hiding somewhere. Perhaps he had used his formulas and amulets to make himself invisible. Could he hear me? Why do you do nothing to disarm the enemy? Conversant as you are with celestial mysteries, why don't you call upon their Creator? Is it not your duty to repel evil? The inhabitants of the ghetto, after all, are doing theirs.

There was generosity and mutual aid; no theft, quarrels, or recriminations, no petty jealousy. Here was Jewish solidarity in action.

My former classmates and I sporadically continued our study of the sacred texts, most often meeting in Ezra Malek's garden. We would sit on the grass under a tree and ponder complex problems relating to fasting or holidays. Perhaps analyzing the positions of Rav and his adversary Shmuel would help us forget the ever more pressing danger.

The Germans demanded that the ghetto supply a daily battalion of Jewish workers. Lists were drawn up, and few avoided this draft —

not out of fear, but out of compassion: If I don't go, someone else will have to, and that wouldn't be moral; it wouldn't be Jewish.

Later I would read much outrageous critical commentary about the Judenrat and the Jewish police in the ghettos. Were they guilty of trying to survive at any price, even while striving to save as many lives as possible? Were they collaborators or martyrs? In general, I would speak in their defense. There were many people like Adam Czerniakow in Warsaw, who killed himself the day the Germans demanded a daily quota of ten thousand Jews for Treblinka. But what about Chaim Rumkowski, "king" of the Lodz ghetto? Is he, too, defensible? No, he lived too comfortably, too "luxuriously," for me to speak on his behalf. Yet I consider him a victim too, a victim of oppression, of the murderous, dehumanizing order the hangmen imposed on the entire Jewish people. Were the Jewish kapos victims too? Yes, they were — with a few exceptions. In those days all Jews were victims, even if all the victims were not Jews.

Some commentators have compared the "elders of the Judenrat" to Pétain, ascribing the same good intentions (the effort to interpose themselves between the conquerors and the conquered) and the same errors (one cannot mingle with the enemy without being drawn into his logic) to both. But I don't like analogies. No Jewish "elder" commanded the powers or resources of a Pétain or a Laval. The Judenräte headed not states but prisons. And let us not forget that the "elders," too, were condemned to death because they were Jews. They enjoyed special privileges and they were able to eat their fill, but did they hold the power of life or death over their fellow Jews? Here we must say no, not really. The killers and their accomplices kept this right for themselves. True, the various Jewish officials could bestow favors, appoint assistants, and issue work permits, ration cards, or housing permits to relatives or friends, who were thereby granted a moment of respite until the next "action." But no more than that. In the end all the ghettos were liquidated, along with their chiefs.

In our ghetto these ethical questions did not arise. Its leaders had no dilemmas of conscience to confront. We stayed too brief a time for a new social structure to be established or for conflicts to erupt. There was barely more than a month: that was not enough for our rules and customs to wither. True, the Germans appointed an assimilated engineer to the post of Judenälteste, or Jewish elder, but it was still the president of the community who had the ear and the respect of its members. We listened to the chief rabbi, not the police. I don't know of a single case in which anyone is alleged to have been beaten or humiliated by the Jewish police or the Judenrat. Despite the overcrowding and strict rationing, there were no incidents of hatred or rancor. There was little or no corruption.

With hindsight I realize that it was in the ghetto that I truly began to love the Jews of my town. Throughout the ordeal they maintained their dignity as human beings and as Jews. Imprisoned, reduced to subhuman status, they showed themselves still capable of spiritual greatness. Against the enemy they stood as one, affirming their faith in their faith. Yes, I know very well that a community cannot be judged on its behavior over just a few weeks. But this is a question not of judgment but of love.

And I do love them, the Jews of my town, the Jews of the ghetto. That's why I glorify them in my writings — and I make no secret of it. Unlike some of my colleagues, I refuse to dwell on ugliness and abjection. My characters are not sexually obsessed or pathologically greedy. Of course, they were not all messianic dreamers and aspiring poets. What of it? The enemy has heaped enough abuse on these Jews without my adding to it. He cast them into the mud and then denounced them as dirty. He starved them and then mocked their weakness. He distorted their features and then ridiculed their appearance. He tortured them, sickened them with sorrow and solitude, then called them madmen.

But to me the Jews of Sighet are neither ugly nor repulsive. Stripped of their property, crushed and mutilated, they still embody the nobility of Israel and the eternity of God, while their enemy — who is your enemy as well — embodies all that is most vile in man. I shall act not as their detractor, but as their *melitz yosher*, their intercessor. But no, I speak too soon. Who am I, what special merit entitles me to intercede on their behalf? They have no further need of that. On the contrary, may they be intercessors for me and mine on high, and may I be worthy of them.

It was a black Saturday in May. I have told the story and will tell it again, will tell it forever, hoping to find in it some hidden truth, some vague hope of salvation.

Events unfolded faster and faster. By imposing his own pace, the enemy became time's master, and time itself became our enemy. Two high-ranking Gestapo officers arrived (we were later told that one of them was Eichmann himself, which is why I think I recognized him during his trial in Jerusalem). The Council of Elders was summoned for an emergency meeting. We waited anxiously for my father, who had gone out in search of news. Neighbors gathered, and a rumor spread like fire — transports, something about transports.

The first convoy was to leave the following morning, but our street would not be part of it. We spent the night helping friends and neighbors get ready. "Do you need clothes? Cookies, eggs, flour?" There were scenes of wrenching resignation, but of tenderness as well. I knocked on neighbors' doors, murmured words of farewell, clasped hands, said goodbye to Yerahmiel, asked the blessing of the Slotvener Rebbe, respectfully kissed the hand of the Borsher Rebbe, went away and came back. Ovens burned everywhere. Everyone prepared for the long journey, comforted one another: We won't be separated long, we'll see each other again soon . . . after the war. At dawn the men said their prayers before slipping their talit and tefillin into their rucksacks. It was a beautiful, unusually hot, sunny day. The streets teemed with distraught men and women. They were thirsty, but the gendarmes prevented them from going back into what had been their last shelter, even for an instant. My sisters and I moved among them with pots and bottles filled with water. Little Tsipouka had never seemed so small, nor so grown up. She gave sick people many times her age a drink of water. At last the convoy set out — in a hush, a kind of religious contemplation. The chief rabbi, his beard cut off, walked wearily, his bag slung over his shoulder. I averted my eyes; to see him like that was unbearable. And my teachers, my classmates — each of them took along a part of me. I felt ill, I had never felt so ill. I wanted to shout, to scream like a madman. I wished I were mad, like my two friends, God's madmen, who had lost their minds on a battlefield strewn with dreams and mystic dreamers. Where was the Messiah now, my friends? Then suddenly there they were, too weak to walk, being carried on stretchers. I said goodbye to them, called out for them to hold on.

Soon it would be our turn, but for now we simply followed the convoy to the ghetto's exit. We were ashamed to be staying behind. Numb, filled with anguish, we went home and gathered in the kitchen, as if in mourning. The convoy had not yet left town. We were told that the people would spend the night at the synagogue, far from us, already so far. An eerie calm fell over the abandoned homes. Those who remained in the main ghetto went from house to house simply to shake hands, to start conversations which reassured them they were still alive.

We spent that night in the yard, listening to Soviet artillery, whose firings lit the mountain-tops. They were only a dozen miles or so away. With a little luck the Red Army would arrive before the cattle cars. One attack, one small shift of the front, and we would be saved. That would be too beautiful, too miraculous. But this was not a time of miracles. God held them back. For whom? For when?

And yet. Human miracles do exist, or rather, they could. That Saturday night someone came and knocked on our shuttered and nailed window facing the street that marked the ghetto's edge. We caught our breath and looked at one another. Who could it be? A policeman ordering us to turn out the light? A friend of my father's coming to warn him, as he had promised, of impending catastrophe? By the time we got the window open, the unknown visitor was gone.

Certainly it had been Maria, gallant, courageous, and loyal Maria, a believer who never complained of her fate. Have I said often enough that she was part of the family? When we went on vacation, she came along. She participated in our festivals and in our mourning, leaving us only when the government forbade non-Jews from working for Jews, and when that happened she wept and swore she would return "as soon as all this is over." In the days of the ghetto she would thread her way through barricades and barbed wire to bring us cheese and eggs, fruit and vegetables. And that night, a Sunday, she appeared again. She had managed to slip through the armed security cordon the gendarmes had thrown up around the half-empty ghetto. "No, it's not witchcraft," she said. "There are ways of getting in and out. I know a safe place. I wanted to come and tell you. . . . To beg you . . . The cabin in the mountains . . . It's ready. . . . Come. . . . There's nothing to fear there. . . . You'll be safe. . . . There are no Germans there, and no bastards helping them. Come. . . ." Dear Maria. If other Christians had acted like her, the trains rolling toward the unknown would have been less crowded. If priests and pastors had raised their voices, if the Vatican had broken its silence, the enemy's hands would not have been so free. But most of our compatriots thought only of themselves.

Barely was a Jewish house emptied of its inhabitants than they descended like vultures on the abandoned possessions, breaking into closets and drawers, stealing bedsheets and clothing, smashing things, looting. For them it was a party, a treasure hunt. They were not like our Maria.

We gathered at the kitchen table and held a last family meeting. Should we follow Maria or stay? We surely would have accepted her offer had we known that "destination unknown" meant Birkenau — or even simply that we would be deported from the country. But we didn't know. All we knew was what we had been told: that the convoys were headed for the interior. "Well-informed" Jewish notables in Budapest had given clear assurances on this point. In light of that, the general view was that we should tell Maria no. "But why?" she implored us, her voice breaking. "Because," my father replied, "a Jew must never be separated from his community: what happens to everyone else will happen to us as well." My mother wondered aloud whether it might not be better "to send the children with Maria." By "the children" she meant the three oldest. Tsipouka would stay, as would Grandmother. We protested: "We're young and strong, the trip won't be as dangerous for us. If anyone should go with Maria, it's you." After a brief discussion, we thanked Maria but . . .

My father was right. We wanted to stay together, like everyone else. Family unity is one of our important traditions, as the enemy well knew. And he now used that knowledge, spreading the rumor in the ghetto that the Jewish population would be transferred to a Hungarian labor camp where — and this was the essential thing — families would remain together. And we believed it. So it was that the strength of the family tie, which had contributed to the survival of our people for centuries, became a tool in its exterminator's hands.

I think of Maria often, with affection and gratitude. And with wonder as well. This simple, uneducated woman stood taller than the city's intellectuals, dignitaries, and clergy. My father had many acquaintances and even friends in the Christian community, but not one of them showed the strength of character of this peasant woman. Of what value was their faith, their education, their social position, if it aroused neither conscience nor compassion?

It was a simple and devout Christian woman who saved her town's honor.

Our turn came on Tuesday, May 16. "All Jews out!" the gendarmes screamed, and we found ourselves in the street. There was another heat wave. My little sister was thirsty, and my grandmother too. They didn't complain, but I did, not openly, but it amounted to the same thing. I felt queasy, ill. I was suffering, but didn't know from what. I was ineffably sad.

127

As in the presence of death, I didn't dare raise my voice. This was where my childhood and my adolescence, my prayers, studies, and fasting had led. These moments would remain forever etched within me. Wherever life took me, a part of me would always remain in that street, in front of my empty house, awaiting the order to depart.

I see my little sister, I see her with her rucksack, so cumbersome, so heavy. I see her and an immense tenderness sweeps over me. Never will her innocent smile fade from my soul. Never will her glance cease to sear me. I tried to help her; she protested. Never will the sound of her voice leave my heart. She was thirsty, my little sister was thirsty. Her lips were parched. Pearls of sweat formed on her clear forehead. I gave her a little water. "I can wait," she said, smiling. My little sister wanted to be brave. And I wanted to die in her place.

I seldom speak of her in my writing, for I dare not. My little sister with her sun-bathed golden hair is my secret. I never even talked to Marion or to my son Elisha about her. It mortifies me to talk about her in the past tense, for she is present. Her presence is more real to me than my own. My little sister Tsiporah, my little angel scorched by a darkened sun, I cannot picture you as death's hostage. You will remain on our street, on the pavement in front of our house.

I gazed at the house — we all did — with

anguish. Here we had lived a Jewish family life that was now gone forever. The laughter and laments, the peace of Shabbat, the prayer of the God of Abraham whispered by my mother and my grandmother, the festival of Sukkoth, the songs of Rosh Hashana, the Passover meals, the community gatherings, my grandfather's visits. The stories of beggars and of refugees, the forbidden broadcasts of Radio London and Radio Moscow that we listened to at night, curtains drawn and shutters closed. I picture myself sitting under an acacia tree, a book in my hands, talking to the clouds. Tsipouka is playing with a hoop. "Come and play with me," she says, but I don't feel like it. And now, as I write these words, my heart is pounding. I should have closed my book and stopped my dream, dropped everything to play with my little sister. Other images rise up: the sleigh in winter, the horse and carriage in summer; a cousin's funeral (a fortune-teller is said to have foretold her death); Bea sick with typhus: she lies in a room of her own, feverish and contagious, hovering between life and death. My grandmother asks me to go with her to the synagogue. It is night. She opens the Holy Ark and sobs, "Holy Torah, intercede on behalf of Batya, daughter of Sarah. She is young and can still accomplish many good deeds for your glory. Tell the Lord, blessed be His name, to let her live. She will be more useful to Him than I." She closes the Ark and backs slowly to the door. There she stops and says, "If I have any years to live, Lord, give them to her. I exchange my future for hers. Let that be my gift." When Bea takes a few steps, I glance at my grandmother. She has offered her life. What will become of her now? I picture our house and see Hilda inside, Hilda the oldest of the children, whose radiant beauty drew all the matchmakers of the region.

I see the people who came through that door day and night to consult with my father — my father who now, bent under the weight of his pack, knows not to whom he might turn for advice. And my mother, always gracious and brave, afraid to look at us, afraid to see the house, afraid to burst into tears only to find she can never stop. So she looks at the sky, the pitiless sky that numbs us with an unseasonable and stifling heat. And the sun? Will it keep its secret? The night before, very late, like makeshift gravediggers, we had dug a dozen holes under the trees to bury what remained of our jewelry, precious objects, and money. I buried the gold watch I had been given as a bar mitzvah present.

For years I dreamed of returning to my native town. It was an obsession. It took two decades, and that trip has now been added to my obsessions. It was night. There was a sleeping town and a sleeping house which hadn't changed: the same gate, same garden, same well. Choked with fear, as though caught in a whirlwind of hallucinations, I wondered whether it had all been a dream, whether our Jewish neighbors were still there, and my parents and my sisters too. Terror swept me away and carried me back. I waited for a window to open and for a boy who looked like the child I had been to call out to me: Hey, mister, what are you doing in my dream?

But strangers were living in my house. They had never heard my name. Inside, nothing had changed: the same furniture, the same tile stove my father had borrowed money to buy; the beds, tables, and chairs were ours, still in the same places. My feverish eyes wandered left and right, up and down. Was it possible that not a single trace of us remained? But there was one, just one. On the wall above my bed had been a photograph of my beloved master, Rebbe Israel of Wizhnitz. I remember it well: I had hung it there the day he died, the second day of the month of Sivan. I can see myself standing there, a heavy hammer in my hand, driving in the nail and hanging the frame. As I write these words, I suddenly realize that my mother died eight years later on exactly the same day, along with my little sister and Grandma Nissel. I cried for the Rebbe's death as I hung his photograph above my bed. The nail was still there. A huge cross was hanging from it.

"We must go now," my mother said. "We must stay together."

It was Tuesday afternoon. We were still in

131

Sighet. Our convoy would not leave for several days. We had been temporarily transferred to the smaller ghetto, whose inhabitants had just been driven out.

We moved into the home of Mendel, my father's brother. My mother cooked our favorite dish, latkes, potato pancakes. This time there was no rationing; we ate all we wanted.

Mendel was my silent uncle. He had married Golda, daughter of my maternal uncle Israel. He was pious and shy. They had three children. Their photograph lies before me, saved by a relative.

Sacred books were scattered on the floor. Someone must have removed them from his bag at the last minute. The table was set, and there was food on the plates. They had been taken away in the middle of a meal. This was what remained of a family.

After the war I questioned every survivor of the second transport I could find, seeking news of Uncle Mendel and his family. I thought I found the answer in 1988, when an elderly man called out to me in the lobby of a Miami Beach hotel. He was, like me, of Romanian-Hungarian origin, from a small village near Sighet, and he told me he had stayed in the smaller ghetto until its evacuation. In fact, he had been in the same camp with my uncle. "Really?" I exclaimed. "You knew my uncle?" "Knew him!" he said. "For years I've seen him, even in my sleep." And then he told me. At first Mendel and his son had been spared, like my father and me, and had been sent to a camp where conditions were relatively tolerable. But they were in different barracks and saw each other only during the day, at work. One night they could not bear to be separated. When the roll was called, the SS Blockführer counted and re-counted the prisoners and ordered: "Let the prisoner who does not belong in this barracks show himself." Mendel's son took a few steps forward. "Closer!" the officer shouted. My young cousin obeyed, halting when he reached the SS man. The officer slowly drew his revolver and shot my cousin in the head, point-blank. My uncle, that sweet and timid man, hurled himself onto his son's body, as if to protect him in death. The SS man stared at him for a long moment and then shot him in the head too. "Ever since then," my witness said, "I see Mendel and his son in my dreams."

And I, I think of the biblical law that, out of compassion for animals, forbids the slaughter of an ox and his calf on the same day. The Germans, however, did not shrink from killing a father and son together, without a second thought, as one would step on two insects.

Fishel and Voïcsi, my cousins from Antwerp, later gave me a different version of their deaths. What is certain, though, is that the enemy annihilated my Uncle Mendel's family.

And what happened to my Aunt Zlati, my father's younger sister? I search my memories of the ghetto for her, but she is not there.

She was married to Nahman-Elye. I don't remember their two very young children, nor do I recall their presence during the weeks before the transport. Nahman-Elye, it seems, was among those the Hungarian army released from the labor battalions to be locked up in the ghetto. It seems he was deported with the first transport and later succumbed to the pressures and temptations of the camp life and became a cruel and murderous kapo. It seems he was tried, sentenced to death, and executed by former deportees. My uncle in the enemy's service? A kapo? My uncle a torturer of his brothers in misfortune? I don't want to believe it.

But yes, that's the way it was.

We arrived at the station, where the cattle cars were waiting. Ever since my book *Night* I have pursued those nocturnal trains that crossed the devastated continent. Their shadow haunts my writing. They symbolize solitude, distress, and the relentless march of Jewish multitudes toward agony and death. I freeze every time I hear a train whistle.

Why were those trains allowed to roll unhindered into Poland? Why were the tracks leading to Birkenau never bombed? I have put these questions to American presidents and generals and to high-ranking Soviet officers. Since Moscow and Washington knew what the killers were doing in the death camps, why was

134

nothing done at least to slow down their "production"? That not a single Allied military aircraft ever tried to destroy the rail lines converging on Auschwitz remains an outrageous enigma to me. Birkenau was "processing" ten thousand Jews a day. Stopping a single convoy for a single night — or even for just a few hours — would have prolonged so many lives. At the least it would have been a warning to the Germans: Jewish lives do matter. But the free world didn't care whether Jews lived or died, whether they were annihilated one day or the next. And so the sealed trains continued to shatter the silence of Europe's flowering landscapes.

Meanwhile, our world contracted steadily. The country became a city, the city a street, the street a house, the house a room, the room a sealed cattle car, the cattle car a concrete cellar where . . .

No, let us go no further. Decency and custom forbid it. I said it earlier, when speaking of my grandfather: In Jewish tradition a man's death belongs to him alone. Let the gas chambers remain closed to prying eyes, and to the imagination. We will never know all that happened behind those doors of steel. They say the victims fought among themselves for a breath of air, for one more second of life, that they climbed on the shoulders of the weakest in the so-called *Todeskampf,* the final struggle among the dying. Much has been said when silence ought to have

135

prevailed. Let the dead speak for themselves, if they so choose. If not, may they be left in peace.

It is unbelievable how fast people adapt. It hurts to admit it, but within hours of first breathing the cattle car's nauseating air, we began to feel at home. "Home" was the edge of the wooden plank I sat on as I dreamed of the Jewish exiles of antiquity and the Middle Ages. More curious than afraid, I thought of myself as their brother. Mixed into my sadness there was undeniable excitement, for we were living a historic event, a historic adventure. The main thing was that we were still together. Had we been told that this journey would last for weeks or even years, we would have replied: May God grant that it be so, for nothing is worse than the unknown, and that was our destination — the unknown. I remember clinging to the thought that nothing is unknown to God, while nothing is truly known to man.

A rumor spread through the train. The Jewish doctors and their families, until recently allowed to live outside the ghetto, had been ordered to return to the ghetto the night before the transport and to join us that morning at the station. But we had seen no sign of them. It was now said that they had gathered at one of their homes the night before and decided to kill themselves. The rumor was apparently false, for in Birkenau I ran into our family doctor, Dr. Fisch, who had helped deliver Tsipouka. But thirty years later I found that the story was true after all. I was lecturing at a large university near Boston when a member of the physics department came up to me. "You're from Sighet, aren't you?" he asked. "So am I." He introduced himself, and the name gave me a start: he was the son of a famous surgeon. In Sighet we had evolved in different circles, but we had been brought to Auschwitz in the same convoy. We had a long talk about our town, and at one point I asked him about the rumor. He confirmed it. The doctors had indeed agreed on a collective suicide pact. "But why? Since at the time we didn't know where they were taking us." It turned out that his father did know. He had operated on a German officer who told him everything. Afterward he had summoned his colleagues to discuss what to do. The majority voted not to board the trains, deciding they might as well die at home. Some of the suicides did not succeed. They were carried to the cattle cars on stretchers.

My new friend the physics professor died one night in June 1991. A suicide, rumor had it. I was struck by the date. I realized that he too had died on the second day of the month of Sivan, exactly forty-seven years after his missed appointment with death in Birkenau.

Life in the cattle cars was the death of my adolescence. How quickly I aged. As a child I loved the unexpected: a visitor from afar, an unforeseen event, a marriage, a storm, even a disaster. Anything was preferable to routine. Now it was just the opposite. Anything was preferable to change. We clung to the present, we dreaded the future.

Hunger, thirst, and heat, the fetid stench, the hysterical howling of a woman gone mad — we were ready to endure it all, to suffer it all. So much so that a "normal," structured social life soon took shape in the car. Families stayed together, sharing whatever came their way: hard-boiled eggs, dried cakes, or fruit, respecting strict rules about drinking water, allowing each member a turn near the barred openings or at the waste pail shielded by blankets. People adjusted with disconcerting rapidity. Morning and evening we said our prayers together. I had brought some precious books along in my pack: a commentary by Rabbi Haim David Azoulai (the Hida), the K'dushat Levi of the Berdichever Rebbe. I opened them and tried hard to concentrate. A phrase of the Zohar, a major work of the Kabala, haunted me: When the people of Israel set out into exile, God went with them. And now? I wondered. How far would God follow us now?

On the last day, when the train stopped near the Auschwitz station, our premonitions resurfaced. A few "neighbors" devoured more than their rations, as though sensing that their days were numbered. My mother kept entreating us: Stay together at all costs. Someone, I can't remember who, asked, "What if we can't? What if they separate us?" My mother's answer: "Then we'll meet again at home as soon as the war is over."

Certain images of the days and nights spent on that train invade my dreams even now: anticipation of danger, fear of the dark; the screams of poor Mrs. Schechter, who, in her delirium, saw flames in the distance; the efforts to make her stop; the terror in her little boy's eyes. I recall every hour, every second. How could I forget? They were the last hours I spent with my family: the murmured prayers of my grandmother, whose eyes saw beyond this world; my mother's gestures, which had never been more tender; the troubled face of my little sister, who refused to show her fear. Yes, my memory gathered it all in, retained it all.

There was sudden trepidation that gripped us when, toward midnight, the train lurched forward again after stopping for several hours. I can still hear the whistle. Elsewhere I have told of what happened next — or rather, I have tried to tell it. But it feels like yesterday. It feels like now. Through the cracks in the boards I see barbed wire stretching to infinity. A thought occurs to me: The Kabala is right, infinity exists.

I see myself sitting there, haggard and disoriented, a shadow among shadows. I hear my little sister's fitful breathing. I try to conjure up my mother's features, and my father's. I need someone to reassure me. My heart thunders in deafening beats. Then there is silence, heavy and complete. Something was about to happen, we could feel it. Fate would at last reveal a truth reserved exclusively for us, a primordial truth, an ultimate postulate that would annihilate or overshadow all received ideas. There was a burst of noise and the night was shattered into a thousand pieces. I felt myself shaken, pulled to my feet, pushed toward the door, toward strange shouting beings and barking dogs, a swelling throng that would cover the earth.

In *Night* I tell of the wrath of the "veterans." They swore at us. "What the hell are you *Schweinehunde* doing here?" I was puzzled. Did they think we had come to this hell voluntarily, out of curiosity? Only years later did I understand. Two of their former companions, Rudolf Vrba and Alfred Wetzler, had managed to escape from Birkenau in 1944 to warn Hungarian Jews of what was awaiting them. That's why they were so enraged. They thought we should have known. Some of them even hit us.

Where were we going? It mattered little, for it was the same everywhere. All roads led to the enemy; it was he who would throw open the invisible black door that awaited us. "Stay together," my mother said. For another minute we did, clinging to one another's arms. Nothing in the world could separate us. The entire German army could not take my little sister from me. Then a curt order was issued — men on one side, women on the other — and that was that. A single order, and we were separated. I stared intently, trying desperately not to lose sight of my mother, my little sister with her hair of gold and sun, my grandmother, my older sisters. I see them always, for I am still looking for them, trying to embrace them one last time. We were taken away before I could tell my mother goodbye, before I could kiss her hand and beg her forgiveness for the wrongs I must have done her, before I could squeeze Tsipouka, my little sister, to my heart. What remains of that night like no other is an irremediable sense of loss, of parting. My mother and my little sister left, and I never said goodbye. It all remains unreal. It's only a dream, I told myself as I walked, hanging on my father's arm. It's a nightmare that they have torn me from those I love, that they are beating people to death, that Birkenau exists and that it harbors a gigantic altar where demons of fire devour our people. It's in God's nightmare that human beings are hurling living Jewish children into the flames.

I reread what I have just written, and my hand trembles. I who rarely weep am in tears. I see the flames again, and the children, and yet again I tell myself that it is not enough to weep.

It took me a long time to convince myself I was not somehow mistaken. I have checked with others who arrived that same night, consulted documents of the Sonderkommandos, and yes, a thousand times yes: Unable to "handle" such a large number of Hungarian Jews in the crematoria, the killers were not content merely to incinerate children's dead bodies. In their barbarous madness they cast living Jewish children into specially tended furnaces.

And if I bear within me a nameless grief and disillusionment, a bottomless despair, it is because that night I saw good and thoughtful Jewish children, bearers of mute words and dreams, walking into darkness before being consumed by the flames. I see them now, and I still curse the killers, their accomplices, the indifferent spectators who knew and kept silent, and Creation itself, Creation and those who perverted and distorted it. I feel like screaming, howling like a madman so that that world, the world of the murderers, might know it will never be forgiven.

To this day I am shaken when I see a child, for behind him I glimpse other children. Starving, terrified, drained, they march without a backward glance toward truth and death — which are perhaps the same. Uncomplaining, unprotesting, asking no one's pity, it is as if they have had enough of living on a planet so cruel, so vile and so filled with hate that their very innocence has brought their death. Do not deny it, I forbid you to deny it. Know, then, that the world that let the killers annihilate a million and a half Jewish children bears its guilt within itself.

That night someone within me, my other self, told me it was impossible that these atrocities could be committed in the middle of the twentieth century while the world stayed silent. This was not the Middle Ages. My very last resistance broken, I let myself be pulled, pushed, and kicked, like a deaf and mute sleepwalker. I could see everything, grasp it and register it, but only later would I try to put in order all the sensations and all the memories. How stunned I was, for example, to discover another time outside time, a universe parallel to this one, a creation within Creation, with its own laws, customs, structures, and language. In this universe some men existed only to kill and others only to die. And the system functioned with exemplary efficiency: tormenters tormented and crushed their prey, torturers tortured human beings whom they met for the first time, slaughterers slaughtered their victims without so much as a glance, flames rose to heaven and nothing ever jammed the mechanism. It was as if it all unfolded according to a plan decreed from the beginning of time.

And what of human ideals, or of the beauty of innocence or the weight of justice? And what of God in all that?

I didn't understand, though I wanted to. Ask any survivor and you will hear the same thing: above all, we tried to understand. Why all these deaths? What was the point of this death factory? How to account for the demented mind that devised this black hole of history called Birkenau?

Perhaps there was nothing to understand.

Suddenly, in my feverish brain, I saw myself with Kalman, my Kabalist master with the yellowed beard. Poring over our ancient texts, we tried to grasp the signs that would herald the coming of the Messiah, especially the most spectacular of them: the ingathering of exiles, Jews arriving from everywhere, from the banks of all rivers, from the most distant places, to meet the Savior. Young and old, employer and employee, the happy and the wretched, in ragged caftans and elegant suits, they cross rivers and scale mountains to clasp one another's hands and greet the blessed day of Redemption. The Third Temple descends from heaven in a conflagration that lights their path. And I felt like tugging at my father's sleeve and whispering: "Look, Father, look: Kalman and his disciples have succeeded at last. Look, it's done!" I felt like turning to our companions and rousing them to joy and hope: "Look, the Messiah has come, we have forced him to hasten His coming! Thank him, then, and let us go to him with a song of gratitude on our lips." But I said nothing. Deep within myself I knew that no Kabalist could ever have foreseen this place.

My intent here is not to repeat what I recounted in *Night* but to review that testimony as I see it now. Was I explicit enough? Did I miss what was essential? Did I serve memory well? In fact, if I had it to do over again, I would change nothing in my deposition.

Logically, I shouldn't have survived. Sickly, timid, fearful, and lacking all resourcefulness, I never did anything to stay alive. I never volunteered for anything, never jostled anyone to get a tin of soup. Coward that I was, I preferred to eat less and to let myself be devoured by hunger rather than expose myself to blows. I was less afraid of death than of physical suffering.

Living marginally, sinking into anonymity, I had no interest in the daily or clandestine life of the camp, nor in its upheavals. The landing in Normandy, the July 20 attempt on Hitler's life, Rommel's suicide, the Liberation of Paris — of these events I perceived only faint echoes. What was the use? One way or another, I did not expect to live through the nightmare. I would not get out alive. It wasn't that I wanted to die, and yet.

Was it the will to testify — and therefore the need to survive — that helped pull me through? Did I survive in order to combat forgetting? I must confess that at the time such questions did not occur to me. I did not feel invested with any mission. On the contrary, I was convinced that my turn would come and that my memories would die with me. When I heard fellow inmates making plans for "afterward," I thought it was no concern of mine.

I repeat: It is not that I wanted to die, just that I knew I would not survive, first of all because I was convinced the Germans would keep their promise and kill us all, down to the last Jew, if necessary in the final hour before their defeat. And also because I knew that beyond a certain point I would be incapable of bearing the hunger and the pain.

If anything motivated me, it was my father's presence. In the camp we were close, closer than ever, perhaps because we thought we might be the last survivors of our family. But there was something else as well: Finally I had my father to myself. At home he had been away often. In the camp I saw him from morning to night, dusk to dawn. I saw no one but him. We depended on each other: he needed me as I needed him. Because of him, I had to live; because of me, he tried not to die. So long as I still lived, he knew he was useful, perhaps even indispensable. In my eyes, he was the same man, the same father, he had always been. If I was gone, he would lose his role, his authority, his identity. And conversely: Without him my life would have neither meaning nor goal.

In this the Germans' psychological methods often failed. They tried to get the inmates to think only of themselves, to forget relatives and friends, to tend only to their own needs, unless they wanted to become "Mussulmen." But what happened was just the reverse. Those who retreated to a universe limited to their own bodies had less chance of getting out alive, while to live for a brother, a friend, an ideal, helped you hold out longer. As for me, I could cope thanks to my father. Without him I could not have resisted. I would see him coming with his heavy gait, seeking a smile, and I would give it to him. He was my support and my oxygen, as I was his.

And yet. Did I really help him, or did I merely sharpen his sorrow? For is there any misfortune, any curse, more devastating to a father than being unable to come to his son's rescue, unable to release him from the lash of hunger and fear? I asked him countless questions in an effort to show him that his authority over his son was still intact, that my confidence in his judgment was as absolute as ever: Should I try to move to a different kommando or barracks? Should I trade my ration of margarine for a piece of bread, or pick up a string I had found at the work site and sell it despite the risk of twenty-five lashes? He didn't know what advice to give me, but my questions did him good.

One day I saw him on the verge of tears. He had noticed how emaciated I had become, and he was afraid he wouldn't be able to pull me through the next selection. He was crying inside, and I felt the weight of his despair. I wanted to console him, reassure him, but didn't see how I could without making him feel even worse. There is no sharper pain, no more shattering grief, than seeing one's father shed tears of impotence.

Being closer to him made me love him more than ever. Sometimes I would offer him a spoonful of soup, telling him I wasn't hungry. He did the same. "My stomach hurts, I can't eat a thing," he would say, handing me a crust of bread. I ached to do something to bring back his smile, his strength, his wisdom and dignity. At night, lying side by side, we would talk about the past: a rabbinical marriage we had attended; the burning of the barracks (who were the saboteurs?); the disappearance of a rich merchant's son — had he fled to Soviet Russia, as people said, or gone to Budapest with false papers, passing as a Christian, as others claimed? We spoke of the problems my timidity created for me, especially here; the roots of anti-Semitism; the virtues of emancipation; the merits of Zionism — was the Satmàr Rebbe right to fight it; the allure of any mystical quest. I talked to him about mine, and he told me of his, which was not esoteric but human. To aid others — that was his watchword, his law, his ideal. A Jew is defined by his actions more than by his intentions. It is his actions that bind him to his community and, through it, to the larger human community.

Did he still uphold his principles, his humanism? Strangely, he came closer to Hasidism. "What we need is a miracle," he would often whisper. "We deserve it. But do the times deserve it? That's the question."

In Sighet I was the one who had believed in miracles, while he, with his rational bent, attached less value to them. Here it was the other way around. The time of miracles seemed long gone to me. I felt that the world had condemned itself and would find no redemption. Why hadn't I asked Kalman, my Kabalist master, to initiate me into the art of making myself invisible? I would have seen to it that my father benefited from my powers too, and I pictured us walking out through the gate under the unseeing eyes of the SS guards. We would climb aboard a supply train, cross cities and valleys, and rouse slumbering inhabitants everywhere: Aren't you ashamed to sleep while they are killing our people?

Like everyone else, I dreamed a lot in those days. It helped.

I was lucky enough — if I may be forgiven that expression — to have a former *rosh yeshiva* (director of a rabbinical academy) of Galician origin as a teammate. I can see us now, carrying bags of cement or large stones, pushing wheelbarrows filled with sand or mud, all the while studying a Law of the Mishna or a page of the Talmud. My teammate knew it all by heart, and thanks to him, we were able to escape. We went to Rabbi Hanina ben Dossa and begged him to pray for us. We accosted Resh Lakish. Would he use his herculean strength to free us? We wandered the alleys of Pumbedita and the hills of Galilee. I listened to sages debating whether the Shma Israel should be recited standing up or lying down.

In the morning my father and I would rise before the general wake-up call and go to a nearby block where someone had traded a dozen rations of bread for a pair of phylacteries (tefillin). We would strap them onto our left arm and forehead, quickly recite the ritual blessings, then pass them on to the next person. A few dozen prisoners thereby sacrificed their sleep, and sometimes their rations of bread or coffee, to perform the mitzvah, the commandment to wear the tefillin. Yes, we practiced religion even in a death camp. I said my prayers every day. On Saturday I hummed Shabbat songs at work, in part, no doubt, to please my father, to show him I was determined to remain a Jew even in the accursed kingdom. My doubts and my revolt gripped me only later.

Why so much later? My comrade and future friend Primo Levi asked me that question. How did I surmount these doubts and this revolt? He refused to understand how I, his former companion of Auschwitz III, could still call himself a believer, for he, Primo, was not and didn't want to be. He had seen too much suffering not to rebel against any religion that sought to impose a meaning upon it. I understood him, and asked him to understand me, for I had seen too much suffering to break with the past and reject the heritage of those who had suffered. We spent many hours arguing, with little result.

We were equally unwavering, for we came from different milieus, and even in Auschwitz led different lives. He was a chemist; I was nothing at all. The system needed him, but not me. He had influential friends to help and protect him; I had only my father. I needed God, Primo did not.

There in the camp, I had neither the strength nor the time for theological meditation or metaphysical speculation about the attributes of the Master of the Universe. The daily bread ration was the center of our concerns. Would it be a centimeter thicker or thinner? Would they give us margarine or jam? Fear of beatings by the guards was greater than fear of heaven. On that score the enemy triumphed: it was the SS, not God, who governed our world and whose shadow fell upon us. The SS wanted their victims to see them not as superior men but as gods, and they acted like sovereign, omnipotent gods. They had every right; we had none. They knew everything; we knew nothing. They fed us or killed us with the merest gesture, but we had no right even to look at them. He who looks God in the face must die. But the faith that bound me to the God of Israel and of my ancestors remained immune to all that, at least for the moment. It remained nearly intact.

For Primo Levi the problem of faith after Auschwitz was posed in stark terms: Either God is God, and therefore all-powerful and hence guilty of letting the murderers do as they pleased, or His power is limited, in which case he is not God. In other words, if God is God, then He is present everywhere. But if He refuses to show Himself, he becomes immoral and inhuman, the enemy's ally or accomplice. The philosopher and historian Gerson Cohen would later show me a moving and terrifying passage in one of our books of martyrology. During the Crusades the Jews of Mainz hid in an underground shelter. One night their spiritual leaders, Rabbi Baroukh and his son-in-law Rabbi Yehuda, heard sounds coming from the synagogue above. When they went to investigate, they found the synagogue empty, but heard voices in the darkness. The two sages fell to their knees and cried, "Is it You, Lord, who wish our death? Have You changed sides? Have You decided to anoint the enemy as Your chosen people?" This is a cruel trap. The suffering and death of innocent children inevitably places divine will in question and arouses men to wrath and revolt. But what if that were just what God intended: that men cry out to Him of their pain and disappointment? Might that be the path to a solution? I prefer to suggest that no solution exists.

There is a passage in *Night* — recounting the hanging of a young Jewish boy — that has given rise to an interpretation bordering on blasphemy. Theorists of the idea that "God is dead" have used my words unfairly as justification of their rejection of faith. But if Nietzsche could cry out to the old man in the forest that God is dead, the Jew in me cannot. I have never renounced my faith in God. I have risen against His justice, protested His silence and sometimes His absence, but my anger rises up within faith and not outside it. I admit that this is hardly an original position. It is part of Jewish tradition. But in these matters I have never sought originality. On the contrary, I have always aspired to follow in the footsteps of my father and those who went before him. Moreover, the texts cite many occasions when prophets and sages rebelled against the lack of divine interference in human affairs during times of persecution. Abraham and Moses, Jeremiah and Rebbe Levi-Yitzhak of Berdichev teach us that it is permissible for man to accuse God, provided it be done in the name of faith in God. If that hurts, so be it. Sometimes we must accept the pain of faith so as not to lose it. And if that makes the tragedy of the believer more devastating than that of the nonbeliever, so be it. To proclaim one's faith within the barbed wire of Auschwitz may well represent a double tragedy, of the believer and his Creator alike.

How was it possible, in that cursed place, to praise the Eternal One for His supposed love of His people? How was it possible, without telling lies, to say in Auschwitz, *"Ashrainu, ma tov khelkainu"* — how happy we are to bear our heritage? How and by what right can we speak of happiness in Auschwitz? As I have said elsewhere, Auschwitz is conceivable neither with God nor without Him. Perhaps I may someday come to understand man's role in the mystery Auschwitz represents, but never God's.

Was I later reconciled to Him? Let us say that I was reconciled to some of His interpreters, and to some of my prayers. If men killed other men, if they massacred Jews, why should Jewish men stop praying? These prayers do not always coincide with reality, and surely not with truth. But so what? It is up to us to modify reality and make the prayers come true. As the Rebbe of Kotzk affirmed: "*Avinu malkainu,* our Father, our King, I shall continue to call You Father until You become our Father."

I will never cease to rebel against those who committed or permitted Auschwitz, including God. The questions I once asked myself about God's silence remain open. If they have an answer, I do not know it. More than that, I refuse to know it. But I maintain that the death of six million human beings poses a question to which no answer will ever be forthcoming.

My Talmudist master Rabbi Saul Lieberman has pointed out another way to look at it. One can — and must — love God. One can challenge Him and even be angry with Him, but one must also pity Him. "Do you know which of all the characters in the Bible is most tragic?" he asked me. "It is God, blessed be His name, God whose creatures so often disappoint and betray Him." He showed me a passage of the Midrash dealing with the first civil war in Jewish history, provoked by a banal household quarrel: And God wept; His tears fell upon His people and His creation, as if to say, What have you done to my work?

Perhaps God shed more tears in the time of Treblinka, Majdanek, and Auschwitz, and one may therefore invoke His name not only with indignation but also with sadness and compassion.

What tormented and revolted me in the physical and moral (or immoral) environment of the camp was the power of evil and its contagiousness. Here was brutality in its purest state. Why did human beings act like savage wolves? Why were even inmates so sadistic? I "understand" the savagery of the Germans, for savagery was their "vocation," their politics, their ideology, their education — I was about to say their religion. But what about the others? The Ukrainians who beat us, the Russians who struck us, the Poles who humiliated us, the Gypsies who slapped us, the Jewish kapos who clubbed us? Why? To show the killers they could be just like them?

Some have tried to explain their behavior by the killer's nefarious influence on his victim, the repressed desire of the oppressed to resemble the aggressor, the innate instinct for survival and respect for power, the metamorphosis engendered by extreme situations. All this is no doubt true, and yet it was very much the exception.

I believe it was Jean Améry who noted that the first to bow to the oppressor's system and to adopt its doctrines and methods were the intellectuals. But not all of them. Not the rabbis and priests, who, after all, were intellectuals too. With a single exception, no rabbi agreed to become a kapo. All refused to barter their own survival by becoming tools of the hangman. All preferred to die rather than serve death. The lessons of the prophets and the sages became shields for them.

On the other hand, how many secular humanists and intellectuals renounced their value system the moment they grasped its futility and uselessness? Sobered, disoriented, and disillusioned, some allowed themselves to be seduced by the ideology of cruelty. The number was significant.

The Communists aided one another in an exemplary fashion, and their clandestine action compels admiration. Whenever one of their own figured on a bad list, his favored comrades — safely working for the camp administration — did all they could to replace him with an anonymous prisoner. From the standpoint of the rescued Communist, the intervention of his political comrades was praiseworthy. But what gave the Communists the right to decide on the replacement comrades' fate?

No one has the right to judge them, especially

not those who did not experience Auschwitz or Buchenwald. The sages of our tradition state point-blank: "Do not judge your fellow man until you stand in his place." In other words, in the same situation, would I have acted as he did? Sometimes doubt grips me. Suppose I had spent not eleven months but eleven years in a concentration camp. Am I sure that I would have kept my hands clean? No, I am not, and no one can be. But having said that, since I did not act badly, why should I feel virtual guilt? Only the guilty must be judged, or at least denounced. Hypothetical guilt has no place here. Those who *could have* compromised themselves but did not are by definition — and by God's grace — innocent.

If I insist on this point, it is because I sometimes hear or read harsh comments about my people. Auschwitz, it is said, is a universal phenomenon; what the Germans, their collaborators, and their accomplices did, the Jews could have done as well. But so long as the Jews have not done it, I forbid anyone to charge them with theoretical, speculative crimes. So long as an individual has not killed, one has no right to see him as a potential killer. This interdiction has even greater force when an entire people is being accused.

Let me make it clear: Not all the inmates with privileges were evil. The Greek *Stubendienst* in my block, Jacob Fardo, wasn't mean. Ask Jackie Hendeli of Salonika — a fellow

Auschwitz inmate — and he will tell you. Fardo never struck a prisoner. The fact is that there were good people even among the ghetto police and the kapos. But then, there were those who were attracted by the killers' power, such as the son of a great Polish Zionist leader, a kapo in Auschwitz who stubbornly tortured, humiliated, and beat his fellow Jewish prisoners, especially if they were religious, and even more if they were Zionists. Was it to "punish" his father and take revenge against those who had believed in him? How to explain my uncle Nahman-Elye? I cannot. All I know is that I utter his name with embarrassment.

And yet, a story. One day two young lawyers from Brooklyn knocked at the door of my office at Boston University to discuss an urgent problem: They had discovered that a respected Hasid had been the vicious person who beat their father in the camp, leaving him half-dead.

"You know him," they told me. "Sometimes you go to the synagogue he attends, and even chat with him now and then." I began to picture the congregation, but quickly decided this was a game I would not play; I would pay no heed to these kinds of accusations. Yet a problem remains: What should be done about the kapos? Should they be prosecuted? Before what court? I have never agreed with Karamazov that "we are all guilty of everything, I most of all." Jewish tradition denies collective guilt, but could there be such a thing as collective innocence? The

Jewish kapos, like their peers, were not innocent. But I will not allow myself to judge them.

I prefer to emphasize the kindness and compassion of my brothers in misfortune. These qualities were found even in the kingdom of darkest night, as I can testify — indeed, as I must. The Jewish soul was a target of the enemy. He sought to corrupt it, even as he strove to destroy us physically. But despite his destructive force, despite his corrupting power, the Jewish soul remained beyond his reach.

I remember a Dutchman who shared his bread with a comrade sicker than he was, a comrade he did not know. "I prefer to be hungry than to feel remorse," he said.

I remember a Lithuanian preacher, a *maggid,* who wandered among us every Friday night, accosting everyone, with the hint of a smile: "Brother Jew — don't forget, it's Shabbat." He wanted to remind us that Shabbat still reigned over time and the world despite the smoke and stench.

I remember a Polish rabbi who tried to console those who had not fasted on Yom Kippur. "Jewish law does not order a person to fast at the risk of his life," he said. "To eat today is more pleasing in the eyes of the blessed Creator than to mortify oneself." But he himself had fasted. Weakened by hunger, he was "selected" soon afterward, and he implored his barracks comrades to say Kaddish for his soul. The entire barracks did so.

I remember a young Hungarian Jew, his shoulders stooped like an old man's, who confessed to some infraction so as to be beaten in his uncle's stead. "I am young," he said, "and stronger than he." He was young but no less weak. He did not survive the beating.

I remember, I remember. Unconsciously I took it all in. Well, not the hangmen. I could not describe the SS Blockführer who summoned us, nor the Lagerführer who attended hangings. Strangely, the murderers did not interest me; only the victims. That is why I never felt the need to become a Nazi-hunter. Though I respect those who did, like the Klarsfelds in Paris and Neal Sher in Washington, my obsession was quite different. Of course, I was shocked by the freedom and happiness enjoyed by these murderers. I saw it as an affront to the collective memory of the victims and as a legal outrage. But I knew that I was incapable by nature and temperament of spending the years left to me tracking them down. The victims alone were worthy of my devotion.

But let me come back to the two Brooklyn lawyers. They wore the kipa. For them the Law of the Torah stood above all else. How to apply it to the Hasid they were accusing?

They told their story. In the camp their father had dared to confront a Jewish kapo who, while distributing soup, exhibited excessive cruelty. "Have you no shame?" their father protested. "Have you forgotten you are a Jew?" That night, the kapo and his acolytes came to punish the impudent man. They wrapped him in a blanket and beat him savagely. It was a miracle he survived. Decades later, walking in Brooklyn one day, he recognized the kapo by his voice. His two sons had sworn vengeance.

I asked them detailed, painful questions, interrogated them. If it was so dark, how could their father, wrapped in a blanket, identify a voice and face? Suppose his memory deceived him. That was possible, was it not? I tried hard to lead them to doubt. As they replied to my questions, my thoughts leaped to the synagogue, reviewing names and features. A kapo among them — if so, how old would he be, and from what country? I asked the young attorneys, "Do you sincerely believe that one can judge and punish a man forty years later, at the risk of ruining an innocent life?" They debated the point and were about to reveal the accused man's name. I stopped them. They then informed me that they intended to report him to the police as well as to the Israeli authorities. How could I dissuade them? I told them of my encounter with a Blockältester in a bus traveling from Jerusalem to Tel Aviv during the Eichmann trial. They knew the story, having read it in *Legends of Our Time.* "Then you know how I acted in virtually similar circumstances. I let him get away." The lawyers were not convinced: "Your man didn't kill your father; this kapo almost killed ours." I answered, "But you aren't sure, you can't be sure." They persisted, and in a sense, I understood them: it was, after all, their father. Still, I persuaded them not to act hastily.

Why did I refuse to hear the kapo's name? Again, only the victims interest me.

Are we to be victims of one another?

The truth is I could spend the rest of my days recounting the weeks, months, and eternities I lived in Auschwitz, abandoning all other subjects and devoting my life, my survival, to testifying for those who died in the storm of ashes. But the student of mysticism within me always holds me back: "Wait! One must not say too much. The secret of truth lies in silence." And that is the dilemma: To be silent is impossible, to speak forbidden. I have therefore chosen to speak of other things — of the Talmud and the Bible, of mysticism and Hasidism. I have written novels and plays about Jerusalem and Moscow. But even while imagining stories ancient and modern, peopled with characters of varying fates, the teller of the tales still lives in the shadow of the flames that once illuminated and blinded him. He sees them, and will see them always. He has sworn never to let them die. Even in heaven, in that world of truth, he will stand before the celestial throne and say, "Look! Look at the flames that burn and burn, hear the mute cries of Your children as they turn to dust and ashes."

January 1945. Every January carries me back to that one. I was sick. My knee was swollen, and the pain turned my gait into a limp. The merciless Silesian winter had buried us in snow; our bodies were half-frozen. It was hard to walk dragging a body dazed with pain, and impossible to report to the kommando given the fever that racked and deadened me. I had nothing left. I knew that whatever strength I retained would soon desert me. My father guessed, but stayed silent. He knew everything, my father, but could do nothing. Still, in the end I asked him what to do. My poor father opened and closed his mouth. Like me, he must have been thinking of my mother. I used to complain of my troubles to her, but now I had only him. His emaciated face was dark gray. Did his eyes still gleam? He hesitated to make a decision for me. Going to the KB, the infirmary, would be dangerous. Few patients ever got out, except to be transferred to Birkenau. But if I did nothing, I would not last much longer. Finally he decided: "Go to the KB. At least we'll find out what's wrong with you."

That evening before roll call, I went to the KB. My father waited for me outside, trembling with cold and fear, arms dangling, alone and more lonely than ever. Would we ever see each other again? I walked as quickly as I could, not daring to turn back. A Stubendienst stopped me. "What's the matter with you?" I showed him my knee. With a sneer of disgust he let me pass. I took my place in line, afraid that my father would catch pneumonia or be driven away with clubs. At last my turn came. A doctor glanced at my knee, touched it. I stifled a scream. "You need an operation," he said. "Immediately." I managed to make my way back to my father, who hadn't budged. "They're going to operate," I told him. He didn't react. "They're going to operate," I repeated. His gaze was lost in the distance. "Remember when we took you to Satmàr?" he murmured. Appendicitis . . . the Rebbe of Borsha's blessing . . . the train ride in the middle of Shabbat . . . the nurse's tenderness — it all seemed so long ago, events in another life. "It'll be all right," my father said. I took his right hand and kissed it, my heart breaking. Every time we separated, even to go to the latrine, I felt the same terror: What if this were the last time? I went back to the infirmary, where another human "miracle" awaited me: One of the doctors, a tall, kind-looking man, tried to comfort me. "It won't hurt, or not much anyway. Don't worry, my boy, you'll live." He talked to me before the operation, and I heard him again when I woke up. I believe he had kept talking the whole time.

Many years later I went to give a speech at the University of Oslo. Afterward, an elegant, distinguished-looking man came up to me. "I believe we were in the same camp," he said in a voice that I could never forget. Dr. Leo (Sjua) Eitinger, internationally renowned psychiatrist, and I looked at each other in silence for a long moment, then smiled at the same time. He was among the speakers at the official dinner following the Nobel ceremony. He spoke simply, as a survivor. That was something else we have in common: He, too, has devoted his life to defending the survivors. And as he spoke, I pictured us back in the camp, among the ghosts.

There is much talk among psychiatrists — possibly too much — about so-called survivors' guilt. It is the height of irony that the hangmen suffer no such guilt. The defendants at the Auschwitz trial in Frankfurt in the sixties laughed during the proceedings. Only the survivors feel somehow accused: "Why did I survive when so many others perished?" But surely survivors bear no guilt for having escaped death. They had nothing to do with their own survival. Only the executioner had the power to decide who would live and who would die. The victims were told to march and they marched. They were told to halt and they halted. They were told to eat and they ate. They were even told to resign themselves to their fate, and they did that too.

Rumors and images. January 18, 1945. The Red Army is a few kilometers from Auschwitz. Warsaw has just been liberated, and Cracow and

Lodz are about to be. Berlin decides to evacuate prisoners to Germany's interior. Feverish activity sweeps over the camp. Storehouses are emptied, blankets and clothing distributed. Each prisoner is given an entire loaf of bread; the favored ones get four.

My father came to see me in the hospital, managing to slip in amid the general disorder. I told him the patients would be allowed to stay in the KB but . . . "But what?" he asked. "The thing is . . . I don't want to be separated from you." And I added, "But you could stay with me, couldn't you?" He asked if that was really possible. I told him it was. There was room, and surveillance had been relaxed. Anything was possible in the mounting chaos. It was a tempting idea, but finally we decided against it. We were afraid. We were sure the Germans would leave no witnesses, that they would kill every last one of us. That was the logic of their monstrous undertaking. They would destroy everything to prevent the free world from discovering the nature and extent of their crimes. We therefore decided to leave with the others, especially since most of the doctors were being evacuated too.

Nearly all the patients who stayed survived, liberated by the Russians nine days later. Had we remained in the infirmary, my father would not have died of hunger and shame in Buchenwald ten days later, and my life would have taken a different course. I would have returned to Sighet. I would have stayed at his side. I would not have gone to France. What books, if any, would I have written?

In 1979, during an official visit to Moscow, I met the Soviet general Vassily Petrenko, whose troops liberated Auschwitz. We spoke about those days. He told me how the units under his command had prepared for the attack, while I told him how we waited for him and his soldiers. "We waited for you the way a religious Jew awaits the Messiah. Why didn't you come a few hours earlier? A breakthrough by a few patrols would have saved thousands of lives." He offered technical explanations having to do with strategy, the weather, logistics. I was not convinced. Was it true that Stalin had deliberately decided not to try to free Soviet prisoners of war? So it was said. The fact is that the Soviet army could have made an effort, but did not. Nor did the American army on its front, later. Historians agree: The death camps did not figure among the objectives set by the general staffs of the Allied armies. Their liberation was not given priority. It happened as if by chance.

To this day I am in mourning for my father, perhaps because I didn't mourn the day I became an orphan. The ordeals that preceded his death remain with me, in all their violence. I described them in *Night*: the death march to Gleiwitz, sleeping in the snow, the train journey standing up in open wagons exposed to the elements, the demented cries of the living dead before our arrival in Buchenwald. Here again, I could spend my life retelling that story. How can I silence the cries that rage within me? I remember being trampled and then pulled to my feet. We were all hallucinating. Walking dead, we no longer dreaded death. We were stronger than death. I don't know why, but I saw myself on the evening of Kol Nidre, surrounded by the faithful draped in their ritual shawls, the living and the dead intermingled, ready to rise to heaven to plead the cause of humanity vanquished by Satan. I remember shouting with the others, howling the words of the Shma Israel and the Kaddish and other incantations that spilled out onto the snow. Borne by the wind, they would cover the earth, the universe, from end to end. Hand in hand, our heads buried in heavy, wet blankets, my father and I swung to and fro, like in the old days in the Beit Hamidrash.

The hot shower on our arrival in Buchenwald did us good. But then we were driven outdoors naked. We were in the "small camp," huge barracks, packed to overflowing. "Let's stay together," my father said as we were shoved forward, echoing my poor mother's words. Like wreckage barely human, we clung to each other so as not to go under. We were both feverish, but my father's fever was different from mine. He was already sick. Dense, irresistible human waves divided us. We shouted, found each other again. They were giving out hot coffee at the gate. Should we go and get some? No, better not. Better not risk being separated in the roiling, hysterical crowd. We decided to wait for soup. It would come, it would come, but we needed it soon. I had my father sit down on a nearby pallet as I ran to the gate where they were giving out food. When I came back, my father was gone. In a panic, I asked around, but no one had seen him. I put the rations down and went looking for him, and suddenly there he was. He had gone to the latrine. He was sick, my father was sick, and I was desperate.

Many years later Jorge Semprun and I were exchanging memories of Buchenwald. He had been in the main camp. Working in the Schreibstube, the office, he did not endure the hunger and cold. He knew the small camp at a distance. The fate of the Jews was unlike that of the non-Jews. We were in the same place, and yet.

My father was getting worse. He was dying. It was the darkest day of my life, a day heavy with meaning. I was weak and sick myself. Though I ached to help him, I did not know how. I would have done anything, would have gladly given him my blood, my life. I was ready to die in his place. Except that my time had not yet come.

I pleaded with the doctors, the Stubendienst, the Creator Himself: Do something for my fa-

169

ther. They were all merciless. Several times we were driven outside to clean the barracks. My father couldn't move. I wanted to stay with him, but was driven out with clubs. I pretended to be sick or dying. My father was calling for me, and I didn't want to let him down. He was talking to me, but his words were incoherent. Was he trying to leave me his last will? At one point he whispered something about the jewelry we had buried, about the money we had given to Christian friends for safekeeping. I refused to listen. I didn't care about all the world's riches. My father was dying and I was in pain. He shuddered and called my name. I tried to get up, tried to crawl to him, but the torturers were there, forbidding all movement. I wanted to cry out, Hold on, Father, hold on. In a minute, a second, I'll be at your side, I'll listen to you, talk to you, I won't let you die alone. My father was dying and I was bursting with pain. I didn't want to leave him, but I did. I was forced to. They were beating me, I was losing consciousness. He moaned, and I waited for the torturers to go away. He was weeping softly, like a child, and I felt my chest coming apart. He groaned, and my body crumbled. Powerless, crushed by remorse, I knew that however long I lived, I would never be able to free myself of that guilt: My father was twisting with pain, dying, and I was near him, but helpless. My father called to me and I could not rush to hold his hand. Suddenly I saw Grandma Nissel. I begged her to accompany me to the House of Study. We opened the ark, prayed to the Holy Torah to intercede for my dying father. She held out her hand, but I touched only emptiness. I bit my knuckles until they hurt, I wanted to howl, but the pain was so bad I could only murmur, the pain was so bad I wanted to die.

I was sixteen years old when my father died. My father was dead and the pain was gone. I no longer felt anything. Someone had died inside me, and that someone was me.

I couldn't cry. My heart was broken, but I had no more tears. I had taken leave of myself: the dead do not weep. Hardly anyone wept in the camp, as though fearing that if you started, you could never stop. Freedom, for us, would mean being able to weep again.

I lurched across the camp, reeling, staggering, my mind numb. I saw myself among the dead, seeking my father as if to tell him, Look, I'm with you, I'm here at your side.

The truth is I had no need to tell him. He knew everything, as I knew everything about him. Just before he died he had a terrifying moment of lucidity. He opened his eyes wide. His ravaged gray face was stamped with dread. He gave a little cry and must have died soon afterward. A minute later or an hour, I'm not sure. I didn't see him die. I saw him dying, and then he was gone. When and where did they take him? I didn't want to find out. I was afraid.

With my father dead, I felt curiously free; free to go under, to let myself drift into death.

Whenever I think of him, I relive his agony and a knot forms in my chest. I feel myself becoming an orphan. Yes, you can be orphaned more than once, no matter how old you are. And every time is the first time.

I picture him and tell myself I will never see him grow old. I am already older than he was when he died.

And the heartrending question keeps coming back. What if we had stayed in the infirmary? He might have survived. Who knows, I might have found a way to make him happy, at peace and proud of his son.

On December 10, 1986, at the Nobel Peace Prize ceremony, as I was about to deliver my acceptance speech in the presence of the Norwegian king and parliament, the diplomatic corps and the world press, I felt unable to utter a word, for Egil Aarvik, president of the Nobel Committee, had mentioned my father in his address: "You were with your father when he passed away; it was the darkest hour of your life. And this is the most glorious. It is therefore fitting that your own son be with you as you receive the highest distinction humanity can bestow upon one of its own." I was shaken by the linking of my father and my son. I saw them standing together. My lips moved, but no sound came out. Tears filled my eyes, the tears I couldn't shed so long ago.

With my father gone, I sank into a lethargy that lasted until liberation, on April 11, 1945. I had no desire to live. I didn't know what was going on in the camp or even in my barracks. I knew nothing anymore, didn't want to know. For all practical purposes, I had become one of the "Mussulmen" drifting beyond life, into death as into water, no longer hungry, thirsty, or sleepy, fearing neither death nor beatings. They were dead but didn't know it. These few weeks, devoid of sense and content, are treated in just a few pages in *Night*. I did not line up for bread and soup. I waited for nothing and no one. I drifted through time and sank into a dreamless sleep. When I woke up, I didn't know where I was. I no longer counted hours or days. They were all the same to me. Now, with hindsight, I remember certain young inmates from Kovno and Vilna with whom I mechanically played chess (with chessmen made of cardboard). I remember that during Passover I attended services in our barracks morning and evening. But it was another person who lived these events.

Was it on the night of April 5 (the seventh day of Passover) that the SS guards ordered all Jews to assemble in the Appelplatz, the parade ground? On the way we were intercepted by the camp police, the Lagerschütz. They were supposed to herd us to the Appelplatz, but instead they warned us to return to the barracks and hide. Prevent evacuation! That was the directive of the Resistance. But I was so detached from reality that I didn't even know there was an underground movement in the camp.

Years later, during an official dinner in Jerusalem, the Norwegian ambassador to Israel told me, "I'm happy to see you again — I say again because we may have seen each other in Buchenwald." Like most of the Norwegian students imprisoned in the camp, he had belonged to the Lagerschütz. "I've been looking for you ever since April 5, 1945," I replied, "to thank you for saving my life."

Several times during the days before liberation, my block was ordered to the Appelplatz for evacuation. In my enfeebled state, I could never have endured even a single day of forced march. Whether it was fate or providence, on each occasion either air raids forced us back into the "small camp," or the daily quota of evacuees had been filled, and my group was sent back to barracks. The Stubenälteste, a certain Gustav, a Polish Jew, ruled over Barracks 66. Of course, he favored the Polish adolescents. There were those who later held it against him.

On April 10 we were back on the Appelplatz, ready to be evacuated. But once again we were told to go back: "Tomorrow will definitely be your turn. The last convoy leaves tomorrow." That day I stayed behind. Someone else took my place. Since then I have often wondered who left because I stayed behind. I will never know him, but I know I owe him my life.

Buchenwald was liberated on April 11, 1945. Actually, the camp liberated itself. Armed members of the Resistance rose up a few hours before the magical appearance of the first American units. Gustav ran from barracks to barracks in our "small camp," his pockets stuffed with grenades. Elated prisoners put the SS to flight. Soviet prisoners of war commandeered American jeeps and drove off to punish the inhabitants of Weimar, city of Goethe. Some of us organized a minyan and said Kaddish. That Kaddish, at once a glorification of God's name and a protest against His creation, still echoes in my ears. It was a thanksgiving for having spared us, but it was also an outcry: "Why did You not spare so many others?"

Strangely, we did not "feel" the victory. There were no joyous embraces, no shouts or songs to mark our happiness, for that word was meaningless to us. We were not happy. We wondered whether we ever would be.

Later I would hear speeches and read articles hailing the Allies' triumph over Hitler's Germany. For us, Jews, there was a slight nuance: Yes, Hitler lost the war, but we didn't win it. We mourned too many dead to speak of victory.

I wandered the camp dazed and confused,

joining one group only to drift to another. Glancing at the sky, staring at the ground, I was looking for something, though I didn't know what. Maybe someone to whom I could say, "Hey, look at me, I'm alive!" Another word that didn't mean much. Would I ever again know what it meant to be alive?

I will never forget the American soldiers and the horror that could be read in their faces. I will especially remember one black sergeant, a muscled giant, who wept tears of impotent rage and shame, shame for the human species, when he saw us. He spewed curses that on his lips became holy words. We tried to lift him onto our shoulders to show our gratitude, but we didn't have the strength. We were too weak even to applaud him.

A soldier threw us some cans of food. I caught one and opened it. It was lard, but I didn't know that. Unbearably hungry — I had not eaten since April 5 — I stared at the can and was about to taste its contents, but just as my tongue touched it I lost consciousness.

I spent several days in the hospital (the former SS hospital) in a semiconscious state. When I was discharged, I felt drained. It took all my mental resources to figure out where I was. I knew my father was dead. My mother was probably dead, since Mengele would have considered her too old to work. Likewise my grandmother. My little sister was too little. I hoped Bea and Hilda might still be alive, but how could I find out? Lists were being circulated. Racked with anxiety, I devoured them. I found nothing but was told not to lose heart: other lists were being drawn up. They came, and I leapt upon them. Still there was nothing. Here and there my eye fell upon a Wiesel, but no Bea or Hilda. Feig, Deutsch, Hollander, Slomowics — some names of cousins were there, thank God. But where were Bea and Hilda? Each list carved a deeper void within me. I was free, but I was more distraught than ever.

We held meeting after meeting. What were we to do now? Where should we go? We could not stay where we were indefinitely.

The American military authorities urged us to make a decision. There were about four hundred of us children and adolescents — the youngest a boy of six or eight, the future chief rabbi of Israel, Israel Meir Lau. The future scientist Izso Rosenman was a little older. Some men from Sighet, who had arrived from neighboring camps, urged us to go home. "We'll be greeted like princes," one of them said. "We'll be able to do whatever we want," someone else added. "We will represent an enormous political force," a dedicated Communist declared. "Let's use it to build a new society." Still another said: "Let's go home, if only to seek vengeance." Only a few were convinced. We were afraid to go back to our empty houses.

"Okay," the American officers said. "We can understand why you don't want to go home.

But where *do* you want to go?"

"Palestine," some answered.

I concurred. It was the only country whose name resonated within me.

"Do you have any family there?"

"Yes," said one of the group. "We do."

"Who?"

"Joshua," he replied. "And Amos. Isaiah. Rabbi Yehoshua ben Levi."

"Not Moses?" the officer asked with a smile.

"No. Moses never made it to the Holy Land."

The officer shook his head sadly. "Neither will you, I'm afraid. You're in the same political and legal situation as Moses: the English really don't want you there."

Then where would we go? Another officer brought good news: "Belgium is ready to accept you." Bravo for Belgium. And I had had family there, cousins who used to send us Rosh Hashana greetings, Shiku and Reizi, brother and sister. I remembered Shiku's sweetness and shyness, and Reizi's haughty bearing. She was beautiful. I wondered what had become of her husband, whom I had run into in Auschwitz soon after I arrived. So be it, off to Belgium.

Had we actually gone to Belgium, I might have met the beautiful young girl who, years later, became the mother of my Elisha. Right after the war, she belonged to a Zionist organization that I might easily have joined as well. But fate decreed otherwise.

One morning we were told that there had

been a change of plans. General Charles de Gaulle, informed of our plight, had invited us to France. France, the country of Rabbi Yehiel and of Rashi (that was more or less all I knew of it). In fact, I had met some Frenchmen in Auschwitz. There were Louis and Charles and André, a marvelous flautist. But since I didn't know their language, we communicated using the concentration camp vocabulary, a mixture of Polish, German, Yiddish, Russian, and Ukrainian. Would I now have to learn French? Well, everything in its time.

First I had to learn — or relearn — to live.

To live far from my father, my father who stayed behind, in the invisible cemetery of Buchenwald. I look up at the sky, and there is his grave. When I raise my eyes to heaven, it is his grave I see.

Don't leave me, Father. No, it is I who am leaving you.

From now on we will be together only in our dreams.

I often close my eyes just to see you.

You are going away, or I am, yet the distance between us is unchanging.

I am leaving the camp, going toward a new life.

And you remain, a fistful of ashes. Not even.

God's Suffering:
A Commentary

Here is what the Midrash tells us. When the Holy One, blessed be His name, comes to liberate the children of Israel from their exile, they will say to him: "Master of the Universe, it is You who dispersed us among the nations, driving us from Your abode, and now it is You who bring us back. Why is that?" And the Holy One, blessed be His name, will reply with this parable: One day a king drove his wife from his palace, and the next day he had her brought back. The queen, astonished, asked him: "Why did you send me away yesterday only to bring me back today?" "Know this," replied the king, "that I followed you out of the palace, for I could not live in it alone." So the Holy One, blessed be His name, tells the children of Israel: "Having seen you leave my abode, I left it too, that I might return with you."

God accompanies his children into exile. This is a central theme of Midrashic and mystical thought in Jewish tradition. Just as the people of Israel's solitude mirrors the Lord's, so the suffering of men finds its extension in that of their Creator. Though imposed by God, the punishment goes beyond those upon whom it falls, encompassing the Judge himself. And it is God who wills it so. The Father may reveal Himself through His wrath; He may even sharpen His severity, but He will never be absent. Present at the Creation, God forms part of it. *Let atar panui minei* is the key phrase of the Book of Splendor, the Zohar: No space is devoid of God. God is everywhere, even in suffering and in the very heart of punishment. Israel's sadness is bound to that of the divine presence, the She'hina: together they await deliverance. The waiting of the one constitutes the other's secret dimension. Just as the distress of the She'hina seems unbearable to the children of Israel, so Israel's torments rend the heart of the She'hina.

What happens to us touches God. What happens to Him concerns us. We share in the same adventure and participate in the same quest. We suffer for the same reasons and ascribe the same coefficient to our common hope.

Now, this community of suffering presents certain difficulties. Its purpose is ambiguous. Does it aim to make our human ordeal easier or more difficult to bear? Does the idea that God also suffers — that He suffers with us and therefore on our account — help us to bear our grief, or does it simply augment its weight? Surely we have no right to complain, since God, too, knows suffering; nevertheless, we can say that the suffering of the one does not cancel out the other; rather, the two are added together.

In this sense, divine suffering is not consolation but additional punishment. We are therefore entitled to ask of heaven, "Do we not have enough sorrow already? Why must You add Yours to it?"

But it is not our place to make decisions for God. He alone has discretion in the thousands of ways of joining His suffering to ours. We can neither elicit nor reject them, but can only seek to be worthy of them, even without understanding. Where God is concerned, all is mystery.

We know that God suffers, because He tells us so. We know of His role as an exile, because He offers us vivid descriptions. Yet we do not even know His name. When Moses asked Him, He replied: *"Eh'yeh asher eh'yeh,"* I shall be who I shall be — in other words, I do not define myself in the present, my name itself is a projection into the future. "And on that day," says the prophet, "God will be one and His name will be one." Does that mean that now, in exile, God has more than one name? Let us say that His ineffable name has been disseminated in more than one place, taking on more than one identity. But this ineffable name eludes us. It is not the Tetragrammaton, but something else. It is the name the High Priest used to pronounce but once a year, during the Yom Kippur service, in the Holy of Holies of the Temple, in Jerusalem. Since the Temple no longer exists and its servants were massacred, God seems to have retaken His name, causing it to escape our awareness. But how, then, are we to speak to Him? God has no need of a name to be present. He is present in our request and its fulfillment alike. He is both question and answer. For us mortals, He is at once link and sundering, pain and healing, injury and peace, prayer and pardon. He is, and that must be enough for us.

I confess, however, that sometimes it is not enough for me. Nothing is enough for me when I consider the convulsions our century has endured. God's role is important in that context. How did God manage to bear His suffering added to our own? Are we to imagine the one as justification for the other? Nothing justifies Auschwitz. Were the Lord Himself to offer me a justification, I think I would reject it. Treblinka erases all justifications and all answers.

The barbed-wire kingdom will forever remain an immense question mark on the scale of both humanity and its Creator. Faced with unprecedented suffering and agony, He should have intervened, or at least expressed Himself. Which side was He on? Isn't He the Father of us all? It is in this capacity that He shatters our shell and moves us. How can we fail to pity a father who witnesses the massacre of his children by his other children? Is there a suffering more devastating, a remorse more bitter?

This is the dilemma confronted by the believer late in this century: by allowing this to happen, God was telling humanity something, and we don't know what it was. That He suffered? He could have — should have — interrupted His own suffering by calling a halt to the martyrdom of innocents. I don't know why He did not do so and I think I never shall. Perhaps that is not His concern. But I find myself equally ignorant as regards men. I will never understand their moral decline, their fall. There was a time when everything roused anger, even revolt, in me against humanity. Later I felt mainly sadness, for the victims.

Commenting on a verse of the Prophet Jeremiah according to which God says, "I shall weep in secret," the Midrash remarks that there is a place called "secret" and that when God is sad, He takes refuge there to weep.

For us this secret place lies in memory, which possesses its own secret.

A Midrash recounts: When God sees the suffering of His children scattered among the nations, He sheds two tears in the ocean. When they fall, they make a noise so loud it is heard round the world. It is a legend I enjoy rereading. And I tell myself: Perhaps God shed more than two tears during His people's recent tragedy. But men, cowards that they are, refused to hear them.

Is that, at last, an answer?

No. It is a question. Yet another question.

Schooling

All aboard, please. No more cattle cars. A luxurious, second-class railroad car had been set aside for us. We walked from the camp to the station. In my desk there is a photograph that shows a long column of children and adolescents with old men's faces. I never looked back. No point in trying to see the invisible. Two Jewish chaplains from the American army went with us. Neatly dressed, carrying generous military rations, we left the Buchenwald station. Several boys from Sighet and its environs made the journey. One of them sat in my compartment. He knew a few words of French, and he assured me that life in France was good. I wondered if there was any place where death was good. I thought about my father. We had arrived together, but I was leaving alone.

The trip took two or three days, I'm not sure which, for I was too absorbed in looking at what there was to see. The train stopped at the border, and they had us get off. A police official made a speech, of which I understood not a word. When I saw people raising their hands, I assumed they were volunteering for some task.

In the camp I had always tried to pass unnoticed, to make myself invisible, and I saw no reason to act differently now. I later found out that the policeman had asked for a show of hands of all those who wished to become French citizens. Since I did not respond, they probably wrote in my file: "Refused French nationality." The consequence of my blunder was endless harassment and administrative hassles every time I renewed my residency permit or applied for travel passes at the Préfecture de Police.

We reboarded, and broke into applause when the train set out again: we were now in France. It was a different landscape, more cheerful and more human. I liked the peasants in berets. People waited for us at every station, showing compassion by offering us hot meals, which the observant among us refused. But we gladly accepted the bread, café au lait, fruit, and cookies. My friend was right: Life in France was good.

Representatives of the OSE, the children's rescue society, greeted us in a splendid château in Écouis, in the department of Eure. There were smiles, plans, and promises. They gave us the same message in many languages: "Here you will recuperate. All we ask is that you let us take care of you." We were given medical examinations. I blushed when undressing for a female doctor. They housed us, clothed us, offered us lavish meals. The weather was beautiful. It was a marvelous June, the first anniversary of the Normandy landing. I went to see the director in his office and shyly asked for a pen and paper. I began a private journal: "After the war, by the grace of God, blessed be His name, here I am in France. Far away. Alone. This morning I put on my own tefillin for the first time in a long while." The group of young believers to which I belonged requested kosher food. Menashe Klein, son and grandson of rabbis of Ungvár, and I asked that we be given the essential books: the Bible, prayer books, a few Talmudic tractates. We were promised these and they were duly provided, as was a study room where we could say morning and evening prayers. We held our first Minha service, and we all said Kaddish together. Though we knew it well enough, that collective Kaddish reminded us that we were all orphans.

How long would we recite the prayer for the dead? The mourning period normally lasts for eleven months after a relative's death. But what if you don't know the date of death? Halachic scholars weren't sure how to resolve our situation.

It was in Écouis that we began to readapt to "normal" life. It was not easy to shed certain habits, certain fears. We had not yet forgotten the camp rules. We didn't finish everything on our plates, instead we would save something for later, hiding a crust of bread or a piece of cake, just in case. Whether the counselors understood or not, they said nothing. They trusted us, and they were right. After several weeks, few "food reserves" remained under our pillows.

The peaceful atmosphere of the home had a lot to do with that. At night we would sit on the grass under the trees. We lit campfires, told stories, recalled songs. The Zionists dreamed of going to Palestine. The Bundists — yes, there were Bundists among us — were opposed. Dedicated socialists, they called for rebuilding a Jewish cultural life in the Diaspora. A Yiddish journalist came to give us a report on the international situation: Germany was defeated. The nightmare was over. One of the members of our team of counselors was a dark-haired young woman of Alsatian origin, thin and graceful, with a seductive smile. Her name was Niny. She understood our Yiddish and even tried to speak it. How many boys saw her in their dreams? Her upbringing brought her closer to our religious group, and we adopted her immediately. Another counselor, Rachel Mintz, a little older, had a face marked by sadness. The OSE had hired her because she was a poet. In the evening she recited verses and told us stories by Itzhak Leibush Peretz. It was she who, in the fifties, introduced me to the work of Nikos Kazantzakis and told me of the secret that bound them together.

Poor counselors, did they think they could educate us? We who had looked death in the face knew far more than they or their teachers about the mysteries of existence and Creation, about the fragility of knowledge and the end of history. The youngest among us had a fount of experiences more vast than the oldest of them. How could they understand our need to hide leftover bits of cake under our pillows? Or the mistrust we felt for strangers? "You wouldn't understand," was the phrase that came most often to our lips. We were polite to them, friendly. We listened to them and obeyed them, or pretended to, so as not to hurt their feelings. But imperceptibly the roles were reversed, and we became their counselors, feigning docile submission to their authority only because ours was superior. We pitied them, but they never knew it, poor things.

The days passed quietly. There were walks, sunbathing, excursions in the forest, and French lessons for those who wanted them. The first crisis was triggered by the arrival of Gustav, who, you might recall, we had last seen in Buchenwald on April 11, his pockets stuffed with grenades.

An elegant, vigorous young man in his thirties, with red hair and a self-satisfied, not to say triumphant, air, Gustav stirred murky and troubling memories in us. In his memoirs, Naftali Lau-Lavi reports that Gustav was the leader of a group of clandestine avengers who tracked down collaborators who had operated in the Polish ghettos. The group tried and executed their prey, strangling them or hanging them in latrines. Gustav was the executioner.

A member of the Stubendienst in the youth block in the "small camp" in Buchenwald, Gustav had not been universally admired. He had been quick to use his fists during the distribution of rations, and he had hit all the harder if the prisoner was Hungarian, hence the charge that he had flagrantly favored his Polish buddies. On April 11 he had been seen parading among the liberators. Then he had disappeared.

And now here he was in Écouis, expressing his desire to stay with "his" Buchenwald children as their big brother, counselor, and spokesman. The leadership saw nothing wrong with his idea. Why not hire someone familiar to us who could maintain discipline without offending our sensibilities? Hence their surprise at the general outcry aroused by his candidacy. Gustav, who was so free with his fists? Some demanded that he be arrested on the spot and turned over to the police. Others, less numerous, defended him: Yes, he was brutal, he got angry, used his fists, but no more than necessary. If he favored the young Polish Jews, it was only natural for him to take care of his own first. How could he be called a collaborator? He was a member of the Resistance, wasn't he? There was yelling and screaming on both sides, and our administrators were booed when they called for silence.

The counselors held an emergency meeting to discuss how to ward off what looked like an impending riot. But their psychology degrees proved useless. Rachel Mintz, probably influenced by the educational theories of Janusz Korczak, made an unusual proposal: that the "children" — that's what they called us — decide Gustav's fate themselves. In other words, have a trial, with witnesses for the defense and the prosecution. Then, after deliberations, we, the tribunal, would issue our verdict.

The "trial" began in the early afternoon and continued late into the night with a recess for dinner and the Minha service. Gustav, proud and arrogant, answered his accusers with shrugs of disdain, and before long the discussion turned from the facts of the case to more general ethical considerations. What was the proper role of a Jew during periods of persecution? Should he accept responsibilities from the enemy in the interests of helping his own? Where lay the boundary that no one must cross, lest he lose his soul? If severity could save lives and limit the power of the murderer's cruelty, was it permissible to reject the use of force inherent in all authority?

All the anger was forgotten, along with the shouting. These "children" who had stared absolute evil in the face expressed themselves without malice. No thirst for revenge motivated them. Despite the defendant's arrogance and the bitter memories he aroused, they would not seek vengeance against him.

In the end the tribunal opted for compromise. Gustav would go free, but he had to leave Écouis. Though we declined to punish him, we did not want him in our midst. No one spoke as we watched him leave the château. Strangely, the man's solitude moved me. I came away with a vague feeling of embarrassment.

It did me good to take up my studies again. Together with Menashe Klein, the leader of our group, and Kalman Kalikstein, a brilliant boy of Polish origin, I rededicated myself to the study of the sacred works. Spontaneously, without thinking about it, I recovered my religious fervor, perhaps as a way of closing the parentheses on my recent past. Most of all, I needed to find my way again, guided by one certainty: However much the world had changed, the Talmudic universe was still the same. No enemy could silence the disputes between Shammai and Hillel, Abbaye and Rava.

Between study sessions I played chess. Sometimes people watched us, which didn't bother me. I was good at concentrating, at blocking out the outside world. It was fine with me if a couple of strangers wanted to take pictures as we played. One of them asked some questions in bad German; I answered in good Yiddish. Someone said they were journalists, but I had never met a journalist before; they were of no interest to me, and I didn't see why I should interest them.

A few days later I went to the director's office to find out whether the books my friend Menashe and I had ordered had come in. He happened to be on the phone. I didn't understand what he was saying, but I assumed he was dealing with our request, because I heard him say my name several times. I waited politely until he finished, then asked my question in a mixture of German and Yiddish. He stared at me, uncomprehending. "I don't know what you're talking about," he said. "Who are you?" I told him, and his face suddenly brightened. "Oh, you're Wiesel? I'm glad you're here. That was a message from your sister." I froze. "My sister! That's impossible." "No it's not. That was her on the phone." When he saw the color drain from my face, he finally realized why I was so upset. Grabbing the receiver, he frantically dialed a long series of numbers. When he hung up, he seemed downcast. "They say your sister called from a post office. They don't know how to reach her." I felt faint. My sister! Which one? "But she left a message for you. She'll be waiting for you in Paris tomorrow." I spent a sleepless night. I told myself it had to be a mistake. Even assuming one of my sisters had survived, what would she be doing in Paris? And even if she was in Paris, how would she know I had survived? And even if she did, how could she possibly know I was in Écouis?

At dawn the next morning I took the train to Paris. I was worried. How would I get around alone? I knew no one and didn't speak a word of French. I was angry at the director and at the OSE. How could they have let me go alone?

199

My sister in France? Hilda in Paris? Bea? It seemed so unlikely, improbable, impossible. I would stand on the train platform, take a quick look around, and catch the next train back to Écouis. Fortunately the director had given me a little money.

When the train pulled into the Gare Saint-Lazare, I thought I was dreaming. Hilda fell into my arms. She introduced me to Freddo, an Algerian Jew who had been deported to Dachau. They met after liberation, and it was love at first sight. When she heard I was dead, she followed Freddo to France. They were going to be married. How had she found me? Simple: she saw my picture in a newspaper, *Défense de la France*, soon to become *France-Soir*.

Hilda took me to meet her future in-laws. It was a large, warm family. I had always had a special affection for Sephardim, and that feeling would now deepen. Hilda and I spent the day and night talking about everything except the things that hurt. We felt a need to censor ourselves, for we were both afraid of being unable to control our emotions. Better to talk about Écouis, the OSE, the train trip — but not our parents or Tsipouka. I was afraid to mention Bea's name. Since she was not with Hilda, did that mean . . . ? No, thank God, Bea was alive. She had gone back to Sighet to find out whether by some miracle I might have survived.

Hilda was worried about my future. She took me to the Consistoire, where we met with the president, Léon Meiss, a patient, affable man. They spoke in French (which my sister knew from high school), so I don't know what they said, but after half an hour's discussion, Hilda told me I could enroll in the seminary and become a rabbi if I wanted. First I would have to learn the language, of course. I said I would think about it. I probably didn't accept immediately because I dreaded being separated from my friends.

Freddo insisted I go see *The Great Dictator* at the Gaumont theater. Here at least my ignorance of French would not be a handicap. It was a packed house of laughing people, but I found Chaplin rather pathetic and sad. True, I had trouble concentrating, for a couple in the row in front of me was kissing. The man was an American soldier. I was wearing khaki, which in the darkness could easily have passed for a uniform. It seemed to me I ought to have the same rights and opportunities. But I had never kissed a woman, and now suddenly I wanted to. It was the first time this had ever happened to me. All at once I was no longer thinking of the film. I wasn't thinking about anything. The past, the future, religious morality — all faded away. My body was doing my thinking for me, and it was drawn to, well, the young woman sitting on my left. I glanced at her furtively, my heart pounding. I told myself not to be a fool — accost a stranger? The very idea! She could make me pay dearly for my impudence. At the very least, I would get my face slapped. And had I forgotten the biblical commandments already? But I wasn't doing anything wrong. I was just thinking, imagining, shyly sliding my hand toward hers. Our fingers barely brushed, as if by accident. When I took her hand in mine, my neighbor did not protest. But then the movie ended, as did everything else. The house lights went on, and I was annoyed at Chaplin. He might have waited five more minutes.

Many months passed before Bea found out I was alive. Someone told someone who saw her in Sighet. We made arrangements to meet in Antwerp, and so it was that I finally found myself in that city of diamond merchants. My beautiful cousin Reizi had died in the camps, but I did find Shiku, who had survived by hiding with a Christian family. It was at his home that the reunion of Sarah and Shlomo Wiesel's three orphans took place.

Shiku could not hold back his tears. We were stronger.

Survivors are often asked, How did you manage to readjust to life, to joy, to love? The truth is, it was not that difficult — less difficult than adjusting to death. Having slept with the dead and spent a lifetime — indeed, many lifetimes — in death's company, we had come to view it as ordinary, expected, a daily presence, the norm, not the exception. We had, after all, been brought to the camp not to live, but to die, and when we stumbled over a corpse, we walked on without so much as a second look. It was like pushing aside a dry twig.

Now we had to reinvent ourselves mentally, reconstructing a system of values so as to understand a Talmudic Law that is permeated with a poignant humanism: If the High Priest happens on an anonymous corpse in a public place, he must drop all other obligations and bury it immediately, even if he is on his way to the Temple. Respecting the dignity of the dead takes priority even over services on the holiest day of the year.

In the camp we were all future anonymous corpses, walking cadavers. Even when a friend or relative died, you didn't cry, didn't mourn, didn't rend your clothes or smear your forehead with ashes. You didn't show your grief. You did nothing to mark the event. You couldn't.

I recall a boy from my region, very tall and thin, who thought he was already dead. "No one will ever convince me that the Germans let even a single Jew escape alive," he used to say. Granted, he ate and drank, but as he pointed out, "Perhaps the dead, too, eat and drink as we do." A constant smile hovered about his lips because he firmly believed that the dead were smiling at him. He therefore returned the favor, out of politeness. In my notebook I gave him a nickname: the dead man.

Where did he get that gentleness? Were all

the dead like him?

One evening we were chatting under a tree, and he shared his happiness with me. Yes, that was the word he used: happiness. "I'm happy because I'm not afraid anymore," he said. "I'm not afraid to die, because I'm already dead."

He is still alive as I write these lines, living in Brooklyn with his wife and children. Those who know him say he believes he's in heaven.

After a few weeks in Écouis, we moved. The leaders of the OSE decided to divide the four hundred "children" into two groups: the observant Jews and the nonobservant Jews. The first group — there were about a hundred of us — was transferred to the Château d'Ambloy, in Vaucelles.

We said goodbye to a third group, the lucky ones who were leaving for Palestine. Among them were Naftali Lau-Lavi (future adviser to Moshe Dayan) and his brother Israel Meir Lau (future chief rabbi of Israel), then eight years old and nicknamed Lolek. Forty years later, during a commemoration ceremony in Birkenau, he mentioned that it was I who taught him to say Kaddish by heart.

I had signed up to go to Palestine too, but the British bureaucrats who issued immigration "certificates" denied my application. The Lau brothers had family in Palestine, while I did not. Who knows if that is why my request was refused?

There was some good news: Niny was to accompany us to Ambloy, and two nice young women, Judith and Mireille, both observant, were put in charge of the new home.

It was an unforgettable summer. Vacation was in the air. Our counselors had no trouble getting the "children" to respect the community, and normal life began. Several minyanim gathered each morning, and study circles and sports clubs were formed. A group of religious Jewish intellectuals, Yeshurun, often came to spend Shabbat with us. Though I sat in on these highbrow meetings, I felt left out, since I couldn't understand their French. Among the participants were Marc Breuer, son and grandson of rabbis; Théo Dreyfus, author of a work on the Maharal of Prague, later director of the Maimonides School before emigrating to Palestine; Benno Gross, another pupil of André Neher, who would later teach at Bar-Ilan University; and Lucien Lazare, who would write important works on the Jewish Resistance and Righteous Gentiles in France.

At night we lit campfires, which the romantic in me loved. They took me back to Fantana, the mountain village near Borsha where we used to spend our vacations. The crackling of the logs, the spray of the sparks, and the solemn, nostalgic songs made us feel close to one another. It was an atmosphere of healthy intimacy, a complete harmony of voice and silence, of the presence of the living and the dead, of memory and what it harbors. If the shadows were too close, they were not menacing. If the stars were too high or their light too cold, nothing frightened us — not so long as the flames bore our songs and voices to heaven. Little by little, cliques had formed. I spent a lot of time with Nicolas. Kalman, Binem, and I studied with Menashe, the most accomplished resident Talmudist. Kalman often surprised me with the rigor of his logic; it was clear that he would become a scientist.

Niny didn't know it, but Kalman and I wrote impassioned, mediocre Yiddish poems to her glory. Our attraction to her, innocent and platonic as it was, seems natural to me today. We lived among boys, and were inevitably conquered by Niny's affectionate, feminine presence. My heart pounded whenever she came within sight.

Judith and Mireille had fiancés and were therefore untouchable. But Niny was alone, and so theoretically open to being loved. Kalman loved her, and so did I. In fact, we all did, though none dared admit it, for we were so sincerely devoted to religious practice that we feared being lured into sin. What is sensuality, we reasoned, if not an invitation to physical pleasure? And what is physical pleasure if not the road to the forbidden and to eventual punishment?

Niny decided it would be instructive for us to meet some of the French "children" (sons and daughters of deportees) who lived in other OSE homes. She therefore invited Kalman and me, along with a third boy, Moshe Kunitz, who was from a village near Sighet, to spend a few days with her at a home called Les Hirondelles not far from Lyons. There I met André Neher, whose sister, Aya Samuel, was director of the home. I was immediately struck by his warmth and thoughtfulness, and by the depth of his knowledge. We conversed in Hebrew. Neher quoted the Midrash and Maimonides, while I simply listened, impressed by the clarity of his ideas. After morning Shabbat services I attended a lecture of his entitled "Transcendence and Immanence," listening intently though failing to understand a word. Neher was kind enough to explain it to me that afternoon, as we walked in the garden. It was in part thanks to him that I turned to philosophy, and he remained a source of light and fervor to me. He introduced me to his future wife, Renée, whose charm and grace were equaled by her erudition and gifts as a historian. Our friendship ended only with his premature death in Jerusalem in 1988.

I also met a girl, Régine, dark-haired, shy, and sentimental. She played the piano. It was the first time I heard a piece by Schumann. I thought of teaching her a Hasidic tune, but she preferred Kalman's company. Such is life.

One evening, during services, a strange man was pointed out to me. Dressed like a vagabond, a tiny hat perched on his enormous head, he stood in a corner, lost in his thoughts. Someone told me his name was Shushani and that he was a genius. "A madman," someone else countered, while a third observer offered a compromise: "A mad genius." As it happens, I was wary of geniuses and drawn to madmen, so I wasn't sure whether to approach him. As I hesitated, he vanished. Too bad, but our paths would cross again.

French lessons were organized for us, but I attended them only sporadically. I didn't see the point. I had better things to do than to puzzle over the conjugation of irregular verbs and the intricacies of the agreement of tenses. There were drawing lessons too, but perspective held no interest for me compared to the Midrash. I managed to get hold of some Hasidic works and treatises on mysticism. I was determined to continue the quest the Germans had interrupted, which I considered more important and exciting than anything in the real world. After all, I reasoned, the events we experience here below are consequences of what is decided on high, are they not? Granted, these were turbulent times: the signing of the United Nations Charter in San Francisco, the four-power occupation of Germany, the Potsdam Conference, the bombing of Hiroshima and Nagasaki, Japan's surrender, Churchill's defeat in the 1946 elections, De Gaulle's resignation. But it was God who governed the actions of men, and if we failed to understand Him, perhaps it was because we were too shortsighted to see what our ancestors would have noticed immediately.

In time, though, our instructors managed to interest us in current events. The Nuremberg trials and philosophy of justice: were retroactive laws legitimate? The Iron Curtain, of which Churchill had spoken at a small college in Fulton, Missouri: were we now to fear our former allies? There was also Jewish terrorism and clandestine immigration to Palestine. We were told of acts of sabotage committed by the Irgun and the Stern Gang, such as the bombing of the General Headquarters of the British Army at the King David Hotel in Jerusalem. Many were killed, many more wounded. Still, the Irgun was said to have warned the British authorities, a local newspaper, and a foreign consulate ahead of time. Why hadn't an immediate evacuation been ordered? Was it just another instance of British arrogance? We debated these questions at length. Would another resistance movement have acted similarly? More debate. Was there any such thing as a specifically Jewish morality? But there were distractions too. We were told that the French and world press were full of talk of a new phenomenon called the "bikini."

It was in Ambloy that we celebrated the first High Holidays since liberation, and during Yizkor, the service devoted to the memory of the dead, the floodgates finally opened. All assembled wept tears of submission to God, of contrition and remorse, incomprehension and despair. I tried to remember the last Yizkor I had attended. Was it with my grandfather at the home of the Borsher Rebbe in Sighet, or with my father on the Appelplatz in Auschwitz? It all seemed so distant now, part of another universe and another history, as though time were no longer counted in years.

I recited the grave, solemn prayers with more concentration than ever. Never had I prayed with such intensity. I saw my father and grandfather as they had stood beside me at services, and I prayed for them. I wept for them.

Questions about divine justice and charity weighed upon me, but they had not yet taken shape. I acted as though my faith in God and His Laws and attributes were still whole and intact, even strengthened, as though my relation to God were untarnished, unshattered.

Today I remember Ambloy with tenderness and melancholy, the more so since our stay there was brief. The OSE soon moved us to Taverny, in the Paris suburbs. I was glad because it meant I could see Hilda more often.

Niny, Judith, and Mireille came with us, probably to reassure us, but they told us it was time to start thinking about the future. The "children" had choices to make. They could leave for Palestine (illegally if necessary), emigrate to America (or to Canada, Colombia, or Australia, if they had family there), or remain in France. But if they stayed, they would do well to learn a trade or to take some special courses before enrolling in the Lycée Maimonides in Boulogne. Many opted for Palestine. Others managed to come up with an uncle in Baltimore, a cousin in Melbourne, or an aunt in Johannesburg. Kalman and I decided to stay in France — for the moment. "Fine," they said, "but in that case you must learn French," which was fair enough. I liked the language, found it musical. But the agreement of tenses was still a source of immense irritation.

Fortunately, in 1947 the OSE arranged for a young teacher, François Wahl, to give me private lessons. Tall and slender, with delicate features, slightly distracted, his head always tilted, François was to play a significant role in my life. He was an excellent teacher, as intuitive as he was erudite, endowed with a vivid imagination. He initiated me into the field most beloved of French teachers: the explication of texts. It was thanks to him that I learned to savor the suggestive power of Racine's poetry and the subtleties of Pascal's thought. He took me to the Comédie-Française and to concerts and guided me through the Latin Quarter. It is to him I owe my passion for classical literature and French culture.

But not everything went smoothly at first. I could have happily forgone the endless, point-by-point analysis of Phaedra's mood swings. Likewise for the Cid and Monsieur Jourdain, and as for Racine's Esther, however much I respected her, I preferred the original. But

François refused to give up. For him the beauty of a text was timeless; to turn one's back on it was to renounce a great source of knowledge. "You sound like a Hasid," I told him. He asked what that was, and I explained it to him. From then on we also talked of things Jewish.

At the time I didn't know that François's father had been deported to Auschwitz and never returned. "I didn't know anything about you," François explained years later. "I didn't speak of it because you never talked about the camps." Though only two years my senior, he seemed much older. I cannot define the nature of the bond between us, except to say that it was deep and true.

Our lessons were held at his mother's apartment, which he shared. She was a physician. I can see her now: distinguished and gracious, with a sober beauty. One day, completely out of the blue, François asked her, "Why do you think I am so taken by Jewish subjects?" Her answer, which reflected her own passionate commitment to Jewish causes, surely affected his future. In 1947, as the underground war raged in Palestine, François performed important secret tasks for a Jewish resistance group. The following year our paths diverged. Later, much later, they would cross again.

It was in 1947 that Shushani, the mysterious Talmudic scholar, reappeared in my life. For two or three years he taught me unforgettable lessons about the limits of language and reason, about the behavior of sages and madmen, about the obscure paths of thought as it wends its way across centuries and cultures. But I learned nothing of the secret in which he enveloped himself.

I remember our decisive encounter. It took place on a Friday, on the train taking me back to Taverny from François's. Still somewhat preoccupied by the conflict between Racine and Corneille, I plunged into the Book of Job, only because I was scheduled to give a talk the next day, after the service and before the Sabbath meal, on the problems it raised.

That was our custom. Each week someone gave a presentation on a subject of his choice, preferably biblical. My very first address was entitled "The Ghetto: Salutary or Destructive Experience for the Jewish People?" Kalman and I worked on it together. I made the presentation and he answered questions. Niny and André, one of our best counselors, helped me prepare the "outline." I had no trouble finding sources, for I knew all about ghettos. But for the talk on Job I hadn't had time to write out anything. That didn't worry me: I would simply read passages and comment, line by line. I felt confident that I knew the subject.

As I sat there on the train, someone suddenly spoke to me in Yiddish in a hoarse, raspy voice. It was the man I had seen at Aya Samuel's in Lyons. He was slovenly, and his ridiculous tiny hat and dusty glasses made him more than a little conspicuous. "Come over here," he said, looking at me. "There's room." When I didn't move, he came and sat down next to me. "What are you reading?" he asked, as if we had known each other for years. Without waiting for an answer, he took the book out of my hands, glanced at the cover, flipped through the pages, and handed it back to me: "The only thing of value here," he said matter-of-factly, "is an innovative commentary on the fifth verse of the fifth chapter." Then he asked me why I was carrying Job around. "Because," I stammered, "I have to give a talk about it tomorrow."

"Oh, you're teaching Job? You?"

"I'm just supposed to talk about it a little," I said, lowering my head.

He asked me — was there a hint of sarcasm in his voice? — whether I knew the subject. Yes, I said nervously, but not that well. . . . "But you've studied it closely?" Well, maybe not closely enough. "In other words, you're going to teach without having studied." I was silent. "You probably figure you know enough to impress your audience, right? Or at least enough to have the right to discuss the subject, yes?" I couldn't think of an answer so I said nothing, but he kept at me until I stammered a few words about the value of dialogue, silence, and the theme of friendship, and the power of Satan. Which was pretty much all I knew. He then proceeded to prove that I had understood nothing whatever about the marvelous Book of Job. In fact, I couldn't even translate the very first verse to his standard. And if I was arrogant enough to believe that this was the only subject about which I knew nothing, I was sadly mistaken, as he now proved by subjecting me to a veritable examination strewn with traps and trick questions. It was clear I was an insolent ignoramus of the worst order. "And," Shushani concluded, "you have the chutzpah to give a speech on Job in public?" All right, enough of that, I thought. I was eager for this ordeal to end. The train moved with agonizing lethargy, but to my relief we finally arrived in Taverny, where I could take leave of his sarcasm. I got up, shook his hand, and politely wished him a good Shabbat. "What do you mean, a good Shabbat?" he said. "We're not done yet. I'm coming with you."

That Shabbat is engraved in my memory like a punishment. No one had invited Shushani, and I wondered whether the sole purpose of his gate-crashing was to ruin my talk. That was his method. He liked to demolish before rebuilding, to abase before offering recompense.

I trembled as I began my presentation. *Ish haya be'eretz Utz.* . . . "There was a man in the land of Uz. . . ." A perfect and upright father, charitable and generous. Almost a *tzaddik*, a man so good that Satan was jealous of him. . . . Supreme injustice: Job suffers without having sinned, and God goes along with

215

the game. . . . Job as a living example of the problem of theodicy. . . . My classmates paid no attention to the strange-looking man who had come for the talk and the meal but not for the service. Ensconced in a corner, he seemed to have dozed off. I half expected him to interrupt me, but he was charitable enough to let me finish in peace. He didn't speak during the discussion either, but an ironic smile fluttered on his lips.

It was during the traditional third meal of Shabbat, late in the afternoon, as dusk gathered, that the thunderbolt fell upon the assembly. Breaking the silence between two songs, he began to talk about the prayers composed in honor of the final hours of Shabbat. His voice was husky, but it commanded attention. What was Shabbat, and who was the queen who bore its name? Over whom did she reign, and with what powers was she invested? Shushani juggled quotations drawn from medieval lyric poetry and the mystic sources of Safed, painting a vivid yet subtle portrait. All at once we pictured the queen; we could feel her presence, were intoxicated by her grace, and became her doting escorts.

Night had long since fallen. We could have recited the prayer of Maariv, performed the Havdalah, and lighted the lamps, but no one dreamed of it. While this orator spoke, we lived outside time in paradise.

In the end he broke the spell himself, putting

his hands on the table, pushing himself up, and emitting a soft grunt as if to say, That's it. We dropped back down to earth, and a new week began.

On Sunday he treated us to a "real" lecture — on Job, of course; to "rehabilitate him," as he put it. It was a dazzling, stimulating, provocative, enriching exposition the likes of which I had never heard: Job and Abraham, Job and the Prophet Elijah, Job and Balaam; the language and philosophy of Job; the Jewish attitude toward suffering and injustice; the commentaries of Rabbi Yohanan and Resh Lakish; truth and myth; the possibilities of the Midrash, but also its limits. Of course everyone looked at me almost as much as at him, as though deriding me: now that's what you call an analysis of Job. I felt ashamed. Having lost face, I wanted to flee. But I stayed, and afterward he buttonholed me as we filed out. "Now at least you'll be able to talk about Job a little more intelligently," he said. I made an attempt to pull away, but he held my arm and added, "Admit you haven't learned anything yet." And I heard myself answer, "Help me learn." He made one last nasty comment and disappeared. It was a game that went on for several days.

But I refused to give up. I sensed in him such great intellectual power and such a deep fund of knowledge that I actually began to pursue him. In fact, I already belonged to him. I gave him my reason and my will. His words banished distance and obstacles. It was as though he were explaining to the Creator Himself the triumphs and defeats of His creation. If he shook my inner peace, that was what I wanted. If he overturned certainties, so much the better, for they were beginning to weigh heavily upon me. Man is defined by what troubles him, not by what reassures him. I needed to be forced to start all over.

In Shushani I had found a master. I would later discover that he had also taught the great French Jewish philosopher Emmanuel Levinas and that his disciples included renowned professors who paid him fabulous fees. What he did with all that money I'll never know.

Everything about him was a mystery. Where had he come from? Philosophy, Marx said, has no history, but what about philosophers? Don't they have a history? This one seemed not to, or else he meant to keep it secret.

No one knew his real name, his origin, or his age. What kind of family did he come from? What was he seeking to achieve, or to forget? Had he ever known happiness, had he ever known a woman? He spoke of himself only to obscure his tracks. Where did he acquire his immense knowledge? Who had ordained him a rabbi? Where had he learned all those ancient and modern languages? Where and toward what end had he studied Sanskrit? He mastered Hungarian in two weeks, just to surprise me. He knew the Babylonian and Jerusalem Talmuds by heart; also Maimonides, Nahmanides, and Crescas, not to mention Yehuda Halevy, the poems of Ibn Gabirol, and the Greek and Latin classics as well. One Shabbat afternoon in Taverny he gave an entire lecture about the very first verse of the Book of Isaiah: *Khazon Yeshayahu ben Amotz* . . . "The vision of Isaiah, the son of Amoz, which he saw concerning Judah and Jerusalem in the days of Uzziah, Jotham, Ahaz, and Hezekiah, kings of Judah." It lasted four hours, and even single words were courses in themselves. *Khazon* means "vision," but is it an image or a word? Was it received from outside or did it come from within? In a waking or a dreaming state? What is its relation to individual piety and organized society? What is the difference between prophecy and vision, vision and hallucination? Can it be that one must be a Jew to have visions? What about Balaam in the Bible or the oracle at Delphi? And who was Isaiah? And why is he called the prince of prophets? What were his complaints against his people? Why was he so harsh with them? If we compare him, say, to Jeremiah, which of the two touches us more deeply? How to define his relation to language and to prophecy? Didn't other prophets, like Moses himself, or Jonah, try to escape their prophetic obligation? More generally, does a prophet have the right to reject his role and mission? Doesn't the law say that a prophet who rejects his prophetic mission merits death? Is that why he died an unnatural death, his body cut in two by King Manasseh? Why did all the prophets die tragically? Without ever departing from the verse, Shushani swept us along at a dizzying pace, as other realms and horizons opened before him and before us. He left us breathless, hovering between the summit and the depths of knowledge, the one as disturbing as the other.

One day he asked us to question him about anything we wanted, the Bible or politics, history or the Midrash, detective stories or the Zohar. He listened to our questions, eyelids drooping, waiting for everyone to finish. And then, like a magician, he gathered it all together to create a mosaic of stunning richness and rigor, harmoniously weaving our questions and his answers together. Suddenly each of us realized that all these themes, raised at random as if for his amusement, were in fact linked to a center, to a single focus of clarity. Yes, Cain's murderous act contained that of Titus. Yes, Jacob's wrestling with the angel heralded the adventure of the Jewish people defying their fate.

The village clock in the distance had long since tolled midnight, but the inexhaustible orator talked on, endowing his words with a thousand shining highlights and his thought with as many shadows, and it was our common prayer that his rough, monotonous voice would never fall silent.

Detractors called him a modern-day Faust. Had he sold his soul to Satan in exchange for

220

limitless knowledge? A daring hypothesis, but I rejected it. I don't know if he was a holy man in disguise, a kabalist wandering the earth to gather "divine sparks" so as to reconstitute the original flame, or an eternal vagabond, the timeless outsider who embodies doubt and threat. But I am sure he did not belong to the powers of "the other side," that of darkness.

One day, unable to contain my curiosity, I foolishly violated his sanctuary, asking him the question that haunted even my dreams: "Who are you? Who are you really? If I have children someday, I would like to be able to tell them about you. . . . I mean later . . ." He froze, and a cruel expression came over his face. I could hear his rasping breath. Then he unleashed his fury: "And who says there'll be a later?" Fortunately, his anger subsided as quickly as it had been aroused.

I sometimes talk about Shushani in my writings and in my lectures. Whenever I mention him, strangers write to me or come up to me adding this or that detail about his life and his mystery — a young rabbi in Connecticut who had met him in Montevideo, a merchant in Paris who told me that Shushani gave him financial advice, the mother of a Jewish beauty queen in North Carolina who remembers listening to him in Taverny. In San Francisco and Montreal, Caracas and Marseilles, when I mentioned Shushani, a smile would appear on some

221

listener's face, and I knew I had just rekindled a spark.

Haim-Hersh Kahan, a childhood friend, wrote from Oslo that he had attended one of Shushani's courses in a synagogue near the Rue des Rosiers: "Everything I had learned till then was as nothing by comparison."

The latest to date is a nuclear physicist, Jacques Goldberg, who shared with me a *khidush* (a finding in biblical exegesis) that he attributes to Shushani. Knowing nothing about physics, nuclear or otherwise, I cannot claim to understand the implications of his communication. In fact, I often felt that Shushani's words were beyond understanding. In fact, I think he liked to be misunderstood.

Menashe attended his courses for a while, but eventually gave up. "Be careful," he warned me. "This man wants to shake our faith. He scares me." Menashe emigrated to the United States and settled in Brooklyn, where he became a *rosh yeshiva,* the head of an academy, and one of the great Halachic arbiters of his generation. Nevertheless, I stayed with Shushani.

I couldn't leave him and didn't want to. He was one of those men who stay with you, inhabiting you and troubling you long after they have gone. Few people have so disconcerted and fascinated me. Clearly, in his role as teacher and master he was intent on transmitting and sharing something, but to this day I don't know what. His certainties? I don't know if he had any. Perhaps his doubts. He used his abilities to perturb established truths.

What were his complaints about man? What did he demand of Jewish thought and history or of man's destiny? On his lips the words "yes" and "no" were equivalent. He developed his own theories and systems in one bold sweep, and used the same arguments to defend or destroy them, leaving the subjugated pupil feeling as though he had been led to the threshold of an adventure that now might cast him into an abyss or take him to towering heights. He was contradiction personified, with all its allure and danger. How to explain his apparent poverty, when his suitcase (which I once chanced to glimpse open) contained a quantity of jewels and foreign currency? What accounted for his taste for wandering? Was he one of those Hasidic masters who must wander in exile before revealing himself, one of the thirty-six hidden Just Men thanks to whom the world exists as a world? I knew of no country he hadn't visited. He had been seen in Algiers, heard in Casablanca, spotted in Nepal. Like the *na-venadnik* of legend, he never slept in the same place two nights in a row. Was he a vegetarian? He refused to take his meals in public. How did he sustain his strength? He could speak for eight hours at a stretch without showing the slightest physical or intellectual fatigue.

During the Occupation he was arrested by an officer of the Gestapo. In perfect German he declared that he was Alsatian, Aryan, and a university professor to boot. The officer guffawed at the sight of this vagabond. "You, a professor?"

"Yes, me."

"And what do you teach?"

"Higher mathematics."

"No luck. It just so happens that I myself am a professor of higher mathematics in civilian life."

Shushani was unfazed. "Well," he replied, "you can of course test my knowledge if you like. But I have a better idea. Let me pose a problem to you. If you can solve it, shoot me. If you can't, let me go." Released, Shushani slipped into Switzerland, where the chief rabbi became one of his most devoted admirers.

Later, having heard that the Rebbe of Satmàr had arrived in Paris, he decided to visit him at his hotel. The hallway was crammed with followers waiting to present their requests to the *tzaddik*. Before entering the room in which the Rebbe was enthroned, everyone lined up to give the secretary the traditional *pidyon,* a banknote. But Shushani tore a leaf out of his notebook, scribbled a few words, and told the secretary, "I order you to bring this message to the Rebbe; otherwise I cannot be responsible." The terrified secretary obeyed. Suddenly the door opened and the Rebbe himself emerged, looking for the visitor in vagabond's garb. They spent several hours alone together, and the content of their discussion was never divulged. But the Rebbe was heard to murmur: "I grant that a human being can know so many things, but how do you manage to understand them?"

Yet I never actually saw him with an open book. Was that because he knew them all, even those he hadn't read? Perhaps it was when he closed his eyes that he could read nonexistent books, or at least books not yet written.

It is difficult to describe our private sessions in Taverny, Versailles, and later in my room on the Rue Le Marois. His knowledge poured down upon me and I devoured his words. It was as though his words came to me from a distant sanctuary I could never approach. We would spend entire weeks on a single page of the Talmud, from the treatise exploring the problems of divorce, for instance, without ever veering from the subject. He spoke, and I followed him in a state of ecstasy and nostalgia. It is to him I owe my constant drive to question, my pursuit of the mystery that lies within knowledge and of the darkness hidden within light.

Why did Shushani accept — perhaps even choose — me as a pupil? Why did he think me deserving? What was it about me that interested him? I have no idea. In general, those are the words I speak most often when talking about him: I have no idea. His disappearances and reappearances, his changes of mood, his feigned or sincere outbursts of anger, all seemed incomprehensible. Why did he never talk about himself? Why did he shroud himself in so much mystery, concealing even his real name? Why did he hide his origins? Why did he live such a bizarre life? Why did he decline to reveal himself to the broader public he surely could have conquered?

I remember that, many years later, he refused to leave Montevideo and come to New York to give courses to a few dozen students. I had suggested it to him, and wealthy friends were ready to finance the project. "Out of the question," he replied. "I swore I would never again set foot on American soil after I lost all that money in the stock market crash." Was it true? Shlomo Malka, a French journalist, and I devoted some fifteen radio broadcasts to Shushani. The series generated voluminous mail from listeners claiming to know "the truth" about him. Now, an eternity later, I think I know the truth, or can at least roughly approximate it.

Born in Lithuania, young Mordechai Rosenbaum (his real name) dazzled relatives and teachers with his prodigious memory. He retained everything he read. Even before his bar mitzvah he could recite the entire Talmud by heart. People came great distances to listen to him, and his father took him even further afield, exhibiting him, for a fee, in various communities. That was how he got rich, and how he traveled the world. Everywhere he went he stunned and enchanted his audience, becoming a formidable acrobat of knowledge. Is there a knowledge that

226

money can corrupt? Does the Torah contain unsuspected perils when turned into a money-making instrument? I have no idea. I still don't know why he disappeared so often, or where he went, or why he left so abruptly for Uruguay. Did he fear another war in Europe? Was it his taste for uprooting himself or his constant need for new experiences? All I know is that he died one Friday afternoon in 1965 in Montevideo, where he was performing, according to some, as a sage, and according to others, as a beadle. I told the story in *One Generation After*. Seated under a tree, surrounded by pupils, he was teaching the Talmud. Suddenly, in the middle of a citation, his head fell upon a female student's shoulder. An instant later he was gone. It happened shortly before the arrival of Shabbat. In Jewish tradition such a death is considered a *mitat neshika*, or gentle death: The angel comes, embraces the chosen one as one would a friend, and takes him away, sparing him every trace of agony and suffering. He was in full possession of his faculties. Since an essay I had written on his teachings was found in his pocket, I was asked to compose the Hebrew inscription for his tombstone: "The rabbi and sage Mordechai Shushani, blessed be his memory. His birth and his life are bound and sealed in enigma. Died the sixth day of the week, Erev Shabbat Kodesh, 26 Tevet 5726."

To Shlomo Malka, who wrote a very good book about Shushani, I confided my conviction that this enigma must be respected. By what right would we seek to unravel it, thereby violating secrets of his personality that he himself protected so fiercely? I simply speak of him as a disciple speaks of his master — with gratitude. I am increasingly convinced that he must be considered one of the great, disturbing figures of our tradition. He saw his role as that of agitator and troublemaker. He upset the believer by demonstrating the fragility of his faith; he shook the heretic by making him feel the torments of the void.

Why was he so determined not to be known? From whom was he hiding, and why? Were his travels motivated by a taste for wandering or the need to flee? Perhaps he wanted to be able constantly to begin anew, with new disciples. Why did he write these indecipherable manuscripts, some of which are in my possession? For whom were they intended? Was it to forge his own myth, as a genius of memory? What I know is that I would not be the man I am, the Jew I am, had not an astonishing, disconcerting vagabond accosted me one day to inform me that I understood nothing.

We didn't stay long in Taverny. No one asked our opinion when we were transferred to Versailles. The new home, known as Our Place, was directed by Félix Goldschmidt, a former mining engineer and a cultivated man of great personal authority. His silent and contemplative wife suffered from a skin disease. They had three daughters, Batya, Eve, and Tilly, and a son, Jules. I got along well with the director. There was never an incident, never a misunderstanding.

This home was different from the others, for it included not only Buchenwald "children" but also other orphans, girls and boys, for the most part religiously observant, who had survived occupation either under false identities or by hiding with Christian families. We observed Shabbat and the holidays, sang the *Birkat hamazon* after meals in the Ashkenazic manner, and went to morning and evening services. But in the garden and cafeteria there was some rather innocent flirting — strolls, smiles, the sharing of secrets — which the counselors, probably for reasons both pedagogic and therapeutic, made no effort to discourage. Clearly we all needed affection, tenderness, and — why not? — love.

I went to Paris as often as possible. Hilda and her husband were living in a small apartment on the Rue Dussoubs, in difficult conditions. Freddo was a portraitist; his art brightened life but put little food on the table. I listened to his plans, and Hilda and I talked about Bea, who was still in a D.P. camp. I thought about her a lot in Versailles, and wrote to her every week.

One morning there appeared in the dining hall a smiling young American Jew named Ted Comet who had just arrived from New York.

He spoke a little French. He had come to serve a one-year internship in the children's homes. He came up to me and said, "Incidentally, I'm looking for someone, a relative of a classmate of mine at Yeshiva University. His name . . . his name . . ." He looked in his notebook and said my name. I would meet his friend and my relative, Irving Wiesel, many years later in Manhattan. And Ted Comet — now a high official with the American Joint Distribution Committee — and I still see each other to this day.

Every day for several weeks I took the train to the Lycée Maimonides. Sometimes I stayed Monday to Friday. And there I met two pupils who later became French television personalities: Marcel Mitrani and Josy Eisenberg. The German teacher assigned me a homework essay about my experiences. I wrote a paper explaining that I couldn't describe them. This earned me some sort of prize, exactly what I don't remember (probably an American chocolate bar). Mathematics lessons, on the other hand, left me cold. In secular schooling I was really only interested in French, and in this François Wahl continued to encourage me.

Marcus Cohen, the director of the Maimonides School, was an unusual character, austere as an ascetic, bearded like a prophet. Unbelievably reticent and slow-talking, he kept his eyes averted and his hands folded in front of him when he spoke to his pupils.

Sometimes he would invite me to his office

to chat, but when we parted I always had the feeling that what was essential had not been broached. His brother Bo, educational director of the OSE, had spoken to him about me. I have no idea what he said, but the director was quite respectful to me, possibly because I spoke modern Hebrew. Cohen was a passionate linguist, the compiler of the first French-Hebrew dictionary. The pupils treated him with affection, though behind his back they made fun of his mannerisms, his self-conscious air, and his obstinate attempts to make them laugh.

I did not stay long at Maimonides. The OSE offered me the chance to move into a small studio in the Latin Quarter. A friend from Écouis, a few years older than I, had enrolled in the Sorbonne and did his best to teach me the facts of life. He introduced me to a young and pretty maid who was prepared to take charge of my apprenticeship, but after just a few days I decided to go back to Versailles.

Kalman, Nicolas, Binem, and I were among the "grown-ups" at Our Place. Nicolas dreamed of putting together a literary review; Kalman was about to set out for Palestine aboard the *Exodus*; Binem was on his way to an internship with Henri Milstein, a choir conductor in Moissac, site of another children's home. As for me, I had all I could handle with Shushani for the Talmud and François for French. But I did find the time to organize a choir with the assistance of Israel Adler, a Palestinian emissary of the Jewish Agency. My childhood violin lessons proved useful, my participation in the Sighet synagogue choir even more so.

My choir attracted quite a few people. The most beautiful girls in the home joined, and suddenly I had more boys than I needed. Some of them sang off-key but insisted on taking part anyway. Just because God gave them thin voices and tin ears, why should they be denied the right to sing? One of them, Nicolas, put forward a more elegant argument: He was hopelessly in love with Myriam, a superb blond choir member, who did not reciprocate his affection. If only I would let him in the choir, he would have a chance of winning her over. "But you sing completely out of tune," I told him. He replied that he would make the effort of his life, that he would learn. "Learn what?" I countered. "It isn't something you can learn." But he was so crestfallen that I gave in, on one condition: that he not sing but only move his lips. He promised but occasionally got carried away and forgot, which was near-catastrophe. But he and Myriam saw each other often, and finally the god of love smiled upon them. Strangely, the boy stopped singing off-key.

As choir conductor I was stupidly and inexcusably severe, doing all I could to appear authoritarian, aggressive, and domineering. The reason was that I was, in fact, painfully shy. If one of the female singers cast a knowing glance in my direction, I lost my composure. If she

232

smiled at me, my heart would pound as if in anticipation of committing a sin. I blushed when I spoke and when I was spoken to. So I raised my voice, striving to affect a stern expression and to project an image of irritability and inaccessibility. I lost my temper easily and reprimanded anyone guilty of the slightest infraction. I was even pleased to be considered harsh. If I aroused anger and hatred, so be it. Anything was preferable to unrequited love. For that's what it was all about. I was convinced that no one I loved would love me back, that anyone I desired would reject me.

Three of the choir members troubled me especially: a brunette with a provocative laugh, a blonde with dreamy eyes, and someone I'll call Hanna. Their mere presence made me lose control. Such was my nature: I dreamed of living on this unlivable earth neither poetically, like Hölderlin, nor piously, like my grandfather, but lovingly.

A need to love and be loved. It seems silly to admit it, but in those days I got crushes far too fast, on everyone at once and on one girl in particular. She was a soloist with an awful personality — Hanna. She was the daughter of an OSE administrator, a fact that embarrassed and annoyed her no end. Rather than assume a false identity, she insisted on being treated like everyone else. She slept in a dormitory, took her meals in the common dining hall, participated in the various activities of the home, and was given the same pocket money as we were. In short, she had the same privileges, the same duties. But of course she added others. She worked more, demanded less, and never complained. She was always the first to show up for rehearsals and was always prepared. Yet we quarreled incessantly, with or without cause. It became second nature to both of us. She challenged most of my decisions and choices. Though friendly enough with the others, she stiffened at the very sight of me, barely deigning to smile hello. No matter what I said, she would grouse. She didn't agree with the schedule, the program, the casting. She claimed I was both stubborn and lax, too authoritarian and too permissive. In other words, the chemistry between us was terrible. She didn't like me. That was clear. The whole choir thought we were divided on everything; we always disagreed. When I said, "Yes," she would roll her eyes and say, "Oy." When I said, "You're not concentrating," she would reply, "How do you know?" When I said, "I can't hear you," she would say, "You're not listening."

The trouble was I loved her. Not physically or erotically, or at least I didn't think so, but not platonically, the way I loved Niny, either. I can honestly say that the fantasies I came to know later I did not have then. Or if I did, they passed through me without a trace. I might even lie and say it was not her body I loved

— but then, why did I get so excited when my shoulder brushed hers? The truth is I loved her self-assured walk and the way she ran her fingers through her dark hair; I liked the way she laughed (rarely) and the way she listened (even more rarely), and the way she glanced over her shoulder to see if anyone was following her when she trotted upstairs. I loved her for herself, and to convince myself that I was capable of loving, of yearning, of living, of existing for somebody else. I loved her because she was my first love.

Of course, in those days I fell in love "for the first time" more than once. Hanna was not the only girl I loved. There was also Niny. Even when I was attracted to other girls, I couldn't tear myself away from Niny. In time I became more lucid and courageous where she was concerned. I learned to deal with it, as the saying goes. I now know what I felt then. Love is no longer taboo, not a vague, murky sensation, but a very precise pain. In other words: Niny meant something in my life. Naturally, she didn't know it. If she had, I would have felt the need to leave Ambloy or later Versailles, though for where I don't know. But for me this was no more than a kind of adolescent game of hide-and-seek, and since it was a game, innocent enough, I allowed myself to play it elsewhere as well, feigning indifference to all women, young and otherwise, that I passed in the street, in the métro, and of course in Versailles. But any woman at all could turn my head if she wanted to. How often did I feel a disturbing yen to walk up to some stranger and tell her, "Love me!" But I lacked the courage, and the experience. To conceal my confusion I wore a Basque beret that was too big for me and struck the pose of the dedicated student devoted only to his courses, the religious neophyte who loves God alone. I remember an encounter from those days. I was on the train from Paris to Versailles, sitting opposite a very fit, athletic-looking woman of about thirty. She was reading a newspaper, I a book. Our knees touched, and suddenly I couldn't read anymore. Our eyes met. She smiled at me and I thought I would faint from happiness.

"Why were you smiling at me?" she whispered.

"Excuse me? I was smiling at you? Me?"

"Yes, you."

"No," I said, "not me," and plunged back into my book, powerless to prevent the infernal dance of the letters on the page. I felt dizzy, but at the same time I was afraid she would move her knee away. I wondered how to do what I was supposed to do, what I wanted to do. Fortunately, my neighbor was persistent. "You're in love," she asked, "is that it?"

"Yes," I said.

"Who with?"

I was about to say, "You," but instead I stupidly replied: "With God."

She must have been shocked. And exactly what I had feared happened. I no longer felt her warmth, the pressure of her knee was gone. Distraught, I ventured a timid initiative. "Stop," she said in a hiss of pique. "I'm not God." I had tried and failed.

Back at Our Place I tried and failed with Arlette and Rachel, Élisabeth and Rita, Denise and Fanny, though of course they didn't know it. When one of them looked at me, I would avert my eyes. Hanna, however, may have been aware of it. Was that why she was always so completely disagreeable, why she detested me so openly? Proud and cowardly, I refused to ask her, telling myself that if she hated me, it was her problem, not mine. But I lost sleep over her. I worried about my newly recovered religious fervor. It was an agonizing contradiction. I lived in two worlds, continuing to say my prayers, eat kosher, and study with Shushani, but in my dreams I beckoned to a finally consenting Hanna.

Nevertheless, sometimes we worked well together in choir. I suffered in secret but was too proud to say anything to anyone, and certainly not to her.

Flash-forward to 1954. One spring day I ran into Hanna in downtown Paris. I decided to take advantage of the chance encounter. We shook hands, exchanged customary pleasantries. It was six years since I had left Our Place. The "children" were scattered throughout the city and the world, flown off like birds or adolescent dreams. The choir had been dissolved. Having become a journalist, I traveled a lot, and had lost contact with the OSE people. But Hanna had kept in touch, probably through her parents. She knew everything. Remember Régine, the girl who was in love with Kalman? Well, she's married. No, silly, not to Kalman. Kalman left for America. Binem? He's in Israel. Rita? Australia. Suzanne got her medical degree. Nicolas was still living in his dreams. And how was she? Very well, thank you. What was she doing? Studying physical therapy. We talked amicably as we walked toward the Place de la République, the neighborhood I lived in. I was so surprised by her lack of hostility that I invited her for coffee. She agreed. I was in seventh heaven and ready to ascend to the eighth.

All at once I forgot her notorious nastiness, forgot all the women I had vainly tried to attract. I fell in love with her again, with her alone. Careful not to show it, I played the great reporter, slightly jaded, a tad cynical, a man surprised and moved by nothing. Striking a falsely humble tone, I told her about my work, my scoops — ah yes, it was important for her to know about them. No self-respecting journalist can refrain from a bit of boasting on that score. I had rarely been so loquacious. Hanna listened, or pretended to, for which I was grateful. I asked her what she was doing that evening, and she answered, "Frankly, nothing." She had always been frank. "Would you like to go to a concert?" She hesitated for an instant, then said yes. Had I heard right? Hanna, the haughty girl who had used all the weapons of femininity to reject me, suddenly friendly? We agreed to meet at the Salle Pleyel at eight-thirty that evening. She was on time, and so was I. She was soberly dressed in a dark gray skirt and white blouse, her hair twisted into a bun held in place by a simple pin. I found it hard to conceal my excitement; she maintained her serene composure.

I used my press card to get two choice seats, gratis. Hanna made gentle fun of me. "So, you're a VIP now." I protested with the requisite false humility. Hanna, unimpressed, changed the subject. We talked about Beethoven and Schubert, symphonic and choral works. I liked the program but found it hard to concentrate. Hanna listened attentively. I felt like taking her hand, but stopped myself for fear of looking ridiculous. During the intermission I tried to charm her with some unoriginal commentary on the various pieces we had just heard. She agreed with this, disagreed with that. We had a friendly discussion. The atmosphere was relaxed, almost warm. I took her arm as we went back to our seats, and she did not pull away. God in heaven, what was going on? Were miracles actually possible? The sounds of the second half of the concert washed over me, dissolving in the air. The hell with Beethoven! I would apologize to him tomorrow. For the moment I heard only the silence of the enchanting young girl seated on my right. Our shoulders touched, and at times her hair tickled my face. Hanna and me, at last. With me at last, all mine. Thank you, Beethoven, for having brought us together. Thank heaven for orchestrating chance encounters. Thank you, Paris in the spring, for inspiring so many lovers.

The concert ended, and the audience applauded. We joined them. Hanna clapped for the conductor, I for destiny. She seemed happy — my onetime nasty beloved seemed happy. I was delighted. I offered the standard — "Fantastic, huh?" — and for once she agreed. I don't know why, but the enthusiasm of the audience seemed to draw us together. Slowly the crowd dispersed, and we went out. I asked if she was tired. No, not at all. In fact, she was rather excited. Once again I suggested coffee. I didn't want the night to end; I wanted it to go on forever. Somehow I sensed that if we separated now, she would be forever lost to me. If I let this God-given opportunity slip away, I would regret it for the rest of my life. I pressed, carefully maintaining a detached tone. "So, do you feel like coffee?" She hesitated, then declined. "Sorry, not tonight. I have to be up early." Her voice was so sweet and beautiful I forgot to be disappointed. "Should we take the métro?" She preferred to walk. "Where do you live?" Montmartre, near Sacré-Cœur. It was a long way, but never mind. I would have happily walked as far as Saint-Cloud, Versailles, or the end of the world.

So we walked. The night sky blinked with bright stars. Passersby smiled at us, beggars thanked me for my generosity, however modest. At last, near the Lapin Agile, Hanna stopped in front of an immense, darkened gate (which I disliked instantly) and held out her hand. I took it and held it for a long moment. And then, idiot that I was, I managed to ruin everything. Striking a dramatic air and affecting a tone of pathos, I looked into her eyes and asked, "Why is it you used to hate me so? Why couldn't you have been like you were tonight, so sweet and nice, so feminine? Really, I wish you could explain it to me."

She suddenly pulled her hand away, her body stiffened, and her face turned blank. "What an idiot you are," she hissed, "an intolerable idiot." She tried to open the gate, but I stopped her. Since she had become an enemy again, I decided to meet her on the battlefield. "Listen, Hanna," I said angrily, "I never understood why you hated me, why you made me suffer the way you did in Versailles. Tonight, for a few hours, I thought that was over. I thought you'd changed. But I guess I was wrong. You still have that chip on your shoulder, still treat me with contempt. If that's the way you want it, fine. As far as I'm concerned, that's it. I've had it. I won't try to understand you anymore. I give up. I hope we never see each other again. Good night."

And I walked away. End of story. Forever.

I was serious, and angry, determined not to look back. Anyway, it didn't really matter. In three days I was due to leave to cover a story in Brazil, and with a little luck I would fall in love on the boat. People fall in love fast on boats, me faster than anyone else. Hanna was over and done with. Good riddance.

Except that . . .

The next day the phone rang. How had she gotten my number? I pictured her, so proud and superior, forced to demean herself, to go to mutual friends with some lame excuse to justify her question. I almost felt sorry for her.

"Who is it?" I asked.

"It's me," she said.

"Me, who?"

"Hanna."

I felt like asking, Hanna who? but she beat me to it: "Versailles Hanna."

"What can I do for you?" I asked in the coldest possible tone.

"I would like to see you again."

Right. Probably to deliver more insults. Last night wasn't enough for her.

"Sorry, but I really don't have time. I'm leaving for Brazil on assignment" — that sounded good — "and I have a million things to do."

She sighed and said, "It won't take long. Give me half an hour."

The voice of the princess was subdued. I dug

in my heels. "I can't."

She insisted. "Give me half an hour."

"What for?"

"To talk to you."

"About what?"

"About . . . Not on the phone."

When I said nothing, she went on, "All right, since you insist. I want to ask you a question."

"A question you can't ask on the phone?"

No, she couldn't. And it couldn't wait. I finally conceded: "At twelve-thirty tonight in the café near the Radio France office. Okay?" I chose that café because I dropped in at Radio France every night to send my cable to Tel Aviv.

"I'll be there," she said, and hung up.

All of a sudden I didn't feel like working. The wire services could supply more information than I could about the siege of Dien Bien Phu and the predictable reactions in France. Hanna's behavior was far less predictable. What could she possibly want to ask me? To pass the time I drafted a cable, tore it up, redrafted it, and tore it up again. My heart wasn't in it. I didn't care about the news that night. It was all the same to me if the planet was in good shape or bad, if politicians howled or fell silent. Hanna's question was the only thing on my mind, but I couldn't very well send Tel Aviv a cable about that, and in the end my professional conscience kicked in. I managed to piece together an article no worse than usual. I looked at my watch. It was time. When I got to the café, I found Hanna sitting in the back. She was the only customer, apart from one man who seemed half asleep. A cup of coffee was cooling on the table in front of her. I ordered one too, and then attacked.

"So what's your question? Do you have it in writing?"

She shook her head. "No need for that. I know it by heart."

"So what is it?" I was still trying to hurt her and succeeding so well it shamed me.

"Well," she said, looking deep into my eyes, "it's this: Will you marry me?"

I would have been less surprised had the ceiling collapsed, had I been named commander in chief of the Red Army, or had I won the Prix Goncourt for a book I hadn't yet dreamed of writing.

The best I could come up with was, "But, but, you don't love me. . . . In fact, you despise me. You've hated me since the day we met."

She smiled sadly. "That's what you thought?"

"Of course that's what I thought. The whole choir thought so."

A flash of tenderness brightened her face. "I can't believe how stupid you can be," she said.

The conversation went on for more than two hours. We left only when the waiter politely showed us the door. "Taxi?" Hanna preferred to walk. I walked her home, and . . .

But no. Let's leave the rest for later.

Back at Our Place life went on: Shabbat meals
and chance meetings, departures and arrivals,
hellos and goodbyes. As in Écouis and Ambloy,
we talked about everything except the past. But
it was the future that dominated our endless
conversations: Learn a trade or go to school?
Stay or go? The director did his best to help.
His wise and silent wife did what she could,
but we saw her only on Shabbat. Nicolas was
studying for his *baccalauréat*. A great future in
literature was predicted for him. Shimon they
said had a great future too, but in science. Méno
was interested in agronomy, Félix in biology.
Israel Adler was already fascinated by Johann
Sebastian Bach but not yet by Salomone Rossi.
I was still undecided. Should I try to enroll in
the Conservatory or the Liberal Arts college?
I heard the call of the Holy Land, but felt I
wasn't ready yet. I was eighteen and living from
day to day, unsure of what to do with my life
and where to live it. I worked with François
and with Shushani and read everything I could
get my hands on. It's funny, but before discovering Malraux, Camus, and Mauriac, I read
The Critique of Pure Reason — don't laugh! —
in Yiddish. I read *Das Kapital* too, and Hegel
and Spinoza. Philosophy monopolized me, devoured me. I irritated all my friends with my
"serious" discussions. I was considered bizarre,
not to mention boring. If I managed to work
up the courage to talk to a girl in the garden

or on the train, I would ask her about the meaning of life and the purpose of Creation. Did infinity exist? And nothingness? Is the soul immortal? What about God? I knew I was tiresome, that everyone laughed at me behind my back, that my interlocutors found me psychologically immature and socially maladjusted. They were right. "Look," a beautiful member of the choir once said to me, "maybe absolute evil exists, but not absolute good or absolute truth. What am I supposed to do about it?" I felt increasingly ill at ease. My body yearned for love, and I retaliated by punishing it. I became even stricter with my choir. I knew I was unbearable. Fortunately, I had my sisters. With them I had no need to play the fool.

My sister Bea was in a displaced persons camp near Kassel in the American zone of occupied Germany. I visited her two or three times, and each trip was a bureaucratic hassle. As a stateless person, I had to fill out a stack of questionnaires, submit several photos, and somehow acquire a travel permit, an exit visa, a reentry visa, authorization from the American army of occupation, and enough money for a train ticket — none of which was easy. In Europe all bureaucrats look alike, but the French are the worst. They detest foreigners if they are refugees, stateless, or without resources, and since I fell into all three categories, I was a source of boundless irritation to them. They would stare at me with hostility, treat me as an intruder. I spent countless hours queuing up at nameless windows in police stations, answering question after question. What was I living on (why was I living?), what did I intend to do, why was I so eager to return to France? After many anxious days I finally had accumulated all the necessary documents, duly signed, sealed, and stamped.

I rode through a vanquished, ruined Germany. The trains were packed. Germans were not allowed to sit in the comfortable compartments, and white-helmeted giants from the Military Police kept a very close watch. I felt satisfaction at seeing the conquerors conquered and the torturers terrified, yesterday's victors on their knees before those they had condemned to death just a few years ago, begging for a cigarette, a chocolate bar, or even just a friendly smile.

Today, as I write this, I think of all those who chided us for our passivity, our resignation, during the war: "Why didn't you resist?" What about the Germans? What accounts for their obsequious cowardice before foreigners after their defeat? There were endless rumors about parents who sold their wives and daughters to the first American soldier for a pair of nylons, former high-ranking Wehrmacht officers who would shine shoes for any corporal, bankrupt merchants who fought over cigarette butts flicked into the mud by drunken soldiers. Their strength was gone, their power dissipated, their arrogance a memory. Yesterday's supermen had become subhuman. But no, I don't like either of those terms, superman or subhuman; both victors and vanquished are no more, no less, than human beings.

A friend of Bea's was waiting for me at the Frankfurt station. Since I had missed the connection to Kassel, he took me to the home of a German family where I was to spend the night. An indigent old couple lived there with their daughter, a woman in her thirties, probably a war widow. She had a big chest, tousled blond hair, and an angular face with chiseled features and sensual lips: in short, she was an adolescent's dream. She glanced at me curiously as she made up my bed. She left and then came back a few minutes later, asking me in German whether I needed anything. I told her, "No, thank you," in Yiddish.

I lay down on the bed, fully dressed, and tried to read, but it was impossible. Too many things were whirling in my head. Back in Auschwitz, if anyone had told me I would one day be treated with so much respect, as a victor, by Germans in Germany, I would have replied that the Messiah must have come in the meantime. I certainly didn't feel like a victor. But in the eyes of the vanquished, we were victors. The widow suddenly reappeared with a glass of wine. "It'll help you sleep," she said. I thanked her but told her I wasn't thirsty, figuring there was no point in trying to explain, in Yiddish, that wine, too, could be ritually impure. At midnight she knocked again. She asked to come in and sit down, and I nodded. When she sat on the bed instead of on the chair near the table, I suddenly felt a knot in my stomach. I was still too religious. Instinctively I drew back, in vain. She reached out and took my hand to caress it. I pulled it away. "We mustn't," I said. "Why not?" she asked. "But . . . your parents are right outside!" That was the best argument I could come up with, and it didn't seem to carry much weight. "Don't worry," she said. "They're used to it."

It would be a lie to say my body did not desire hers. I was young, and had never made love. Why not seize the opportunity? But some obscure force held me back. Should the first woman in my life be a German, perhaps the wife of an SS officer or a camp guard? I would never be able to forgive myself. "For ten cigarettes or two Hershey bars I'll stay all night," the woman said. I leaped out of bed, opened my suitcase, and took out a pack of cigarettes. "Here," I said. "Take them." I had trouble speaking because she had begun to take off her blouse. "No," I said, "don't do that." She didn't understand. "As you like," she said with a shrug. "Let me know if you change your mind. My door is the one near the staircase." She left and I lay back on the bed. My body was angry at me, and I tried hard to think about something else — my presence on German soil, the Jews who once lived in this city, Rabbi Shmelke's brother, the great Rebbe Pinhas, Meyer Anshel Rothschild, Rabbi Samson Raphael Hirsch. I dared to hope I had not shamed them.

The next day I felt uneasy as I put on my tefillin and said my prayers. The door opened and the woman came in with my breakfast. She stared at me, obviously stunned. Surely she had never seen a practicing Jew say his prayers. I wondered whether she had ever seen a Jew at all, other than in anti-Semitic films. She put the tray on the table and left. An hour later she was back. "Can I ask you a question?" Yes, she could. "Is the reason you didn't want me because I'm German?" "Because I'm Jewish," I told her. "You hate us, is that it? You want to hurt us, humiliate us, get revenge?" "It's more complicated than that," I said, still in Yiddish. I saw fear in her eyes. Was I really so terrifying to her? Suddenly I understood. She had offered herself to me not only for cigarettes but also to appease me. The Germans were afraid of us. The mere sight of a free Jew must have filled them with terror. They must have been afraid that camp survivors and underground partisans would return as avengers and make them pay for the torments they had inflicted. That was why these old people bowed before me, and that was why this woman wanted to spend the night in my bed: if not to redeem themselves, at least to divert and perhaps even disarm my anger.

But they were wrong. Jewish avengers were

few in number, their thirst for vengeance brief. I thought about the liberation of Buchenwald. Jewish survivors had every reason in the world to seize weapons and go from city to city, village to village, punishing the guilty and terrorizing their accomplices. The world would have said nothing, everyone would have understood. But with the exception of a few units of the Palestinian Jewish Brigade who swept through Germany tracking down and punishing the murderers of our people, the Jews, for metaphysical and ethical reasons rooted in their history, chose another path. Later, this absence of violence among the survivors, this absence of vengefulness on the part of the victims toward their former hangmen and torturers was widely discussed. Of course, the setting was a Germany barely able to breathe under the weight of its ashes, a nation humiliated as few have ever been.

There were no bloody reprisals, few summary executions, no public beatings. There was no collective vengeance, except for the Nuremberg trials and a few other prosecutions (of criminal doctors and the Einsatzkommandos). De-Nazification wasn't really serious. The German judicial system was scarcely affected by it. Nazi judges sat in judgment of Nazi defendants, and no one seemed to care, not even in the international Jewish community, which seems incomprehensible. In 1492, when they were forced to leave Spain, the Jews were quick to excommunicate the country that had expelled them,

251

a ban the entire Jewish people observed for nearly five centuries. There is one very pragmatic explanation for why we didn't act with equal rigor against Germany, whose crimes were far more monstrous. After the exodus from Spain, the Marranos were the only "Jews" who remained, whereas tens of thousands of survivors were unable to leave Germany in 1945, for they had nowhere else to go. All doors were closed to them. Lodged in camps for refugees and displaced persons, often in the very places they had been held by the SS, they waited for travel permits to Palestine or visas to America. It was a painful ordeal that lasted for some until 1950. It was therefore impossible to impose a public ban on a land where Jews were forced to go on living, even if in a state of misery and humiliation.

Yes, the fate of the "displaced persons" was shameful indeed, as was established in an official American report ordered by Harry Truman and drafted by Earl Harrison, former dean of the University of Pennsylvania Law School and American representative to the Inter-governmental Committee on Refugees. The September 30, 1945, issue of *The New York Times* devoted a long and devastating article to this report. Some excerpts:

President Truman has directed General Eisenhower to clean up alleged shocking conditions in the treatment of displaced

Jews in Germany outside the Russian zone and in Austria. . . .

The report declared that displaced Jews were held behind barbed wire in camps guarded by our men, camps in which frequently conditions were unsanitary and the food poor and insufficient, with our military more concerned with other matters.

Some of the displaced Jews were sick and without adequate medicine, the report stated, and many had to wear prison garb or, to their chagrin, German SS uniforms. All were wondering, it was added, if they had been liberated after all and were despairing of help while worrying about the fate of relatives.

They were in many cases, [Mr. Harrison] said, behind barbed wire in camps formerly used by the Germans for their prisoners, including the notorious Bergen-Belsen camp. Nearly all had lost hope, he stated. . . .

The Germans in rural areas, whom the Jews look out upon from the camps, were better fed, better clothed and better housed than the "liberated" Jews, the report declared.

It also noted:

As matters now stand, we appear to be treating the Jews as the Nazis treated them except that we do not exterminate them. They are in concentration camps in large numbers under our own military guard instead of SS troops. One is led to wonder whether the German people, seeing this, are not supposing that we are following or at least condoning the Nazi policy.

As I read and reread this article, feelings of shame, frustration, and sorrow sweep over me. American Jewish leaders, intellectuals, and humanists must have read this report. They knew — they must have known — that their brothers and sisters were suffering in Germany, yet they did little to relieve their plight. I don't like to criticize fellow Jews, but their passivity seems incomprehensible.

And what about the Allied governments? In Henri Amouroux's book *La Page n'est pas encore tournée* (The Page Has Not Yet Been Turned), he recounts with indignation the outrageous conditions as French inmates left Bergen-Belsen, with the bitter memory of having been treated scarcely better by the British than by the Germans. The same for Flossenburg, Dachau, and Buchenwald. For too many deportees, liberation meant no more than the possibility of dying free.

But let us leave all that aside for now, and return to Frankfurt, and to Kassel.

When I visited the camp in which Bea worked in the office of UNRWA (the United Nations agency created to take care of refugees) while waiting for her visa for Canada, I felt a growing anger not only toward the Germans but also toward the "friendly" countries. They were treating the "displaced persons" like lepers or criminals. The situation had improved somewhat since Truman's letter to Eisenhower, but the sensation of oppression persisted. Every prospective emigrant was subjected to endless requirements and interrogations before being granted a visa. They had to prove that they were in good health both physically and mentally, that they were able to take their places in a "normal" society, that they would not go on public assistance, that friends or relatives could guarantee them jobs in their adopted countries. So much for our dream, in our rare moments of optimistic delirium, that if we survived we would be treated as long-lost brothers, carried in triumph to show how deeply humanity regretted what had been done to us.

This truth must be stated and restated: The suffering of the survivors did not end with the war; society wanted no part of them, either during or after. During the war all doors were closed to them, and afterward they remained shut. The evidence is irrefutable. They were kept in the places where they had suffered. Granted, after some delay they were housed (in barracks), fed (badly), and clothed (pitifully), but they were made to feel that they were beggars and poor relations, extra mouths to feed. Time does not heal all wounds. Some remain open and raw.

Those who were stupid or naïve enough to return to their countries of origin sometimes faced outright hostility from their former neighbors and countrymen. Instead of greeting them with flowers (as was done in Denmark), instead of hailing their survival, begging forgiveness for their indifference or worse, their compatriots regarded them with suspicion and rancor. "What, you're back? Auschwitz must not have been so terrible after all." In many places, they were denied compensation for their homes and property. When Bea went back to Sighet, she found strangers living in our house and had to stay with friends. A sociologist has argued that in Hungary the predominant motive for postwar anti-Semitism was that the populace feared the return of deportees whose apartments and factories they had confiscated. Kielce, in Poland, was the site of a genuine pogrom: more than fifty Jewish survivors were massacred in broad daylight. Elsewhere the number of victims was lower, apparently too low for the press to take notice. But everyone knew the Jews were being subjected yet again to hatred and terror. No, the tragedy of the survivors did not end with the liberation of the camps.

The ordeals Bea endured in the camps left her with damaged lungs, and the United States consequently denied her a visa. Like thousands of other survivors, she was considered "undesirable." Canada, where there was a labor shortage, was less recalcitrant, its immigration laws more flexible. Bea therefore applied for a visa at the Canadian consulate. Here, too, no one was eager to be burdened by her lungs, but in the end she got a visa to work as a housekeeper for a Jewish family in Montreal.

As I wandered through the camp and chatted with refugees, I told myself that the citizens of the free world might someday be forgiven for having done so little to save the Jews of Europe. After all, perhaps they didn't know, and if they knew, they didn't believe it, and if they believed it, they didn't understand it, and if they understood it, they were powerless to change anything. Besides which, there was a war on. The Hitler regime had to be destroyed. So perhaps there were extenuating circumstances. But they will never be forgiven for their treatment of the victims after the German defeat. After the war they knew everything, could no longer lie to themselves or to others. All you had to do was open a newspaper or a magazine, or watch a newsreel at a movie theater, or listen to the radio, and you would know of the tens of thousands of men and women eking out an existence in the same camps, in a German environment, under German eyes, because America and Canada, France and Britain, were unwilling to help them rebuild homes and futures.

But despite all this — astonishingly — I encountered neither anger nor spite in the camp itself. There was no trace of bitterness. On the contrary, the community showed a boundless spirit, and an unparalleled joie de vivre.

In several barracks young people were organizing to combat the British occupation of Palestine. Elsewhere in the camp plays by Sholem Aleichem or Peretz Hirshbein were staged. Humor and satire were dominant. There were cultural conferences, political meetings, evening concerts. The camp was a whirlwind of ideas and calls to action. An atheist intellectual introduced me to the works of Hugo Bettauer, another had me read Karl Kraus and Otto Weininger. I attended morning and evening services at the synagogue, where they studied the Mishna and pored over the Hasidic tales of the Besht. It was the same in other D.P. camps. People were getting engaged and married, schools and nurseries were opened, newspapers published. Yossel Rosensaft — about whom I will have more to say later — talked to me at length about the "Jewish kingdom" of Belsen. The Jewish poet H. Leivik described "The Marriage of Föhrenwald." If some traded on the black market, what of it? What other kind of market was there in occupied Germany? If some merchants got rich, more power to them. I confess there was a time when I resented those survivors who dreamed of personal fortune instead of working for the honor and memory of our people. But later I changed my mind. Who was I to judge them? If they sought wealth while a few friends and I devoted ourselves to study, that was their right. They had lost enough, suffered enough. Let them seek their happiness however they saw fit. Indeed, I am proud of their defiance and success. Instead of nihilism, they chose society. But where did they find their confidence in the future? How could those who had seen so many families annihilated now rebuild homes? How could they hope to integrate their children into a society whose murderous and dehumanizing end they had every reason to fear? I cannot account for their faith in man or in themselves, but I am eager to state how proud I am to be one of them.

I knew that someday it would be my duty to testify. And that the fate of those in the D.P. camps would be part of my testimony.

Bea was much appreciated by her superiors in UNRWA. Serving as executive secretary and personal assistant, she had many languages and was a jack-of-all-trades, drafting requests and documents, answering mail, serving as liaison between various agencies. She was like our father in that she liked everyone and everyone liked her. She was always ready to do a favor. I was moved by her popularity. She was known in all the barracks, in all milieus. Religious Jews, Zionists, intellectuals — everyone spoke of her with warmth and gratitude. She gave them all advice, information, and assistance. In the office she dealt with ten visitors at a time, giving each of them the impression that she was concerned only with him or her.

Her quarters, which she shared with several friends from Sighet, were so crowded late into the night that it was hard for us to find time to see each other alone. When we did, we held hands in silence.

The day of my departure came too soon. The night before I left we spent a moment alone, and I was finally able to ask some questions. I wanted to know about Sighet. Who had survived? What had she found in the house? She told me that very few Jews had come back, about a hundred at most — disoriented, lost, seeking a father, a mother, a husband. Who in our family had survived? She said there were only a few cousins, some distant relatives. What about those Nyilas bastards, those hate-filled anti-Semites? Only a few had been arrested, tried, and imprisoned. What else could we expect? The Red Army had given control of the police to some young Jewish Communists returning from Bucharest, the labor battalions, and the camps. Whom else could they have any confidence in? (One of them, Aczi Mendelowics, later became Amos Manor, chief of the formidable Shin Beth security service in Israel.) As a result, there was some settling of scores with the fascists. That's all? No public executions? No hangings? Not that she knew of. Acts of vengeance? None. And the house? The less said about that the better. The jewels? Gone. Other objects of value? Stolen. Everything was stolen. After we left, our good neighbors had swarmed over the vacated Jewish homes, looting them all. She stayed with the Davidowics family, distant cousins. In any case, survivors tried to stay together. Out of fear of ghosts? Out of fear, period. Drunken Russian soldiers sowed terror. A friend of my father's, a clockmaker by trade, had his throat cut by a Russian soldier who fancied his watch. His daughter, who had arrived from Germany a few days earlier, found his decapitated body in the street. Surely we could not go "home." What would become of the two of us? How long would Bea have to stay in this camp? How long could I stay in France? The future seemed far from promising.

Last night — July 10, 1991 — I saw my mother in a dream again. She seemed upset, and I realized that something serious had happened. She motioned me to follow her. Then suddenly I saw my father. He was wearing my gray suit. It looked good on him. We were all there, everyone from before and from now, standing at a river that all at once began to swell, its level rising from moment to moment. "It's the flood," someone said, quite calmly. It's the flood, but I'm not afraid. So, I said to myself, it's possible to watch the rising tide and not feel fear. Just then my father waded into the murky, blood-colored water, and I said to myself, So rivers of blood exist after all. I waited for my father to come back so I could point this out to him, but he stayed beneath the water. I began to shout for help, but everyone was suddenly gone. I don't know how to swim, so I panicked, screaming louder and louder. But I was all alone. I began to search for my father in the waters that now reached my shoulders, and I found him. I don't know what power aided me. All I know is that I managed to save him all by myself. I helped him stretch out on the grass, listened to his breathing. In my dream he was alive. My mother too. She was alive in my dream.

Back in Versailles I found that my friend Kalman and two or three other "children" were about to set out for Palestine illegally aboard the *Exodus*. It meant I would be separated from my inseparable friend. "Why now, Kalman?" I asked. He shrugged. "I don't see any point in staying here. I don't like this transient life, so I might as well go. Do something useful, something true. As soon as possible." Though mischievous by nature, he had become serious and romantic. I went with him to the station, and we talked while waiting for the train, though in muted voices so as not to be overheard by any British spies who might be roaming the platforms. I understood him, but I didn't understand myself. I tried to. Why this desire to stay behind? I, too, loved the land of our ancestors, loved it passionately. Jerusalem had always figured in my most ardent and luminous dreams — Jerusalem my lullaby, my prayer. The mere evocation of its song made me feel elevated, transformed. What held me back? Hilda? Bea? François? Shushani? The latter answered my discreet request for advice with this comment: "If you're going so as to know yourself better, fine. If it's to learn, you'd do better to stay here with me." "But if Eretz Israel needs me," I replied, "what right have I not to heed its call?" He shrugged. "The people of Israel need intelligent, erudite Jews capable of learning and teaching. What would you take with you to Palestine? Your ignorance? Your spiritual poverty? Your doubts and neuroses?"

I asked to see Bo Cohen, who, after all, was the educational director of the OSE. It was his duty to guide us. A timid yet demanding man, he was our older friend. He and his young wife, Margot, attended to us with a devotion bordering on sacrifice. They were always ready to listen to us and support us. Bo's view was that we should complete our studies first. A diploma was always useful, one way or another. Kalman did not agree. He ached to leave.

I also confided in Israel Adler, who was not only from Jerusalem but also a *shalia'h*, or emissary, of the Jewish Agency. His response was unequivocal: "When the time comes we will 'ascend' together." For the moment he helped me with the choir. Our most beautiful songs were for Jerusalem.

I continued my studies. Shushani led me surreptitiously toward a subject that had always fascinated me: asceticism, the lure of and quest for suffering, the will to suffer so as to infuse one's own suffering and that of others with meaning. We talked of the ascetic and his self, enriched or mutilated by suffering, the relation between suffering and truth, suffering and redemption, suffering and spiritual purity, suffering as a gateway to the sacred; the prophetic, rabbinical, mystical point of view. Was it necessary, even indispensable, to punish the body so as to allow the soul to soar to new heights? Why was the *nazir* (ascetic) considered a sinner in Scripture? Why was he compelled to bring a sacrifice to the Temple? How to understand the variety of ascetics? Even Samson, the greatest womanizer of his generation, was a born ascetic. It took me a long time to understand: Asceticism warns us that language is sacred, that words must never be uttered lightly. I took copious notes and then began to write, pages and pages. Maybe someday it would make a book. Why not? I had wanted to write ever since childhood. In Sighet I often went to the offices of the Jewish community to write a page of Bible commentary on the only available Hebrew typewriter.

Of course, I could write my memories of the camp, which I bore within me like poison. Though I never spoke to anyone about this, it weighed upon me. I thought about it with apprehension day and night: the duty to testify, to offer depositions for history, to serve memory. What would man be without his capacity to remember? Memory is a passion no less powerful or pervasive than love. What does it mean to remember? It is to live in more than one world, to prevent the past from fading and to call upon the future to illuminate it. It is to revive fragments of existence, to rescue lost beings, to cast harsh light on faces and events, to drive back the sands that cover the surface of things, to combat oblivion and to reject death. All this I knew. And because I knew it, I told myself I should write. But I had to be patient. Someday, in years to come, I would celebrate memory, but not yet. Even then I was aware of the deficiencies and inadequacies of language. Words frightened me. What exactly did it mean to speak? Was it a divine or diabolical act? The spoken word and the written word do not reflect the same experience. The mysticism with which my adolescence was imbued made me suspicious of writing. Rabbi Itzhak Lurie set nothing down on paper. His disciple Rabbi Hayyim Vital did it for him, perhaps without his approval. Rabbi Nahman ordered that his writings be burned. The Zohar speaks of *galut hadibur*, the exile of the word, for words, too, are exiled. A chasm opens between them and their content; they no longer contain the meanings they once harbored. Having become obstacles more than points of reference, words broke my spirit. I had no confidence in them, for I sensed what I would later come to feel with greater certainty: Human words are too impoverished, too transparent to express the Event. The problem was clear: how to surmount the dilemma that either the teller lies or the words do. Why proliferate lies? The Hebrew poet Bialik was right: "Words are whores. Decked out in their finery, they offer themselves to the first passerby." I decided to wait, to make a kind of vow: Ten years would pass before I would speak, before I would come forward with my deposition. If I enjoyed writing, then thank God there were countless other subjects awaiting redemption — love, for instance, by which I mean love of the people of Israel and of its hope and suffering, or, better, love of Israel's hope and suffering. Anyway, you get the idea.

One of the OSE volunteers — Joseph Milner, from the famous village of Chelm (all of whose inhabitants, legend has it, were innocents), a physician and a Yiddish writer in his free time — became interested in my writing. He gave me a letter of recommendation to the editor in chief of a Yiddish daily. Armed with that letter, I visited their headquarters and was shown into an office in which disorder was not king but emperor. Someone was hard at work behind a mountain of files, newspapers, and books. Only his head was visible. When I said hello, he didn't answer. I cleared my throat, but he didn't look up. It was as if I weren't there, as if he himself weren't there. Was this his way of initiating a beginner into the delicate craft of journalism? I coughed loudly, simply to see if he was alive. After one last attempt to attract his attention — a loud and clear *"Bonjour, monsieur"* — I tiptoed out, unaware of how lucky I had been. The newspaper in question, *Neie Presse,* was the organ of the French Jewish Communists. We were hardly made for each other. I would not be a Communist journalist.

That year the OSE organized a summer camp in Montintin, in the Limousin region. Bo Cohen suggested I go along as a counselor, a proposal Israel Adler urged me to accept. For one thing, I could use the money; for another, it would be a valuable experience. Adler planned on going too, for the same reasons. Ted Comet, the young volunteer from New York, would be part of the leadership team. At first I couldn't make up my mind. I waited for a sign, and finally it came: Hanna was going too. Was that why I said yes? Anyway, I never regretted it. Early every morning I worked (in Hebrew) on "my book" on asceticism, and after breakfast I gave Bible and Midrash classes. I organized discussions on the situation in Palestine. I liked to listen as much as to speak. At night I was the last to leave the campfire site. Life seemed fruitful and promising. I discovered the true joy of teaching, that of confidence and sharing.

Hanna, of course, remained true to her nature, treating me with special unpleasantness. I did my best to avoid her. Fortunately, the other girls were not without charm. I indulged in some serious flirting, by which I mean that I talked to them of things too serious to achieve the desired result.

When summer ended, Bo advised me to leave the comfort of Versailles. Except for Shabbat, which I would regularly celebrate at Our Place, I would now live in a small room near his home at the Porte de Saint-Cloud. Nicolas, Shimon, and Félix were given the same advice and identical rooms in the same building. Bo was right. I was nineteen years old. It was time to strike out on my own. But to do what? I forget whose brilliant idea it was to urge me to go into science. It was hard to see how someone incapable of solving a simple algebra problem could become an engineer. I refused. There was a future in engineering, but not for me. Then someone got me to sign up for a course in chemistry, and one fine morning I found myself in a laboratory surrounded by colored test tubes. An anarchist would have felt as much at home among dervishes or Trappist monks. I loved my white smock, but that was about all. I dropped out two weeks later, embarrassed but relieved.

I continued my courses with Shushani and François. My room was a gloomy little box without running water. Visitors had to sit on the bed. Fortunately, there were Shabbat, Versailles, and the choir. The choir and Hanna, so cold and beautiful.

Naturally, I followed Jewish current events closely, participating in various Zionist meetings and demonstrations at the Salle Pleyel and other, less distinguished places. Elated, I read reports and articles in *Franc-Tireur* on the heroic odyssey of the *Exodus* and Britain's outrageous exclusionary policy. I cursed British foreign secretary Ernest Bevin. How dare he send survivors of Bergen-Belsen back to Germany?

Kalman reappeared in Versailles. He had fallen ill and disembarked in Port-de-Bouc. His exuberance was gone. He seemed sad and discouraged. He gave me a firsthand account of the voyage of the *Exodus*, of the courage of the clandestine passengers, the complicity of the French authorities, and the duplicity of the British. For a brief moment the world's heart beat to the rhythm of that ship, which has become part of Israel's legend.

With hindsight we have a better sense of the historic dimensions of that epic journey. More than the debates in the United Nations and as much as the battles waged by the Jewish resistance groups in Palestine, the saga of the *Exodus* fascinated and swayed public opinion on several continents. There was much admiration for these men and women without weapons or resources who had chosen to tear themselves from the graveyard that was Europe and to reclaim the land of their ancestors.

Sometimes I stare at photographs taken at that time, looking for familiar faces, and I still wonder: How was it that these refugees from so many lands, survivors of so much persecution, of so many massacres and so much hatred, found the courage to confront the perils of that crossing, not to mention His Britannic Majesty's invincible navy? They were survivors of death camps, women with veiled eyes, stooped old men and eager adolescents, students drawn by the Torah or inspired by patriotic faith. How did they manage to transform themselves into heroes? Kalman's only answer was a shrug. "That's how it was."

Of course, they were inspired by a common ideal: to break with the vicissitudes and temptations of exile, to build their homes in joy rather than in fear, to render unto Jewish destiny and Jewish history their due. They could not know, they could not have guessed, that their dream, once realized, would entail new challenges and fresh perils.

I study their faces in candid photos, taken later on Israel's liberated soil. Sober, melancholy, do they regret that true redemption, ultimate messianic deliverance, has yet to come? No, they are used to waiting. They have been waiting for centuries. Some demand peace, all dream of it. "We have done our duty," they might easily say. "Leave us alone." But they don't. Peace — peace with the Arabs, with the Palestinians — is now their goal, for they have children and grandchildren who also must live, just as the other children, on the other side, must also live. There is enough sun to warm all hearts, enough dew to freshen all flowers. How to explain the generosity of the people of the *Exodus*? It was thanks to them, and people like them, that the Jewish state was born.

Israel: nearly fifty years of social turmoil, of wars, victories, and burials, and now, as the century draws to a close, its anguish grows ever more violent. What can be done, what must be done? How I would love to be able to discuss that with my friend Kalman.

He emigrated to the United States, where he became an authority on radar. I saw him in Brooklyn during my first visit to the United States. "How's your work on asceticism going?" he asked. Much later we met again at Hunter College, where he was teaching and I had come to make a speech. He hadn't changed; he was as reserved and delicate as ever, and as frail. Some years later I got a call from Harav Menashe Klein, our old friend from Ambloy. "Call Kalman immediately," he said. "He's not well." It was cancer. "Do you know Professor Steven Rosenberg?" my childhood friend asked in a whisper. "He's the man who operated on President Reagan. He alone can help me live. Without him I'll die." My heart breaking, I did all I could to make contact with the famous oncologist. Kalman beat me to it, but in vain. He died soon afterward, and once again I got the news from Menashe. I was out of New York, too far away to make it to the funeral the next day. We had shared so much: Écouis, Ambloy, Taverny, Versailles. His sense of humor, the rigor of his thought had sustained me so often. Kalman, my old friend, why did our paths diverge? We lived in the same city so long yet saw each other so rarely.

With François's help I enrolled in the Faculty of Letters of the Sorbonne. At last I found my vocation.

I have happy memories of my student years. There were lectures by Daniel Lagache in the Descartes or Richelieu amphitheater, and by Louis Lavelle at the Collège de France. I devoured books on philosophy and psychology, Plato's dialogues, Freud's analyses. I wandered from bookstore to bookstore, from park to park. I remember the silence of the Sainte-Geneviève Library and the chance encounters and inevitable rendezvous in the Sorbonne courtyard. François, my tutor, guide, and friend, did his best to initiate me into the life of the Latin Quarter, taking me to hear Sartre and Buber, whose lecture on religious existentialism was an event. The hall was packed, the audience enthusiastic. Buber was treated like a prophet. His listeners were elated, conquered in advance, ready to savor every word. There was just one problem. Had Buber spoken in Hebrew, Yiddish, English, or German, there would have been some people in the hall able to follow his address. But he opted for French, and his accent was so thick no one understood him. Everyone applauded just the same. No matter, they would read the text when it was published. But I was delighted to have seen the handsome face and heard the searching voice of the author of *I and Thou*, one of the great Jewish spiritual thinkers of our time.

At that moment, however, I was more concerned with material problems than with theology or existentialism, for I had nothing to live on. My sole means of support was the meager OSE subsidy: eight thousand francs a month (sixteen dollars today). "You have to learn how to get by," Bo told me. Easier said than done. I sent some "philosophical" articles to the Zionist daily of Paris, which did not bother to reply. I didn't know what else to do. I was good at nothing: I would never find a way to make a living. Success required daring, which I lacked, for I feared rejection; better to die of hunger than of shame. (I knew all about hunger. I had no wish to become acquainted with shame.)

Like everyone else, I had ration cards. When I wasn't broke, I ate corn bread and cheese. The young salesgirl at the cheese shop always gave me an extra-large slice of Brie. She was probably a romantic who liked helping starving students.

Bo got me a job tutoring a doctor's son in Hebrew and Bible studies in preparation for his bar mitzvah. I was paid just enough to feel useful, but the truth is I wasn't worth my salary, for I left my twelve-year-old pupil hopelessly confused. The problem was that I used Shushani's method, far too complicated for a boy his age. Instead of teaching him to read the sacred texts, I decided to help him discover the mystery of their genesis. "In the beginning God created the heaven and the earth," my pupil would murmur, and I would stop him. In the beginning? What does "beginning" mean? Can there be a beginning for God? Or an end? And suddenly I was talking about the Ancients and their concepts of creation, citing Nahmanides and Abrabanel. My poor pupil seemed unsure whether he should pretend to listen or run crying to his room. His father happened to sit in on one of our early lessons and politely shared his discontent with me. For the time being, he said, his son could do without my metaphysical imaginings. Perhaps I might come back when he was grown up, after his marriage, for example.

There remained the question of questions: How would I pay my rent? Food was a problem too, but I found a way around that. Sometimes Bea would send me cans of condensed milk or cookies, and I ate at Hilda's from time to time: bread and french fries. Hilda had no idea how precarious my situation was. She was preoccupied with problems of her own.

Every morning I had to decide whether to walk to the Latin Quarter and eat a snack or sandwich at the kosher restaurant on the Rue de Médicis or take the bus or métro home on an empty stomach. Wretched economist that I was, I wore out my shoes walking. Having them resoled cost more than the métro.

The end of the month was the worst time. I trembled at the idea of being unable to pay my rent and sometimes, to avoid going home, spent the night walking along the Seine. I was vaguely afraid of my landlady. I was still too pious, too imprisoned by taboos, not to be afraid of women, who, after all, had been created to seduce us and to incite us to sin. I was afraid she would take advantage of my economic and emotional situation to . . . to do what exactly? It was stupid, ridiculous, I know that now. Though I was hardly a Don Juan, I had the terrifying impression she was trying to seduce me. When she came to do the room, I would slip out like a thief, and if I accidentally brushed against her, it made me sweat and shiver. She was young and not lacking in charm. To put it more bluntly, her charm was her chest, and it was always in my way. Whether I went left or right, I could never avoid it. My fears may well have been based solely on my repressed desires, but they felt real to me — real and upsetting. Even if my landlady acted the same with all her tenants, when we were in the room together I changed to the point that I didn't like myself, disapproved of myself. I wanted to be somewhere else, to be someone else. I wished I could disappear.

There came a time when I decided to put

an end to the sterile life I was leading, laden with apprehension and remorse as it was. For the first time, the idea of suicide occurred to me. I would stare at myself in the mirror and wonder whether the moment had come to put an end to my worries and misery. If I didn't die of starvation, I could throw myself into the Seine or in front of the métro. Wherever I turned, I saw death staring back at me with its countless eyes. How could I repel it? In ancient Greece condemned prisoners had to whisper verses of Euripides in the tyrant's ear to be spared. Were there other verses that could appease the angel for whom tyrants and their subjects are equal prey?

This wretched despondency lasted several weeks, perhaps several months. I no longer recognized the man I hoped to become or already was. He eluded me, he was shrouded in fog. Contact between us was severed. My self no longer belonged to me. I doubted him and all others, doubted everything — except my memory. Though it, too, was threatened with death, it had nothing to fear, for it was protected by the dead who inhabited it. They seemed to beckon me. In fact, it was not death that lured me; it was the dead who called out to me. I saw them and questioned them ceaselessly. I sensed, was imbued with, their presence. I lived among them more than among the living. When I speak of suicide in my novels, it is this period in my life that provides the inspiration.

But there was no hurry. Death drew back, and the dead wanted no part of me, perhaps because I had as yet done nothing with my survival.

I fell ill. I ate sardines without bread, and my stomach tormented me, my intestines burned. I vomited constantly. Rarely have I suffered so much. As a child I had enjoyed being sick, but now I was terrified by it. I was so ill my landlady didn't dare come in. Then one morning, miraculously, François dropped in to see me. He may have suspected the state I was in. "Suppose we study *Le Malade imaginaire* today?" he suggested, but I lacked the strength to appreciate the joke. He went downstairs to call his mother the physician and returned with some medicine. Then he helped me claw my way out of my state day by day. I don't know what would have happened without him. The pain gradually eased, and I was able to take an interest in something other than my own body.

The newspapers, which I devoured regardless of the expense, were filled with reports of clashes and turmoil in Palestine. My sole regret was that I had not emigrated clandestinely, with or without Kalman. I wished I could have been part of the heroic, historic war waged by the Jewish people against the British in the Holy Land. Then came the dramatic event at the United Nations, the passing of the resolution granting Jews the right to a sovereign homeland, the famous partition plan of November 29, 1947. I felt I could no longer remain on the sidelines. I looked up the address of the Jewish Agency in the phone book — 183 Avenue de Wagram — and rushed over. When I rang the bell, the porter asked me whom I wanted to see. I told him I didn't know. He asked whether I had an appointment. I told him I didn't. When he asked what I wanted, I said, "To become a member of the Haganah." He hesitated briefly between laughter and indignation, then slammed the door in my face. I was angry not at him but at myself. What a fool! I should have realized that the Haganah was an underground movement, not a football club. I needed a contact, but knew no one in official Zionist circles. By chance I came across a Yiddish weekly called *Zion in Kamf*, a newspaper of the Irgun. There was no editorial address, of course, since this was the organ of a Palestinian resistance group. But French law required that the address of the printer be given. The printshop, I soon learned, was owned by one Marc Gutkin, a leading militant of the movement led by Vladimir Jabotinsky. Gutkin was a cultured, athletic man who spoke Hebrew and who loved life and its pleasures, but his true passion was the Palestinian Jewish cause. I wrote a letter in Yiddish to the paper's anonymous editor. In it I explained simply but clumsily — in a pompous, patriotic style — that my most ardent wish was to aid the Jewish resistance in Palestine. I mailed the letter to the printshop and instantly regretted it, certain it would only make me look ridiculous to some stranger. I was convinced nothing would come of it. Press barons surely had other fish to fry. Even if the letter reached the editorial office, a secretary would toss it in the trash; if it happened to get to the editor, it would wind up in *his* trash.

I was wrong. That very week I was invited to the newspaper's secret editorial headquarters, in an undistinguished building on the Rue Meslay, near the Place de la République. I arrived at the prescribed hour, and an elegant gentleman with carefully combed hair and tortoiseshell glasses, who looked like the typical Middle European intellectual, rose and warmly shook my hand. "My name is Joseph," he said. "Please have a seat. So, you're a student and you want to help us, is that right?"

And that's how I became a journalist.

Journalist

I felt like singing. I considered myself the luckiest and happiest of all my comrades and friends, of all the brothers in misfortune I had met since the torment. I speak of happiness quite consciously, as if issuing a challenge to myself. I who detested drink felt like laughing and drinking, telling the world the good news, as if the world would care. I wanted to tell my sisters, François, Shushani. But of course I didn't. Absolute discretion was the first rule of clandestinity. Anonymity was obligatory, as were caution and vigilance. You had to seem sad when you were happy, and if you were sad, you had to say it was because you were unlucky in love or had lost money gambling.

I was happy, but I knew very well why I should not have been: Was I not turning my back on the dead and on my studies and religious observance? Could a journalist have an inner life? Did a survivor have any right to be happy? But I also knew there was justification for my happiness. For one thing, my financial worries would soon be over. I was to receive a millionaire's salary: about thirty thousand francs (sixty dollars) a month. Until then I had been living on a quarter of that amount. I would be able to move. The end-of-the-month worries were over, along with the discomfort that gripped me in my landlady's presence. No more walking from Saint-Cloud to Odéon. I would now be able to live closer to the center of town. I found a room — with a sink, no less — on the Rue de Rivoli near the Hôtel de Ville, close to the editorial office. Long live journalism! Long live the future! Frantically I grabbed my valise, stuffed it with the few clothes and books I possessed and the tefillin from which I was never separated, and hurriedly settled into my room in the Hôtel de France. Bursting with energy, I felt like a future conqueror. Except I wasn't sure what I wanted to conquer.

But I did know I was joining the fight, and that gave me a sense of joy I had never felt before: the joy of action — even better, the joy of underground action.

For me the Resistance was the essence of everything that was ethical and noble in society. Physical courage, self-sacrifice, and solidarity could be found even in the lower depths; total compassion, rejection of humiliation either suffered or imposed, and altruism in the absolute sense were found only among those who fought for an idea and an ideal that went beyond themselves. Nobility of action was found only among those who espoused the cause of the weak and oppressed, the prisoners of evil and misfortune.

In my eyes, the anti-Nazi Resistance embodied that kind of nobility, and it disturbed me that I had not been part of it. True, I was too young to join the underground Communist network that distributed leaflets against the bourgeoisie in Sighet, and in Buchenwald I was too fearful and apathetic to join the clandestine organization of whose existence I was in any case unaware. Still, I felt frustrated and deficient, not whole. Now I had the chance to redeem myself.

The Irgun, of course, had nothing to do with the French Resistance. For one thing, the enemy was not the same. For another, I was quickly disabused of any romantic ideas about secret meeting places, passwords, nighttime journeys, pretty girls serving as liaisons. There may have been some of this in the Irgun, but I didn't experience it. Nor was there in my experience any intrusive interrogation, detailed examination of my past, or oath with one hand on the Bible and the other on a revolver. There was just a friendly conversation and a handshake, nowhere near enough for a suspense film. If I imagined that I would be living a life of danger, I was soon disappointed: I was risking neither death nor imprisonment. Even deportation from France was unlikely. Stateless persons were rarely deported; that was one of the few advantages of the status. In the worst case, I would join Bea in the displaced persons camp. But underground or not, I was happy, for I was now part of a Jewish resistance movement.

Overnight I had a job, a way of life I would grow to love for was there any more absorbing vocation or fascinating prospect for a boy of nineteen in this time of postwar turmoil? I read Joseph Kessel's news reports, Camus's editorials in *Combat* and Altman's in *Franc-Tireur*, François Mauriac's polemics in *Le Figaro*. I wanted to follow in their footsteps, stand at the nerve center of events, live in the midst of life, inform, explain, and participate in the planet's upheavals. I pictured myself as a star foreign correspondent taking planes and ships, penetrating the Sahara or the jungles of Africa, making contact with lost tribes anxiously awaiting discovery. Only, reality did not tally with the dream.

The following Monday I presented myself at the editorial office. Joseph, the boss, showed me to a desk, handed me an article in Hebrew, and asked me to translate it. The article, published in the Irgun's newspaper in Israel, was a denunciation of David Ben-Gurion and the Haganah and a paean to Menachem Begin, commander in chief of the Irgun. I translated the Hebrew words into Yiddish without grasping their meaning. I knew that the Haganah was fighting the British as hard as the Irgun was, and I couldn't understand why the two movements hated each other so much. The article also mentioned the Lehi (the so-called Stern Gang), but what was its role? Perhaps I was too politically naïve to understand. I pictured the Jewish fighter as an idealist striving for the redemption of our people, a man of purity, motivated by the poetry of his dreams, almost a Just Man who would give his life to save a brother or a comrade. But then why accuse Ben-Gurion and the Haganah of "collaborating" with the British police by turning in Irgun patriots? I translated and retranslated, but did not understand. The article talked about a certain "season" during which atrocious acts were allegedly committed by the Jewish political establishment. I didn't dare ask Joseph about this. He probably assumed that the political situation in Palestine held no secrets for me and that I had deliberately chosen to work for the Irgun. But he was wrong. I didn't know one underground group from another, and if the gatekeeper at the Jewish Agency hadn't turned me away, I might have been sitting at a desk working for the Haganah, translating an insulting article about the Irgun. Obviously I had to find out what was going on. For the moment, however, I simply translated, the need for translators apparently also being part of the underground patriotic struggle.

The task was far from easy. I read Hebrew well and spoke fluent Yiddish, but my Germanized written Yiddish wasn't good. My style was dry and lifeless, and the meaning seemed to wander off into byways lined with dead trees. That was not surprising, since I was wholly ignorant of Yiddish grammar and its vast, rich literature. I had not yet read — except for a few fragments — the works of Peretz, Sholem Aleichem, or Mendele. The names Leivik and Markish, Bergelson and Der Nister, Glatstein and Manger, were still unfamiliar to me. I had a lot to learn.

Joseph edited my translation and told me he was ready to teach me. He soon became my professor of literature and political science, explaining that Yiddish had its own grammar and idiosyncrasies, with countless nuances and as many pitfalls. "If you want to hold the reader's attention," he said, "your sentence must be clear enough to be understood and enigmatic enough to pique curiosity. A good piece combines style and substance. It must not say everything — never say everything — while nevertheless suggesting that there is an everything."

I learned that Polish Yiddish differed from Lithuanian Yiddish, and that Romanian Yiddish had a rhythm distinct from Hungarian Yiddish. The Yiddish of the Hasidim was not the same as that of their adversaries, and the Yiddish of intellectuals was not that of fairground workers and lumberjacks.

I talked about this with Shushani — whom I was still seeing in the evening — and once again he astonished me. His own accent was Lithuanian, but he knew all Yiddish variants except Hungarian. On the same occasion he asked about my work, but, faithful to my oath, I evaded his questions. He wasn't offended. "I love secrets," he said. "Think of the alchemists trying to turn sand into gold in their underground hideouts. All great projects are conceived in secret." Though he abhorred violence, he was hardly indifferent to the Jewish struggle in Palestine. Whenever the British arrested a member of an underground organization, Shushani tried to get information about his fate. One day he seemed extremely agitated. He interrupted our lesson, pacing back and forth, bumping into walls, blowing his nose, panting, and wiping his forehead with the biggest handkerchief I had ever seen. It was the day a member of the Lehi and a member of the Irgun committed suicide together just a few hours before their scheduled execution.

I also continued to meet with François. Joseph allowed me to pursue my studies with him and at the Sorbonne. But we spoke less about *Hernani*, Victor Hugo's play that marked a turning point in French theater, than about the fighting ravaging the Holy Land. How and why did François suddenly decide to join the struggle for an independent Jewish state? Had he, too, knocked on the Jewish Agency's door on the Avenue de Wagram? Though he joined the Lehi, and I belonged to the Irgun, our friendship was unaffected. In any case, each of us kept his activities to himself. We both agreed that the less we knew about each other, the better.

I confess I enjoyed my "clandestine" life. To be the bearer of a secret gives your life purpose and intensity. You play the part of a potential hero and feel vaguely superior to those around you. No one asked questions at the synagogue I attended on the Rue Pavée. To them I was a student like any other. If only they knew.

But knew what? The truth is there was nothing to know. I worked in an ordinary office, translating articles that had already been published elsewhere, and spent long hours in a small printshop engaged in thoroughly legal activities. I had no information on arms sales or chartered ships; I asked no questions and was privy to no rumors. In fact, after the United Nations vote there was hardly any underground activity in Palestine anyway.

But I felt privileged, important, and useful. Though I was in no danger, I thought of my situation as problematic, and somewhat heroic: militant journalist, fighter for Jewish freedom. I was very young and very enthusiastic and in search of a cause.

The choir had been dissolved and I went less and less often to Versailles. But when I did, I had to restrain myself from strutting around like a "resistance fighter," especially in Hanna's presence. How could I convey to her that I was worthy of her attention if not her affection, that she might be interested in what I was doing, that she ought to ask me certain questions so that I could reply that I had no right to reply? There was no need to pretend with Niny, whom I still saw in Paris. She had guessed. Did she approve? I suppose so. "Be careful," she told me one Sunday morning, and added with a wink, "Don't neglect your studies too much."

I didn't. Perhaps there is some truth to the American saying that the busier you are, the more time you have. There were Shushani and the Talmud, François and Kierkegaard, asceticism and *Zion in Kamf*. I did what I had to do. I would have liked Hanna to have noticed the toll that lack of sleep had taken, but when she looked at me it was in order not to see me. Or so I thought.

The newspaper took up more and more of my time. With Joseph's encouragement, I got better at choosing news stories and articles to translate or adapt. I began to suggest headlines and to carry manuscripts to Gutkin's printshop. I composed the front page and the cultural section. Week by week, I was learning the trade.

At the office Gutkin and I chatted about religion, culture, and Zionist politics. I remember Jacotte, his daughter, still young but so dynamic, impish, and tireless. I remember the linotypist named Sam, an Auschwitz survivor who worked relentlessly into the night, concerned that every issue be worthy of its mission. His assistant, Jackie, would be the last Yiddish linotypist in Paris.

Through work I met Shlomo Friedrich, the leader of Betar, Jabotinsky's Youth Movement. He was a tall, vigorous man with a rapid gait, a former prisoner in the Gulag. Remarkably intelligent, inventive, and inspired, he led his

291

movement with passion and imagination. There was great kindness in his smile, and I loved his voice. Friedrich could do everything, from singing in Yiddish, Russian, and Hebrew while accompanying himself on the accordion to drafting a political agenda. When young members of his group wanted to get married, he presided over the ceremony and made sure there would be gifts. If a cantor was needed for the High Holidays, he willingly volunteered, performing the task to perfection. He spoke to government ministers as easily as to the lawyers who came to see him. I met his wife Shoshana and later his children. (I was living in New York when Shlomo died of cancer in a Paris hospital. When I heard the news, I was immensely saddened.)

The process of becoming a journalist involved attending press conferences, public meetings, and demonstrations, and offered a chance to meet such "colleagues" as Henri Bulawko. As we talked, we discovered that we had been in Auschwitz-Buna at the same time. And I met Léon Leneman, one of the first to sound the alarm for Soviet Jews. I kept learning about my new craft. I was still translating but soon I would be writing articles.

The world was in flux. Young King Michael of Romania was forced to abdicate and abandon his country to the Communists. Burma won its independence. Gandhi was assassinated, Jan Masaryk pushed to his death. British soldiers were being killed in Palestine, and so were Jews. Arab terrorists blew up the Jewish Agency building in Jerusalem: eleven dead, eighty-six wounded. In Paris people mourned the death of Antonin Artaud, the great poet who died in an insane asylum. At the time I didn't even know his name.

Envoys from the Irgun came to the editorial offices every day. All were from Palestine and I was supposed to know only their aliases. Their commander, Élie Farshtei, was shrouded in mystery, but, after swearing me to secrecy, Joseph told me of an incident from his past. In 1946, when Élie was head of the Irgun's intelligence service in Jerusalem, he was captured and tortured by agents of the Haganah. It seems he spent months chained to an iron cot in a kibbutz run by Mapai (Ben-Gurion's party). He and his aides, Aryeh and David, would often closet themselves in Joseph's office. I ached to know what plans they were hatching. Military attacks? If so, against whom? A new wave of illegal immigrants? When and from what country? I was flattered when Élie Farshtei stopped by to ask whether I wasn't working too hard, whether my studies weren't suffering. I told him that everything was fine, and that I hoped he was pleased with my "contribution" to "Zion in Struggle."

I remember a man called Marcel, who spoke English, which at the time I didn't understand, as well as Hebrew. He gave the probably false impression that he was always armed. There was Zeev, who served as the link with the Irgun groups in Germany, and Saul, more professor than man of action. There was Mendel with his poet's air. In the corridors I might have encountered a young Jewish girl from Vienna, beautiful and daring, who transported documents and provided a hiding place for guns: my future wife.

The situation in Palestine grew increasingly tense. A wave of terror swept over the Jewish communities in various Arab countries. The synagogue in Aleppo, Syria, was burned by a mob. Dozens of Jews were slaughtered in Aden. Jerusalem was besieged, and gangs loyal to the grand mufti, the pro-Hitler Haj Amin el-Husseini (former ally and protégé of Himmler), attacked Jewish villages and convoys. It would soon be May, and the day of independence. Mobilized units of the Haganah, the Palmach, the Irgun, and the Stern Gang united their efforts and their wills. It was imperative to protect every kibbutz, every settlement. The Zionist organizations in the Diaspora worked tirelessly to supply our brothers in Palestine with political and financial support. In France, and in the United States as well, we were mobilized. Young and old, rich and not so rich, all felt the fever our ancestors had known in antiquity. Representatives of all the resistance groups worked day and night, though separately, procuring arms and ammunition, raising funds, recruiting volunteers who would set out for the various fronts of the nascent Jewish state. Élie and his aides no longer found time to sleep. Out of solidarity, neither did we.

My personal circle narrowed. Kalman left for America; Israel Adler was recalled by the Haganah and was now in a training camp for volunteers, the Grand Arenas, near Marseilles. He was an officer in charge of cultural activities. My friend Nicolas informed me that, despite his love for French poetry, he planned to abandon his studies: "Our people are fighting for our homeland. How can I stay here doing nothing." He was going to fight. What about his parents? They would understand. "And Myriam? She loves you, you know." He knew it and didn't. In Versailles he had loved her madly, but now it was the other way around; he loved her a little less. No problem: she could join him in Israel and it would all work out. Whether out of a desire not to be separated from Nicolas or a pang of patriotism, I suggested we go together. I discussed the possibility with Joseph, who cleared it with his superiors. Naturally, they would have preferred that I enroll in the Irgun, but they told me to do as I pleased.

Deep down, I had reservations. Military life was not for me. The routine of training, the sergeants' shouting, the overcrowded barracks, the dissolution of personal identity in the mass — I sensed I would find all that intolerable.

And what if I died in combat? I hadn't yet done anything with my life, had written nothing of the visions and obsessions I bore within myself, hadn't yet shared them with anyone. Even at the newspaper all I did was translate and transmit the thought, demands, and wrath of others, the frustrations and aspirations of others, but nothing of my own, nothing of myself. My history threatened to die with me. Besides which, I felt I still belonged to the Diaspora. Nevertheless, I decided to heed the call to arms.

Nicolas and I signed up at the recruitment office on Avenue de la Grande Armée. There were so many eager volunteers that we had to stand on line. The atmosphere was one of camaraderie. People greeted one another, gossiped, passed on rumors and jokes. We were already part of the Jewish army. Everything seemed fine, except that a problem arose during the medical examination. The doctor was "displeased" with my state of health. He suggested a minor operation, not serious but necessary. "Take care of yourself," he told me. "You're not in good shape. Come back another time." I didn't feel sick, so why was the doctor trying to scare me? I envied Nicolas, who was declared "fit." I pictured him joining Israel Adler in the south of France. He would disembark in Haifa and don the uniform of the resurrected Jewish army. He would be a warrior, a hero, unlike me.

Disappointed, in utter disarray, I went to Versailles for Shabbat. I was among the last of the "children" who still visited the home, and the old atmosphere was gone. I had the feeling they all looked at me askance and even that some were passing judgment on me. That probably included Hanna. It was what she had been doing ever since we met. At table we sang the usual songs, but my heart wasn't in it.

I also went to Orsay, where Léon Ashkenazy (nicknamed Manitou) headed a modern (Sephardic-style) yeshiva. By then he was already a well-known and charismatic leader, his teachings a seamless poetic blend. I liked both his method and his songs. I felt a need to celebrate Shabbat by praying, singing, and studying. In Paris that was difficult. In Orsay I learned Ladino tunes and taught Hasidic songs.

At the editorial office we worked around the clock. We talked about having mounted the seventh wave, the highest of all. The Jewish state was being born, the ancient dream on the point of realization. Of all the peoples of antiquity, Israel alone had reestablished its national sovereignty in the land of its ancestors.

Then came the much-awaited day, the dawn of our dreams. It was a Friday. May 14, 1948. All the world's radios broadcast David Ben-Gurion's speech. In a museum in Tel Aviv, a few hours before the onset of Shabbat so as not to violate its sanctity, he read the Declaration of Independence, and as I listened, as I read and reread it, I was unable to contain my emotion. When had I last wept? It was in an almost painful state of reverence that I greeted Shabbat, the most beautiful and luminous Shabbat of my life. That day Shabbat was not an offering to Israel. That day Israel was an offering to Shabbat.

The world held its breath, suspended as it was between wonder and anguish. Would the Jewish people, realizing its ancient dream, finally change its destiny?

At nightfall I hurried to synagogue to greet the Queen of Shabbat, not so much to pray as to mingle with a living community. The service had not yet started. The elated faithful were discussing politics and strategy. An aged master in a broad-brimmed felt hat drew me aside and asked, "Do you believe in miracles now?" I told him I did. "And you will no longer deny the beneficence of heaven?" I wouldn't. He stared hard at me, and his voice turned harsh. "Well, young man," he said, "you're satisfied with very little. You forgive and forget too fast." But I needed this turning point, or at least this sign. "No," the master exclaimed, full of scorn. "Though I have no right to reject salvation that comes too late, I cannot call it salvation, for we paid too dearly. A true, redemptive salvation would have had to have come sooner." He began to pray, his teeth clenched, while in Israel, despite inferior numbers and insufficient weaponry, they were already fighting as in the days of the Maccabees. To lose would mean the end of a dream, the end of Eretz Israel. (I recalled this conversation often when visiting Israel. Israel as recompense for the Holocaust is a far too expedient explanation, one that borders on blasphemy. The two experiences have in common only the people who lived them.)

Public opinion was favorable to the newborn Jewish state. Truman and Stalin vied for the honor of being first to recognize its existence de facto and de jure. The French press dispatched its best reporters and most prestigious commentators. I envied them. War correspondent — what I would have given for that title. Insofar as "Zion in Struggle" needed my services, it was in Paris, as an ordinary journalist-copyboy-editor-messenger.

I therefore lived the historic events from a distance, vicariously: Israel at war, Israel greeting its repatriated children from distant camps and prisons, Israel structuring its government. I read the wire-service dispatches, compared political reports and military analyses, underscored particularly significant images, listed especially striking expressions. I learned to associate names and events: the death of Abdelkader Husseini near Kastel; the attack on Deir Yassin (whose bloody details we did not yet know); the fall of Kfar Etzion; the massacre of a convoy of doctors. I "accompanied" the glorious units of the Palmach as they fought to open the road to Jerusalem and of Brigade 7, famous for its victories in the south. I shouted for joy when the Irgun conquered Jaffa, applauded when Menachem Begin proclaimed his commitment to democracy by creating a new political party, Herut, which succeeded the Irgun, whose officers and soldiers were integrated into Tsahal, the Israel Defense Force. I screamed with rage and sadness when I learned of the surrender of the Old City. And then, in June, I was finally given the right to publish an article of my own, a fictional commentary on the incomprehensible tragedy of the *Altalena*, which aroused fury even more than pain at *Zion in Kamf*, for we considered it not only a tragedy but a crime — namely, murder and treason.

After the declaration of independence, Tsahal absorbed all the underground movements on national soil, except in Jerusalem, which was internationalized by the UN and where the Irgun and Lehi preserved their autonomous infrastructures, bases, and commands. The Irgun, short of men and matériel, chartered a ship, the *Altalena*, that carried about a thousand refugees from displaced persons camps and enough arms and ammunition (donated by the French government) to equip all its own units and others besides. But this initiative posed a twofold problem. On the one hand, it violated the embargo decreed by the UN; on the other, there was Prime Minister Ben-Gurion's fear (whether real, imaginary, or politically useful) that the detested Irgun commanders might attempt a coup d'état. The prime minister's entourage claimed the two camps had not reached an agreement, while Begin's swore they had. The Irgun's argument: If we were planning a coup, would we have informed the government of the date of the ship's arrival? Subsequent testimony from many witnesses confirmed that there had indeed been negotiations about the distribution of the arms. The talks failed either because of the provisional government's fear of being condemned for violating the UN embargo, or because of Ben-Gurion's unconfessed desire to liquidate the separate armies of the Irgun, the Lehi, and especially the Palmach.

The *Altalena* arrived off the coast of Israel at Kfar Vitkin, but, strangely, was denied permission to drop anchor unless all of its cargo was handed over to Tsahal. The Irgun commander decided to take the ship to Tel Aviv. There, on Ben-Gurion's orders, the Palmach greeted it with artillery fire, sinking it. The operation was commanded by high-ranking officers whose names would later shine in the Tsahal firmament: the future general and minister Moshe Dayan; future archaeologist, general, and minister Yigal Yadin; future minister of foreign affairs Yigal Alon; and a young officer as staunch as he was shy, the future chief of staff, minister of defense, and prime minister Yitzhak Rabin. Ben-Gurion was stubborn. His directives spoke of an "enemy" that had to be liquidated at all costs. He demanded unconditional surrender, seeking to humiliate as much as to defeat. Respected rabbis and political leaders tried to convince him that mediation was not only desirable but possible. In vain. There would be no mercy for the "enemy." Anglo-American volunteers refused to open fire on the ship. "We didn't come here to kill Jews," they said. Some officers (among them Dayan's aide) took a similar position. But these acts of conscience were exceptional. For the Irgun, this battle was lost in advance. There was talk of twenty victims, nearly all of them camp survivors. Was it true that some Palmach officers drank to their victory? Begin, in tears, issued an appeal to his troops: "No vengeance, no civil war, no fratricidal struggle!"

During a stormy Knesset debate Ben-Gurion made a speech that to this day I find hard to comprehend, let alone forgive. Justifying his order, he declared: "When the Third Temple is rebuilt, the cannon that fired on the *Altalena* will have a place of honor." I was angry at Ben-Gurion. Later — much later — I came to feel lasting admiration for him and for his political vision (in spite of the *Altalena*).

In its issue devoted to the event, *Zion in Kamf* published a polemical article brimming with prophetic indignation by Israel's leading editorialist, Dr. Azriel Carlebach (translated from *Maariv* by a rabbi, Eliézer Halberstam, a member of the Irgun and scion of a prominent Hasidic dynasty). Inspired by this text, entitled "The Sacred Cannon," and deeply moved by the event itself, I wrote a piece that appeared under the byline Ben Shlomo. In it I recounted the tragedy of two brothers belonging to opposing camps. The Irgun fighter becomes the victim of his brother, a Palmach soldier.

Thinking back on it now, I find it curious that my first published article dealt with an evil that has always afflicted my people's history. Was it merely an accident that Cain and Abel, the first two brothers of the Bible, were murderer and victim, and that the children of our patriarchs quarreled incessantly? There was scarcely a generation not cast into turmoil by some internal Jewish schism, scarcely a century not marked by some Jewish ideological conflict, by various splits and sunderings: Isaac against Ishmael, Jacob against Esau, Judah against Israel, the Pharisees against the Sadducees, Maskilim against Hasidim, Bundists against Zionists, Communists against everyone else. What about the Jewish solidarity so praised in our literature and decried by enemy propaganda?

Yet I believed in it. I wanted to believe in it. In my eyes, to be a Jew was to belong to the Jewish community in the broadest and most immediate sense. It was to feel abused whenever a Jew, any Jew anywhere, was humiliated. It was to react, to protest, whenever a Jew, even an unknown Jew in some distant land, was attacked for the simple reason that he was a Jew.

It never occurred to me that a Jew might be capable of spilling Jewish blood, of waging war on other Jews, and surely not on Jews who refused to fight back. The renegades of the Middle Ages were exceptions, as were the kapos during the war. In both cases the perpetrators were marginal figures lacking all authority. But here were good Jews — indeed, Jewish soldiers, even Jewish heroes — firing on their brothers, survivors of hell who had come to aid them, to join their cause, to fight alongside them, to participate in their marvelous adventure.

I couldn't accept it. I told myself it wasn't true even as I read the articles and dispatches and examined the photographs. It couldn't be true. The prime minister of the newly risen Jewish state had not issued such orders. The officers of the Palmach had not carried them out. They had not denied the wounded medical care. The soldiers had not fired upon camp survivors and former partisans floundering in the sea. The dead were not dead.

Like a disillusioned lover, I sought in vain for some reasonable explanation. The Irgun people had one: Ben-Gurion has always hated what we are and what we stand for. They cited his official program during what was called "the season," when his opponents were persecuted and hunted. To combat the Irgun all those suspected of membership were to be fired and refused aid and shelter. Their threats were to be resisted, if necessary by collaborating with the British police. At the time the main enemy of the Jewish establishment in Palestine was not the British occupier but the Irgun fighter. That's how it was, I was told. The leopard does not change his spots, nor the Haganah its tactics.

I could not accept this portrait of Ben-Gurion. A great Zionist, a Jewish idealist like him, could not be a monster. But I would not be seen again at the recruitment office at Avenue de la Grande Armée. I bore a secret wound whose scar would be a long time healing. It was a case of loyalty not so much to the Irgun as to my adolescence. In any event, there was no Irgun in Israel anymore, no Lehi either. Both were dissolved. But they still functioned in the Diaspora, carrying on activities that today would be considered public relations.

I decided to visit Bea again. She was still waiting for her visa, and I had to go through the usual procedure: long lines at the police station, requests for visas, irritating, humiliating interrogations, lifesaving stamps.

Bea's camp was gradually emptying. Many people left for Israel, others for more distant lands. The Germans seemed happy to be rid of these Jews. Ben Shlomo — yours truly — wrote an article on the subject, entitled "Victors and Vanquished," which raised the question: Even if the Germans are vanquished, are we the victors?

I was now writing a lot, mostly for the trash can. Joseph didn't want me to deal with politics anymore, and I too had had enough of issues that divided the Jewish people. To support one side while criticizing another, to defend one group while condemning another, was not at all to my taste. I was more interested in literature and philosophy. I wrote a long study on Spinoza and another on Muhammad and the Koran. Neither, of course, had anything to do with the Irgun or current events, and one of our "superiors" was kind enough to call attention to that fact. What was the renegade of Amsterdam doing in a paper in which "renegade" meant Ben-Gurion? Fortunately, Joseph backed me up. He hoped to broaden our readership by appealing to intellectuals. We were no longer an underground publication — if indeed we ever had been — and, like any self-respecting newspaper, we could no longer be content with tendentious news reports and polemics. Thus reassured, I prepared several cultural articles and background pieces for the months to come. But in January 1949, shortly after the *Altalena* catastrophe, the Irgun offices in Europe shut down. Élie Farshtei and his lieutenants, Joseph among them, were recalled to Israel. I received no orders or aid from anyone. "Why don't you come with us?" Joseph asked. I promised to think about it.

Now unemployed again, I turned back to my studies with renewed vigor, reading everything I could get my hands on. I finally discovered modern French literature: Malraux's *La Condition humaine*, Mauriac's *Le Baiser des lépreux*,

Roger Martin du Gard's *Jean Barois*, and of course the existentialists. I devoured novels and memoirs about the Resistance. There were days when I was so absorbed in my reading that I never left my room. I had nothing to seek in the desert.

Shlomo Friedrich came to my rescue with a few translating and editing jobs that allowed me to pay my rent, but my situation remained precarious. The OSE had long since suspended its subsidies. Sometimes I couldn't afford to eat. I thought about going back to Porte de Saint-Cloud to smile at the salesgirl in the cheese shop, but the prospect embarrassed me. I wondered how long I would keep feeling sorry for myself. I felt uprooted and out of place. I no longer belonged to Europe. Bea had finally left for Canada. Shushani had disappeared, probably for good. Hilda and her husband were barely getting by. I often went to their home in the evening to baby-sit for their son Sidney, whose crib took up the whole "living room." They wanted to go into business, but in the meantime they had just enough to live on. Sometimes I went back to Versailles for a decent Shabbat dinner, but Our Place had changed completely. Only Hanna hadn't changed. She was as distant and sarcastic as ever. So be it. I had other worries. Nicolas sent me a long letter urging me to join him. Israel Adler sent me a one-word message: Come. The weeks passed quickly, and soon it was Passover, springtime. Suppose I went to Israel for the summer? I discussed it with Georges, Hilda's brother-in-law, who held an important post in the Amaury press group. He thought it was a good idea and said he would arrange to get me a press card. The war in Israel was over, but there was still the armistice, which was not the same thing as peace. It would be the fulfillment of my dream: at last I would be a war correspondent. But how would I report on a war without war? Well, I would find plenty of other subjects, like the life of the new immigrants, and Israel as a land of refuge for all the sons and daughters of the Diaspora, Israel, the beginning of redemption. There was no way to tell how long I would stay. The important thing was to be there.

To make sure that my plan could work in practice, I went to the Jewish Agency and met with a deputy director who was enthusiastic. "By all means," she said. "A good sentimental, romantic story is always useful for aliyah. The doors of the country are open, but too few Jews are entering."

The mother of Méno Horowitz, a Versailles comrade who was studying agronomy, worked with me. We prepared a plan. In May or June I would join a group of immigrants and make the trip with them, from the train station in Lyons to Haifa. After that we would see. The group happened to include a few Irgun veterans, but they were leaving Europe for good, and I was ashamed to admit that I was less idealistic and above all less courageous than they. Then there was the detail of what I would live on in Israel. Surely the paper would employ me only on a free-lance basis. Still, my wallet was not quite empty: a few thousand francs (my life's savings) plus one pound sterling, a gift from Freddo.

Arriving at the station carrying a suitcase stuffed with my tefillin, a few articles of clothing, books, and my unfinished manuscript on asceticism, I ran into my friends Baruch and Louis. The former adored Jack London's novels, the latter fine food. Everyone was in excellent spirits. The elated young *olim*, or immigrants, sang and drank, alert and open to camaraderie as never before. They talked laughingly of their amorous conquests, while I dreamed of Hanna and Niny. I never said goodbye to either of them. In Niny's case I had a good reason: She was on a training program in the United States. "What about you?" someone asked in the dark of night. "Come on, what's with the secrecy? Some woman must have made you happy. Or miserable." I pretended to be asleep. My buddies felt good. I should have, too, but I was unable to share in their joy. I pictured myself at the station in Sighet, waiting for my dead father, gripped with anguish, wondering whether the train would come. At last it did. The locomotive gave three long whistles, but no one opened the doors. The train was empty.

Trucks were waiting at the station in Marseilles to take us to the transit camp. As we drove through a tunnel, Baruch asked me to close my eyes. I did. "Now open them," he said. When I obeyed, the sight of the sea took my breath away. Coming from the mountains as I did, I was stunned by its immensity and mysterious power. My heart beat faster, as though I were on my way to a lovers' rendezvous. I would never escape its grip.

Our first stopover was a lodging house near Bandol. There was an atmosphere of permanent excitement. Families were reunited; couples formed, fell in love, and promised each other eternal bliss. I took notes. People gathered in groups according to political affinity and spun countless projects and plans. I scribbled. That's what I was there for. Some went into town to shop or have fun. To complete my image as a great reporter I bought myself a leather jacket and a pair of sunglasses.

Feverish discussions were held in the shadow of every barracks. Would we all be housed together when we got *there?* How were we going to make a living? Was military service tough? "Sure it's tough," said a stocky man with lively features, "but consider this: Once I was a partisan, an underground fighter hiding in the woods like a hunted animal, not daring to come out except after dark, and now I'll proudly wear the uniform of the Israeli army." His companion, a stooped man with pinched lips, disagreed: "Yes, a very pretty picture, but I've had enough fighting for one lifetime, spent enough nights standing guard, faced death too often. I wouldn't mind a little peace and quiet." Voices were raised in agreement and disagreement. Some feared the armistice would drag on, others that it would be broken, but everyone was concerned about it.

At night I sat on my cot, listened to conversations, and jotted down notes. It must be a way to relieve tension — when men gather among themselves, invariably someone tells a locker-room story. Everyone laughs, and then someone tries to top him, going for bigger laughs. But I didn't feel like laughing. I thought about all the girls in Versailles and all the unknown women in trains who didn't know how much I loved them, and about all the sins I lacked the courage to commit.

Eventually, the conversation died down, the final murmurs eliciting no more than weary sighs. The barracks dozed off. It was late, but I couldn't sleep. I can't imagine why, but it seemed like a good time to draw a kind of balance sheet. I pictured myself back home, listening to my father wonder aloud whether we should leave everything behind and set out for Eretz Israel. I heard him whisper, "Do I have the strength to start all over again at my age?" How many fathers in how many towns felt that same fear? And then there was our lack of imagination. We had entrusted our future to God, never suspecting that the enemy had already taken possession of it. How could my father and all the Jews of Europe have been so naïve and blind? Nothing could have prevented them from emigrating to Palestine fifty years or even thirty years before. Back then you didn't need visas or travel permits. What bound us to lands so consistently thirsting for Jewish blood? I thought about all the people of my town and of my life who could not be with me on my journey.

There were sunny days and fragrant evenings, an atmosphere of dreams and expectations. Strangers formed friendships more readily on the threshold of great adventure. But not I. My shyness isolated me. I yearned to strike up a conversation with Inge, a young Jewish girl of German origin whose melancholy beauty disturbed me — no surprise there. She had neither friends nor family. Clearly she was destined for me. Suddenly I forgot all past temptations. It was over with Hanna; Inge alone occupied my thoughts. She was surely sweeter than Hanna. Oh, how I could love her! Sometimes I found myself standing behind her in line. If only I could manage to speak a word, just one word. But I was paralyzed. I knew I should reach out and touch her arm, offer her my warmest smile, explain a difficult passage of the Bhagavad Gita or of Schopenhauer to her. I should whisper to her, convince her. I didn't want to leave Europe never having made love. But I didn't dare. I was afraid, afraid of being rejected. I promised myself I would be more daring on board. Surely at sea everyone becomes more daring. Everyone but me.

The ship, the *Negba*, was packed. There was no room to stand on the deck and no place to be alone. All of us were housed in the hold. From time to time we were allowed onto the deck for air, and I would search for Inge, my new obsession, in the unwieldy crowd. But there were too many people, many young children. Someone told me that a few women had moved into cabins. Had they suddenly gotten rich, or perhaps accommodated someone? Maybe if I showed my press card to a crew member, he would let me take a look at the other decks. But I was too shy. As always. To make such a request would mean drawing attention to myself. Ever since the camp it had been my watchword to lie low. I promised myself I would be more daring in Israel, where everyone is daring.

It was an uneventful crossing. I prayed, read, wrote in my journal, took notes for my articles, observed others and myself, counting the hours and keeping busy so as not to get seasick. The night before we arrived I didn't sleep. I wanted to be awake, eyes and ears wide open, all my senses honed, to catch my first glimpse of Mount Carmel. With a little luck I might even glimpse the Prophet Elijah.

I hoped to be the only one with this idea, but of course I wasn't. Dozens of couples came out onto the deck. Some had brought blankets.

"Wake us as soon as the mountain appears on the horizon," they asked. But we didn't have to wake them. They couldn't sleep either.

I leaned against the railing and scoured the starry sky, rocked by the waves. A sadness as deep as the ocean enveloped me, so oppressive that I found it hard to breathe, so powerful that I had a sudden urge to end my life, to throw myself overboard and be swallowed up and carried off by the waves. I had never felt the lure of death so strongly, not even in my wretched room near the Porte de Saint-Cloud. Just then a man unknown to me, his face shrouded in shadow, spoke to me, and thus unwittingly saved me. I didn't understand what he said, but I knew he was talking to me, or perhaps to himself through me. History, religion, poetry — he talked and talked, and when, in the end, I turned to him, Lord be praised, I caught sight of Inge next to him, staring off at the same waves, perhaps summoning death just as I had. I prayed that the man between us would go away, that he would speak to one of the many other passengers on the deck. And God heard my prayer. I should have stopped the man to thank him for saving my life, but Inge was right there, so very near, and I was afraid to lose her. Gently I moved closer to her, absorbing the silence that reigned over sky and sea, a silence broken only by whispers of love and prayer. I was sure, absolutely sure, that to take her hand would be to embark on an unforgettable love story. We would begin a new life together, have beautiful, mischievous children, and be together always, never separated, not even by death. I needed just one gesture, just one. But unsurprisingly, I remained paralyzed, imprisoned by my inhibitions. The blessed moment passed. It had lasted an hour, perhaps even two, but it passed, and all at once a powerful cry of triumph sprang from a thousand throats: "There it is!" I peered out at the horizon that would soon be tinged with the flames of dawn, and then I saw it: Mount Carmel, looming high, menacing the enemy but beckoning to us, the faithful, to approach. My cheeks were suddenly and not surprisingly damp.

Was it our imminent arrival that had moved me so deeply, or bitterness at once again having let my chance slip away? I looked to see whether Inge had been as moved, but when I turned she was gone.

I felt alone in the crowd that thronged the deck, stupidly and irrevocably alone. As always.

I still have my notebook from those days. The handwriting is choppy and illegible, for I was elated as never before. In a few moments I would tread the soil of Israel and breathe the air of Galilee. It was like reliving my childhood dreams. Just imagine: Isaiah and Habakkuk, Rabbi Yehuda and Rabbi Ishmael, Rabbi Moshe ben Nahman and Rabbi Itzhak Lurie may have walked this very ground. Then, too, this was my first news assignment. Observing everything around me and within myself, I was determined to absorb and retain it all — the color of the sky (is there such a thing as biblical blue?), the slow and steady shifting of the clouds, the deafening sounds of the port mingled with shouts and cries in countless languages. The heat. The excitement. The officials wearing shorts!

The police and customs formalities were quick. Here no one was treated as an alien. Still, there was an assembly line of stamps, forms, and money-changing. People smiled and winked at me, not because I was a journalist but because I was a Jew, because we were all Jews. Immigration officials shook my hand and welcomed me. A disturbing thought crossed my mind: How could they be sure no spies had slipped in among all these immigrants from the four corners of the earth? Anyone could have told them any story; it was impossible to check. I made a mental note to look into it. In the meantime, I followed the immigrants to a reception center with the highly poetic name of Bat-Galim, "Daughter of Waves."

Everyone in our group slept in the same tent, and — yes, there is a God — I was lying on a cot next to Inge, and all at once she reached out to me in the darkness. Truly, this was a land of miracles. Trembling, I took her hand in mine and held it for an eternity; perhaps an entire minute. Was this why I had come to Israel? To find out what it was to hold a delicate, sweet, and open hand, a feminine hand?

I grew up in a tradition that denies chance. Though not everything is predetermined, everything is linked. Nikos Kazantzakis once said, citing an Etruscan proverb: "It is not because two clouds are joined that the spark ignites; two clouds are joined so that the spark may ignite." Yet, free will and the possibility of choice exist. Rabbi Akiba tells us that all is foreseen, though human beings have free choice.

Holding Inge's hand in mine, I was free to keep it or to let it go, to kiss it or caress it, to let my own hand wander. Would I dare? Yes, I would. I felt her breast, and the blood rushed faster in my veins. Then I stopped, perhaps out of modesty, or out of fear. Looking back, I think of what Oscar Wilde said: Our greatest regrets are for the sins we didn't commit. I had made a fool of myself in Inge's eyes, and now she proved it to me, sighing and withdrawing her hand. Feeling mutilated and empty, I could not fall asleep.

The next morning I couldn't face her and promised myself that the next night would be different. But there was no next night. Someone came to pick her up and take her to a kibbutz. She never even said goodbye, and for the first time since Écouis I forgot to say my prayers before breakfast, not even realizing it until nightfall, by which time it was too late to put

317

on the tefillin. Yet the sky did not split; no
bolt of lightning struck me. But it happened
in Israel.

A few days later I left Bat-Galim, having gathered enough material to write my first article
on the immigrants' arrival. I went to Tel Aviv
to register with the foreign press service at the
Kete Dan Hotel, but first I took a walk along
the shore, and suddenly I felt as if I had been
slapped in the face. Aground off the coast lay
a hulking wreck: all that remained of the *Altalena*. Someone had written in gigantic white
letters on its blackened flank: "Herut, you will
end like the *Altalena*." Why had that relic of
a shameful episode not been erased? Herut, after
all, was a democratically constituted, legal party.
Why call for its doom?

I introduced myself to the officer in charge
of press relations and was issued a "foreign correspondent" card, which, I admit, impressed me.
The provisional government of Israel, no less,
requested that civil and military authorities aid
and support me in the performance of my duties.
The young state was eager to please. All doors
were open to overseas journalists. I traveled by
jeep, bus, and truck, listening in a trance to
war stories and dramatic tales real or imagined.
An incorrigible romantic, I felt transported back
to the days of Judah Maccabee. I crisscrossed
the small country, bemused by its diversity and
of course by its Jewishness, but most of all by
its openness. No words could express the

people's courtesy and warmth. No one locked their doors at night. Had they no fear of thieves? They have to make a living too, people told me with a laugh.

In Tel Aviv I tried to contact Nicolas, but he was in the army. I did manage to locate the two sisters of André Bodner, a former OSE counselor. In Haifa I ran into my cousin Leizer Slomovic, a future professor of Talmud in Los Angeles who had married a girl from Sighet. I spent a Shabbat with them, and their happiness was contagious. They gave me the address of our cousins Reshka and Leibi Feig in Tel Aviv, and I spent another Shabbat with them. Reshka knew my taste for latkes, which I had not eaten since the ghetto. They were happy, though their material circumstances were difficult, but so were everyone else's. Individual problems didn't seem to matter much, given the historic events the country was living through. My cousins talked like Zionist propagandists: A good Jew, a real Jew, ought not to spend even one day more than necessary in the Diaspora. Everyone here said the same thing. I was in no mood to argue and couldn't have even if I had wanted to. I was conditioned to see only the good side of Israel. Call it sentimental, but I was moved when I spoke to a Jewish official, questioned a Jewish politician, saw a Jewish policeman or a Jewish army officer, or listened to a Jewish cabinet minister.

I loved the Galilee, so much so that I felt

like settling down in Safed, city of mystic visionaries, or perhaps in Tiberias, of whose charms the Talmud boasts. But then, why not settle in the Negev, a desert unlike any other, of which so many poets ancient and modern had sung? And Jerusalem, most beautiful, most silent and inspired of cities — why not spend the years remaining to me there? Of course, I could not visit the Old City, the true Jerusalem; it was still in the hands of the Jordanian army. To see it I climbed the tower of Notre Dame, the Lamentations of Jeremiah ringing in my mind: How solitary, how abandoned, is the city of God.

For the first time since its founding in the days of King David, there was no Jewish life nor any Jew within its walls. Even after the Temple's destruction, not everyone had deserted it. But now the Israelis seemed to have forgotten it, an inexplicable, disconcerting phenomenon I decided to investigate. But it wasn't easy, for the witnesses to Jerusalem's tragedy refused to speak. Faces went blank when I asked questions. I did not write on the subject, at least not yet. Much later I would speak of it in *A Beggar in Jerusalem* (1967) and *The Forgotten* (1989).

The fall of Jerusalem in 1948 haunts me still. Can it be compared to its fall in the year 70, after the Tenth Roman Legion, commanded by Tiberius, nephew of Philo of Alexandria, laid siege to the city? Who were the men who defended her to the last? What happened during her last hours of sovereignty? I was riveted by the merest detail.

In my notebook I recorded what I managed to discover about her more recent fall. Here are excerpts from a chronicle:

. . . And that morning a strangely sad scene unfolded beneath Jerusalem's blue sky.

Two old rabbis, Minzberg and Hazzan, approached the Zion Gate, in the Old City, bearing a large white sheet stretched between two poles.

It was Friday, a luminous Friday, the twenty-ninth of May 1948, nine-fifteen in the morning.

On the other side the Arabs . . .

When the Jordanians occupied the Old City, defended by a tiny group of poorly armed Jews, they vented their frustration. "Had we known how few you were, we would have driven you out with sticks."

Why were the Old City's defenders so few in number and so poorly armed? At the start of the siege, two thousand Jews lived there with their families; most were ultraorthodox, rabbinical students and Kabalists. The defenders, members of the three resistance movements, exhibited unparalleled courage. Young and old participated in the fighting. A twenty-year-old boy was wounded. "How long will this take?" he asked the doctor trying to treat him. "Twenty minutes," was the reply. "Too long," he said. "Give me something to kill the pain and I'll be back." They brought him back an hour later — dead.

Still, not everyone was prepared to sacrifice himself for the city. Religious anti-Zionists prodded the population to despair; they wanted defeat. They were few in number, but it hurt.

Who will console the violated and defeated city? When will it be consoled?

That was my last entry.

The religious anti-Zionists reminded me of Flavius Josephus. He, too, sought to demoralize the inhabitants by preaching resignation and inciting fighters to despair. Is there nothing new in the annals of our history? The question fascinated me, but I doubted it would interest my employers in Paris. They wanted a reporter, not a historian. I had been sent here to speak of living Jews, not dead Romans, of a wandering, dispossessed people who had become proud citizens. Flavius Josephus could wait. He had waited this long, he could wait a little longer.

The new immigrants had some surprises for me. As I talked to them in the absorption centers, towns, and villages, I began to hear complaints and recriminations that left me disappointed and disillusioned. There were protests against bureaucracy, economic hardship, and housing shortages. That much I could understand. But the problem ran deeper. "They don't like us, won't accept us," some told me. Astonished, I asked them to elaborate, and when they did, it hurt.

They said "it" had been going on since 1945. That in Palestine too, survivors of the camps were treated like outcasts, victims to be pitied at best. They were given housing and commiseration, but little respect. They were made to feel that they themselves were to blame for their suffering: They should have left Europe earlier, as they had been advised to do, or risen up against the Germans. In other words, the immigrants were seen to embody what young Jews in Palestine refused to be: victims. As such they represented the saddest image in Jewish history: the weak, stooped Jew in need of protection. They personified the Diaspora and its indignities.

"We came here hoping to escape humiliation," a former teacher from Lodz told me. "But in their eyes I am human wreckage," a former merchant from Radom told me sadly.

Things had gotten steadily worse since 1948. Proud Israelis sometimes openly manifested their contempt for the new immigrants, the *olim 'hadashim*. "Six hundred thousand of us defeated six well-equipped Arab armies. Six million of you let yourselves be led like lambs to the slaughter." How to explain it to them? How to tell them that they didn't understand, could never understand?

They looked down on the new immigrants, who were seen as cowards and smugglers, and schemers who dreamed only of enriching themselves illicitly, of deceiving the government and sowing disorder in the land. Some were even told that they weren't fooling anyone, that since they survived, they had probably been members of the Judenrat or, worse, kapos.

It doesn't seem possible, but at school pupils called their immigrant classmates *sabonim*, little "soap cakes." It wasn't their fault. It is never the children's fault. They were only repeating what they had heard at home. Zionism's heroic virtues had been so lauded and the disasters of the Diaspora so decried that the two now seemed incompatible: Zionism was great, beautiful, and honorable; the Diaspora had perverted and dishonored man, leading him to Auschwitz. In the kibbutzim surviving children and children of survivors were urged to forget the past, to jettison the memory of their suffering. That was not only healthier but essential if they were to refashion a new life within the community.

In this atmosphere little attention was paid to the Holocaust. For many years it was barely mentioned in textbooks and ignored in universities. In the early fifties, when David Ben-Gurion and his colleagues finally decided to pass the Knesset bill creating Yad Vashem, the Holocaust Memorial, the emphasis was on courage.

Resistance fighters were presented as a kind of elite, while the victims — the dead and survivors alike — deserved at best compassion and pity. Allusions to the fate of the victims were rare, especially in public. The subject was considered embarrassing.

This unhealthy, demoralizing state of affairs aroused in me an uneasiness that I could not shake. It tarnished my joy at breathing the air of Jerusalem. I vainly sought to regain my equilibrium. It occurred to me that it might help to write an article on the subject, but when a former Irgun emissary I had known in France asked me not to mention him in any article I might write, I understood. I decided to keep my disenchantment to myself.

Still, I decided to extend my stay, and the old question of what I would live on reasserted itself. I stayed with cousins and friends here and there. Itzu Junger, my friend from Sighet, loaned me his room in a Tel Aviv suburb, a sort of windowless cage in which you could spend no more than a few hours without risking suffocation. But it was better than nothing. I went to see Joseph, my first employer, who now worked in the editorial offices of *Herut*. He offered me a temporary position until I could find something else. "But I don't plan to stay long," I told him. "Besides, I'm not a member of this political party." He smiled. "You expected to be writing editorials, maybe?" At least it would help me perfect my Hebrew. For three or four weeks I was half proofreader, half errand boy. Then one day I ran into a friend from Paris in the hallway, and he suggested I come with him to Beer-Yaakov, where there was a children's home. I jumped at the chance, and soon became a full-time counselor. I wondered what Niny would think if she saw me in her role.

The "children" were adolescents of Romanian and Bulgarian origin. I spent a few enjoyable and instructive weeks with them. There were campfires, of course, as at Fantana and Ambloy, and songs and tales. We studied Scripture and ancient Jewish history as well as modern European philosophy and literature. I was astonished at these young people's breadth of knowledge. The Romanians in the group were remarkable for their fervor. There were many evenings of music, lectures, and discussions in the orange groves. There were also some flirtations. As usual, they came to nought.

The autumn rains arrived, and I withdrew further and further into myself. A wave of depression courses through my notebooks. In Shushani's absence I made little headway in my study of asceticism. And once again I was at a crossroads, and once again I forced myself to draw a balance sheet. I was not yet ready to settle down in this, the country of my dreams, in which I felt not alien but useless and superfluous. I loved Israel with all my heart, and yet I felt it was time to go back to France. I needed friends. Nicolas was still in the army,

Israel Adler had resumed his studies in Paris. A little love affair would have been just the thing, but there was nothing on the horizon. Solitude weighed heavily upon me. I dreamed of love and yearned for Paris, where surprises happen every day. I missed the sidewalk cafés, strolling along the Seine, dropping in at little shops. But here it was again: How would I get by? What would I live on?

I had an idea. Why not become a "foreign correspondent" in France? I made the rounds of all the dailies: *Haaretz, Haboker, Maariv*. All had representatives in Paris, all except *Yedioth Ahronoth*, the smallest and poorest of Israel's daily papers. I set out in search of a recommendation and found someone who knew someone who knew the editor in chief. I telephoned, and was granted an interview.

Dr. Herzl Rosenblum, a signatory of Israel's Declaration of Independence, was a man of great political erudition. A funny man, eyes glinting with irony and intelligence, he treated me to a detailed history of this once rich and influential paper that had lost its fortune and its prestige in a stunning putsch.

One morning in 1948 the then editor in chief, Dr. Azriel Carlebach, left his post and launched his own evening paper, *Yedioth Maariv* (he changed only one word in the title), taking with him the whole editorial and administrative staffs. Most readers went with Carlebach. This left *Yedioth Ahronoth* in dire straits, but its owner,

Yehuda Mozes, was determined to keep it alive at whatever cost. In a matter of hours, he created a whole new editorial team. *Yedioth Ahronoth* appeared the next day, a bare two hours late. Unfortunately, Rosenblum explained, the paper lacked the resources to employ a correspondent in Paris. "If you went to Moscow it would be different," he said slyly. I couldn't imagine what he meant, since he could pay no more rubles in Moscow than francs in Paris. But this Lithuanian Jewish intellectual had a nostalgia for old Russia. Indeed, in his memoirs he misses no opportunity to evoke the glorious era of Kerensky, whose talents as an orator he admired. ("If only he had been a little more decisive in 1917, the world would be very different.") I listened with great interest, since I love stories and history. The bottom line was that he would be pleased to have me as a correspondent, but as for a salary . . . that was another matter. I would have to work as a freelance. So be it. As long as I had a press card, I would manage to get by.

I sailed back to Paris on the *Kedma,* older sister of the *Negba,* and this time I was violently seasick. I cursed the day I first dreamed of the sea, swore I would never again set foot on a boat. By the third day I felt better. I forgot my vows and stood on the deck, loving the soft and soothing song of the waves, letting my thoughts ride them to the end of the world and beyond.

I was not alone on deck. Once again — no surprise — there was a beautiful young girl who intrigued me. Neither Inge nor Hanna, she could easily have taken their place. I spoke to her of destiny, and of Dante for good measure. She told me not to be a fool. Nothing had changed. There was no point in even trying. Also on deck was another girl, probably Moroccan or Tunisian, surely Sephardic, with long dark hair, treating a crew member to a voluptuous kiss. Maybe I should join the Navy. Behind me a young woman, very blond, sobbed desperately, refusing to part from a boy she had probably just met. Other couples were engaged in similar exercises. I could hear their whispered promises. The next day I noticed with some glee that the blonde had acquired a new suitor. And what about me? For them I didn't exist. I didn't exist for anyone. I was the only passenger on board not to have had even the slightest flirtation. The less said about my self-esteem the better. I promised myself I would be more enterprising in Paris. I would be a new man. I owed it to myself.

I arrived in Paris on an overcast day in January 1950 and moved back into the Hôtel de France on the Rue de Rivoli. I paid a visit to my editor to give a lame explanation as to why I hadn't sent the series of articles on immigrants in Israel, and then hurried to see Hilda, Israel Adler, and Friedrich, all of whom congratulated me on my new status. When I showed Niny my press card, I was moved to see how proud she was. I caught a train to Versailles and, once again, returned disappointed. Hanna had treated me to a quick "You again?" and turned to talk to someone else. I never went back to Our Place again.

I had lost track of Shushani and François, but decided it would be a mistake to interrupt my studies on that account. I made a promise to myself: I vowed I would never spend less than an hour a day studying.

My first article was a portrait-interview of Emile Najar. The former lawyer and Egyptian Zionist activist, a minister-counselor to the Israeli embassy in Paris, a passionate talker and lover of political and literary anecdotes, took me on a grand tour of Franco-Israeli relations and the political and cultural situation in France. It was not a traditional interview — I was too shy to press my subject for personal revelations — but that didn't matter. The important thing was being able to quote him.

With images of Sartre and Hemingway dancing in my head, I plunged deeper into the ambiance of Paris, picking a table at a sidewalk café at which to work, perhaps to be accosted by an unknown woman who would ask me in which language I was writing and whether I was a novelist. "No," I would reply nonchalantly, "a journalist." But no one showed any interest in my efforts.

I read and reread the published version of

my article, "from our Paris correspondent." I showed it to Israel Adler, who marked the event by treating me to coffee and a kosher salami sandwich. This became a tradition. Every time I had an article published, he would buy me a sandwich, which meant he was paying me about as much as the paper was. He knew I was broke, but he was almost as broke as I was.

I expected a note of thanks from Najar for all the nice things I had said about him, but instead he called me to convey his displeasure. I had described him as middle-aged when he wasn't even forty. Terrified of losing a precious source of information, I began to stammer apologies, but he burst out laughing. He had a wonderful sense of humor, and as the years went by, this future ambassador to Tokyo, Rome, and Brussels, one of the most brilliant minds in the Ministry of Foreign Affairs, continued to be generous with his time and his counsel.

Money remained the problem. Once again, Shlomo Friedrich, my angel of mercy, managed to steer some free-lance translations and editorial work my way. As a favor to him, a Hebrew monthly that would soon become a quarterly before disappearing altogether asked me for an article on any cultural subject I chose, provided it was long. I chose to write about Beethoven. Yerahmiel Viernik, the magazine's editor in chief and sole staff member, stared at me as though I were mad. "Did I miss something here? Did

Beethoven speak Hebrew? He was Jewish, maybe? What am I supposed to do with a biographical text about a poor deaf composer who had nothing to do with Zionism? Yehuda Halevy, Bialik, Jabotinsky, Herzl, Nordau — you forgot about them?" But since he had nothing else at hand, he had to make do. I never loved Beethoven as much as I did that day. Without him I couldn't have paid the month's rent.

I worked in my hotel room, a sunless cubicle overlooking the courtyard. Fortunately, the rent was on a par with the amenities. More than once I wondered whether the hotel rented rooms by the hour. I kept running into new customers on the stairway.

My press card, issued by the office of the Président du Conseil, was my most precious possession. It should have been all I needed, but the French were enamored of cards. In the United States the only document one carries is a driver's license, but in France you are constantly called upon to prove your identity. Like all foreign correspondents, I had to obtain, in addition to the indispensable pass from the Préfecture de Police, a red card (for the theater), a blue card (for concerts), and a green card (for movies). These cards also gave me the right — this was France, after all — to bring along my legal spouse or lady friend of the moment. Most often I went alone.

Though he was a musician by training, Israel Adler had a passion for movies. And so it was

332

he who most often accompanied me to the cinema. We preferred the small neighborhood houses that showed "old" French or Italian films, in particular the masterpieces of Carné-Prévert-Kosma. *Les Enfants du paradis* and *Les Portes de la nuit* had a great impact on me. I saw them two and three times each.

My big problem was that *Yedioth Ahronoth* would publish only articles directly or indirectly related to Israel and/or the Jews, or at the very least to their enemies. This was the result not so much of indifference to the rest of the world as of lack of space, caused by a paper shortage. Newborn Israel, weakened by a merciless war, was racked by an unending economic crisis. For my newspaper, poorer and weaker than the country itself, the outside world existed only insofar as it was good or bad for the Jewish state.

But there was no lack of subjects for any self-respecting foreign correspondent. All you had to do was open your eyes, leaf through a magazine, attend a political demonstration, or read the obituaries. There was the beginning of the war in Indochina; the death of Léon Blum, who, like me, had been in Buchenwald; the death of André Gide. A succession of strikes and political scandals was erupting. Governments rose and fell at a pace no playwright would have dared attempt. The chasm between the Communists and their adversaries widened. The literati debated whether collaborationist writers whose works had been banned should be pardoned. François Mauriac pleaded for compassion, Louis Aragon for severity. Eventually, the National Committee of Writers was torn apart by tensions dating from the Occupation era. It was also the heyday of existentialism: Sartre, Camus, and Simone de Beauvoir, the Café de Flore and the cellars of Saint-Germain-des-Prés. Long live polemical literature and the philosophy of commitment! Later I wrote of this period in my novel *The Town Beyond the Wall.*

I was intrigued and stimulated by the intellectual and artistic ferment of Paris. Still working on my education, I was an insatiable patron of the library. Never have I read so much. I devoured the works of Malraux, Mauriac, Paul Valéry, Georges Bernanos, Ignazio Silone, and Roger Martin du Gard. I read everything by Camus (why did he submit to German censorship and agree to delete the chapter on Kafka from his *Myth of Sisyphus?*) and Sartre (couldn't he have waited until Liberation to have his *No Exit* performed?) and was fascinated by the break between them. I discovered de Beauvoir, Arthur Koestler, and William Faulkner; Cervantes and Miguel de Unamuno, and of course Kafka. I compared their questions to mine. Could one be holy outside religion? Was there a secular priesthood? Where did man's responsibility end and God's begin? Would existence be absurd without God? I needed to be guided, but François was nowhere to be found. Nor was

Shushani. I went back to my manuscript on asceticism determined to finish it, but doubt assailed me. What was so urgent about that theme?

Strangely, with the exception of the moving testimony of David Rousset and a few works by surviving resistance fighters (among them Robert Anthelme's *L'Espèce humaine*), there was practically no concentration camp literature. It was as if people were afraid or ashamed to broach the subject. Were they still too close to it, too busy reintegrating themselves into society, too busy remaking their lives? As elsewhere in Europe, many books appeared on the Occupation and the Resistance. That was the great theme. Plays, films, documentaries, essays, novels — the source seemed inexhaustible. The men and women who had valiantly confronted the occupier and driven him out were glorified. The heroism of the few obscured the cowardice of the many, concealing the suffering of the victims who had been so readily sacrificed by a defeated and passive France tainted by collaboration. It was more expedient to depict the courage of underground fighters than the humiliation and betrayal of the Jews who were persecuted not only by the Germans but also by the gendarmerie and the police. The letters of denunciation recovered from German archives were taboo. Likewise, references to the notorious site of the most extensive roundup of Jews, the Vel d'hiv, the camps Gurs and Drancy, and the deportation of Jewish children, which, though the Germans had not demanded it, was suggested by Pierre Laval.

Others would later denounce this complacency. But *Yedioth Ahronoth* wanted only articles on current events. How could I convince my employers to grant me some freedom of action? If only I could return to Israel. Come to think of it, why not? I was a journalist, was I not?

I went to see a man called Loinger, a former resistance fighter and OSE official and now director in France of Zim, the Israeli shipping company. I explained my problem: I had to get to Tel Aviv, but . . . Loinger understood immediately. "If it's for pleasure," he said, "there's nothing I can do. But if you're going to write . . . You're going to write, aren't you?" He winked at me. "No," I replied, "what I mean to do is —" He interrupted me. "A journalist can't help but write. If not immediately, then later, right?" Without waiting for my answer, he picked up the phone and issued instructions to his staff. I was to be given a round-trip ticket on the *Kedma* that very day. He showed me to the door and said, "You're a journalist, but you still don't know how to pull strings. Don't worry, you'll learn." Loinger was a nice man, but he was wrong. Some people never learn.

This crossing was very different from the last one. I had a comfortable cabin larger than my hotel room, a private shower, fruit and flowers on the table. But all the luxury was lost on me. Seasickness kept me in bed most of the time. I didn't even get up to see Mount Carmel.

When we disembarked in Haifa I caught a bus for Tel Aviv and arrived unannounced at the editorial offices in Re'hov Finn, near the teeming central station. The warmth of Dr. Rosenblum's welcome was worth more than a star reporter's monthly salary. He was happy with my articles, though he would have been happier had they come from Moscow or Tashkent. He introduced me to his colleagues, few in number at the time, and now I was part of the team, the youngest member. Everyone gave me advice, for they all knew the ropes better than I. Over coffee they let me in on their "secrets": who was on the way up, who was in trouble. One editor urged me to be careful. The enemy, he said, was everywhere. I thought he was talking about the Arabs, but it turned out he meant our rival. Everyone warned me. *Yedioth Ahronoth* had one and only one enemy, and that was the usurper, the traitor, *Maariv*. Our paper was so short of funds that people must have worked there for the honor and pleasure of it — or because they couldn't find anything better.

Devoted as he was to Russian ways, Dr. Rosenblum offered me tea instead of coffee, along with another masterly lecture on literature and politics. He invited me to his home. His apartment breathed culture. He informed me that "the Old Man," Yehuda Mozes, the paper's

337

owner, wanted to meet me, right away. Wondering if I had done something wrong, I hurried to Sderot Rothschild, climbed the steps, and rang the bell. The door opened and a woman silently showed me in. A man in a white goatee and a black kipa came toward me, his hand extended. I remember the clarity of his blue eyes. We sat down in the living room and looked at each other in silence for a long moment, I because I didn't dare open my mouth, he because he was weighing my character and temperament. Then he, too, began to tell me about "our" newspaper. He would have liked nothing better than to be able to pay me well, but unfortunately since the "coup" . . . On the other hand, there was more to life than money, wasn't there? What is money, after all? It is an illusion, nothing more. You make it, you lose it. Besides, as we all know, it corrupts. But enough of that, because in any case, between you and me, everything was about to change. "They" (the competition) would soon find out what we could do. He was convinced of that, and he wanted me to be convinced as well. Injustice cannot endure eternally. There is a God in heaven, and it is He who rules the world. God is just, God is good, God will set things straight. I wondered whether God was a banker. I preferred to think of Him as a philosopher.

The Old Man soon put me at ease. He asked about my life, my studies, my plans. He talked about his own past, in Kalisz (whose Jewish cemetery, it seems, is the oldest in Poland) and in Lodz. I wondered what, if anything, he knew about me or my story. Suddenly he asked me a question that stunned me: Did I believe in God? — an intrusive inquiry that would have pained me coming from anyone else. I blushed as I answered, and a bond was forged between us not professional, but personal and human. Then the Old Man changed the subject. We spoke of the Talmud, the Midrash, Hasidism. He cited a passage, which I timidly corrected. To demonstrate my error he rose, left the room, and returned with a volume. He opened it, glanced inside, closed it immediately — I was right. But he wasn't offended; on the contrary, he seemed pleased. To use an ancient Hebrew expression, "I had found grace in his eyes."

He insisted I stay at his home, which was a real help, since the hotel would have cost me three months of my wretched salary. I ate at his table and participated in the discussions after meals. While under his roof I formed a friendship with Dov, his nephew, also a camp survivor, and later with his son Noah. The Old Man took me to Jerusalem in a *sherut* (collective) taxi. On the way he told me of his childhood and youth and of his encounters with the poets Shneur and Bialik, the painters Soutine and Mane Katz, and one Mrs. Reid, former owner of the *New York Herald Tribune*. He shared with me his disappointments, joys, and aspirations, and I became a member of his family. The Old

Man set the tone. Everyone feared him except his wife, but to me he was unfailingly courteous. Later he would sometimes phone me in Paris, often on a Friday afternoon to wish me a peaceful Shabbat, to share a Hasidic saying, or simply to chat. There were times when I wished he would give me the money he spent on those calls, but money isn't everything, is it?

The Old Man encouraged my friendship with Dov, and to this day I wonder why. Perhaps he hoped it would make Dov more Jewish, more involved in Jewish life. At the time Dov was more interested in the latest issue of *Time* than in the Torah reading of the week. For a while Dov and I shared a room, and after his marriage to Leah they invited me to live with them. The Old Man magnanimously allowed me to accept their hospitality, or Noah and Paula's, but no one else's. When I happened to be in the country for the High Holidays, I had to go to services with him. I remember a Rosh Hashana in Jerusalem in his wife's absence. I recall the solemn service with the Hasidim of the Rebbe of Guer. The Old Man wept as he recited certain litanies, and I averted my eyes respectfully. During meals we discussed liturgy and repentance.

The Old Man, I now realize, was not all that old. Today I have the strange feeling that the whole world is younger than I.

Foreign correspondents move around a lot, and I loved to travel. I was always ready to accept an invitation to go anywhere, to change habits and time zones, to discover new lands, court adventure, and seek impromptu encounters.

By chance in Paris I met an official of the Jewish Agency who invited me to accompany him on an automobile trip to Morocco. I hurried to the Préfecture for an exit visa, then to the Spanish consulate for a transit visa. Luckily, I had enough photos on hand and quickly obtained the necessary papers. But what about money? I had one month's rent on my room saved up. I took the money, stuffed everything I owned into an old valise, and that was that.

There were three of us in the car. The first stop was Marseilles, where we stayed in the transit camp near Bandol. Things had changed since I had passed through the year before. Now it was Moroccans who were waiting to "ascend" to Israel. I questioned them about their abandoned homes and told them of the land of their dreams, of the joy of feeling Jewish and of living free of anti-Semitic threats, of the beauty of dusk in Jerusalem. Since I spoke fluent Hebrew, they thought I was Israeli and didn't ask why I had chosen to remain in the Diaspora. The camp director was so pleased with my little speeches that he insisted on paying me ten thousand francs (two hundred dollars). At first I refused, but I finally said thank you and put the money in my pocket.

We set out for the Spanish border. I was terrified of the police and customs officials who examined my stateless person's travel permit. Would they take me for a Communist agent, a veteran of the International Brigades? True, I could tell them I was only eight to ten years old during their filthy civil war, but did fascists know how to count? I pictured myself in a Spanish jail. I should have taken a different route, I thought to myself. But it was July, and they seemed to be in a state of lethargy. They let me pass without a problem.

Spain enchanted me — the landscape, the singing, the dancing, and especially the women, the Spanish women with their sensual lips and their dark, passionate eyes. Since childhood I had dreamed of this country where our greatest poets and philosophers had lived and sung, where the Inquisitors tortured and humiliated my people in the name of a bizarre love of God. I recalled reading their manual. They thought of themselves as God's protectors punishing the enemy.

Haunted by tales of the Marranos, I searched for their descendants. Any passerby I encountered on the *ramblas* of Barcelona could be one of them. Barcelona and its crowds, Barcelona and its ghosts. I was strolling down a deserted street when suddenly a young boy stood before me. Perhaps he had come from some neighboring hovel. He held out his hand, palm open, and said, very softly, "Señor, I'm hungry."

Instinctively I reached into my pocket for a

few pesetas to give him, but my hand refused to obey. The boy's words — and, more than that, his voice — paralyzed me. I froze, unable to take my eyes off the hand that seemed to accuse me of all the sins committed since the first man turned his back on his brother, not far from paradise.

"Señor," the boy repeated, "I'm hungry." I wanted to ask him his name, but didn't know how. Juanito, Alfonso, José? Once again I tried to give him what I had in my pocket, and once again my fingers refused to move.

The scene lasted but a few seconds. Time had stopped, all Creation concentrated in the motionless Spanish boy. Believing that I was refusing to help him, he dropped his hand and disappeared. Only then did I emerge from my trance, my heart pounding so loud it might have roused the slumbering city.

I began to call the boy, crying out for him to come back, telling him I wanted to give him what I had, that I wanted him to understand how much I hated societies in which children have to beg strangers for bread. But it was no use. Discouraged, he must have gone off to try his luck elsewhere.

I never saw him again. But no — he has a hundred faces and as many names, and he is always hungry.

Madrid: I wondered whether all those people in the streets found what they were looking for. They seemed to spend more time outside than at home or at work and to be suspicious of strangers. One definitely felt the dictatorship, but no one followed us, or at least that's what we believed. Later we learned we were mistaken. In a police state everyone is suspect, tourists most of all.

We visited the Prado. The madness depicted by Goya, so human and yet so grotesque, would long haunt me, as would the dignity in the portraits of Velázquez. We visited Arias Montana, an institute of Jewish studies. I wanted to read and reread all the documents and archives on Spain's Jewish past, but there wasn't time.

On Friday night I went to synagogue. A small minyan gathered in a cellar. I closed my eyes and imagined that I was back in the age of Ferdinand and Isabella, the days of Torquemada. The worshippers prayed in soft voices. I mingled with the congregation and listened to their remarks in Yiddish. Almost all were refugees. To my astonishment, they praised Franco. True, he was a fascist; true, he had strangled the republic; true, the Jewish religion was not recognized in this country, but . . . But what? During the war Franco had treated Jews honorably. A conscientious reporter, I conducted a minor inquiry, interviewing Spanish officials, foreign diplomats, and American and British colleagues. The evidence was clear: Unlike "humanist" Switzerland, Spain never rejected Jews fleeing persecution. The philosopher Walter Benjamin had been wrong to commit suicide:

The Spanish would not have handed him over to the Vichy police. In fact, Franco had instructed his legations in the countries occupied by Germany to issue Spanish passports to Sephardic Jews. "And yet," a high official of the Ministry of Foreign Affairs complained, "Israel refuses to establish diplomatic relations with us." For David Ben-Gurion, Spain was a fascist country, and that was enough to disqualify it. Later Israel would change its position, but then it was Spain that demanded concessions. Nevertheless, as I walked through the streets of the capital, I was annoyed at myself for feeling so content in this land. The memory of the victims should have affected me more.

We spent unforgettable hours in Toledo. A beautiful old synagogue had been turned into a church, but the Hebrew letters refused to disappear from the walls. (In 1992 and 1993 the banker and philanthropist Edmond Safra tried to buy the building back from the Church to restore it to the Jewish community.) The former residence of Shmuel Hanagid — where El Greco had also lived — had its own underground tunnel. If the priests broke in, the Jews could escape toward the sea.

Saragossa: city of the renowned mystic visionary Rabbi Abraham Abulafia, who in the late thirteenth century conceived the idea of hastening the ultimate redemption by converting all humanity to the Law of the Torah. It was a perfect idea and a fine solution, but where to begin? In Rome, of course, with Pope Nicholas III, no less. After that, things could only go smoothly. Sadly, the poor dreamer died before he could bring about redemption.

While visiting the immense cathedral, I was approached by a thin, middle-aged man with an angular face and deep-set, somber eyes. We conversed in French, which he managed with difficulty. He asked me where I was from and what I was doing in Saragossa. I told him I was a Jew living in Paris but that I worked for an Israeli newspaper. He was astonished. Do Jews still exist? Yes, they do. And Israel — that has something to do with the Bible, doesn't it? Yes, I said, but with history as well, including contemporary history. He listened to me intently, then invited me to his home to show me something he thought might interest me. I went with him, and when we got to his house he handed me a small, rolled parchment. It took me some time, but eventually I managed to decipher the Hebrew text: One Moshe ben Abraham called upon his descendants to remember their origins. I wanted to buy the document at any price, but the man refused to sell. And when I persisted, he became angry. This parchment, he explained, was an heirloom, handed down from father to son; it had never left his family. I was so overcome by emotion that when he began asking me questions, I couldn't answer. Then, standing with him at the window, I read and reread for him the contents of the testament, first in Hebrew, then in French.

Years later I met him again by chance in Jerusalem, where he was living modestly with his family. As I was leaving, he said to me with a smile, "By the way, I never told you my name. It is Moshe ben Abraham." Whenever I think of Saragossa, it is him I see.

We continued our travels, which became a pilgrimage to the sources of our collective memory. Every stop was marked by a discovery, an encounter.

In Algeciras we spent the night in a small hotel near the port. I couldn't sleep. My journey through this country, with its Jewish, Christian, and Muslim past, haunted me. I spoke of it in *Legends of Our Time*, though perhaps not enough.

We took a boat to Tangier. It was a stormy crossing, and I got the worst case of seasickness of my life. I told myself it was a punishment. I never should have left Saragossa.

I was dazzled by the subterranean nightlife of Tangier, a cosmopolitan city of countless entrepreneurs, from the most honest to the shadiest. My impressions and memories would later go into *The Town Beyond the Wall*. Tangier by night, the *soco chico* — thieves were so resourceful it was hard to get angry at them. They were just doing their job. There were kids offering you all the gold of the Orient for a few francs; fire-eaters; smugglers trying desperately to pick up easy money; adventurers eager for dangerous missions in lands that often existed only in their imagination. There were Arab storytellers entertaining ecstatic crowds, arousing emotion, admiration, for a few pennies. Tangier, for me, was Pedro, my friend, the man who to me embodies the ideal of friendship, as much madman as sage, as brave as he was philosophical, as sad as he was triumphant over all sadness. I created Pedro because I missed him. I still do.

We crossed Spanish Morocco at breakneck speed and, arriving in Casablanca, encountered a blinding but somehow soothing whiteness. There were mischievous little shoeshine boys, and blanket merchants who stared at us openly.

It was 1950 and I was too ignorant to notice the tensions dividing the various communities. Foolishly, I was convinced that everyone respected and liked everyone else. National and ethnic identity, the right of self-determination — these ideas were not yet current. What was current was much poverty.

My traveling companions had contacts within the Jewish community. A young man, in tattered clothes, offered to serve as my guide. His name was Ifergan. He knew rabbis, merchants, and Jewish activists. All doors were open to him. He couldn't understand why I wanted to be introduced to rabbinical masters. "Are you a journalist," he asked, "or a yeshiva student?" He wanted me to meet the notables of the community. The erudite old men I met were astonished when I asked them more about their traditions than about contemporary political issues. I accommodated them by asking about the contemporary value of tradition, and their answers, steeped in wisdom, were far more stimulating than any politician's pronouncements. A *dayan* (rabbinical judge) showed me some unknown mystical writings attributed to the sages of Fez. A rabbi told me little-known anecdotes about Maimonides's years in Morocco. Here, as in Spain, the Jewish past was pervasive.

The Jews in Morocco seemed attached to their soil and to their sovereign. I was surprised at their praise for the sultan, Mohammed V, but I should have known better. The sultan had protected his Jewish subjects during the war, standing up to Vichy and the Germans alike. Not a single Moroccan Jew was deported. Rich Jews maintained friendly relations with rich Muslims. And yet. Many Moroccan Jews planned to make aliyah, to "ascend" to the Holy Land, because the future was uncertain. Signs of dislocation were appearing in this energetic, exuberant community. My companion, the emissary of the Jewish Agency, predicted that few of its 250,000 souls would remain. But if things were so good in this beautiful land, why would the Jews want to confront the unknown? Ifergan's answer: "For a Jew Israel is never the unknown." I recalled the Jews of my city. How was it that the Moroccan Jews were more perspicacious and audacious than those of Sighet in 1940–44? And thanks to the World Jewish Congress, and the Jewish Agency, nearly the entire Moroccan Jewish community emigrated to Israel between 1952 and 1956.

I became attached to them — not surprisingly, since I love the Sephardim. As a child I pictured the Messiah with dark skin, a black beard, and dark eyes — in a word, a Sephardi. (May the Ashkenazis forgive me, and if the Messiah is an Ashkenazi, may He forgive me as well.) I also loved the familial, patriarchal spirit that governed their relations. On Friday night the synagogue was full. Children kissed their fathers' hands, and fathers, in turn, kissed *their* fathers' hands. Despite the differences in customs and languages, I pictured myself back home, far away.

On Saturday afternoon I attended the meetings of Zionist clubs, for songs, lectures, prayers. It was like being back in Versailles or Orsay. I taught them a few songs, and my friend from the Jewish Agency, declaring that he was pleased with my "influence" on the youth, handed me an envelope containing a modest sum that seemed princely to me: no more money worries for two or three weeks. Even better, there was a member of the choir who reminded me of Hanna, though they did not really look alike. This one, small and very dark, was a soprano, whereas Hanna was an alto. She was calm and sweet, not volcanic like Hanna. I was not surprised to find myself spinning dreams and talking to her — you guessed it — about Nietzsche and about nostalgia in the works of Yehuda Halevy. She seemed friendly and interested. One night we were alone in the street. Shyly, I took her hand. She expressed a desire to ride in a carriage. In love as never before, I gazed at the stars, witnesses to my happiness, imploring them to glitter in the dreams of this beautiful young woman. But when I escorted her home I didn't dare kiss her good night.

The next day the faithful Ifergan confessed that he had followed us, and he chided me: You are courting danger. I thought he was mad. What danger? "You held that girl's hand." So? "Here that means you intend to marry her." Marry her! "What are you going to tell her father or her brother if they show up at your hotel tomorrow?" Thanks to good old Ifergan, I may have escaped fleeting happiness and lasting misfortune.

A conscientious guide, he was constantly underfoot, awkward but accommodating. Little by little I was initiated into the real life of Casablanca, learning to distrust appearances and ready assertions. My reports became more balanced, more subtle and objective. I now understood better why so many of these Jews were ready to uproot themselves.

Back in France I received a telegram from Ifergan: "Your articles aroused considerable anger. I am now in the hospital, with a few broken ribs."

I felt responsible and wanted to do something for him, but I didn't know his address. I sent two or three letters "in care of the Jewish community," but they were returned marked "addressee unknown."

Twenty years later, in an article on repentance for the Rosh Hashana issue of *Yedioth Ahronoth*, I mentioned the unwitting wrong I had done to Ifergan so long ago. It was a sincere but humorous apology. Ifergan responded immediately: "Don't blame yourself. I was only doing my job when I followed you. I was working for the Mossad at the time, and they told me to keep an eye on you. The chance of having my ribs broken was part of the deal."

As for the young girl who liked carriage rides, I happened to run into her in New York, years later. Her husband and children were with her.

"How is your father?" I asked.

"My father?" she replied, surprised. "He's no longer alive."

"When did he die?"

"Oh, a long time ago. When I was five."

"And your brother?"

Her eyes widened. "Brother? I'm an only child."

Last night, after midnight, I saw my mother in a dream. She held me by the hand, and that seemed strange to me. I've grown up, I told myself, I'm a man, but for her I'm still a child.

We were walking slowly down a street, and I asked her where we were going. She seemed not to hear. Or perhaps she did, and preferred not to answer. Suddenly I realized we were alone. "Where is everyone?" I asked. "It's as though a storm has swept them away." My mother shook her head, though whether in approval or denial I didn't know. We continued our trek across the city. I recognized the houses, but something bothered me: Though plunged in darkness, the windows lit our way, as though a mysterious hand were lighting a candle in each one. "But they're Yahrzeit candles," I said to my mother. She nodded, as though telling me I was right, or that she had heard me. "But who died?" I asked. She did not reply, and I asked again, "Who died, Mother?" Suddenly she let go of my hand, and I was alone again, the sole extinguished candle among a thousand flickering flames.

Dov, the Old Man's nephew, was now in charge of all departments of the paper except the editorial page. He suggested I write a column entitled "Sparks from the City of Light." I accepted immediately, not only for purely material reasons — I would now draw a monthly salary of twenty-five thousand francs, modest enough, but better than before — but also because I would at last be able to break out of the "ghetto" to which my newspaper had previously confined me. Twice a week I recounted amusing anecdotes, gossip, and stories from the world of arts and letters. I attended openings, but not receptions. I was invited to various performances, but not to banquets. Neither *Yedioth Ahronoth* nor its correspondent was important enough for that. I was refused an interview with the winner of the Prix Goncourt but was granted one with a novelist who had just been awarded a less august literary prize. I had a brief exchange with Louis Jouvet, whom I went to see in his dressing room after a performance of a play by Molière. "Monsieur Jouvet," I asked, "what do you do when you're not being Louis Jouvet?" His reply: "I call him to show you the door, young man." I scoured the weeklies, looking for sensational reports. Dov was happy with the column, and so was I.

Mira Avrech, Israel's most famous gossip columnist, later told me a secret that pleased me: When she was hired by the paper to write a column on society and politics, the Old Man recommended that she read my "Sparks" for inspiration. And so I found out that I had at least one reader in Israel.

I had one in France as well. Dana, an Israeli woman of Romanian origin, worked with my friend Shlomo Friedrich. She had many suitors, whom she attracted and discarded with great frequency. Hers was a quick and stinging intelligence, and she had lots of charm. I didn't dare pursue her; it would have been hopeless. I was therefore content with her company. She had a bawdy sense of humor that would have made a regiment of soldiers blush. She had opinions on everything and hated being contradicted. I loved the fact that she enjoyed my articles and sometimes invited me to share her meals in a small restaurant near the Grands Boulevards. She was almost as broke as I was, but the "almost" made all the difference. She often acted as my banker, helping me make it to the next payday.

It was around that time that I saw Rachel Mintz again, the poet who had recited Yiddish verses for us in Écouis. She wanted to see me, and when I asked why, she told me it was "personal."

She lived not far away, near the Place de la République, in a small, well-appointed apartment filled with books and flowers. There was a samovar on the table. As I looked at her, the thought crossed my mind that she must once have been very beautiful.

"I've been reading your articles," she told me. "Some are good. You will be a writer. That's why I phoned you."

I waited to find out more about her intentions.

"I want to ask you a favor," she continued. "But you have to promise me you'll say yes."

A strange request, but what did I have to lose? I replied with a phrase from the Book of Esther: "Ask for half my kingdom and it shall be yours."

"This favor is rather more modest," she said

with a smile. "All I want is for you to listen to me, then write, and then publish. But not until after my death."

My mind raced ahead while she stared at me calmly, waiting for my answer.

"Madame Mintz," I said, "I promise you the second half of the kingdom."

"Good," she said. "Then listen . . ."

She began to tell me of her love affair with Nikos Kazantzakis in Berlin after the First World War, how they had met in an archaeological museum filled with Egyptian statues. "Nikos was convinced I was a reincarnation of Nefertiti," Rachel said. "He thought I looked like her."

It was she who introduced him to the Jewish tradition, teaching him to fast on Yom Kippur, persuading him to go to Palestine and to learn the sacred tongue. The hero of his novel about Africa is called Toda Raba ("thank you very much" in Hebrew). The widow in *Zorba the Greek* is partly based on Rachel. In fact, she figures in each of his novels.

She let me read the letters the Greek writer had sent her in the twenties. They were love letters of stirring beauty. Though their liaison lasted just a few years, it seems their passion never died.

From that day, I plunged into Kazantzakis's work and read it all, in one vast gulp. The great writer carried me into an enchanted universe in which man pursues with equal stubbornness his battle with himself and with God.

I spent a week listening to Rachel and then we parted. But our relations had changed. She became too touchy, too demanding. In her frequent letters she complained that I didn't write often enough.

Years later I was on the French Riviera, covering the Cannes Film Festival. I decided to visit Kazantzakis. I obtained his address in Antibes and soon was knocking on his door. He answered in person and asked me what I wanted. When I said, "Nothing," he closed the door in my face. A moment later he opened it again and said, "Come in." He led me to a sofa, sat down next to me, stared at me intently, and asked, "Who are you?" I told him I was a journalist. "What do you want to know?" "Nothing," I replied. "I just wanted to meet you." He leaned toward me until our foreheads almost touched, and then he said, very softly, "You know her, huh?"

They had not seen each other in twenty-five years.

There was talk in Israel about the upcoming negotiations with the Konrad Adenauer government, and Dov asked me whether I would be ready to go to Germany. I wasn't, but I said yes anyway.

After visiting Bonn, I spent a day in Dachau alone. I was troubled and depressed, for the Jewishness of the victims was barely mentioned.

In Hitler's day Jewish life had been in danger. Now it was Jewish memory that was at risk.

It was around that time that an unexpected source of income opened up for me: simultaneous translation. Molière was right: Sometimes you have talents you don't know you have. I was completely unaware of the craft that would now supply me with desperately needed funds.

The telephone had rung. A man with a pleasant voice and a slight drawl — "My name is Teddy Pilley and I am in need of your services" — asked me whether I would be interested in a position as an interpreter at the upcoming conference of the World Jewish Congress in Geneva. "Let me add that it's well paid," said the voice. "Two hundred dollars a day." I thought I was hearing things. Two hundred dollars a day! At the time I was making fifty dollars a month. I'd be a millionaire. Teddy Pilley listened to my silence and then said, "But of course that doesn't include the per diem." I was speechless. What was a per diem? When I still hadn't said anything, Pilley went on, "Come to the Congress offices tomorrow morning at eleven. You know the address? On the Champs-Élysées. We'll talk. Are you interested?"

Was I interested! My only problem was I wasn't sure I could do it. I had never done any "simultaneous" interpreting, didn't even know what it was. I had never been to an international conference either. Why had they picked me? Well, I had nothing to lose. But the next morning I panicked. There were six candidates, and they apparently meant to test us one at a time. Well, I don't like tests, and I said so to the pleasant man who greeted us as we arrived. "Don't look at it that way," he said. "Think of it as a game. We're going to have some fun, that's all." I wanted to protest, but he quickly led me to a room where two booths had been set up, and a moment later I found myself sitting in front of a microphone wearing huge earphones. "I'm going to read something in French," Pilley told me, "and you translate into Yiddish. A word of advice: Don't think about the words too much. Let yourself be carried by the rhythm of my voice. It's easy, you'll see." He began to read a political article from a morning paper. I felt trapped, but somehow Pilley's voice forced my own out of my throat, and then I don't know what came over me. I departed from the text, making things up, saying whatever came to mind. I expected my examiner to lose his temper, but it turned out Pilley didn't know Yiddish. All he wanted was to hear me speak. I decided to make him happy. When he stopped, so did I. Next he read a speech by Nahum Goldmann, president of the World Jewish Congress. Once again I took flight, especially since I had met Goldmann and was familiar with the subject. After about ten minutes Pilley took his earphones off, and I followed suit. "I have made my decision," he said, smiling. "You will be part of the team. But to appear fair, I must test all the candidates." I must have shown my worry, for Pilley reassured me: "I don't know them, but I doubt they're better qualified than you. I'll get back to you this afternoon."

He kept his word and we had dinner together that very evening. "Call me Teddy," he said. We liked each other. He made an interpreter's life sound very fine indeed: well-paid trips, a good salary, exciting meetings with world figures. He said it was better than journalism. I protested. I loved my trade and would not let him disparage it. We had a lively discussion, arguments for and against. Teddy was a brilliant, funny man, a born raconteur. He told me of his life as a young Jew in Poland. He remembered Lvov with nostalgia, and seemed to have a great need to speak of his father, who had been an important lawyer there. He had had many protégés, among them a classmate of Teddy's two years his junior for whom he bought books and clothing and for whom he paid tuition, with a generosity Teddy believed to be motivated by the friendship between the two adolescents. Years later he learned the real reason: The boy was his half-brother. They met again in Lvov after the war. "I'll never forget how much I owe your father," his friend said. And Teddy had corrected him gently: "You mean our father."

Then it was my turn to talk, of Kalman the

360

Elie, age 15, not long before the deportations.

Elie with his mother and his sister Tziporah, shortly before the Nazis entered Sighet.

Elie Wiesel's childhood home in Sighet, Romania, as it looked in 1965.

Elie with his friends Dov and Lea Judkowski in Florence, 1953.

Sharing some light moments with friend Teddy Pilley (with bow tie) and other interpreters, Geneva, 1953.

With four Israeli Prime Ministers *(counterclockwise)*: David Ben-Gurion, Levi Eshkol, Golda Meir, and Yitzhak Rabin.

On the boat taking him to Israel for the
first time, 1949.

At the Western Wall in Jerusalem with Dov, immediately after the Old City was recaptured in the Six-Day War.

At a rally for Soviet Jews in New York, 1968.

Kabalist, Shushani, Pedro. Of all my characters, it was Pedro he found the most fascinating. I was delighted to have met Teddy; we had much to talk about, many things to share. He asked me how well I knew Geneva. When I told him I had never been there, he described its tranquil mood, its serenity.

Finally, we talked about the job. Teddy filled me in on practical details and offered useful advice. When he gave me a letter confirming our agreement, I felt rich. This would pay the rent for months. I was still uneasy about whether I would be up to the task, but Teddy reassured me. "Don't worry, most of the speeches will be in Yiddish, so you'll have less work than the others." At that point I confessed the trick I had played on him that morning. He burst out laughing. "I love it! What a lesson. That ought to teach me." I promised not to do it again.

The conference opened two weeks later. I arrived by train, traveling first-class, in princely style. The eight interpreters (English, French, Hebrew, and Yiddish) were housed in a luxury hotel, along with our chief, who invited us to organize our work over coffee. "I have confidence in you," he said. "Just make sure you don't translate the opposite of what the speaker says. For the rest, we can always work it out."

We worked it out by splitting up into four teams of two for each language, but so many of the speeches were given in Yiddish that my teammate and I had little to do. We therefore tried to help out the French team. That was when something happened that cost me quite a bit of money and caused considerable dissension.

It happened two days before the close of the conference, at a closed-door session of the executive committee. I was translating President Nahum Goldmann's speech into French. He was reporting to the delegates on his negotiations with West German chancellor Konrad Adenauer about the reparations and indemnities the Bonn government was to pay Israel and the survivors of Nazi persecution.

Here I must explain that while Goldmann had a reputation as a good speaker, as head of the World Jewish Congress (which he had founded in the thirties with the American rabbi Stephen Wise to combat the Nazi peril in Europe), he was known to solicit the views of others only rarely, preferring to impose his own. Though he encouraged discussion, he would not tolerate being contradicted. He considered himself the person most qualified to manage the complex affairs of the Jewish people. He claimed not only to be on a first-name basis with all of the world's leaders, but to be singularly adept at interpreting their intentions.

On that particular day the session was stormy. Some European and Israeli delegates feared the negotiations would result in the practice of "forgive and forget." Tempers flared. I had never seen such a disorderly, tumultuous debate. Everyone was talking at once, and we interpreters were swamped, unable to decide whom to translate. I passed a note to Teddy, who sat in the next booth. He passed a note back to me: "Translate Dr. Goldmann, he's paying the bills." So I concentrated on the president as he pressed his case like a general facing mutinous troops; but hardly anyone was listening, and those who were, shouted their disagreement. Goldmann hurled slogans and reprimands, but to no avail. I vaguely heard him say to a former Latvian minister, Rabbi Mordechai Nourok, a bearded old man with a prophet's face: "This is not a matter of sentiment; the point is to save the economy — and therefore the existence — of the Jewish state." The rabbi tried to answer, but Goldmann cut him off: "That's why I wanted this to be a closed-door session. If the West German government found out the tenor of what you're saying here, they might take it badly." To which Rabbi Nourok, with a strained voice, responded, "And you're more concerned about German sensibilities than about our brothers'?"

The discussion grew more and more violent. Would there be a commemoration of German crimes or not? In the end Rabbi Nourok asked: "We won't even say Kaddish?" Goldmann's response: "Which will profit Israel more, the Kaddish or German financial compensation?"

When the session ended, I asked my colleagues

whether I had heard Goldmann right. Was he really against saying Kaddish for the victims? I needed confirmation, because when you are translating so fast, it is not easy to retain what is said. My colleague in the booth reassured me. I had heard right.

Now I had a big problem: As an interpreter I was sworn to secrecy; but as a journalist did I have the right not to report to the Israeli and Jewish public the outrageous words I had just heard? I asked Teddy for advice. He too was troubled. He could not fathom Goldmann's position, but thought he must have had his reasons, reasons of state perhaps. "In any case," Teddy said, "I wouldn't blame you if you decided to report this in your newspaper. But you would have to resign from the team first."

I panicked. Was I ready to give up two hundred dollars a day, not to mention the per diem, be poor again, go back to sleepless nights? It seemed too heavy a sacrifice. There were, on the one hand, food, the rent, the laundry, the métro, the shoemaker; on the other, the duty of informing my readers and, most of all, fidelity to memory. "So, what do you say?" Teddy asked. "What are you going to do?" Feeling myself go pale, I finally murmured, "I have no choice. I resign."

Teddy's face lost its habitual smile. He put his hand on my shoulder and said, "You know, I'm proud of you," as though I had performed some heroic deed. But there was nothing heroic about it. A few hundred dollars just wasn't worth it. My new friend continued to tell me how rare idealism was these days, but I listened with half an ear. Delegates were coming and going around us. The session was soon to reconvene — but without me.

I went to the telecommunications center and feverishly drafted a brief, indignant cable. It was a scoop, and naturally it made the front page, touching off a storm in both Israel and Geneva. Goldmann had to call a press conference, where Jewish journalists assailed him with questions. Was it true that he was opposed to saying Kaddish at the solemn closing session, that he now preached forgive and forget, that he had betrayed Jewish honor for pecuniary reasons, to please the Germans? Was it worthy of a Jewish leader to act this way? Goldmann, trying to maintain his calm, said he didn't understand. How could anyone suspect him, a Jew of Galician origin, a friend and collaborator of Rabbi Stephen Wise, of wanting to forget the victims of Nazism or of sacrificing memory to a rapprochement with German leaders? The question of the Kaddish had never even come up in the Executive Committee. What about the story in *Yedioth Ahronoth*? It was utter fantasy, he said. There was not a word of truth in it, on his honor. Moreover, it had been a closed-door session, and all the participants had sworn they had not breathed a word to the press. In other words, the *Yedioth Ahronoth* correspondent had made the whole thing up. Goldmann, of course, didn't realize I had been present. I could have, should have, stood up and set the record straight. But I was afraid to harm Teddy, who might have been reprimanded for having hired a journalist. And also I felt incapable of speaking in public. I left the press conference sick with shame.

I went back to the hotel and called Dov, who tried to console me. He suggested I go see Rabbi Nourok and ask him to testify, which I did. "Listen," I said. "Dr. Goldmann is calling me a liar. My professional future is at stake. You were there. Tell them I wasn't lying." The rabbi gave me a fully satisfactory statement. But of course it got far less coverage than Goldmann's denial.

Over the years Goldmann and I came to know one another well. Though I criticized him often — sometimes perhaps unfairly — he never held a grudge, and I learned to appreciate his true worth. He had the courage to shock. The ambiguity of his relations with Israel was such that he once allowed himself to express doubts about its very survival: "Perhaps Israel will turn out to be but an episode in Jewish history." Ben-Gurion didn't like him (calling him a Jewish Gypsy), and Golda Meir wasn't too fond of him either, as she was suspicious of his overtures to the Soviets and the Arabs. He was an agitator ready to challenge received ideas and principles. And while he was not a good listener, he was a great speaker, able to place events in a historical context in a way that both exasperated and fascinated me. We often talked about the dark years of the war. I asked him why the American Jewish lobby hadn't done more, acted more decisively to save European Judaism? At first he tried to convince me they hadn't known what was happening in the countries occupied by the Nazis. Then he admitted that they had known and had remained silent. He claimed extenuating circumstances: Up until 1941 the American Jewish community itself feared anti-Semitism; it would have been dangerous to oppose Roosevelt; the Jews didn't have the power they came to possess — or were believed to possess — in later years; and finally, Roosevelt had a gift for convincing Jewish visitors that he was the best advocate for and protector of their people.

One evening, as we dined at his favorite restaurant in New York, I recalled the incident in Geneva. "How could you lie like that?" I asked. "What did you think a young journalist like me would think of you?" He laughed. "First of all, I didn't know you were in the room, so I thought I could say whatever I wanted with impunity. Second, the difference between us is that I'm a politician and you're not." He then gave me a piece of advice: "Write your novels, tell your Hasidic tales, but don't ever get involved in politics. It's not for you." At another dinner, as if forgetting his own advice, he suggested that I succeed him as president of the Memorial Foundation and the Claims Conference, both financed by the Germans. I refused. (But I remained close to the World Jewish Congress, especially after Edgar Bronfman, seconded by his aides Israel Singer and Elan Steinberg, assumed the presidency.)

My friendship with Teddy Pilley deepened after Geneva. He worried about me, and whenever I found myself in pressing financial need, he would come up with some international conference where I could exercise my talents as an interpreter.

In the spring of 1960 I visited him in London. The telephone rang, he answered, and I heard him say in French, "What's the date? Okay, I think I have someone for you. Wait a minute, let me check." He turned to me. "What are you doing next week?" I told him I had no plans. "Can you get away for some urgent, well-paid work?" Of course. "He says it's all right," he told his caller. "Come over tomorrow, and I'll introduce you." He hung up and told me, "That was Prince Andronikov, De Gaulle's personal interpreter, a wonderful man. . . . His problem is that Ben-Gurion is coming to Paris on an official visit next week with his own interpreter, and De Gaulle hasn't one. The General thinks it's a question of national prestige." Andronikov had called on my friend to find a Hebrew interpreter. I agreed, of course. To be De Gaulle's interpreter, to be present at his talks with Ben-Gurion, was an honor, a privilege. "Promise me you won't pull another Geneva," Teddy added. I promised.

The next day we had dinner with the prince. Teddy was right: He was quite a man, cultivated and well informed, capable and efficient, a master of his craft. He explained in detail how the summit would be organized. He, too, insisted on confidentiality, and I gave him my word. It was a full evening, and I was too excited to sleep. I pictured my encounter with the Israeli prime minister, and suddenly I froze. I realized I would have to back out of the project.

I had covered Ben-Gurion's most recent visit to Washington, and he and I had played a kind of private game. I had a friend in his entourage who informed me of his whereabouts, and wherever he went, I would be there waiting for him: the White House, Vice President Nixon's home, the Senate, the House of Representatives. And every time he saw me, Ben-Gurion would exclaim, "What, you again?" I was terrified at what would happen if he saw me standing alongside the General at the Élysée Palace, and I decided I couldn't do it to him. Especially since, in a way, I would be part of the opposite camp.

Despite the late hour, I called Teddy and told him of my decision. He tried to reason with me. "All you have to do is inform Ben-Gurion in advance. I'm sure he'll agree." I stood my ground and finally came up with a decisive argument. "Teddy," I said, "I may not be able to resist temptation. It would be a fantastic scoop and I wouldn't want to embarrass you or your friend the prince." There was a long silence. "Idiot," Teddy finally said in his warm drawl. "This is going to cost you a lot of money and a historic opportunity to see two great men at work." He sighed. "What you say is foolish, but once again I'm proud of you." Professor Samuel Sirat, a future grand rabbi of France, acted as De Gaulle's interpreter.

With hindsight I regret this decision. But perhaps I just wasn't sure of myself. Perhaps I feared I would be unequal to the task.

I had similar worries when Maurice Carr, correspondent for the *Jewish Chronicle* of London, asked me to replace him for a few months. I was dying to accept: not only was the Anglo-Jewish weekly prestigious, it paid its correspondents well and reimbursed them for their expenses. But what about the language barrier? My English was inadequate. "Don't worry," the editor in chief declared. "You can send us your articles in Yiddish." I finally accepted and was very unhappy when Carr returned.

The first official negotiations between West Germany and Israel opened in early 1952 at the Vassenaar Château in the Netherlands. My paper was eager for me to cover the event. Dov knew I was personally as well as professionally interested in these negotiations, and he made what he considered a generous offer: The paper would pay my travel costs. Visa formalities were settled in twenty-four hours. I was beginning to feel like a real reporter.

Only four journalists were accredited to both delegations: Sam Jaffe of the Jewish Telegraphic Agency; Marcel Rosen, editor of the official organ of the Jewish community of Düsseldorf; Alfred Wolfmann of Berlin Radio; and myself, the only correspondent working for an Israeli daily. The Dutch authorities advised us that for security reasons we, like the delegates, would remain virtually sequestered throughout what promised to be a highly dramatic conference. Despite the political and economic issues at stake, the event was of greatest import for its historic significance. For the first time, German and Jewish officials would confront the consequences of a common past marked by the former's legalized brutality and the latter's acknowledged suffering.

The Israeli public followed the negotiations closely, and was divided by the ethical questions they posed. Passions were aroused, as though a religious war had erupted. Should money from the Germans be accepted? Ben-Gurion and Goldmann said yes; Begin shouted no. Ben-Gurion quoted the Prophet Elijah: "Thou hast killed, shalt thou also inherit?" — meaning the victim's possessions. Begin affirmed that Jewish blood was not for sale and that the Jewish dead were not bargaining chips. Survivors, even the leftists of Mapai and Mapam, were generally against. There were daily demonstrations and petitions. Debates raged in every community, every kibbutz, every family, arousing antagonism and scorn.

I personally was against. To take this money — the sum of a billion dollars had been mentioned — would be the first step toward a normalization I considered premature, for it would surely lead to economic and political collaboration between the two peoples. And I believed that both would inevitably lead to a betrayal of the memory of the dead.

When Israeli delegates asked me whether I would prefer that stolen treasures remain in German hands, I replied: Why not let the government of the United States serve as intermediary? Let Bonn consign the sums in question to the Americans, who could pass them on to the state of Israel. But even so, surely, the Germans would never give back everything they took from us.

(The Israelis now say that without German reparations there would have been no heavy industry in their country. Possibly not. But many of those projects nourished with German money went bankrupt. The luxury liners of the Zim shipping company, for example, were all sold.)

Passionate discussions filled our hours of waiting in the corridors of Vassenaar, as the delegates dealt with technical aspects of the accord. Marcel Rosen was for, Sam Jaffe was in the middle. Alfred Wolfmann participated in the discussion only in my absence. That was because at our first encounter he had insisted on introducing himself to me "honestly," as he put it, as a former Wehrmacht officer who had served in occupied France and very briefly in Russia. He had never been a Nazi, but described himself as a loyal citizen of the former Reich and the present Bundesrepublik. He said he wanted things to be clear. "Very well," I told him, "let them be clear. You will of course understand that under these circumstances there can be no relations between us. Of course, if I knew for certain that you committed no crime against my people . . . But since I don't, it's better for us to keep our distance." I never spoke a word to him after that. The Israeli officials also treated him with a distrust he grudgingly accepted. "Look at the Germans," he said to Sam. "Look how friendly they are with you Jews. . . ."

There was solemnity and drama in the opening session. The two delegations, equally grave, stood facing each other without shaking hands. The symbolism was inevitable. Yet Professor Franz Boehm, who headed the German mission, was a democrat above all suspicion. It was thanks to him that relations between the two sides grew more relaxed, becoming first cordial and later even amicable.

But between Wolfmann and myself, the situation was unpleasant. I could not bring myself to treat him as a colleague. I could not fraternize with an officer who had pledged loyalty to Hitler. Still, I would sometimes steal a glance at him. He was a wonderful craftsman, his analyses were clever, and usually accurate. He and Sam became buddies, to the point that one day I heard them arguing about something that had nothing to do with politics: Was Hebrew a difficult language to learn? Sam claimed it was. Alfred arrogantly insisted it was no more difficult than any other. In fact, he was prepared to bet a hundred florins that he could master Hebrew within a few months. Sam turned to me. "Did you hear that?" I advised him to take the bet. Alfred asked me if I too would like to bet. I pretended I hadn't heard him.

"How much is a life worth?"

"I have no idea."

"Think about it, please."

"I can't."

"Try. You have to admit it's an important question. The Germans are ready to pay for murdered Jewish lives, so we have to draw up some kind of price list, don't we? For instance, does a child's life go for as much as an old man's? Do a university professor and a beggar fetch the same price? I mean, you can't just toss all these Jewish lives in the same bag, can you? We're businessmen here, aren't we? So let's do business."

"Shut up."

"Why, am I being unreasonable? Illogical?"

"Shut up. For the love of heaven, shut up."

374

Both sides considered the conference a success. When it ended, our little group broke up. Alfred held out his hand, but I turned away. He frowned. "I thought the war between our peoples was over." I didn't reply. Sam took a plane for Paris, Rosen for Germany. I went home by train, stopping in Antwerp, where I wanted to see my cousins, the Feigs and the Dicks. I checked into a modest hotel on Pelikaans Straat, filed my last dispatch, and went to bed. Early the next morning someone knocked on my door. When I opened it, there stood Wolfmann. I asked what he wanted. He said hello and made a move to come in, but I stopped him. "Go away," I said. "I don't want to see you. Not here, not anywhere." He smiled, then shrugged and left. I went back to bed, but could not fall asleep.

A few weeks later he showed up at my lodgings in Paris. I was about to throw him out when he started talking — in Hebrew. It was surreal, a nightmare. "I win," he said calmly. Taking advantage of my surprise, he came into the room and sat down in a chair near the unmade bed. Certain that he had practiced a few phrases just to impress me, I asked him to say something else. He did so without the slightest hesitation. The former Wehrmacht officer spoke fluent Hebrew. I waited for what might come next. Was he going to try to convince me he had learned Hebrew since our meeting in Vassenaar? He let me wait a long moment, then said, slowly and deliberately, still in Hebrew: "I lied to you. I was never a Wehrmacht officer. I'm a Jew." I wanted to grab him and shake him. Was he telling the truth in Vassenaar or in Paris? "I'm a Jew," he repeated.

He was a strange character and his story was anything but ordinary: childhood in Germany; emigration to Palestine, where he joined the Communist Party; return to East Germany, where he became a high party official; ideological disenchantment; flight to the West, where he was now a (anti-Communist) journalist.

But why the lie, why the game? His answer seemed insane: "Two reasons. First of all, for revenge. All you smart-ass Jews from Poland or Russia think you're so superior. In Palestine they made fun of me because I was a Yekke, a German Jew. I was treated like a well-bred imbecile who would believe anything. So I wanted to show all of you that I could fool you." And the other reason? "To show you it's wrong to judge others too hastily. An hour ago you found me contemptible because I was German. Now you like me because I tell you I'm a Jew."

I looked at him and burst out laughing. He had invented that entire ridiculous, childish story, erecting a barrier between us, for "vengeance" and to win a kind of oratorical joust.

"Look," I told him, "let's call Sam. He's probably at the office by now." He was. "You owe

376

me a hundred florins," Alfred said to him in Hebrew. Now it was Sam's turn to laugh. "I don't believe it," he kept saying over and over.

Alfred and I spent the day together. I liked him, but found him disconcerting. How could a Jew leave Palestine for Germany? "You forget I was a Communist," he said. "The whole world was my country." "Even Germany?" "Even Communist Germany." But why did he stay in Germany now? "Because I'm waging a battle I consider just — a battle against Communism and anti-Semitism." Why couldn't he wage that battle elsewhere? "It wouldn't be the same."

The truth is I didn't understand him. I found it disturbing that Jews (many of them survivors) still lived in Germany. He told me I would understand someday.

After a silence he went on. "I was miserable and unhappy in Palestine." Because he was a German Jew? "Because I was a Communist. I was a member of the most extreme faction, more Stalinist than Stalin. Close to the Arabs. People didn't like it, and they made me pay. I couldn't find a job. I was humiliated, treated like a traitor, dragged through the mud like a pariah."

I introduced him to colleagues. We went to a press conference at the Israeli embassy together and had lunch with Sam Jaffe. It occurred to me that *Yedioth* had no correspondent in West Germany. I asked him if he would be interested. He said yes. I promised to discuss it with Dov, who agreed, but added, "Tell him the paper is not as rich as it used to be," a tune I knew by heart. Alfred was delighted. He requested and obtained Israeli citizenship. He seemed at peace with himself. But then, as the years passed and he fought the Nazi resurgence in his country, his fear began to grow and he fell ill. In the throes of paranoia, he thought he had to be constantly armed. He saw Nazis everywhere, in the street, in front of his house. We talked often on the phone, and I tried to calm him down, to bolster his morale. I asked about his wife and daughter, whom I had met. Dov invited him to come and rest with his family in Israel. He went, but soon left again. Dov suggested he settle down in Israel, but he refused. He was afraid to leave Germany and afraid to live there. I called him from Tel Aviv to try to convince him, but he had become a prisoner of his fear. When I asked him what he was afraid of, he seemed incredulous. "You of all people ask me that? Don't you know they're here? They want to kill me, they want to kill all the Jews. Don't tell me you don't know it. It's starting all over again. But this time I'll be ready. This time I'm armed."

The next day he put a bullet in his head.

Alfred and I had talked often about the question of forgiveness. Should — could — the Jews forgive their former enemies? Years later I was asked the question directly after a speech to German students: "Do you forgive us?" I replied that Ivan Karamazov was right: I could conceivably forgive the evil the Germans did to me personally, as an individual, but not the suffering and death they inflicted on my parents, on all the dead Jewish parents and all their murdered children. No one could grant forgiveness in their name. It must be noted that in any case, the German people never asked it of us.

I was now working full-time. Israel was increasingly in the news. Israeli government officials visited Paris, and so did actors, colleagues, and members of the Knesset. They kept me busy. The Israeli economy was improving, and so was the paper's position. I was writing more articles, on more varied subjects: the funeral of André Gide, the death of Charles Maurras, the work of Gérard de Nerval.

And then — don't laugh — there was Miss Israel, who filled my evenings and my daylight hours, in the apparent belief that my time belonged to her as much as I did. I guess I should explain. The Miss Israel contests were organized by La'isha, Yedioth Ahronoth's women's weekly. The lucky winner was awarded not only a crown but also a trip to Paris, where she needed a guide, if not a chaperon. Naturally, the task fell to me.

It must be said that I had some limited experience in the field. A few weeks before Miss Israel was elected, the Old Man asked me to interview Miss Europe. I remember her well:

dark, thin, and beautiful the way some Spanish women are beautiful. She graciously received me in her apartment near the Champs-Élysées. Sitting with me, hands poised delicately on her knees, she was delighted to answer my questions. Unfortunately, I didn't have any. I had no idea how to interview a beauty queen. What was I supposed to ask her? Her views on German disarmament, her favorite authors, what she thought of the winner of the Prix Goncourt? I fidgeted, and she waited, serenely at first and then with mounting impatience. I was so confused I couldn't see straight, and in the end I opted for frankness. "Mademoiselle," I stammered, "I don't know what I'm supposed to ask you. Could you give me a little help?" She burst into applause, as though she had just heard the best joke of her life. "You really don't know? Well, that's the first time this has ever happened. Okay, take this down. . . ." She proceeded to tell me about her diet and exercises. Then she cited some figures. I asked if it was a phone number, and that produced a fresh burst of laughter. "You claim to be a journalist? And in Paris?" It wasn't my fault. How was I supposed to recognize her measurements? I wrote it all down like a student and, sweat running down my face, pieced together an article I hoped no one would read, or whose byline, at least, no one would notice.

Fortunately, I would not have this problem with Miss Israel; I wasn't supposed to write anything about her. But she did cause trouble of another kind. The paper had forgotten to send me the money required to show a young Jewish beauty queen the hospitality due to one of her exalted status. I had to borrow left and right, for, unfortunately, this queen was cultured and intelligent. She wanted to see the real Paris, not just the Eiffel Tower and the Folies-Bergère. She wanted to go to the theater, to concerts, and so on. My various press cards came in handy. I must also admit that I rather enjoyed the envious glances; it wasn't so bad being the attentive escort of Israel's most beautiful woman, especially since Miriam (that was her name) had plenty of character and spirit. She asked many questions about Paris, which I was delighted to answer, improvising with an aplomb that I am ashamed of today.

Perhaps this is the moment to make a confession. In those days I often made up stories about Paris, descriptions you won't find in any guidebook. The problem was that too many Israeli visitors insisted I show them the Louvre and the Place de la Concorde, Montmartre and the Russian cabarets. At first I was a conscientious guide, telling only what I knew, but then I realized that my tourists were disappointed. They wanted more interesting stories. The façade of Notre-Dame, with its Jews in pointed hats, was not enough for them. Nor was the Palais de Justice, where, in 1240, by order of King Louis IX, the first disputation on Judaism between Rabbi Yehiel and the convert Nicholas Donin was held.

Did my visitors know that the king and queen attended the event and that it was Donin who persuaded Pope Gregory IX and King Louis IX to order the Talmud burned? "We learned all that in school," they said. "We want to hear about other things." So I began inventing anecdotes for every statue, stories for every square, memories for every monument. I didn't see how rearranging the capital's past for an hour or a morning could do France any harm. Until one day the inevitable happened. I was at the Place de la Bastille addressing a small group of French speakers who listened raptly to my description of the Revolution. I was in top form. I even gave them the names of the officer who first threw open the prison gates and the prisoner who fell to his knees to beg for mercy. In the next cell a princess awaited death. She was ready to die, but changed her mind at the sight of the officer. Suddenly, to her friends' chagrin, she began to shout of her love of life and the living. I could easily have gone on until the next revolution but for the cry that then came from a gentleman unknown to me. He was, unfortunately, a professional guide, and he proceeded to tear me apart. "How dare you!" he blustered. "How dare you tell such lies in my presence, I who know this city and the history of each stone?" We slipped away as quickly and quietly as possible. "Pay no attention to him," one of my charges hastened to console me. "He's just jealous. Nothing could be more obvious."

Dr. Rosenblum and his wife visited too. I met them at the airport and would have loved to have taken them to dinner, but I had no money. They guessed as much, so instead they invited me to their hotel room for anchovy sandwiches. It was the first time I ate anchovies.

Paula Mozes, the Old Man's daughter-in-law, was the next to inform me of her impending arrival by train from London. She came with a compliment: "I read the article in which you said that Paris is the only city in the world where the first day of spring is front-page news, so I came to see." I would have liked to have shown her the hospitality she deserved, but I was still broke.

I was having increasingly violent migraines, and if that was not enough, a toothache was killing me. I found a dentist on the Place de l'Opéra, a royalist who regularly flew into a rage at the mention of the word "democracy." While working in my mouth, he preached the virtues of monarchy unopposed.

At about that time I discovered the vast resources of the film industry. I wrote Hebrew subtitles for the film *Clochemerle* and was paid for each line approximately what *Yedioth* paid for an entire article. Through Marc Gutkin, I found yet another job to make ends meet. He introduced me to Aaron Poliakoff, a Yiddish actor originally from Warsaw, who wanted Marc to publish a Yiddish monthly to be called "The Mirror of the Theater." He suggested I work with him on the project. "For the moment we're not exactly Rothschild, so we can't pay you a real salary, but . . ."

"But what?"

"You'll have a real title: editor in chief."

"Who else is on the editorial board?"

"Very prestigious names, I promise you."

"Like who?"

"Well, you. And maybe me."

I liked Poliakoff. He had charm and a sense of humor that reminded me of all that was most appealing in Eastern European Judaism. In fact, he was so persuasive that I agreed to become the new monthly's secretary, typist, reporter, commentator, critic, and editorialist. There was just one outstanding practical question: Had he rented editorial offices? "Of course." Where? "Come with me." We went to a corner café, took an outside table, and ordered a café-crème. We talked about Yiddish culture and literature, Yiddish playwrights (of whom I knew little) and actors (of whom I knew even less). After about an hour I grew impatient. When were we going to the office? Poliakoff laughed. "We're here."

Once a week we met at the same café to plan the next issue. Poliakoff and his wife belonged to a famous family of actors, and they initiated me into their world with tact, talent, and tenderness. I loved hearing their anecdotes, amusing or sad, about the stars of the Yiddish stage. I read the plays of Ansky and Leivik, Pinski and Hirschbein, became familiar with the names of Adler and Granach, Kaminska and Schwartz. And so I became the head of a Yiddish theater review, even though I had attended perhaps three Yiddish productions in my life. It's amazing what one will do for a "real" title.

Around the same time another idea occurred to me. Why not launch a French-language Jewish weekly patterned on *Time*? This would be nothing like "The Mirror of the Theater," in which I wrote under ten different names, but a real magazine, with a real editorial team. I discussed the plan with Ilan, an Israeli friend, a sound engineer by trade, as ignorant of my craft as I was of his. I sounded him out simply because we happened to cross paths that evening. For my sake he declared himself enthusiastic, and we sat over our café-crèmes dreaming of years to come, when Henry Luce would be knocking at our door seeking advice. All we needed was a millionaire backer ready to invest in youth.

Interviewing an Israeli industrialist, I summoned up the courage to raise the subject. He was interested, but wanted to see something in writing — a prospectus, a budget, and preferably a dummy issue. I hurried to see Gutkin. Sam helped out, and a dummy issue was soon ready.

But in the meantime my visionary potential angel had left France. I later tried the experiment in the United States, with no less disappointing results.

Of course, I continued to cover current events. There was fighting in Indochina, strikes in France, and we learned with dismay of anti-Semitism in the Soviet Union, where "cosmopolitanism" was treated as a crime against the people and the state. Trials were held in Moscow, Prague, and Sofia, with supposedly freely given confessions. Laszlo Rajk confessed in Hungary, Rudolf Slansky in Czechoslovakia. Their submission seemed inexplicable. How could all these glorious Communist leaders be spies, saboteurs, and traitors? We tried to understand. Arthur Koestler's *Darkness at Noon* offered the simplest of explanations: In the USSR the end justified the means. Then came the arrest of Jewish doctors, state anti-Semitism. And the Communist press hit new lows. How could they parrot *Pravda*'s lies about Zionism, cosmopolitanism, and the Jewish charity organizations without disqualifying themselves? There were even some Jewish Communists (such as André Wurmser) among the propagandists, and they showed special zeal. Had they no shame? As yet we were unaware of the murders of Solomon Mikhoels, Peretz Markish, Dovid Bergelson, Itzik Fefer, Der Nister, and other Jewish writers and poets. Stalin signed their death warrants personally. Among the leading Jewish intellectuals arrested, only academician Lina Stern was spared. She later described her encounters with her codefendants in prison — Itzik Fefer, for one: unrecognizable, doubled over, half mad, his hands bloodied and trembling, he had urged her to confess. There were disturbing, murky rumors about others who were driven mad. Only Peretz Markish was not broken by torture. "I am not guilty," he shouted at his accusers. "None of us is guilty. You are trying us only because we are Jews."

Even before these revelations we knew that Jews had been publicly denounced, threatened, persecuted, and humiliated. Yet Communist writers in Paris continued to glorify Stalin. What were they afraid of? Did they really believe that Slansky and London had sold out? It was in an effort to understand the Communist mentality that I later wrote *The Testament*. Was I right to advance the hypothesis that communism was a kind of religion, a messianism without God? It is enough to examine its vocabulary: expiation, confession, redemption — the words sound like entries in a dictionary of mysticism.

One day I went to a Communist demonstration. Its aim was to mobilize the party of the workers against "filthy bourgeois Zionist intellectuals" who dared to criticize Stalin, father of all oppressed peoples, of the poor yearning for peace and freedom, and probably of an illusion or two as well. The truth be damned! Tirelessly — ecstatically — they repeated the same slogans, the same gestures. The crowd applauded frantically. At the end they stood tall, fists raised, and sang the "Internationale."

I was never attracted to communism. And yet, had I been born at the beginning of the century, I might have succumbed to the lure of its original prophetic message. In the thirties I was too young and too religious, and after the war I had other problems. I often wondered, had I joined the movement, would I have had the courage to break with it in 1952–53? I think Soviet anti-Semitism would have forced me to do so. I have discussed this more than once with the writer Howard Fast, who tried to explain his long delay in leaving the party by explaining how difficult it was to break with an ideal, a religion, and a family, and that communism had been all those things to him. I was not convinced. Communism, like Nazism, ended in inhumanity. And Stalin hated Jews almost as much as Hitler had.

Whether it was a mere coincidence or a consequence of my disillusionment with things European, I decided to turn over a new leaf. I set out for India.

Traveling

I had long dreamed of visiting India, drawn to it by a desire to meet not maharajahs but sages, yogis, and ascetics, for I had never abandoned my project of the Shushani years, my study of Jewish asceticism. Why not compare it to Hindu asceticism, contrasting the Jewish idea of redemption with the Hindu concept of nirvana?

I was fascinated by the Hindu tradition. I studied mantras, yoga, and most of all tantrism, but from afar. I loved the beauty of the Bhagavad Gita, the Upanishads, the Vedas, and the cosmic connections they described. The Talmud's Angel of Death and Shiva, god of destruction of Hindu texts, were both enemies of ignorance as much as of facile pleasure. Despite its apparent polytheism, Hindu mysticism was close to Jewish mysticism, except that my tradition rejects images, while they proliferate in Hinduism. A statuette of a Jewish Brahma would be inconceivable. Was the Vedanta a Hindu version of the Zohar? Was the world no more than a dream of God, and Creation but a wheel in eternal rotation?

The truth is that all mystical traditions have similar origins. It is only on the surface, on their most superficial levels, that religions seem opposed to one another or even incompatible. I wanted to find out if this was also true of Hinduism.

Travel expenses were a problem. *Yedioth* had no money, so I didn't even bother asking. I wrote ten articles for various Yiddish newspapers, promised ten more for later, did a few translations, and bought a lottery ticket for the first time in my life. Miracle of miracles, I won a modest amount, and at last I had a ticket in hand, but not much more. The two hundred dollars in my wallet would not take me far.

There remained the question of a visa. Dan Avni, press attaché of the Israeli embassy and future writer and professor, phoned his Indian colleague and settled that matter for me.

During the crossing — with stopovers in Suez and Aden — I studied English, read translations of Rudyard Kipling and Somerset Maugham, and reread the teachings of Sakyamuni and the commentaries of Sri Vivekananda and Sri Aurobindo. A fellow passenger — whose visiting card bore his name and profession: "future physician" — gave me the name of an inexpensive hotel in Bombay. Except that for me everything was expensive. The medical student advised me to play the ponies. Aboard ship? You didn't need horses to play. My instructor showed me how. At first I lost, then I won, then lost again.

Games of chance are not my forte. The future physician didn't do well either. Broke, he asked me to lend him two hundred dollars, my entire fortune, promising to pay me back in Bombay. I should have known not to be a fool, but I could never say no. The night before we docked, I felt panicky: I should never have trusted the future physician, should never have set out on this "spiritual" adventure in the first place. I would have done better to look for the mysteries of India in Paris. How would I pay for lodging in this vast country? What would I live on? But it was too late to turn back.

On a wet January morning, after three hours of interrogation and negotiation with the border police and customs agents (the inspectors couldn't understand why I was the only passenger without a trunk), I finally disembarked in Bombay, carrying a battered suitcase and my typewriter. I searched for the future physician in the crowd, worried that he was a crook and convinced that I was an imbecile. But there he was, two hundred dollars in hand.

Near the harbor, as I looked for a taxi or, preferably, a bus, I was suddenly surrounded by a swarm of half-naked waifs ravaged by various diseases ancient and new, known and unknown. One wept with tearless sobs, another muttered incomprehensible words, a third pointed to the stump of his amputated left leg. Some were young, others ageless. Despite their condition, they seemed beautiful and mysterious

— black, disheveled hair, eyes like tombs reflecting nothingness, their only clothing shirts that might have once been white. Palms extended, they begged: "Sahib, a few annas . . . a rupee." They were hungry. I remembered the boy in Barcelona. This time my hand did not fail me — it reached into my pocket. These were the children of hunger, the world's most wretched, utterly devoid of hope. In *The Oath* I devote to them a passage I copied directly from my diary.

I met children like this, God's most wretched orphans, all over India. Devoured by leprosy, missing arms or legs, they were all starving. Some were still crying, others lacked the strength even to speak.

My thoughts were with them as I questioned first an old man with a delicate face, then a gravely silent spiritual master, and finally a prudent and reserved official. How could a civilized state like India tolerate such misery and agony? I became more concerned with this question than with theosophical research. I was answered with smiles, shrugs, and long speeches about the transmigration of souls, about India's quest for self-improvement, its striving to approach perfection at whatever cost. I wasn't satisfied. In Judaism it is in his earthly life that man is supposed to accomplish something: by participating in the life of his fellow men, by doing good, by combating the injustice inherent in existence. After that, it is too late. Surely the doctrine of reincarnation is not a valid response to suffering. I can accept and bear my own suffering, but not that of others.

Granted, national independence requires its share of political sacrifice. And yes, considerable progress had already been made. The system of castes had been officially abolished. Jawaharlal Nehru's decision to name an Untouchable as minister of justice was both daring and ingenious. But what about the multitude of rickshaws hauled by men resigned to their misfortune? What about the shelterless people lashed by the bitter Bombay monsoon, awash in the detritus of Calcutta, infected by the pollution of the Ganges? What of the tattered men who slept in the streets, whom passersby stepped over with an air of indifference? What about the widows in the country's heartland, who were still being burned to death along with their husband's bodies, or the countless lepers roaming the streets? I was unable to consider their distress within any value system I knew, religious or otherwise. This mass of suffering hit me hard. I had no right to ignore it or to make my peace with it through specious rationalizations or magic formulas.

Sometimes curiosity got the better of me and I tried to talk to one or another of these poor souls. But since I knew neither Hindi nor Urdu, I could do no more than mumble in a jargon incomprehensible even to myself or utter a few undoubtedly mispronounced and inappropriate words of Sanskrit, a language that in any case has not been current in India for centuries.

I set out in search of the country. The beggar-monks who roamed in processions from place to place reminded me of the wandering righteous. All masters look alike: you recognize them by the quality of their disciples. I met several Parsis, whose temples are off-limits to strangers and in whose cemeteries, known as Towers of Silence, bodies are not buried but exposed to the sun to be devoured by vultures. These towers confirmed how distant I was from this religion. I kept thinking of the biblical phrase "Born of ashes, to ashes man returns." A Parsi journalist wondered at my astonishment: "Isn't this more useful? In my tradition man nourishes living creatures even in death."

I was revolted by the caste system, with its rigid, immutable rules. There were four castes, each with specified powers and privileges. At the summit of the hierarchy reigned the Brahmins; at the bottom were those without caste, the pariahs — or Untouchables — whose lot was misfortune. I got a better understanding of Gandhi, the towering apostle of nonviolence, whose philosophy, sadly, is rarely applied. But I couldn't comprehend his anti-Zionism, despite everything I read about it, including his correspondence with Albert Einstein and his dialogue with Yehuda Nedivi, a Zionist emissary, in the mid-1930s. Why did he oppose Jewish immigration to Palestine? He wanted the Jews to stay in Europe, where, he felt, they enjoyed full human rights.

One day I met a rich and influential Parsi (most of them were). We chatted about this and that, and he found something about me intriguing. He was acquainted with several Jews but knew nothing of our customs, laws, and traditions. I told him of the Persian influence on Jewish culture in antiquity, especially during the Babylonian exile. I pointed out the curious similarities in our respective mysticisms. Several hours later, as he left to return to his associates, he gave me a calling card on which he had written a few words. "India is a vast country," he said. "You will undoubtedly move around a lot. With this card you can take any domestic flight to any destination." I didn't know how to thank him. In fact, it took only a few weeks for me to appreciate the true value of his gift. Whenever I was hungry, I would get on a plane. By then I had discovered the identity of my benefactor: He owned the airline.

I regret that I did not go as far as Tibet. In the 1990s, when I met the Dalai Lama, I told him of that frustration. "Do you need me to tell you never to give up hope?" he asked with a smile. In 1992, when I was asked to introduce him at a gathering in his honor in Washington, he questioned me about the secret of Jewish survival, wondering how it could be applied to his own people, also exiled, its religion also threatened: "Despite the persecution and hatred that surrounded you, you managed to keep your culture and memory alive. Show us how." In his meetings with Jewish intellectuals he would often repeat: "We Tibetans have much to learn from our Jewish brothers and sisters."

India is a country that makes one dream. Naïvely, I thought then that the nightmarish civil and religious wars might be things of the past. At the time it seemed so. Who would have predicted that forty years later, in 1993 and 1994, the country would again be ravaged by bloody rioting? Eleven bombs exploded on a single day, killing some three hundred and wounding about a thousand. In those days I was too optimistic. I thought hatred would at least recede. India was casting its spell on me: Hyderabad, Amritsar (site of the Golden Temple of the Sikhs), Jaipur; Varanasi and its sacred river carrying offerings of ashes to the sea; Calcutta and its dense and stifling crowds; Bombay and its B'nei Israel, the Jews of India whose ancestors served in King Solomon's merchant marine; Cochin and its Jewish past, Cochin and its legends.

From the fourth to the fourteenth century an independent Jewish principality flourished in Cranganore in southern India. The leader of this Jewish state, a map of which is still on display in the synagogue of Cochin, was one Joseph Rabban. The prince of Cranganore, who was his friend and protector, ordered him to pass down his duties and privileges from father to son.

Where did these Jews of Cranganore come from? Palestine, of course. But opinions differ as to when they arrived. Were they among the Ten Tribes King Salmanasar III led into captivity, or were they among the people deported by King Nebuchadrezzar? Some say they were sent on a commercial or diplomatic mission by King Solomon.

What is "certain," at least according to legend, is that in Cranganore they lived in peace. It is said that Rabbi Yehuda Halevy and Rabbi Abraham Ibn Ezra were so curious to see a Jewish monarch in the flesh that they came to visit. Even the great Saadiah Gaon speaks of India, expressing his conviction that anyone who went there got rich. According to one theory, Christopher Columbus set out for India solely to discover this Jewish state, which he thought might agree to accept future refugees and exiles from Spain and Portugal.

In Cochin there were memories of glory and distress, including the occupations by the Moors and by the Portuguese. Yet India has enjoyed a reputation as a tolerant, clement land. I have often heard Jews in Bombay and elsewhere assert that there has never been anti-Semitism in India. It is a country of spiritual defiance and conquest, a land of infinite probabilities just as Israel is a land of infinite improbabilities. Could a European, a Jew like me, truly find his bearings here, and perhaps even fulfillment?

A sage approached me outside my hotel in Bombay. "For five rupees I'll tell your future." I told him I would give him ten if he could tell my past. Taken aback, he asked me to write down my date of birth and any other date on a piece of paper. He snatched it from my hand, turned his back, and remained still for a moment. What was he calculating? When he turned to face me, he looked terrified. "I see bodies," he said. "Many bodies." Now it was my turn to be taken aback. How could he have known what April 11, 1945, meant to me? And yet.

I spent a Shabbat with a Jewish family in Bombay. I went to synagogue. My hosts proudly told me of their success. The Sassoons and the Kadouris were super-rich families, veritable dynasties. But it had never occurred to anyone to discriminate against them because of their origins or their ties to Judaism. There were so many ethnic groups, languages, cultures, and traditions in this vast country that Jews did not attract special attention. In one of the synagogues I met a Jewish American student who wanted to convert to Buddhism. I asked him why, and his answer saddened me: "Judaism is egocentric while Buddhism is universalist." Had he ever really studied his people's tradition? Probably not, but . . .

I spent an unforgettable evening in an ashram learning to listen to the stars, and to listen to Him who listens in silence. I learned to receive offerings of smiles. I plumbed and absorbed the teachings of old sages. At night it was hard to tell whether I was dreaming. In the morning it was hard to tell whether the light came from above or from higher still.

This sort of pilgrimage was not yet as fashionable as it became later. In one place I was the only foreigner among one hundred young monks contemplating the meaning of suffering. When our eyes met, they would greet me with the graceful Hindu gesture of raised hands, smiling and nodding as I smiled back. I attended their prayers. Their chanting of *om* still echoes in my ears. One old master invited me to join him in his walks, yet I left the ashram without ever having heard his voice.

I was drawn to India and to the spiritual force and intellectual possibilities it represented. But in the end I had to tear myself away. Its concepts of existence and of God were too different, too distant from mine. A Jew considers pain an insult to man. I have no right to turn my back on the suffering of others. Jews must "choose life," in the here and now, and the living. In fact, the same word — *hayyim* — means both "life" and "the living." I have no right to postpone my salvation for an eventual reincarnation.

I returned from India even more Jewish than before.

Grandma Nissel, her black scarf knotted under her chin, chats with Tsipouka. Grand-

mother is somber, my little sister serene and pensive.

They are sitting quietly on a bench covered with dead leaves. I tell myself it must be autumn. It is always autumn in the cemetery.

I approach the bench on tiptoe, with gliding but annoyingly noisy steps. I try to listen. But all I hear is the rustling of leaves. I tell myself the leaves are speaking for the dead, and that when they fail to rustle it means the dead don't feel like talking.

The dead invade my sleep even more often these days, plowing it up as if to reap images of themselves, images undistorted by time.

I awake early in the morning, exhausted. In a panic, I strive to grasp a word, a call from that world from which I so reluctantly escaped.

I close my eyes.

She is pale, my grandmother.

And so is my little sister.

In my dream I walk with them to the point beyond which the living may not advance. I turn back.

And begin again.

A free ticket from El Al enabled me to visit Montreal. Bea seemed happy enough; she was now working at the Israeli consulate. Here, unlike in occupied Germany, we were often alone. I desperately wanted to ask her a question that had haunted me for years: What was it like before the selection, those final moments, that last walk with Mother and Tsipouka? But I didn't dare. It was the same with Hilda. I didn't dare.

While in Canada and the United States, I wrote a series of articles on the life of the *yordim*, a pejorative term for Israeli emigrants, people who had decided to leave the country — in other words, "to descend." In 1953 and 1954 you could meet them everywhere, particularly in Paris, Montreal, and New York. They had abandoned their recovered homeland mainly for economic reasons. The "American dream" had its devotees in Israel, as elsewhere: Get ahead, make money, show "them" what you can do. Nobody, especially not a non-Israeli, had a right to judge or even to criticize them.

The time has come to tell you about Joseph Givon. I am sure you don't recognize the name. He was the man who supposedly gave Stalin strategic planetary advice, who was both the confidant of Mao Zedong and the mediator between Ho Chi Minh and Pierre Mendès-France and between General de Gaulle and the Algerians.

The story begins in Israel in 1953. I had planned on staying a month. I would finish my articles on India and get better acquainted with the *Yedioth* editorial team and the country itself. I stayed at a hotel, since chaos reigned in the Old Man's apartment, where the family was preparing for my friends Dov and Leah's wedding. The Savoy is near the beach. I would rise at dawn and take long walks along the seashore. I loved those moments of peace.

And so, for ten busy days, I would spend mornings in the editorial office and evenings with the Old Man's son Noah, Dov, or Dr. Rosenblum. I met dozens of writers, journalists, and artists. Dr. Shimshon Yunitchman, a veteran of the Revisionist movement whom I had met in Paris, told me that my articles on India had been well received at the Ministry of Foreign Affairs. It was my first compliment from an important personality, and it felt good. I was invited to the theater, concerts, and receptions and introduced to members of the Knesset. The Old Man insisted I accompany him on his travels through the country. In Jerusalem he introduced me to a Lubavitch Hasid who was a doctor and who taught me "the" melody of the movement's founder, Rabbi Shneur Zalman of Lyady. I was also introduced to the Old Man's younger daughter. He was scheming . . . but Rachel was even more bashful than I. Besides, how do you flirt with a pious girl?

On the morning of the eleventh day I got an urgent phone call from Dov. Prague, he said, was about to release an Israeli citizen, a man called Furmand, who had been with Mordechai Oren, an important Israeli left-wing leader, in the Pancracz prison. *Maariv* was sending its best reporter to Paris to interview Furmand, and Dov

404

wanted me to catch the first plane out. It would be a scoop.

The magic word — most journalists would give their right arm, or at least their left, for a good scoop. It was the way to get noticed and earn a bonus, or, if you worked for *Yedioth*, get warm congratulations. O God of Moses — first reporter and editorialist of our turbulent history — give us this day our daily scoop, or at least a weekly one should you be too busy.

I washed, dressed, gulped down some coffee, jumped into the car the paper had sent for me, and headed for the airport without even stopping to say goodbye to the Old Man. Our Lod correspondent was waiting to shepherd me through the passport and customs controls. Within five minutes I was in the air, seated — where else? — beside my rival from *Maariv*. Innocently, I asked him why he was going to Paris. "Personal reasons," he replied. "Visiting a sick aunt."

"And you?" he asked after a brief silence. I looked at him. "My uncle the doctor," I explained, "is taking care of your aunt." We burst out laughing.

As it turned out, our respective employers were equally satisfied, for we both interviewed the former prisoner that very afternoon. (In the interests of historical accuracy, I must admit that my colleague beat me by one hour.) His information about the situation in Prague was sensational. Oren was linked to the Slansky trial. In fact, everything beyond the Iron Curtain was linked to everything else. Prague was Moscow, Moscow was Stalin, and Stalin was mad. The left in Israel (which no longer had diplomatic relations with the Soviet Union or any of its satellites) was in utter disarray, unable to comprehend the fierce anti-Semitism of Stalin and the Stalinists. So when Oren was indicted for espionage and subversion, the newspapers waged a merciless battle for any scrap of information about his trial, confession, and sentence. But Prague was an inaccessible fortress into which no one could venture. The sole person for whom that city would open its secret doors was the great, the all-powerful Joseph Givon.

But who was Givon? Was he a kind of journalistic Shushani, a world-class adventurer, or an ingenious spinner of tales? Don't ask. If you don't already know, you never will. He was, in any event, a great character, a remarkable, bizarre personality. Like myself, the Israeli poet Haim Guri and the mayor of Beersheba, Izso Rager, will swear that never in their life did they encounter anyone like Joseph Givon.

I first met him at a reception at the Israeli embassy. He was still young, a man with the light blue eyes of a startled child. He moved his left leg and right arm with apparent difficulty. He wore an elegant blue suit with a golden Palmach insignia on the lapel. When I first saw him he was deep in conversation with an actress from the Israeli National Theater. I couldn't help but overhear bits and pieces. The actress wanted to know who had given him his decoration. His murmured response: "Yitzhak, General Yitzhak Sadeh in person." The former commander of the Palmach himself? "Yes. I was a colonel and he was my superior officer. The decoration was bestowed on me at a special session of the General Staff." The actress, her cheeks flushed, asked what it was for. "Excuse me, but I regret . . . I'm not allowed . . . Surely you understand." She understood, and so did I: He must have been a member of the security services. He strolled through the embassy as if in familiar territory; he knew the ambassador, the military attaché, all the advisers and secretaries, and everyone seemed to know him. Intrigued, I asked an attaché who he was. "I have no idea," was the reply, "but maybe I'm not supposed to know." So my guess was right. Surely he was a heroic wounded veteran who worked for the "services."

A group of people were exchanging the latest news about Oren. I strained to listen. You never know. Someone might unwittingly offer a little scoop. Suddenly I heard our hero say, "But I did warn him. I told him they were going to arrest him." Told whom? someone asked. "Mordechai Oren," he replied nonchalantly. I jumped. Did he know Oren? "Know him? Of course I know him. We were in East Berlin together. And Prague too. I have friends there, you know, friends in high places. And one of them advised me to let Mordechai know they were watching him. That he should leave as soon as possible. 'Mordechai,' I begged him, 'think of yourself, your family. Get the first plane for Paris, Vienna, Bangkok, wherever. You're in danger. Can't you feel it?' The idiot refused to listen. But I have to admit I was no less idiotic than he was. In the end they arrested me too."

By now I was uneasy, annoyed that he had said all this out loud. There were colleagues of mine in the room, and they might well join us. That was all I needed. I wasn't sure what to do, but for once I had the guts to act on an idea. I whispered to Joseph Givon that I had a confidential message from the beautiful actress he had just charmed. We withdrew to a corner, and I introduced myself. "I read *Yedioth*," he said with a faint smile. He then introduced himself in turn. "You have the advantage," I told him. "I don't know what *you* do." Ignoring my comment, he said: "So what's the confidential message?" I lowered my voice: "She says you should trust me."

"That's all?"

"No. She also says you should tell me about your experiences in Prague."

"That's it?"

"No, she also says you shouldn't tell anyone but me."

He uttered a strange, almost silent laugh. "Did anyone ever tell you you're a poor liar?" he said. "But all right, let's go." I felt like dancing for joy. "Okay," he said once we were out in the street, "since it's the wish of a beautiful woman, and an actress to boot, I'll tell you a thing or two." We looked for a quiet café. As we walked, he talked about life in Prague. He had known the Czech Communist leaders Rudolf Slansky and Artur London. In fact, he was on intimate terms with both of them. Before anyone else he had known that they would be arrested, indicted, and tried. "Since they were Jewish, I thought it would be a good idea to tell Moshe." Moshe who? "Moshe Sharett, of course," he said. "The minister of foreign affairs." Did he know him too? "We've done a few things together," he confided. "Next you'll tell me you know David Ben-Gurion," I needled him. "He's the first person I see whenever I come to Israel. He made me promise that, and I've always kept my word."

We sat over black coffee and I showered him with questions, which he answered in the self-assured voice of a man who knows whereof he speaks. I felt like a child in a toy store, but I wasn't sure what to believe. "Malenkov sent a military aircraft for you? Why?" Was Givon an adviser to the Kremlin, an interlocutor of Marshal Zhukov? Why was Mao Zedong so insistent on seeing him? Was he really Slansky's intimate confidant? When had he seen him last? My head was spinning, but Givon remained serene, and cautious. Before answering a question, he would look from side to side as if to make sure no one else was listening. You could never be too careful. Certain "services" would pay dearly for his whispered confidences, but I was receiving them free of charge. Every one of his revelations was worth a thousand times the value of my newspaper, and he was offering them to me gratis. No doubt there is a God who watches over poor and timid journalists.

Everything he told me had the ring of truth, yet I knew I might be dealing with a fabulist, a compulsive liar. Was I supposed to believe that Malenkov, Ho Chi Minh, Stalin, and Ben-Gurion were intimates of this gentleman who looked more like a vagabond striving vainly for elegance? He must have noticed my skepticism, for at one point he casually reached into his jacket pocket and handed me a pack of photographs. All at once my incredulity vanished. Here were Givon and Stalin, Givon and Mao, Givon surrounded by Soviet generals. Wait a minute, I said to myself. Don't fall for it. How could he have negotiated the fate of humanity with the great men of this world without anyone ever knowing it? The photographs were probably fakes, however astonishingly well done. When I examined them carefully I had to admit (amateur though I was) that they seemed genuine. But I still thought the man might be manipulating me. Did he really know Rudolf Slansky? Had he really had words with his accusers and judges, really met Oren before and after his arrest? Yes. Indeed, he could describe the prison, and he told me behind-the-scenes stories about this case which the whole world had been talking about for months. I decided Givon was an invaluable source, a gold mine. I wondered whether I should make him an offer of some kind. I could wire Dov for money, but would he believe me? I was afraid to look ridiculous. Suddenly Givon stood up. "You'll have to excuse me," he said casually, "but I must go now. I have an urgent appointment with Sartre."

The philosopher? "Yeah. An old friend of mine."

He seemed not to notice my surprise. Actually, why shouldn't a man who knows heads of state be friends with a famous writer? I asked when I would see him again. "Tomorrow. I'll call you." In the meantime could I use what he had told me for a cable to *Yedioth Ahronoth*? "Oh no," he cried. "Anything but that! That would expose me to risks you couldn't possibly imagine." But he promised that tomorrow he would bring me information for a sensational story. Something told me that it would be better not to press the issue. Better pretend to trust him. "Okay," I said, "take my phone number." His childlike blue eyes rested upon me. "No need," he said. "We know how to reach you." We? "Be at your phone tomorrow morning at 10:35." Then he added, "Let's synchronize our watches." We shook hands and walked off in opposite directions.

411

In my dispatch I told Dov I might soon have important — indeed, sensational — revelations about Oren. He called back at five in the morning. "What's this all about?" I told him I couldn't say any more on the phone. He insisted I at least give him a hint. Now it was my turn to act conspiratorially. "Not on the phone."

At 10:32 I took up my position at the phone. It rang at exactly 10:35. I recognized the drawling voice. "It's all set," he said. I realized I had forgotten to breathe. "That's great, but . . ."

"But what? You're happy, aren't you? Be downstairs at 16:48 this afternoon." And he hung up.

My head was spinning. I must have looked pale, because Léon Leneman, at whose home I was living at the time, seemed worried. "Bad news?" he asked. I told him everything was fine, but I wasn't so sure of that. I didn't think my new friend was lying, but I was afraid he might be drawing me into some kind of conspiracy. Why all these complicated arrangements? I decided to wait — did I have a choice? — until 4:45 — excuse me, 4:48 — that afternoon.

But waiting was not easy. I paced my room as if it were a prison cell, chain-smoking. Madame Leneman offered me coffee, but I didn't feel like it. I tried in vain to read the papers, and to write an article.

Finally, it was time, or almost. At 4:40 the

412

phone rang. "It's for you," Leneman said. I asked him to take a message. I had to go downstairs, Givon would be here any minute. "He says it's urgent." I took the receiver and recognized the now familiar voice. "I'm at the airport," he said. "I've been called back to Prague, so we'll have to postpone our meeting. Is next Monday all right?" Crushed, I stammered a feeble yes. Of course Monday was all right. "I might call you from there," he added just before he hung up, "so don't stray too far from the phone."

I went to my room and locked the door. I didn't want to see anyone, hear any news, send any dispatches. I was going to resign from the paper, go back to India, and become an ascetic.

It was a very long week. Then, on Saturday night I got a call from Prague. "Is Monday still all right?" Absolutely. "By the way, I set it all up." Set what up? For whom? "For you, idiot." What could he have set up for me in Prague? "I'll tell you Monday. Downstairs. Same time." Madame Leneman was worried about me. "You don't look well. Is anything wrong?" I reassured her, thanked her for her concern. "Could it be love?" I smiled awkwardly and didn't reply. Let her think what she wanted.

Unnerved, depressed, I spent the rest of the weekend waiting for the rendezvous, convinced it would be postponed again. I was wrong. At exactly 4:48 in the afternoon a taxi pulled up in front of 8 Avenue de la République. Givon invited me to get in. He put his finger to his lips, suggesting that we needed to be careful. We stopped near the Châtelet. He allowed me to pay for the cab, then pointed to a sidewalk café. "Do you think it's all right?" I whispered. He looked around and decided it was.

"So," I asked after we sat down at a table, "how was Prague?"

"Like always. I did what I had to do. Saw Mordechai. Gave him a package."

The blood pounded in my head. "You saw Oren? In prison?" Yes. "Can I publish that?" No. "Why not?"

"Because I have something better." Who wanted something better? That scoop was just fine. I could see the front page now: "Message from Oren, Exclusive to *Yedioth Ahronoth*." My colleagues would not only be green with envy but also red with embarrassment. "No," Joseph repeated impatiently. "Besides, you want to know everything, but you don't give me a chance to talk." I could feel he was closing up. I had to find a way to put him at ease. "Look, Joseph," I said, "I'm sorry for interrupting. Go on, please. How is Oren getting along? Tell me, is he depressed? Confident? Is he alone in his cell? What is he eating? Do they let him read?" Givon pretended not to be listening. He finally halted my flow of questions with a wave of his good hand. "What would you say to an interview with Oren?" I was stunned. "Is this some kind of joke? How am I supposed to meet him?"

"I asked the authorities in Prague," Givon calmly replied. "At first they were somewhat reluctant, but I managed to convince them it was necessary. You understand, the prosecutor's secretary likes me. In fact, I think she has a crush on me." He paused. "Come with me next week." I had to force myself not to shout. "How am I supposed to get to Prague?" I asked.

"By plane," he replied evenly. "I'll pay the fare." And the visa? "I'll take care of it." With what passport? As a stateless person, I couldn't just up and go where I wanted, especially not behind the Iron Curtain. No government would come to my aid if I was arrested. "Don't worry," he said. "I'll take care of that too. By the way, would you prefer a Swiss or a Belgian passport?" I thought it was a tasteless joke. How dare he offer me a false passport? "Oh no," he said. "It wouldn't be false. It'd have your photo, name, signature." In other words, it would be a real false passport, or a false real one. But wasn't that illegal? "No, it isn't. Sometimes they let us do this kind of thing. Legally. Rarely, but it happens." Again the plural. Who were "us"? I told him I would think about it. He seemed offended. Didn't I trust him? I tried to mollify him. Yes, of course I trusted him implicitly, but he had to understand my situation: I couldn't make any decision without informing the paper. He was amenable: "I'll give you five days. If you come with me, you'll have the scoop of the year — no, of the decade. You'll be the first — the only — Western journalist to penetrate Pancracz and to interview Mordechai Oren."

I didn't know where to turn for advice. Dov was too far away. It wouldn't have been smart to talk about this over the phone. I had an idea. Colonel Yehoshafat Harkabi, chief of Israeli military intelligence, happened to be in Paris at the time. Why not explain the situation to him? After all, he would know what was going on, since Givon was working for him, or for a service related to his. A friend from the embassy arranged a meeting for me. The colonel listened attentively and then confessed, "The name Givon sounds familiar, but I'm having trouble placing it. Let me look into it. Call me in forty-eight hours." When I did, his response was brief: "In my view, you should say no." That's all? "Yes, that's all." But why? Who is Joseph Givon? Where does he get his power? Is he a double agent? And what about his friendship with Yitzhak Sadeh, Sharett, and Ben-Gurion? What about the photos, his trips to Prague, his relations with world figures? The colonel would not satisfy my curiosity. Was it possible that Givon was an agent so secret even the chief of military intelligence was unaware of his identity? If he wasn't working for Israel, whom was he working for? What obscure organization employed him? Was he involved in some illegal, reprehensible activity?

416

Was that why I was advised not to go with him?

"So, are you coming?" Givon asked when we next got together at a café on the Champs-Élysées. I invented a thousand excuses: A stateless person can't be too careful, I could be imprisoned or deported if I were caught with a false passport. "You're afraid, is that it?" I admitted that yes, I was a coward. I didn't want to risk my freedom and my future for a scoop, no matter how sensational. Givon seemed disappointed. I was too.

He left by himself, or at least without me. He called me from Prague several times, usually to tell me overtly or in code that he would call again. But the missed opportunity left me bitter and troubled. Dov tried to make me feel better. "These things happen." Still, I felt like a fool.

I was to see Givon again, there were to be more "adventures" with him. But the Oren chapter was closed. I now had to turn my attention to other situations. I was sent on several European trips related to the Israeli-German conference on reparations, then on another journey to Israel, and finally to Brazil.

Brazil was Dov's idea. It seems the Catholic Church was conducting suspicious missionary activities in Israel, particularly among Jews recently arrived from Eastern Europe. They were poor and unhappy, and Rome's emissaries offered them visas for Brazil, free passage, and two hundred dollars each, provided they converted to Catholicism. "I want you to go and see what's going on," Dov said.

I was happy to go. My poet friend Nicolas, now immersed in South American literature, proposed to go with me. A resourceful Israeli friend somehow managed to come up with free boat tickets for us. But before sailing, let me pick up the thread of another story. If you recall, we left Hanna in front of her building near the Sacré-Coeur, in the middle of the night. She had just asked me to marry her.

Back in the café, when she popped the question, I instantly began to imagine our future together. I tried to picture us as a couple, united by common plans and obligations. We would leave the house together in the morning, she for her job, me for mine. We would go to dinner with friends. On Friday night we would celebrate Shabbat. There would be candles on the table and songs with the meals. I tried to picture our home. What would it look like? Would it resemble that of my childhood? Would we live in Israel, France, or somewhere else? I tried to picture our children. I imagined Hanna at thirty, at fifty. Would I still love her? Did I really love her, or was I only attracted by her beauty and inaccessibility? "Listen, Hanna," I finally said. "The answer is yes. I'm ready to marry you. But I don't want you to regret it someday." There were tears in her eyes. "I won't regret it," she whispered. I wasn't so sure, but I didn't want to humiliate her. I felt trapped. At a loss for what to do, I suggested we postpone the decision.

"Why?" she asked.

"To give you — give us — time to think."

"I've already thought it through."

"Even so," I insisted.

She swallowed, smiled sadly. She was as beautiful as ever. I felt myself wavering, but she was asking: "When you say put off the decision until later, what do you mean?"

I reminded her that I was leaving for Brazil in two days. "I'll be gone six weeks. When we see each other again, you'll ask the same question, and I'll say yes, and it will be a yes without reservations. But you'll have to ask it again. Okay?" She agreed.

I walked her home. A strange peace mingled with disquietude swept through me. We walked hand in hand, like lovers, slightly embarrassed, confused and silent. I felt close to her but wasn't sure how to act. It was late. The streets were empty, the windows shuttered. Was there any couple in Paris like us? All lovers in this city made for lovers must have wondered the same thing. We were sure we were different. For the second time in forty-eight hours we arrived at the gate of Hanna's building, and once again we didn't know what to do. Go upstairs? Embrace? I wanted to, of course, more so than at Versailles, more so and differently. In a sense, we were almost engaged. "Should we kiss?"

Hanna asked. We kissed. Not on the cheek, but on the mouth, shyly, our lips barely touching. It was the first time. How I had dreamed of this moment. How many sleepless nights had I spent imagining how it would be to hold her in my arms. I loved her, there could be no doubt.

She called me the next day, and the day after that. I gave her my itinerary, including the addresses where she could write to me.

Her first letter was waiting for me in Marseilles, where I embarked on *Le Provence*. Her letter was hesitant and cautious, mostly about the past: Versailles, the choir, the evenings. "How could you have been so blind so long?" she asked. As for the future: "Let's try to be happy, let's make up for all the lost years." I was touched, and happy, but anxious too. I wasn't so sure I wanted to get married right away. How would I provide for a family's needs?

These questions haunted me during the crossing. I was worried sick that I might be making the greatest mistake of my life: Should a man marry a beautiful, intelligent, and impulsive woman with a marvelous voice just because he had once loved her and because she had now proposed to him? And because he did not want to hurt her?

I spent most of the voyage in my cabin working. I was writing my account of the concentration camp years — in Yiddish. I wrote feverishly, breathlessly, without rereading. I wrote to testify, to stop the dead from dying, to justify my own survival. I wrote to speak to those who were gone. As long as I spoke to them, they would live on, at least in my memory. My vow of silence would soon be fulfilled; next year would mark the tenth anniversary of my liberation. I was going to have to open the gates of memory, to break the silence while safeguarding it. The pages piled up on my bed. I slept fitfully, never participating in the ship's activities, constantly pounding away on my little portable, oblivious of my fellow passengers, fearing only that we would arrive in São Paulo too soon.

We were there before I knew it. Nicolas, an Israeli citizen, was quickly cleared for disembarkation, but as a stateless person, I was an object of suspicion. As I waited to go ashore, I suddenly heard shouts in Hebrew. I turned around and, to my surprise, saw a group of some forty Israeli emigrants who had made the crossing in third class. I was furious at myself. My subject had been right here at hand, and I had wasted my time recording memories that could easily have waited a week or a month. I went to speak to them and found them dismayed, even desperate. They had been forbidden to disembark. A local priest pleaded for them: "But their visas are in perfect order." Sorry, the officials replied. "Their visas have been annulled. We're just following orders." While the priest went for help, I asked one of the ship's officers what would happen to these poor people when the ship lifted anchor. He said that if their visas were not reinstated, they would have to remain on board. "For how long?" He frowned. "Until someone gives them visas." My journalist's instinct was aroused. If I stayed with them, I would get my story.

We sailed from port to port, pariahs rejected everywhere. Since my cabin had been reassigned, I traveled with the others in the hold. For one hour a day we were allowed on deck to get some air. I envied the passengers with passports. What wouldn't I have given to be granted Peruvian or Salvadoran nationality! Stateless persons were regarded not only as noncitizens but as somewhat subhuman as well.

Down in the hold, children cried and parents vented their anger. Some cried out at having let themselves be duped by the missionaries. Others might have felt a similar bitterness but dared not admit it. I was at a loss to understand them. How could they give up Israel for a little money, a visa, and a boat ticket? Were they that unhappy? How could Jews like them, with their past, have agreed to convert? Their ancestors chose death by sword and fire rather than renounce their faith. And they gave it all up for a trip to Brazil? They protested. "We never renounced our faith. The God of Israel is still our God." But hadn't they promised to convert? "Promised? So we promised. Don't we have the right to make promises?" Haim'ke the tailor remembered that it was the anniversary of his mother's death. We formed a minyan so he could say Kaddish. Baruch the shoemaker tried to justify himself: "I spent two years in the ghetto and fourteen months underground with the partisans. I didn't have what it takes to stay in Israel. Life's too hard there." Others joined in. "Too much hardship . . . Too much suffering . . . Don't judge us too harshly. . . . We're not traitors to our people. . . . We're good Jews. . . ."

At the stopover in Montevideo I contacted a Jewish journalist and told him of my companions' tragic odyssey. He promised to alert the community. In Buenos Aires my cousins Voïcsi and her husband Moishe-Hersh Genuth came to meet us. I gave them some articles for *Yedioth Ahronoth*, unaware that they would be reprinted or quoted in the American Jewish press.

Yehudit Moretzka, a Yiddish singer and friend of the Lenemans, came aboard with Mark Turkov, a Jewish book publisher. Having by then become a sort of spokesman for the exiles, I shared my concern with them: Someone would have to let them disembark somewhere; they couldn't possibly go on like this. They were sick and exhausted. As we talked, Turkov noticed my manuscript, from which I was never separated. He wanted to know what it was and whether he could look at it. I showed it to him, explaining that it was unfinished. "That's all

423

right," he said. "Let me take it anyway." It was my only copy, but Turkov assured me that it would be safe with him. I still hesitated, but he promised not only to read it but "If it's good, I'll publish it." Yehudit Moretzka encouraged me by telling me she would make sure the manuscript was returned to me in Paris — with or without a rejection slip. I was convinced Turkov wouldn't publish it. I couldn't see why any editor would be interested in the sad memoirs of a stranger he happened to meet on a ship, surrounded by refugees nobody wanted. "Don't worry so much," Yehudit Moretzka told me as she left. But I felt lost without my manuscript.

The South American Jewish communities proved equal to the task. The refugees were finally allowed to come ashore in São Paulo. But the priest who greeted them could not contain his anger when he learned they would be taken in charge by a Jewish charity. Baruch embraced me and asked me to come and visit him once he was settled. He would present me with a pair of handmade shoes. Haim'ke, too, embraced me and promised to make me a fine suit. A third passenger told me of a beautiful cousin who wanted to get married, suggesting that —who knows? — I might make a good husband. They were all relieved and happy, and so was I.

In the meantime, Hanna's letters, which had piled up at the American Express office in São

Paulo, betrayed mounting unease. Because of my change in itinerary, I had not written to her. She wondered about my prolonged silence and whether I had changed my mind. Nearly six weeks had passed, and now I had to postpone my return. I wrote to her explaining why, but by a quirk of fate my letter was delivered after a serious delay. I had been away for two months when Dov recalled me to Paris to cover Pierre Mendès-France's accession to power. I flew back, anxious to see Hanna. I would explain the exceptional circumstances, find a way to make her forgive me. She would understand, for I had missed her. I would tell her that I had been faithful to her, even in my thoughts.

As soon as I arrived, I hurried to Leneman's office and asked whether there were any messages for me. He handed me a sheet of paper with a list of names. Nothing from Hanna. Then he gave me my mail. The first letter I opened was from her: "You didn't write and didn't come back when you said you would. I realize what that means; I'm not angry with you." I rushed to her apartment, where the concierge told me she was sorry but Hanna had left. Where had she gone? "To Palestine, I think." When? "Ten days ago." I was both sad and relieved.

Fifteen years later I saw her in Jerusalem. She was still proud and beautiful, though a little subdued. She was married and had children. I wondered whether I should tell her that my delay and my silence had not been my fault, that I had come back to Paris ready to marry her. I decided to say nothing. There were two possibilities: Either she was happy, in which case there was no point in reopening old wounds, or she wasn't, in which case there was no point in kindling regrets.

I never saw her again.

The last thing there is to say about my Brazilian expedition is that it ended on a comical note. Ever since my arrival, colleagues and acquaintances had been telling me about a man called Assis Chateaubriant: "If you're writing about this country, you must meet him." The name meant nothing to me, so they explained that he was a vivid and influential personality, the owner of several newspapers, radio stations, and art galleries; a friend and confidant of members of government and high society. I would have been delighted to meet him. Unfortunately he wasn't interested. I spoke to an army of secretaries but was unable to persuade them to put me through. I asked diplomats and clergymen for help, but to no avail. The great Chateaubriant was too busy. If he wasn't traveling, he was in a meeting or delivering a speech or writing an editorial. In short, he was never there, and if, by chance, he dropped by his office, he was not to be disturbed.

But sometimes the good Lord has a wry sense

of humor. On my way home to Paris, as I was waiting to board my plane, I noticed excited activity around a short, unimpressive-looking man. Obsequious assistants and secretaries trailed him all the way to the gate. As soon as he came aboard, the captain rushed out to greet him, and the stewardesses fell all over themselves to charm him. Curious, I discreetly asked one of them who he was. "Oh, didn't you know? That's Chateaubriant." As he eased into the seat next to mine, I thought that I would get my interview after all. But then I had a better idea. I decided to pay him back for the time I had wasted pursuing him. With what I hoped was great nonchalance, I took out a French book and began to flip through it. Evidently, he was in the mood for conversation.

"Oh, are you French?"

"No," I replied curtly.

"Algerian?"

I shook my head.

"But you read French?"

"It would seem so." Realizing I was disinclined to chat, he fell silent. An hour went by. I took out an Israeli paper and began taking notes intently.

"What's that?" he asked.

"Hebrew."

"Are you Israeli?"

"No," I replied, not deigning to look at him. Another hour passed before he returned to the attack. "What brought you to Brazil? Business?"

"No."

"Vacation?"

"No."

"An official mission, perhaps?"

I shook my head, and then, after a silence, added, "I'm a journalist."

He was delighted to hear it. "Really? In that case we're colleagues. I'm a journalist too."

My eyes widened. "Oh, what's your name?"

He brightened. "Surely you've heard of me. Assis Chateaubriant."

I pretended to search my memory. "Chateaubriant, Chateaubriant. . . . Like the great writer, you mean?" Yes, he said, that's it. "But with a *t* instead of a *d*. And not René. Assis."

I looked at him more closely. "I'm sorry, sir. The name doesn't register. No doubt it's my fault, but I don't think I know you." Disbelief crept over his face. "I cannot believe that nobody mentioned my name," he said. I pretended to search my memory. No . . . "I met with a lot of important people in Rio and São Paulo. Senators, industrialists, high officials. I visited the editorial offices of the great dailies, but . . ."

He seemed dejected. "And no one spoke of me?" I drove in the final nail. "No. No one." He muttered something in Portuguese that I didn't understand. Some of his certainties had crumbled. He was silent for several hours.

Just before we landed in Madrid, I took pity

on him and confessed the truth. He was as famous as he had thought, after all. "Thank you," he exclaimed, clasping my arm. "Thank you for the lesson. From now on I'll meet with any foreign journalist who wants to see me." Between Madrid and Paris he offered me a job with one of his papers. I promised I would think about it.

Perhaps I should have accepted. If I had married Hanna, as I was then ready to do, my meager *Yedioth Ahronoth* salary wouldn't have paid for the wedding or anything else. Nor would there have been a shortage of articles to write for Chateaubriant, for in that year, 1954, Paris once again became important and newsworthy. Pierre Mendès-France — charismatic, popular, energetic, and imaginative — intrigued not only the French, but newspaper readers throughout the world.

Paris

Pierre Mendès-France: a magical, legendary name that aroused enthusiasm and hatred in equal measure. Was he too intellectual to serve as prime minister? Perhaps he had too much integrity. A man of obsessive honesty, determined to honor his ethical and political commitments, he attained his position thanks to his *Weltanschauung* and his philosophy of social justice. François Mauriac often spoke to me about him. He admired and loved him as he admired and loved De Gaulle, for each proved capable of ending the absurd violence of war, one in Indochina, the other in Algeria, and each succeeded in imposing his own concept of man's destiny.

In Tel Aviv there was a sudden surge of interest in foreign news, especially from France. The war in Indochina had entered its final phase. Dien Bien Phu dominated international politics. There was speculation about its geopolitical and strategic implications, about what China and the Soviet Union would do. The atmosphere was supercharged, with stormy debates in the French National Assembly. Power was up for grabs, and Mendès-France declared himself a candidate. "What, another Jew?" howled anti-Semites who in the 1930s had shouted, "Better Hitler than Blum." Their obvious hatred for the new prime minister, who put himself forward as a man of peace, provoked uneasiness in all political circles.

It was a busy time for me. I was happy, involved, and fully absorbed in my work. I had found my true vocation. I would finally complete my break out of the exclusive domain of Jewish or Israeli issues. I hurried from press conferences at the Quai d'Orsay to meetings at the Palais-Bourbon, sometimes skipping lunch, but never the papers. I devoured the dailies, scanned the weeklies. Dov, my employer and friend, asked me to interview Mendès-France. Naturally, I tried, and naturally I failed. And naturally Dov refused to give up. He sent me daily cables urging me not to give up either. I laid siege to the press office of the Hôtel Matignon, bombarding them with written requests. Still no reply. Finally, I wrote Mendès-France a despairing, pathetically naïve letter. "Mr. Prime Minister," I pleaded, "if you refuse me an interview, one of two things will happen: Either my newspaper — which is spending a fortune on cables — will go bankrupt and I will be unemployed, or I will be fired. In either case, the responsibility will be yours." Evidently unconcerned with this burden of guilt, he answered with a hastily scribbled note assuring me that, although there would be no interview, if either of the predicted misfortunes befell me, he would personally help me find another job. Dov was encouraged. "See? You're already in direct contact with him. Just keep trying."

It was around this time that Givon reappeared. "I just got in from Geneva," he announced with his usual phlegmatic intonation. I knew he wanted me to ask what he was doing there, so I did him the favor. "Oh, nothing," he replied. I was, of course, meant to feign incredulity, and so I complied. "Well," he said, "since you insist . . . I had to set something up for Pierre." An alarm went off in my head. There was, of course, no dearth of Pierres in France, but by now I knew Givon's style. He wanted me to keep asking questions, and I decided to oblige him. "Pierre who?" I asked. He stared at me as though I had just asked whether Paris was the capital of Togo. "What do you mean, Pierre who? Pierre Mendès-France. Who else?" Playing the game, I asked, "You know him?" Once again I was treated to a withering look, as if to say, Who do you think would know him if not I? He went on as if talking to himself. "In fact, I'm going to see him tomorrow — no, the day after." In spite of myself, my imagination ran away with me. I pictured myself in the prime minister's office asking probing questions and jotting down confidential replies that would make the front page of *Yedioth Ahronoth* and all the world's press the next day.

But my optimism failed me soon enough. Who was I to Joseph Givon that he would let me go with him? Hadn't I disappointed him by refusing to go to Prague? He kept on talking. "Actually, if you feel like it, maybe I could take you with me."

I told him I would give him anything he wanted if . . .

He bristled. "You don't have to give me anything. There's nothing I need."

He suddenly seemed annoyed. Once again I felt my chance slipping away. I kicked myself for having offended him by trying to bribe him. But he decided to let it go. "I like doing favors," he said. "So come with me to Pierre's. I'll phone you tomorrow morning and give you the go-ahead." He spoke as if it were a military operation. Here we go again, a voice inside me whispered, but I silenced it. I wanted to show my gratitude, but before I could thank him adequately, he extended his injured hand (I never did figure out why he shook hands sometimes with the right and sometimes with the left), said goodbye, and limped away. When I realized he hadn't said what time he would call the next morning, I ran after him. "You'll see," he muttered. I started to ask again, but I could see he was getting annoyed. So be it. I would wait all morning, all day if I had to.

Givon kept his word. If he was a liar, he was as anxious to be believed as an artist is to be admired. My notebook indicates that he

436

phoned at precisely 11:38 A.M. "Be ready for an urgent communication," he said. So he was still intent on playing the conspiracy game. "When?" I whispered. In an hour. Once again he kept his word. "I dropped in on Pierre this morning," he said. "We had breakfast alone together." In other words, the meeting had already taken place, without me. I tried hard to swallow my bitterness, but Givon explained, "I had to speak to him about you first. I couldn't just show up with you in tow without warning, could I?" So the plan was still on. "Pierre told me he would be happy to meet you. I even translated some of your articles for him. He was touched by the one about his investiture." So I would see him tomorrow? "Absolutely." There was a long pause, and then: "I'll call you tonight. Will you be in?" "What time?" I asked, but he had hung up.

I was supposed to write an article for *Yedioth* that evening, but it could wait. Givon's call took precedence. A man on intimate terms with the masters of the Kremlin and Peking, who visited Mordechai Oren in prison and had been photographed in the midst of a throng of Soviet officers, was worth the sacrifice. I sat home and waited, annoyed when Leneman used the phone. I wished I could have kept the line open by telling him the truth, but Givon never would have forgiven me. So I invented a tale: A beautiful friend of mine, a girl I loved, had promised to meet me tomorrow. It would be a catastrophe if I missed her call. Leneman and his wife both smiled. They wanted to know who the girl was and where I had met her. They didn't go so far as to ask if she was Jewish, but I felt myself blush. "Shyness becomes you," Madame Leneman said. Meanwhile, I bit my nails in anticipation. To keep him off the phone I got Leneman to talk about his wartime experiences in the Soviet Union. He succeeded in distracting me from Givon and his mysterious exploits as we discussed the stages of his interminable march to the depths of Siberia and Stalin's insane anti-Semitism. Leneman had been first to speak of the Jewish tragedy in the Soviet Union. Actually, I listened with some skepticism. Labor camps in the USSR? Courts doing the bidding of the NKVD? Summary executions? It was like listening to Victor Kravchenko in Yiddish. It all seemed impossible, unthinkable. Yet Leneman was an eyewitness. Originally from Warsaw, he was a war refugee in Moscow, where he became the correspondent of the Jewish Telegraphic Agency. He had known Solomon Mikhoels, the great theater director whose murder in Minsk in 1949 sounded the alarm. In Moscow Leneman had associated with Jewish novelists who were later shot on Stalin's orders: Peretz Markish, Dovid Bergelson, Der Nister. Despite everything I already knew — the so-called Doctors' Plot, the anti-Zionist and anti-cosmopolitan campaign that had swept through the Communist world — I still could not get used to the

438

idea that so many intellectuals could have gone on worshiping and remained faithful all these years to a viscerally racist despot. And then there had been the infamous Ribbentrop–Molotov Pact. . . . And yet, how could one forget the heroism and sacrifices of the Red Army and the Soviet partisans, the misery of an entire people? I didn't challenge what Leneman said, but I did wonder about it.

Finally, it was almost eleven, and Madame Leneman went to bed. Leneman retired at midnight. I went to my room and stretched out on the bed, fully clothed. I tried to read but found it impossible to concentrate. I had never waited so anxiously for a phone call, even when I thought I was in love. I picked up the receiver to make sure the line was working. Everything was fine except me. Joseph was driving me crazy. It was already two in the morning, and I was facing another sleepless night. Okay, the important thing was to meet Mendès-France, but would the damn phone ever ring? I talked to it, harassed it, and finally it rang. In my excitement, I woke everyone up: "Joseph?" Givon waited an interminable moment before saying: "I'll pick you up tomorrow at noon on the dot." He hung up before I could say a word. I wondered whether to call Dov. An inner voice urged caution. With Givon you never knew. Tomorrow could mean next week or next year. I had to get some sleep. If the meeting came off, I would have to be in good form. But I couldn't sleep. I felt like talking to someone so I went downstairs to the corner café, which was still open.

I stood at the counter and drank a scalding café-crème. A muttering drunk was sipping wine. A woman looked at me invitingly. I smiled, thinking of Givon. She smiled back. The waiter gaped at me, incredulous. He often teased me for being too straitlaced, and here I was . . . The woman walked over to me. "Problems, honey? Something bothering you?" I told her that, on the contrary, everything was fabulous. "In that case," she said, "why don't you tell me all about it?" "Leave him alone," the waiter broke in. "Can't you see he's not interested?" I ordered another café-crème, bought her one, and we chatted about this and that — in short, about life. The drunk joined in, for he knew a thing or two about life himself, and pretty soon the waiter put his two cents in as well. We philosophized until dawn. My throat was dry when I got home, but I felt good, at peace with the world. Madame Leneman, up earlier than usual, knocked on my door and invited me to breakfast. "How did it go?" she asked. I looked at her, uncomprehending. "You know, your beautiful friend . . ." I thanked her for her interest, assured her that the girl was still beautiful and that I loved her with all my heart. But we had decided to stop seeing each other. That made poor Madame Leneman very sad. "Don't worry," I said. "It's just a lovers' quarrel." Her face brightened.

At noon a taxi pulled up. "Let's go," Givon said, as though the driver had known the way since childhood. We set out in silence. Givon was a great lover of silences. Perhaps he was a mystic. His meditative air made him seem present yet remote, as though he were listening to voices he alone was worthy of hearing. I was dying of curiosity. Were we going to see Mendès-France? The signs were good. We seemed to be on the way to the National Assembly. Place de la Concorde. Excellent. My heart pounded. But why were we turning onto the Champs-Élysées? This wasn't the way. Where the hell was my silent torturer taking me? We turned off the main boulevard, drove along the Seine, passed several intersections, and turned into the Rue du Conseiller-Collignon, where the taxi came to a full stop in front of an austere but elegant building. A policeman standing guard at the door recognized Givon and saluted him amicably. Givon finally spoke as we waited for the elevator: "I thought it would be better to see him at home, in private. There are too many people at his office at Matignon." In other words, Givon, not the prime minister, had decided where the interview would be held. Mendès-France was at his beck and call! I had not yet recovered from my astonishment when Givon added, "I asked if we could have lunch. It's better that way. More private."

Givon rang the bell, and the maid who answered also recognized my friend the miracle-worker. She showed us into a salon where Givon obviously felt at home. The young woman was happy to see him. "I'll tell Madame you've arrived," she said, and a moment later there was Lily Mendès-France, the elegant, lovely, distinguished wife of the prime minister. "Sorry to keep you waiting," she said, kissing Givon on both cheeks. I felt like I was dreaming. "My husband will be here any minute now," our hostess announced warmly. I prayed that there would be no hitch, that the French government would not be ousted by a no-confidence vote before lunch. "What would you like to drink while we wait?" Givon had an aperitif.

We were shown to comfortable chairs, but I couldn't sit still. Two adolescents joined us. Our hostess looked at her sons proudly. Givon chatted with them about their studies. I nodded, agreeing with everything they said. A relaxed, intimate atmosphere was suddenly interrupted by the ringing of a telephone. Madame Mendès-France went out. My heart pounded. It was bad news. "My husband asks you to excuse him. He's been detained at the National Assembly." End of dream. I felt my stomach turn over but managed to conceal my disappointment. Oh well, I would write an article about how I almost met Mendès-France, a sort of interview in absentia.

Dov's reaction: "Why give up? You're a friend of the family now." I intended to prevail once more upon Givon, who, after all, really was a friend of the family. Unfortunately, he had to leave Paris. International developments required his presence elsewhere. Ho Chi Minh? Khrushchev? I bombarded him with questions, but he merely shrugged. I wasn't sure whether to believe him or not, but he had brought me to Mendès-France's home, and if he knew the French prime minister, he might well be on speaking terms with other world leaders too. In any case, he vanished from Paris.

He reappeared at Orly Airport sometime later, when the Israeli ambassador and his entourage came to welcome General Moshe Dayan, who was on an official visit to Paris. The rest of us had to stand in a special waiting room, but there was Givon, limping out onto the tarmac and shaking hands with the illustrious visitor just as he came down the ramp. Who had given him authorization? The ambassador was as puzzled as I was, and his advisers knew no more than he did.

I saw Givon again in Geneva in 1955, during the summit conference attended by Soviet marshals Zhukov and Bulganin (covered with medals), British prime minister Anthony Eden (more elegant than his colleagues), French prime minister Edgar Faure (the most intellectual of the group), and Eisenhower (godfather, if not father, to the meeting). I was most interested in Zhukov, conqueror of Berlin, the man who had vanquished Hitler. If only I could approach him,

I would ask him to confirm Givon's claim that they were friends.

Givon intrigued the press by accompanying the chief of East German intelligence everywhere. From that moment on we communicated only through the mail: cards and letters from Warsaw, Peking, Prague, and Moscow, where he became a movie producer. It was also in Moscow that he married the daughter of one of the physicians imprisoned on Stalin's orders during the time of the so-called Doctors' Plot. "I will never return to the West," he wrote to me. "It's too late to turn back now." *Izvestia* (or was it *Pravda*?) published an article denouncing him for dealing in "contraband." Arrested as a smuggler, he was sentenced to ten years in prison. "I'm innocent," he told me in a pathetic letter. "The truth will out in the end." The truth — the word seemed flexible coming from Givon. But he was right. He was released — "thanks to the intervention of several Western ambassadors" — with the court's apologies. Disgusted with the Soviet system, he returned to Prague and then resurfaced in Paris, where he lived in my old room at the Lenemans' home. After that, he settled in Israel, where he died of a heart attack.

Newspapers and magazines in Tel Aviv published many obituaries and articles about him and the many sides of his character. Haim Guri wrote a book called *Who Knows Joseph G.?* The public yearned for clarification of the Givon mystery, but received little satisfaction.

I often think of him with affection. I came close to sharing a few of his adventures, real or imaginary. Adventurers don't always tell the truth; they prefer to invent it. But he did take me to lunch at the home of the Mendès-France family, didn't he?

In those years Paris teemed with strange characters: genuine vagabonds and fake warriors, currency smugglers, impoverished princes, men intoxicated with holiness, others with debauchery, men of many trades and of none. Listening to their real or fabricated memories, I gathered stories for my novels to come.

Like most of my foreign colleagues in search of the exotic, I spent a lot of time in the Latin Quarter (remembrance of existentialism past) and Montparnasse (hoping to encounter starving artists on leave from their garrets). I would sit at an outdoor table at La Coupole and jot down ideas and impressions. Looking up from the page, I hoped to discover the next Soutine or Modigliani, or even Chagall. Some had talent but no luck, while some of the lucky ones were sadly lacking in talent.

I liked to wander around with my friend Avigdor Arikha, the painter. Born in Romania, he had endured the ghettos and camps in the Romanian-occupied territory of Transnystria. He often accompanied me on midnight visits to Radio France to send my dispatches. I tried to get him to talk about Mogilev, for not enough is known of the history of that ghetto that became the site of massacre. Arikha, a great artist (delicate drawings, stunning portraits), evolved from abstract expressionism to a classicism of rare originality. He was a man of great esoteric erudition. A friend and confidant of Samuel Beckett, he was interested in everything: philosophy and literature, science and history. At once naïve and arrogant, sweet and rigid, he was capable of losing his temper over nothing. You had merely to disagree with something he said. I envied him for having taken part in the war of independence in 1948. He had arrived in Palestine with the Youth Aliyah. Naturally, we often talked about the situation in Israel. He would have liked to have been able to rewrite history and live in a Jewish kingdom. He imagined himself as "Prince of Jerusalem," and, in his magnanimity, he crowned me "Prince of Galilee."

If there was a "Prince of Lithuania," it would have been our friend Izis, an exceptional, inspired photographer, intimate of the poet Jacques Prévert and André Malraux. Nicolas, my friend from Ambloy and Versailles, helped research the text for his album on Israel, a masterpiece.

I also spent time with Mane Katz, an old friend of Yehuda Mozes, the owner of *Yedioth*, who had asked me to get in touch with him. Short and bubbly, astonishingly agile for his age, he skipped as he walked and talked. He liked to tell anecdotes (true or invented) about his vague resemblance to Ben-Gurion. A woman supposedly fell in love with him when she mistook him for the Israeli prime minister. A spy offered him Arab military secrets in exchange for a recommendation addressed to the Good Lord Himself, who, as everyone knows, lives somewhere in Jerusalem. A crook offered him a large sum of money for the treasury of the Jewish state. "Funny thing, the moment I reveal my true identity, they disappear," he added with a chuckle.

His apartment looked like a storehouse of Jewish antiques. Ritual objects and ancient books were scattered everywhere, in indescribable disorder: on the floor, on the bed, and even under it. I wondered how he managed to sleep, live, and paint in such chaos, but somehow he did. There was always a bottle of whiskey or vodka under his blanket, and we would drink out of cups as we chatted. He told me of his childhood in Kremenchug, his nomadic adolescence, and his early years in Paris, where he came into contact with the greatest names in the art world. He was jealous of Picasso and especially of Chagall. He knew countless stories about the former's love life and the latter's intrigues to advance his career.

One day when he was in an especially good mood, he told me he had a present for me. "I'm alone in the world," he explained, "for all practical purposes without an heir. The jackals will get their claws on my canvases. So why don't you take a few?" Without waiting for an answer, he brought them out to me, and I don't know which touched me more, his generosity or the atmosphere that permeated his work. His pictures were of old Hasidim and their young disciples, and resonated with the melodies that filled my memory. I needed the warmth that seemed to pour from his paintings, a warmth that carried me back to a world swallowed by history. "What about it?" Mane Katz asked. "This present will be worth millions someday, and you don't even say thank you?" He laughed, while I was so gripped by emotion that I felt like hiding. "Thank you," I finally managed to stammer, "a thousand thanks, but I cannot accept such an extravagant gift." He was speechless. "What, are you crazy?" he said. "I offer you treasures and you turn them down? You don't like my work? If Chagall or Picasso gave you some canvases, would you refuse them too?" He shook with anger. "I love your work," I told him. "Really I do. It's just that as a journalist I can't accept gifts. It's a question of professional ethics." He exploded with indignation, telling me that ethics had nothing to do with it. We argued about it for a while. Finally, he sat down on his bed, legs folded under him, and pointed to a stool. "Okay," he said. "Explain your ethics to me." I tried to beg off, but he insisted. Citing ancient sources that had nothing to do with the matter at hand, some drawn from Scripture, others from my own imagination, I spoke for an hour or two, or perhaps until dawn. I talked about the duty of objectivity, the pitfalls of complacency, explaining that a reporter is both witness and judge, and that the Bible is scathing in its criticism of judges who take gifts. I don't know if I convinced him, but I do know I wasn't telling the truth. Actually, I turned down his gift because I was too poor; I had no place to put such valuable works. My only possessions were a typewriter and a suitcase. What would I do — hang the paintings in my suitcase?

Another "gift" I declined torments me to this day. The Yiddish poet Abraham Sutzkever and my colleague Léon Leneman were both close friends of Marc Chagall. One day they sent me a message from the artist. It seems he liked my book *Souls on Fire* and proposed that we collaborate on a book about the great masters and their disciples. He would do the illustrations.

I hesitated and procrastinated, delaying my response. Finally, I let this project, a chance to work with one of the century's great painters, slip away.

One gift I was lucky enough to reject was a pair of shoes. At a Zionist meeting an elegant, seemingly educated man approached me. He spoke halting French but perfect Yiddish. He told me he was from my region and asked if we could have coffee together. We went to an outdoor café and he told me an interesting tale. He remembered Sighet, which he had passed through during the war. Drafted into the labor battalion, he had followed the Hungarian army through Poland and into Ukraine. Now he was an international businessman. Import-export — the magic words. He was making so much money he didn't know how to spend it. "Listen," he said. "I have a brand-new pair of expensive shoes. They're too small for me, and I'd be delighted if you would wear them." I refused. He insisted, but to no avail. No longer a starving Sorbonne student, I owned a perfectly good pair of shoes. But he refused to take no for an answer, acting as though his future were at stake. I therefore fell back on my standard argument: professional ethics. It sounded less convincing in Yiddish than in French, but I can be stubborn when I have to be. I don't remember exactly how we parted, except that he asked for my card.

A few weeks later I was summoned to the Quai des Orfèvres, national police headquarters. My heart was in my throat as I walked in. Kafka was right: You can feel guilty even when you don't know what you're accused of.

The *commissaire* who received me looked like a detective in a crime film: impassive face, icy voice, penetrating stare. He asked to see identification, and I showed him my press card. "Citizen of?" Stateless, I said. "I see." He pondered in silence while examining a file on the desk in front of him. I would have given a lot to know what was in that file. "So," he finally said, glancing at me sidelong as if to see if I would fall into the trap, "tell me about Vargas." I told the policeman I didn't know any Vargas. "Are you sure?" His voice seemed threatening. "You maintain you don't know Vargas?" My brain whirled. If I gave the wrong answer, I was obviously in deep trouble, but I didn't know any Vargas, except for the president of Brazil, which is what I told him. Did the *commissaire* think I was toying with him and with the authority he represented? "Okay," he said. "Forget Vargas. Tell me about Jacques Rubinstein." Rubinstein? I knew a tailor named Rubinstein on the Rue Vieille-du-Temple, but his name was Boris, not Jacques. I also knew a medical student by that name whose father had just died, but that was Albert. The *commissaire* was obviously displeased. "All right," he said. "Let's forget Jacques Rubinstein too. What do you know about Kurt Zeligman? And don't tell me you don't know him either." Unfortunately, I was forced to admit that I knew Zeligman no better than I knew Vargas or Rubinstein. Surely this *commissaire* was anti-Semitic. What did he want from me? I was so tense I thought I would eventually confess to every unsolved crime in Paris. Without taking his eyes off me, he opened another file and slid a photograph across the table to me. "I suppose you don't know him either," he said sarcastically. I gave a start. "But that's . . ." The *commissaire* jumped. "That's who?" The man with the shoes, I said. "Shoes?" he exclaimed, clearly excited. "Did you say shoes?" I told him the whole story, and he picked up the phone and issued instructions that were later explained to me. The man in question had been traveling from continent to continent on false passports. He was wanted by Interpol. He had just stolen some diamonds which, thanks to me, would now be returned to their rightful owner. When I asked the *commissaire* how they had connected me to all this, he explained with a smile, "Your card. We found it in his pocket. If you hadn't mentioned that business about the shoes, we would have had to let him go." The *commissaire* invited me to attend the trial. The thief did not act guilty. He claimed to speak only Yiddish, and after considerable effort the court managed to come up with a sworn interpreter. The defendant was convicted and sentenced to several years in prison. I'm not sure why, but I avoided looking at him as I left the courtroom.

Years later he sent me an angry letter. "If you had agreed to wear my shoes, we would both be millionaires today."

I finally met Mendès-France at a reception at the Weizmann Institute in New York, but by then he was out of power. So I never did get that scoop, though not for lack of trying. But there is always a reason for everything in this life, even if it takes time to see the links. It was thanks to Mendès-France that I made the acquaintance of François Mauriac, whom I had initially contacted in the forlorn hope that he might help me get an interview with Mendès-France, whose intellectual master he was. Yet it was my encounter with the great writer and Nobel laureate that turned out to be one of the most important in my life.

I first saw Mauriac in 1955 during an Independence Day celebration at the Israeli embassy. As always, he was surrounded by a throng of people hanging on his every word, and I wasn't sure how to approach him. Plagued by my usual cursed timidity, I stood on his right, on his left, and finally directly in front of him, not daring to open my mouth. Constantly underfoot, I was unable to utter a single word. At last he said goodbye to his official hosts. "Now or never," I said to myself, but he was already on his way out. I followed. Someone handed him his overcoat, and I helped him put it on. He must have thought I was part of the embassy staff, because he shook my hand and thanked me for the warm welcome. "No," I began to stammer, but he went on, "I'm delighted you invited me. Israel is dear to my heart, and I enjoy participating in its celebrations. God knows it has every right to celebrate."

Overcoming my embarrassment, I told him I was not a diplomat but a journalist. He asked which paper I worked for. I told him and quickly asked for an interview. I expected him to plead lack of time or to tell me to call his secretary, but instead he took out an appointment book, and an instant later, I was the world's happiest journalist. "Are you sure you're not busy that day?" he asked. I was sure. "But you didn't even check your book." No need, I told him as we shook hands. You only had to dare, I told myself, and the rest was easy.

It was easy, that is, except for the usual waiting. To make time pass, I wrote a few pieces: Paris by night, Paris on Sunday, Paris at dawn. A colleague of mine — Yerahmiel Viernik, a former leader in Jabotinsky's party and editor in chief of the review that had published my long piece on Beethoven — joined me for an all-night walk through Pigalle, the Parisian red-light district. We bought some french fries and stood under the glaring lights of a café counter drinking coffee and discussing (don't laugh!) the poetry of Chaim Nahman Bialik, the man who had said that words were whores. Not surprisingly, none of the working girls approached us. No doubt they realized at a glance that we were not prospective customers. Luckily, they didn't understand our Hebrew, or they would have collapsed in laughter. Back home I faced the astonished smiles of the Lenemans sitting at their breakfast table. It was the first time I had stayed out all night, but they were too discreet to ask questions. "I was out working on an article," I told them. I had completely forgotten that I was supposedly involved in a complicated love affair. They must have thought me a wretched liar.

The next day I was invited to a performance of the Marquis de Cuevas dance company. In truth, I am not a lover of dance. But that night I was the guest of a member of the Israeli parliament — Shraggai, a politician friend of Viernik's and mine. He adored ballet, and for me it simply meant spending a couple of hours in his company. A tireless emissary of his movement, Shraggai had clear blue eyes, a thick, drooping moustache, and incredible charm. If he didn't know everybody, he knew everything everybody wanted to know about everybody else. I loved listening to his gossip, predictions, and analyses. Besides which, he told me he had a pleasant surprise for me.

He was right about that. The surprise was a young American student whose beauty left me breathless. Her name was Kathleen and that night she tiptoed into my life. I liked her name, its melodious sound. Everything about this girl was attractive: her dark brown eyes, silky black shoulder-length hair, a discreet, mysterious smile. I knew if I lowered my guard I would be hit by one of those thunderbolts I never knew how to handle. So of course I lowered my guard.

I pretended to be absorbed in the show and to ignore the young American girl seated between Shraggai and me. But suddenly I forgot all about my appointment with Mauriac. I forgot

455

about Mendès-France. I even forgot about Givon. A single question popped into my mind: Was she Jewish? But then, did it really matter? After all, I wasn't going to marry her. Just the same, I was curious. During the intermission she left us for a moment. "So?" Shraggai asked. "Not bad," I lied, "but believe me, I'm not interested." He wanted to know what I was interested in. Mauriac and Mendès-France, I told him. He didn't believe me, and I tried to convince him. In the meantime, Kathleen came back. Having overheard snatches of our exchange, she asked me about Mauriac and about my work. My English left a lot to be desired and her French wasn't great, so Shraggai acted as interpreter. She asked me why I thought Mauriac was "underrated" in her country. The word was unfamiliar to me, and there followed an incongruous but intense discussion about the difference between "underrated" and "underestimated." Suddenly Kathleen took my arm and asked, "Would you like me to give you English lessons?" Ask a child if he wants candy, a sick man if he wants to live. "And you can help me with my French, all right?" Shraggai watched, amused; I had fallen into the trap he had set for me.

The bell rang to alert us to return to our seats. I continued to feign enthusiasm, applauding in all the right places, admiring the choreography and the ballerinas. It's amazing what you'll do for someone you're about to fall in love with, someone you already love. Had Kathleen suggested we go onstage for a few *entrechats*, I would have followed her without fear of ridicule. Maybe that's what love is: not to fear. But I had feared it all my life, and when the curtain came down, the old inhibitions resurfaced.

I invented an excuse to disappear. Professional duty, I said. It was time to send my cable. Shraggai tried to persuade me to go with them to a restaurant. I resisted. I owed it to my readers, I said. In fact, I had no dispatch to send that night, and Shraggai probably guessed as much. "If you stay with us, I'll give you a scoop tomorrow," he said. Of course, I had no wish to leave, but I dug in my heels so as not to lose face. It was a suggestion from Kathleen that saved me from myself: "Why don't you send your cable and then join us? We'll wait for you, won't we, Shraggai?" Of course, he said. "But hurry." "Yes, hurry," Kathleen pleaded. Was she already getting attached to me?

I set out for the métro station at a run, but Shraggai's voice stopped me: "Don't you want to know which restaurant?" Idiot. He named a well-known café, adding, "It's not far from the telegraph office, Rue Montmartre." True, it wasn't far, but I had nothing to send anyway. I decided to wire Dov a brief message: "Project Mendès-France on track again." Let him have a sleepless night for a change. He would definitely call me in the morning, wanting to know more, but there was time enough to think about that. For the moment I had to hurry. Shraggai and Kathleen were waiting. I repeated her name to myself as I walked. *Kath-leen, Kath-leen.* It seemed the most beautiful name in the world. Sure, it wasn't Jewish, but so what? The important thing was that she was waiting for me and that she was beautiful. And there she was, keeping an eye on the entrance.

She smiled when she saw me come in. "Thanks for being so quick," she said. "We've already ordered," Shraggai said. "What do you feel like?" Coffee. "That's all?" Kathleen asked. "Aren't you hungry?" I wasn't. "Try," she urged. Okay, I would have what she was having. "A sandwich?" Fine. "A ham sandwich?" Uh-oh. There's your answer, I said to myself: She's not Jewish. "Cheese, then?" she suggested. Fine. At which point Shraggai launched into a discussion about dietary laws in the Jewish tradition. Kathleen asked pertinent questions. Her voice set me dreaming and her glance intoxicated me. I told her I would explain the complicated dietary laws some other time. "So there'll be another time?" she asked in an innocent, anxious voice. "Of course," Shraggai said. "What about tomorrow night?" "Sorry," Kathleen replied, "I can't." I added that I couldn't either, that I was busy. "I was lying," she whispered to me as Shraggai paid the check. "Actually I'm not busy. I was going to suggest we start the English

458

lessons tomorrow night, but if you're not free
. . ." I told her I had lied too — I was at
her service. I came close to confessing that I
was free every night. "Call me in the morning,"
she said joyously, giving me her number. When
Shraggai came back he announced that he was
taking Kathleen back to Neuilly. It was two
in the morning, and I walked home borne by
a new happiness.

The next morning was ruled by the telephone.

"What's up?" an excited Dov wanted to know.
"It's not that crackpot Givon again, is it?" I
reassured him without giving anything away. My
evasiveness only sharpened his excitement. "Be
patient," I said. He laughed. "Don't tell me
you're not impatient too." But it was no longer
Mauriac or Mendès-France I was dying to see
again.

Anxious, I called Kathleen. "I didn't wake
you, did I?"

"No, I wasn't sleeping."

"What were you doing?"

"Thinking about last night."

"I owe you a confession. I don't know a thing
about dance."

"I know, I could feel you looking at me."

"But I didn't look at you either."

"I felt it anyway."

There was a long silence. "Do you really want
to see me again?" she asked, in her touchingly
sweet voice. I threw the question right back
to her. Another long silence, and then she said,

"Yes, very much." We made an appointment for me to pick her up in Neuilly.

Next came an amused call from Shraggai. "So, don't you want to thank me? Don't tell me you didn't find her beautiful, charming, cultured — in a word, extraordinary." I said nothing. "If you want to ask me anything about her," he went on, "don't hesitate." But I had only one question: How had he met her? He said it was a long story. "Why don't you come and have coffee with me?"

Shraggai looked tired — pale and drawn, his eyes bloodshot from insomnia. "She thinks a lot of you," he said without further preamble. I thanked him and reminded him that he had promised me a scoop today. He laughed. "Isn't Kathleen the most beautiful scoop a journalist could ask for? She told me she was afraid of you. Afraid to fall in love with you." And that frightened her? "Yes, because she's not free." I almost choked. She's married? "No, engaged." My anticipated happiness was vanishing. I don't know how I managed to get out the words: "So where did you meet her?"

He had noticed her a month ago standing in line at the Salle Pleyel box office. By chance, they had bought adjoining seats. During the intermission Shraggai was approached by a friend of his, a Mossad officer, who questioned him about his neighbor. How long had he known her? What did he know about her? Shraggai explained that he had never seen her before.

The Mossad agent was disappointed. "Too bad. We thought you could help us. She's German, and she lives with someone we're interested in, a German scientist who's working for Syria." Shraggai was skeptical: "Even the Mossad can make a mistake. On the way in, I struck up a conversation with her, so I can tell you she's not German but American. I doubt she knows anyone who works for an Arab country. In fact, she just arrived from the United States."

Shraggai accompanied her home and since that evening had become her chaperon, guide, and bodyguard. She treated him not so much like a father as like an old friend of her father's; he was her confidant. Why had he wanted to meet her? "I like helping fate," he said. And that's why he wanted to throw us into each other's arms, even though she was engaged? "Sometimes fate opens a door, sometimes it closes it. And sometimes it stands aside without doing anything."

Then Shraggai asked me some questions about his protégée. Had I found her sufficiently attractive? Did I want to see her again? If my profession had taught me anything, it was the art of sidestepping questions with a minimum of elegance but a maximum of caution. I knew how to keep a secret and didn't breathe a word about my appointment with Kathleen.

The afternoon seemed interminable. I had a terrible migraine and found it hard to breathe. I canceled all my appointments. I would not

461

attend the press conference at the Quai d'Orsay tomorrow, nor tonight's reception. Leneman suggested we take in a premiere at the Théâtre Antoine. "No thanks," I said. "Something has come up." Suddenly it was impossible for me to sit down at the typewriter and concentrate.

That evening I took the métro to Neuilly. Feeling like a smitten teenager, I rang the bell. Kathleen let me in. "Do you mind if we go to my room instead of the living room?" I didn't mind at all. Her room would be more private. Besides which, Shraggai had told me that Kathleen had a live-in landlady, and landladies made me nervous. The room was not too large but tastefully furnished. Kathleen sat on a blue sofa and invited me to sit beside her. I didn't know how to begin. A gaping hole swallowed all the words and ideas teeming in my brain. I was about to call on my old friend Kant, who had always served me well as conversation fodder, when a voice inside me screamed, Don't be a fool! One stupid remark and she'll show you the door.

Kathleen came to my rescue. She began to talk about her life, her quiet childhood and turbulent adolescence. Her father was Irish and her mother Indian, and she felt torn between two traditions, two cultures, two loyalties. I wondered when she would get around to her fiancé. She spoke as though he didn't exist. Shraggai must have made a mistake. I loved her slightly husky voice. As her eyes carefully

462

examined the tip of her shoes, she spoke slowly, as though fearful of revealing a buried secret. At one point her hand touched mine, perhaps inadvertently. I took it. She said nothing, nor did I. She raised her head. I could feel her hair. Her face was very close to mine. Her breath burned my eyelids. Her lips sought mine. I didn't know a kiss could last so long, nor that it could blossom so deeply. Kathleen was teaching me a lot about my capacities — but unfortunately not enough. When she whispered softly that it was time to make love, the fool that I am protested. "We mustn't," I said almost indignantly. "Believe me, we mustn't." Her eyes widened. "Why not?" Why shouldn't a man and woman who will love each other, who already love each other, make love when they feel like it? My body, tense with desire, wanted to — I was certainly attracted to Kathleen — yet I resisted her. Was it lack of experience or fear of disappointing her? She guided me to her bed, under a purple canopy. We embraced, falling onto the thick bedspread. I felt her body's warmth. I would have given anything to receive what it offered me. But I was not ready to give — or receive — anything. Imprisoned by my inhibitions, religious or otherwise, I rejected the offering. Caresses, kisses, yes. But no more. I stopped myself at the last instant, on the threshold of joy, for deep down I was sure Kathleen was still a virgin. In those days I was convinced that all women were virgins until they married, and how could I, my father's son, "sully" them? "What we do must be pure," I whispered to her. "Do you understand?" She didn't. I launched into a philosophical lesson on love's theological components. Did she know that in the Bible the terms *kedosha* and *kedesha*, which are strangely related, mean "saint" and "prostitute" respectively? Did she know the Gitas? Now I was back on familiar ground. Between two passionate embraces I told her what I had learned in India about sacred eroticism. And had she ever heard of Jewish mysticism? Did she know that every union is a re-union? Is there any union more mysterious and pure than that of two beings imbued with the same need, the same desire? I expressed myself awkwardly, speaking many words but saying nothing, becoming agitated without doing anything she expected of me or anything I expected of myself.

At about three in the morning she gave up, exhausted. "Will I see you again?" she asked. Maybe she was afraid she had disappointed me. I reassured her: I loved her more than ever. I loved her body's beauty and grace as much as the purity of her soul. So of course we had to see each other again. We kissed one last time, and I left.

The métro had stopped running, and the rare taxis were expensive, so I walked home. Hardly anyone was in the street, even on the Champs-Élysées, though it was spring and the weather

464

was fair. I was accosted by prostitutes. An old woman, heavily made up and leering unpleasantly, touched my arm. I jerked it away. Farther on, near the Madeleine, a much younger girl tried to lure me: "I have a baby and no money to feed him." I wondered why I didn't take her up on it. She could give me lessons I sorely needed. But I thought about Kathleen and kept walking. The young prostitute began to cry. Had I insulted her? I turned back and told her that, unfortunately, I wasn't rich. She cursed me and told me to get lost. I was sorry she misunderstood. I didn't mean to hurt her. On the contrary, I was in love, and I wanted to love the whole world: the sleepy passersby, the derelicts, the last customers in the last open cafés, the trees, the clouds, and the wind that drove them. Yes, blessed by a young Indian-Irish woman from Ohio, I would gladly offer blessings of love to all Creation.

The few days that remained before my visit to Mauriac were devoted almost exclusively to him. Kathleen, whom I now saw every evening, did not object, for she knew what was at stake. I rediscovered Mauriac by delving anew into his novels, reencountering his favorite themes: the power of sin and the weight of hatred, forbidden love, and grace. I reread his polemical essays on current affairs for *L'Express* and *Figaro*. I admired his mordant style, his fierceness toward his opponents, whom he demolished before offering them his pity. I disagreed with his absolution of collaborationist writers who had preached hatred and demanded death for the Jews. By what right did he pardon them? I knew, of course, that as a Catholic, he was prepared to forgive anything. But as a Jew, I found it disturbing. God Himself refuses to efface the sins one commits toward others: only the victim may do so. If I questioned him on this issue I might offend him. What questions should I ask? How to overcome my fear of seeming stupid or ignorant? Kathleen watched me and worried about how nervous I seemed. I was ashamed to admit my doubts to her, but finally did so in an effort to elicit her tenderness. It worked. She took me in her arms to boost my morale. When her lips touched mine, my apprehension vanished. The interview with Mauriac suddenly seemed inconsequential. The important thing was that I had at last been allowed to live a real love story. And what a story it was. As always when I transgressed the rules of my own making, a shiver ran through me: what if my father saw me now, what if my grandfather knew. . . .

On the designated day I arrived an hour early at the Avenue Théophile-Gautier. I walked nervously through the neighborhood streets, stopping at shopwindows and outdoor cafés, chain-smoking, mentally rehearsing the questions I wanted to ask. One thing was clear: I had to get him to talk about Mendès-France.

The rest would follow. I didn't think it would be difficult, because he spoke constantly of Mendès-France in his columns.

I was glad it was a slow elevator, for I needed a moment to collect myself. I rang the bell. An elderly housekeeper told me I was expected and led me to the living room. "Please be patient for a few moments," she said. I went to the window and gazed out at the passersby: two schoolgirls in uniform, a housewife walking a recalcitrant dog. A hoarse voice came from behind: "Excuse me for having kept you waiting." I was immediately impressed by Mauriac's simplicity and warmth. Both the writer and the man inspired respect. I knew of his exemplary conduct during the Occupation. *Le Cahier noir de Forez* was testimony to the man, as *Thérèse Desqueyroux* was to the novelist. I felt intimidated.

He was quick to put me at ease, speaking intimately of his work as a journalist. He became ferocious when he mentioned the "spitefulness" of this rightist agitator or that leftist editorialist. In ten minutes I learned more about Parisian politics than I had in five years. I wanted to ask him about Mendès-France but was loath to interrupt him, especially since I found his monologue fascinating. He had read and studied everything associated with the great men who shaped the literary and political destiny of this century, but his favorite theme was the life — and, more so, the death — of a young Jew from Nazareth. When he spoke his name his smile seemed to turn inward. Once started, he had no wish to change the subject. His words were brilliant, but . . . In my essay "An Interview Unlike Any Other" (in *A Jew Today*) I described my reaction, my indignation. Later I was angry at myself, for having said that I knew Jewish children who had suffered more than Jesus and of whom we did not speak. I had no right to hurt him, especially since he never sought to use his faith as a sword against mine. On the contrary, it was because he loved Jesus that he defended Jews, because he suffered at Jesus's suffering, that he strove to assuage ours. But I came to understand that only later. In the end he didn't get me an audience with Mendès-France (for the simple reason that I never asked him), but in the meantime we became friends, and that friendship meant more to me than all the scoops in the world.

A man of integrity whose personality was riddled with contradictions, he was by turns humble and ironic, acerbic and compassionate, a rich bourgeois but a friend of the dispossessed, charitable but fiercely polemical, a devout believer who understood those who doubted faith. "We should have met sooner," he confided to me one day, a tinge of sorrow in his voice. "I'm an old man now, too old to start over."

He wrote of our first meeting in his column of Saturday, May 14, 1955, referring to a "young Israeli who had been a Jewish child in a German camp." Of course, I wasn't Israeli. Perhaps in his mind, Jew and Israeli were the same thing.

I owe him a lot. He was the first person to read *Night* after I reworked it from the original Yiddish. He submitted it to his own publisher, promising to write a preface for the book, to speak of it in the press, and to support it with all the considerable means at his disposal. "No one's interested in the death camps anymore," he was told. "It won't sell." He then took my manuscript to Jérôme Lindon at Éditions de Minuit. The ever-daring Lindon ignored commercial considerations and gave my story a chance.

I don't know how I would have fared without Mauriac. He kept a watchful eye on my literary efforts. During each of my trips to France I went to see him, just to talk. I needed his approval, his trust. He always began with a summary of what people had been talking about in France while I was away. I will never forget his account of a woman's failed suicide against the background of an ill-fated love affair; she was a great journalist for whom he felt true tenderness. Then there was the story of his granddaughter's marriage to a film director. But we also talked about such matters as his latest conversation with General de Gaulle, or the verbal thrashing he had administered to an insolent writer. He spoke often of his confessor, whom he considered a true confidant. Mauriac wept

469

as he spoke of his brother Pierre, an ardent Pétainist accused of collaboration, who had been arrested and imprisoned in Bordeaux in 1944.

Excerpts from conversations with François Mauriac:

"But you were among the few who discerned the evil and refused to compromise."

"Not at first, not at first. Like everyone else, I thought Pétain had the interests of France at heart. I believed that, and even wrote two articles that said so."

"You were not alone."

"No, I wasn't. Others went further, longer, and deeper into error. But that's no excuse."

"Still. You stopped in time. Then there was *Le Cahier noir* . . . ."

"Yes, of course. But let's tell it as it was, as it is. In those days no one was innocent — I mean entirely innocent."

"Except those who resisted. And the victims."

"The victims, yes. Their innocence was absolute."

"You told me I had to speak, to write."

"Yes, I suggested that. You belong to a people who has survived by and through the Word."

"What word?"

"The Lord's Word."

"And the Lord needs men to communicate His will?"

"It would seem so. Otherwise He would not

470

have done it. The Jewish people have been invested with His word, have they not?"

"We are supposed to testify for Him. But how? Christians say, through suffering. We say, through faith."

"But is that enough? You are not the only ones to have suffered, nor to have rejected heresy. In what way are the Jewish people different from others?"

"All peoples are different, each in their own way."

"But only the Jewish people offered the world and its history the man capable and desirous of saving them from themselves."

"Jesus of Nazareth? I know you believe that. But for me — forgive me for repeating it — he is not the Savior."

"For me He is. I recognize it by His suffering, His agony. I belong to Him because He is Love."

"The Jew in me is obliged to say that he belongs only to God. And God is one."

"Any Christian believer would say the same. For us too, God is God, and He is one. But Jesus is His son."

"All human beings are His sons."

"In that case, how do you explain the existence of evil?"

"I distrust explanations."

"And the Nazi hangmen? Those who massacred the Jewish children you knew? Were they, too, God's sons?"

"That is for God to answer."

"Sometimes God prefers to ask questions."

"The answer is beyond me, *Maître*. But I do know that the Nazi killers and torturers were baptized."

A long silence.

"Let us not blame Jesus for that," Mauriac said, lowering his voice. "It is not His fault if we betray His love for us."

"I'm not blaming Jesus. He was crucified by the Romans, and now it is Christians who torment him by committing evil in his name."

At La Méditerranée restaurant:

"I brought you here so you could finally eat something. They don't serve meat. Just fish."

"I am grateful."

"So how would you like some lobster?"

"Sorry, that's not kosher."

"But it's not meat!"

"Some seafood is also forbidden."

"I don't understand."

"It's complicated. It's a matter of having scales or not."

"Shrimp?"

"Forbidden."

"It sure is complicated being a Jew."

"And not only in restaurants."

I settled for a cheese sandwich.

"How did you manage it?"

"Manage what?"

"To survive."

472

"I don't know."

"It was God. God's will. The Lord chose you."

"No, don't say that."

"Don't you believe in God?"

"Yes, I do."

"It was your faith that saved you."

"Don't say that, I beg you."

"Faith can offer support and comfort. It can be a kind of nourishment, a higher nourishment. Faith embodies life and life's power. Perhaps it was faith that made you strong."

"Strength had nothing to do with it."

"Or God?"

"Not God either."

"Then what?"

"I don't know."

There was a long sigh, followed by his usual little smile.

"It is when one knows not that faith arrives."

I felt obliged to reply: "Does that mean when faith arrives, you do know?"

Mauriac, a man of tolerance, never sought to entice me toward Christianity, never made any attempt to proselytize. In one of his columns he recounted a conversation we had about Jesus. I told him that in my view Jesus surely began as a pious Jew who put on his phylacteries every day and that it was because he was a Jew that the Romans condemned him to death and crucified him.

Let me quote from Mauriac's text, for it requires some commentary:

Wednesday, May 29, 1963.

Never have I felt such joy in crowning a book, or rather, a work. The Prix de l'Universalité de la Langue Française, awarded annually to a foreign author writing in our language, was given this year to my friend Elie Wiesel, born in a Jewish community in Transylvania, now an American citizen, New York correspondent for an Israeli newspaper and French novelist.

In a preface to his first book, *Night* (Éditions de Minuit), I told of how we met. When I described to this young journalist from Israel, who had come to interview me, the train packed with Jewish children that my wife saw in the Austerlitz railway station during the Occupation, he said to me, "I was one of them." Our friendship was born of those few words. Elie Wiesel returned from the camps after seeing his whole family burned — a mystic child having lost, or believing to have lost, his faith in the God of love and consolation.

How I love Jewish mystics, witnesses of the first love! Perhaps many still exist, but not within the Israel we know today, whose genius is wholly devoted to conquest and domination. . . .

Someday Elie Wiesel will take me to the Holy Land. He desires it greatly, having a most singular knowledge of Christ, whom he pictures wearing phylacteries, as Chagall saw him, a son of the synagogue, a pious Jew submitting to the Law, and who did not die, "because being human he was made God," Elie Wiesel stands on the borders of the two testaments: he is of the race of John the Baptist. . . .

I thanked him for the warm friendship with which this text is imbued, but when we next met I drew his attention to certain inaccuracies. To begin with, *Night* is not a novel. Second, having never been at the Austerlitz station during the Occupation, I could not have said that I was on that train packed with Jewish children. I probably remarked that I had been in a camp with Jewish children. Third, his criticism of Israel (which aroused no negative reaction within the Jewish community, which trusted him) was unjustified. Fourth, concerning Jesus Christ he ascribes to me a thought that is not mine but his: I believe it was Basil of Caesarea who said that man's aim is to become God. In the Jewish tradition we aspire to greater humility: Man's aim is to be human. Finally, I don't know why he added that "Elie Wiesel stands on the borders of the two testaments," like John the Baptist, but I felt I had to clarify my position for him (as I later did for my friend Jean-Marie Cardinal Lustiger, archbishop of Paris): Where I come from and from where I stand, one cannot be

Jew and Christian at the same time. Jesus was Jewish, but those who claim allegiance to him today are not. In no way does this mean that Jews are better or worse than Christians, but simply that each of us has the right, if not the duty, to be what we are.

We had already discussed this latter point several years earlier, when he did me the honor of dedicating his book on Jesus to me: "To Elie Wiesel, who was a crucified Jewish child." On the whole, however, our relationship was free of conflict. I responded to his friendship with friendship.

Mauriac was interested in Judaism, the Jews, and their enemies. He was perturbed by the anti-Semitism of some of his peers. We spoke often, very often, of Israel, its mission and its ordeals. I invited him to visit the Promised Land: "Let us go together where it all began, for you and me alike." He agreed immediately. I got in touch with the Israeli ambassador, who sent him an official invitation, which he accepted in principle. But he feared the emotional upheaval he might feel at seeing the places where Christ lived his agony and his death. He postponed the journey repeatedly.

A single disagreement briefly troubled our relations when General de Gaulle in 1968 uttered his famous "little phrase" about a "self-assured and dominating people," possibly inspired by Mauriac's comment about genius devoted to conquest and domination. Except that Mauriac was referring to the state of Israel, de Gaulle to the people of Israel and therefore the Jewish people. I felt it necessary to criticize de Gaulle for this, while Mauriac defended him: "No one will convince me that de Gaulle is an anti-Semite." I replied: "A man in his position is responsible not merely for what he says but also for how his words are interpreted. And his comment was interpreted as anti-Jewish." Our quarrel did not last long. Mauriac was not only a great writer but a sincere humanist as well. He found a way to disassociate himself from the general's comment without distancing himself from him. (His son Jean Mauriac later told me of de Gaulle's warm admiration for the Jewish people.)

I happened to be in Paris on the day of Mauriac's funeral. My publisher Paul Flamand and I went to Notre-Dame, but there were too many people. We stayed outside in silence.

My friendship with Mauriac continued until his death. My liaison with Kathleen lasted but a few months. For one thing, there was her fiancé, who was Greek. Then there were the French classes she was supposed to be taking at the Alliance Française. In her spare time she evidently preferred something other than my philosophical monologues on love's "essential purity." During the time we were "together," she also "saw" other men. To make me jealous? To force me to change? We broke up — painfully — in the summer of 1955.

I saw her again, years later, in the United States. She had read the review of my book *The Town Beyond the Wall* in *Time* magazine. Excited, she phoned me at the *Jewish Daily Forward*. She was passing through New York and invited me to join her at the Sherry Netherland. Having converted to Judaism to marry an industrialist from the Midwest, she treated me to a lively account of her new life: Passover seders, Bar Mitzvahs, fund-raising for Israel, receptions, cocktail parties, dinners. She offered to buy a thousand copies of my book to help it climb onto the best-seller lists. I asked her whether she had that many friends or just that much money. She tactfully spoke of her marriage, but not of her husband. "Do you love him?" I asked. She blushed and moved to another subject, telling me of her conversion under the guidance of a reform rabbi, and she paid me a compliment: "In becoming a Jew, I felt closer to you." In other words, it was to please me that she married her super-rich husband. What happened to the Greek fiancé? On that subject too she was discreet. But she took my hand. Here we go again, I said to myself. And yes, she was still attractive, and I was still receptive to her beauty. Our rediscovered "love" endured one afternoon.

Feeling once again the need for a change of scene, I decided to return to Israel. I had a reservation on an El Al flight but a friend of

Bea's from Montreal pleaded with me to yield my seat to her since she had had trouble getting three seats on that flight for herself and her two children. The plane was shot down over Bulgaria by the Bulgarian air force. I felt awful and vaguely responsible. I thought of the legend of the Grand Vizier and his escape to Samarkand. The same fate that saved me doomed them. Who had taken my place? Bea's friend? One of her daughters? All I knew about them was the voice of the mother. It remained with me.

I went by sea. Despite my tendency to get seasick, I enjoy traveling by ship. The lure of the sea is such that desperate people often succumb to its promise of peace. It was the lure I had felt during my first crossing, and now, as I leaned against the railing, I was overwhelmed by the darkly powerful idea of letting go, of allowing all bonds to unravel once and for all. I was convinced that, rocked by the waves, I would at last be at peace.

I spent several weeks in Israel, staying with Dov and Leah but making many trips through the country. I went to Bnei Brak, the most religious suburb of Tel Aviv, which some call Israel's least religious city. But I had a sudden desire to see the "young" Rebbe of Wizhnitz, for he represented an essential part of my past to which I needed to cling. I have spoken of the love and respect I felt for his father, Rebbe Israel.

Slumped in his armchair as if crushed by the

weight of years, he gazed at me with a mixture of tenderness and frustration. Perhaps he was looking for the adolescent who had spent exhilarating shabbats under his roof.

"I look at you," the Rebbe said, "and wonder who you are. I know who you were, but not who you are." I didn't answer. I was thinking of his father. Had I really changed that much? Yet, like the adolescent who went on a pilgrimage to the neighboring town, Grossvardein, I contemplated the Rebbe with respect and devotion. All at once I forgot everything I had learned in philosophy about being and about the immanent forms of transcendence. I felt guilty, and I now understand why. In days past I had visited the Rebbe that he might question me; but this time I had come to question him, about such things as fate's place in existence and about the all-powerful Creator and His devastated creation. But I didn't know how to articulate my doubts and apprehensions. My lips stubbornly remained sealed. To put me at ease the Rebbe began to smile, as his father once had long ago. He invited me to explain how I had changed.

"Times, too, have changed, Rebbe," I said.

"What of it? If times have changed, that's their business, not yours. Times change because God, blessed be His name, makes them change. But you yourself are responsible for what happens to you. And for how you look. I liked you better the last time I saw you."

The last time had been in Antwerp. He had arrived from Romania. A Hasid had told me that it was my cousin Avrom Feig of Arad who in 1944 had saved the Rebbe from deportation by sending a guide to lead him and his family across the border. In Antwerp he was as lonely and melancholy as I. But he was probably thinking of a time long before that.

"You liked me better before, Rebbe? Why? Because I wore side curls and feared heaven?"

He did not reply. Instead, he leaned forward, as if to examine me more closely. "Tell me," he asked, "what is the relation between the man you are and the man I see?"

I fell back on philosophical double talk: "Being is not necessarily visible, and that which is visible is not necessarily part of being."

He was silent. He looked unhappy, disapproving. "Where did you learn that?" he asked, his voice muffled.

"In books, Rebbe."

"What books?"

I didn't know what to say. He understood or he guessed. Profane works had displaced the sacred texts on my desk. The Talmud was no longer my sole concern.

"And if your grandfather, may he rest in peace, could see you, what would he say?"

The blow registered. "And you, Rebbe, who do see me, what do you say to me?"

His next question was one I asked of myself as well: What would I like to hear him say?

Was I seeking his blessing? He closed his eyes, then opened them.

"The great Rebbe Nahman of Bratslav," he said, "tells the story of a child lost in the forest. Gripped by panic, he cries, 'Father, father, save me!' So long as he cries, he can hope his father will hear him. If he stops, he is lost."

All trace of severity was gone from his face and from his voice. I looked at him and saw his father, and suddenly I felt better.

"Rebbe," I said, "believe me, I have never ceased to cry out."

A smile brightened his face. He seemed relieved, perhaps even happy, happy to have brought me back.

"May the Lord be praised," he said. "Then there is hope."

The conversation became more relaxed. He asked me about my work. He wanted to know if the stories I told in my books were true, had they really happened. I answered not too convincingly: "In literature, Rebbe, certain things are true though they didn't happen, while others are not, even if they did."

I would have loved to have received his blessing.

In Jerusalem, as always, I climbed the towers of Notre Dame and the YMCA to look at the Old City, peering through binoculars at Jordanian soldiers strolling in the city of David. Later Yehuda Mozes (my employer and friend) and

I revisited Galilee. Safed and Tiberias were now regular destinations in our personal itinerary.

My friend Paula Mozes kept me informed of developments at the paper. She was the confidante of all the journalists. Anyone in need of help or advice turned to her. The poet Uri-Tsvi Grinberg, whose work is among the most powerful in Israel, owed the comfort of his last years to her.

Paula was an exceptional woman, intelligent and courageous. During the Occupation she had escaped from her native town, Zhdanov-Lubelsky, and reached Smolensk, where she joined a unit of Russian partisans. Disguised as a peasant, she kept house for the local Kommandantur. Having convinced the Germans that she did not understand their language, she was allowed to remain present when officers chatted among themselves. She risked her life often and her information contributed to the success of many acts of sabotage, especially those that targeted railroad tracks. After the war she made her way to Budapest, then to Vienna. When she left for Palestine, she brought four hundred orphans with her.

Today a great sadness comes over me when I think of Paula and Noah and the tragedies they suffered. Their twelve-year-old son Adi was hit by a car and killed in Ramat Gan. The following year they had another son, Nonni. As a young adolescent he was in a car that skidded and killed a neighborhood boy in the very spot where Adi had died. Many years later Noah himself was struck by a truck near the newspaper's offices in Tel Aviv. An ambulance brought him to the hospital, where he was operated on by the same doctor who had tried to save the two adolescents. But it was too late. I miss Noah. He was a character; as smart as he was, he loved to act the fool; wealthy, he loved to pass for being penniless. The journalists adored him. Paula died some ten years later in early 1994, just before Passover. The holiday became a time of mourning.

At the end of my stay in Israel, Dov proposed that I leave Paris and go to New York, not just to write a few articles, but as a permanent correspondent. "That way Leah and I will be able to visit the United States," he said with an impish smile. But I had no desire to leave France. I didn't know anyone in America and wasn't sure I could make enough money to get by there. Dov told me they would raise my salary to $160 a month. When I politely inquired whether he thought I could make ends meet on that, he replied, "No, but you can do what other people do." I asked what other people did, and he said, "Make speeches." That was a fine idea for someone who broke into a cold sweat whenever he had to open his mouth in public. "You'll learn," Dov said. I told myself he couldn't be serious, but decided to wait and see.

When was it that I realized I was not in control of my destiny? It was by chance that I had survived, by chance that I had followed one road rather than another. It was by chance that I had become a journalist. Events unfolded outside me and beyond my will. Very often I simply let myself be carried along.

Back in Paris I began to prepare my move. I arranged for Shaike Ben Porat, a young Israeli intellectual who wrote for one of the ideological weeklies, to cover Paris in my absence. At Dov's request I set up a whole network of European correspondents. In Geneva I appointed Edwin Eytan, a likable bon vivant who gave up his medical studies to assume the post. Alfred Wolfmann kept the position in Bonn, and Abraham Rosenthal his in London. They were all happy, and so was I. In my new capacity as chief foreign correspondent, I paid them visits, feeling not only useful and influential (with Dov) but also vaguely superior, though why or to whom I couldn't say. I had never given anyone an order and wouldn't have known how to.

In December I received from Buenos Aires the first copy of my Yiddish testimony "And the World Stayed Silent," which I had finished on the boat to Brazil. The singer Yehudit Moretzka and her editor friend Mark Turkov had kept their word — except that they never did send back the manuscript. Israel Adler invited me to celebrate the event with a café-crème at the corner bistro. He was wearing my raincoat. Why? One day I had gone into a store to buy a bathing suit. They didn't have my size, but since I was too shy to say no to the salesgirl, I had left with an ill-fitting raincoat. So I had passed it on to Adler, half-price. "Tonight," he announced, "you're coming with me to hear some Brazilian music." I told him I couldn't. I had an appointment with Amos K., a young, wooden-faced journalist who was for many years the *enfant terrible* of the Israeli press. I knew he wanted to see me because he was hoping I would intercede with Yehuda Mozes on his behalf. He wanted to write for *Yedioth*, but the Old Man wanted no part of him, for reasons both ideological and personal. "Bring him along," Adler expansively suggested. Amos said he would come if there would be drinks.

A lover of food and drink, Amos was a tireless talker who became brilliant when drunk. But when he was sober, his smile was forced. In fact, everything about him seemed forced. He aroused discomfort the way some people spread warmth. That night he complained steadily about the service, the singer, the food, the drinks, even the cigarettes. By two in the morning he was not so much unpleasant as grim and incoherent. He was shouting obscenities at shuttered windows on a street behind the Boulevard Saint-Germain when suddenly he noticed two young women approaching. "What do you say we go for them?" he suggested. My cowardly heart sank. "I'm exhausted," I said. Whereupon Amos turned to Adler. "What about you?" he asked, challenging him. Israel wasn't tired. They accosted the two women and the four of them walked off without so much as saying good night to me. One of the women became Amos's long-time companion. The other — Michelle — became Israel Adler's wife in Jerusalem.

My intercession with the Old Man worked. He withdrew his veto against Amos, who then made a career at the paper that hadn't wanted his byline. His pieces were original to the extent that they were hurtful. In *Yedioth Ahronoth* he wrote on Chinese cuisine, pornography (political and otherwise), abstract painting, the greatness of his friends (who feared him), the stupidity of his enemies (who were legion), the ambitions of leaders and the frustrations of their critics. He liked to hit, and he hit hard. As it happens, he was often right. But why did he detest all those who wrote about the Holocaust when he himself referred to it more frequently than they did?

Over the years he would drop in on me during his visits to New York, downing a bottle of whiskey while asking me to find him an American publisher. Once he mentioned in an article that he had never seen me laugh, and it's true that in his company one really didn't feel like it.

Later I will have occasion to come back to this eternal adolescent who aged so badly. Our paths have not crossed since 1986. My friendship with Israel Adler, on the other hand, has withstood time.

But let me return to the preparations for my trip to America. I planned to be away for only a year. That was what I told Shaike Ben Porat and Poliakoff, my actor friend. "Look at it this way," I said, "our monthly will now have an office in the United States." I promised to send them articles about Broadway. And, I promised, when I came back, everything would resume as before: I would resume my duties as *Yedioth* correspondent and editor in chief of *Le Miroir du Théâtre*. The Lenemans assured me that they would receive me again as a lodger; I could leave with peace of mind.

The night before my departure Amos and Israel insisted I join them in a café. As usual, Israel drank a little, Amos a lot. I knew that journalists should be able to tolerate whiskey and cognac, but I wasn't much of a drinker. That night, however, I did drink a little, and for me a little was too much. When I got home, I felt so sick I vomited. I didn't have the strength to get undressed. Through it all, my great worry was what the housekeeper would think when she came to make up my bed the next day.

In a flash of lucidity, I told myself this was my farewell to Europe.

New York

On the interminable El Al flight to New York I struck up a conversation with one S. L. Schneiderman, a journalist of Polish origin, who wrote for a Yiddish daily and worked part-time for the United Jewish Appeal. I asked him whether it was true that this philanthropic association organized lectures and paid the speakers. He said it was, and that he could introduce me to the right person. I phoned him from my hotel room, and he made an appointment for me with the secretary of the speakers' bureau. I went there the same day, wondering whether Dov was right. The secretary's secretary kept me waiting for an hour before agreeing to see me. She was in her forties, her hair was pulled back into a bun. From her piercing gaze I could see that she was used to refusing requests of all kinds.

She subjected me to a formal interrogation: age, profession, titles, personal tastes. "Schneiderman said you would like to speak in Yiddish about your experiences in the camps, is that right?" I hastened to correct her: I had no intention of dealing with that subject. "But Schneiderman said you wrote a book in Yiddish about the camps. Was that wrong?" No, it wasn't wrong, but writing was one thing, speaking another. "I don't get it," she said, shaking her head. "You're an author, aren't you? Your work is autobiographical, isn't it? You want to be known and to make a little money, don't you?" Since my wretched English left me incapable of explaining the limits of language and the possibilities of silence in a hundred words or less, she coolly announced her verdict. "Look, I'm just asking you these questions to please Schneiderman, but I really don't think you're suitable for us." I understood. It was her job to say no. I wasn't a famous writer and I wasn't even an Israeli. I had done nothing heroic or spectacular. So why should anyone want to come and listen to me and make donations to the UJA?

My trip to America had certainly begun auspiciously. Back at the hotel I called Schneiderman and told him about my lack of success. He was sorry. "Don't be sorry," I said. "It could be worse. I'll find something." But I was curious to know how much I would have made had the secretary seen me as a young Yiddish Demosthenes. Schneiderman thought for a moment and replied, "Fifty dollars a speech, maybe a little more." It was my first setback in the States. Fifty dollars was more than a week's pay and there was no point in asking Dov for a raise. Finances were handled by the Old Man, who would tell me the paper wasn't rich, not yet, and that I should be patient.

I hope readers will forgive me for talking so much about material concerns, but it's hard not to think about such things when you're broke.

Here I can't resist another leap ahead in time. In 1972, just after the murder of Israeli athletes by Palestinian terrorists at the Munich Olympics, the top leaders of the United Jewish Appeal asked to discuss an urgent matter with me. Having had virtually no contact with their organization, I wondered what they wanted. They came to see me in my office. Their spokesman, Irving Bernstein, was impressive, and came straight to the point: "There's something we've been concerned about for quite some time. You've never come to speak for us. Our local groups ask for you and you seem to reject their invitations automatically. What do you have against us? Aren't you close to the state of Israel, which needs our support? Don't you want to help the American Jewish community, whose hospitals, nursing homes, and schools could not exist without our financial aid?" I tried to evade the question. I said I was too busy, too tired, had too many other commitments. The truth was that I had decided as a matter of principle to avoid any kind of fund-raising. I didn't like the hard-nosed, show-biz approach to it in America.

Irving did not give up. "We are organizing our national conference," he said, "and the

Munich tragedy will occupy a central place within it. Please be our guest on Shabbat afternoon. We'll pay double, five times, your usual honorarium. In fact, name a sum, any sum. Five thousand? Ten thousand?" As he pleaded with me, I suddenly saw myself sitting opposite the UJA secretary who specialized in rejections. I smiled. "Okay," I told Irving. "I'll come on Shabbat afternoon." The UJA leaders looked at me in surprise, no doubt wondering why I had changed my mind and what fee I was going to demand. "Consider it a gift," I said. Of course, they couldn't appreciate the irony of the situation. That was their loss, and my reward.

After two nights at the Alamac Hotel (which almost bankrupted me), I decided to rent a studio. Some I looked at were too expensive, others too dirty or too far from midtown. Luckily, a relative agreed to put me up while I looked for something more permanent.

Samuel Wiesel and his wife lived in uptown Manhattan. People of modest means, they both worked for a necktie company and swore by their trade union, which to them represented a kind of secular religion. Though strictly observant, they also believed in the benefits of emancipation. One Friday evening after Kiddush, Sam told me how he had come to the United States. "It's thanks to your father that I'm here," he explained, his voice curiously tense. "He had obtained an American visa — yes, a visa for all of you — but didn't want

494

to use it right away. He preferred to wait, hoping not to arrive empty-handed. But you know the old saying: Man proposes, God disposes. . . . The Romanian army was about to draft me, and I was in no mood to oblige. So I asked your father to 'loan' me his visa. He had a good heart, your father. Always ready to help anyone, especially family members. Do you understand now what I owe him?" Stooped after long years of hard work, my distant "uncle" suddenly seemed much closer.

Sam was not my only New York relative. There was another, on my mother's side. My sister Bea in Montreal had reestablished contact with him and urged me to pay him a visit. Meanwhile, he had learned of my presence in the city from an item in a Yiddish paper and immediately called Bea, who then insisted that not to see him meant offending a family member. I promised I would drop in on "Uncle" Morris, as she called him. I have a stinging memory of this "reunion."

To begin with, my "uncle" was rich, very rich, and to put it in the nicest possible way you could say he didn't hide it. His personality was defined by what he possessed. Now, I have nothing against wealth, unless it is flaunted so as to humiliate those less fortunate. My "Uncle" Morris lived in a luxurious apartment in a luxurious building in a luxurious neighborhood. The two doormen, in uniforms that made them look like Swiss guards out of a Russian novel, greeted me and escorted me down the hallway. The elevator boy, also in uniform, his silver epaulets gleaming, was excruciatingly polite. He asked if I was well, whether I did not find the New York winter too arduous. Wishing me a pleasant evening, he pointed to my uncle's door. I was admitted by a maid, who put a finger to her lips to indicate I was not to speak loudly. Was someone sick? Was a performance under way? In any case, no noise was allowed.

Uncle Morris was visible in the living room, but was not to be disturbed. He was playing cards. There were a dozen or so guests. I whispered hello to him, and he replied without looking up from the table: "Do you play poker?" Disappointed to hear that I didn't know how, he shrugged and said, "So what's the point of writing in newspapers?" I failed to see the connection, but his guests, more sophisticated than I, laughed heartily. Dear Uncle Morris evidently possessed an admirable sense of humor in addition to his considerable fortune. Well, let them laugh if that's their pleasure, but I didn't appreciate the joke. Having decided to sulk, I sat down in a corner. The maid, more polite than her employers, offered me a drink. Whiskey? No thanks, soda would be fine. Cigarette? I had my own. Half an hour passed. Preoccupied with the game, the guests exhibited not the slightest interest in me. An hour went by, and I began to find the situation less than funny. But it was not my style to make a scene, and I didn't want to cause Bea any embarrassment, so I sat patiently. I didn't think they would let me wait on that elegant sofa until dawn. Sooner or later they would get tired or hungry. Finally, I went over to the table and respectfully whispered to Uncle Morris that, to my great regret, I had to go. Professional obligations required my presence at the United Nations (a lie, but it sounded good). "One more minute," said Uncle Morris, fidgeting in his chair. "I'm winning big here, and the UN isn't going anywhere, is it?" Twenty minutes later he cried victory, pocketed his winnings, and got up from the table. The others followed. My "uncle" then solemnly asked me to come closer and at once launched into a speech. "Look at him," he said proudly. "You know who he is? He writes in the newspapers. Thousands of Jews read him in Israel. In France too. Even in South Africa. Anyway, that's what they tell me, and listen, I believe it. He's my nephew, or cousin, or something like that, it doesn't matter. What matters is that he's here. He's here to tell you who he owes his career to. Go ahead, tell them. Tell them who helped you, who sent you money, who paid for your studies. Come on, what are you waiting for?"

I felt myself blushing with shame and anger. All at once I remembered that in Ambloy I had indeed received a letter from him, followed by a package. In the letter he told me how happy he was to have tracked down a member of his family and announced that he was sending me something that would surely make me happy. The package contained a pair of phylacteries. I wrote back thanking him for his concern for my spiritual well-being and informing him that I already had tefillin. And that was the end of our correspondence.

Before Morris could finish his speech, his guests were overcome with admiration: how generous he was, what a good heart he had, dear Morris. A saint, that's what he was. Yes, I had a saint for an uncle.

That was too much. I interrupted the saint and his guests: "Excuse me, but it's getting late and I must go." I invoked the UN, an emergency session, international crisis. Morris was adamant: "At least say a few words. Just to show you can do it. Words are your trade, aren't they? What'll it cost you to make a little speech? If only to show my friends I was right to invest all that money in your career. Come on, you owe me at least that much, don't you?" "I'm truly sorry," I replied, "maybe some other time. The Security Council, the Trojan war, world peace — you know what I mean." There were mutterings: What a lack of gratitude; he can't even say thank you.

All I wanted was to get out of there. I couldn't take much more of this. "Come with me," my uncle ordered. I asked where. "To my room," he said. I broke out in a cold sweat. I was sure he was going to offer me money, which I damn well needed but could not allow myself to accept. I thought about my sister as I followed him uneasily into his bedroom. He went to his closet, opened it, and began rummaging through his shirts and suits. He must think he's back in Sighet, I said to myself, keeps his money stuffed under his shirts. "Where is it, where is it?" Morris mumbled. "Ah, here it is!" he finally announced, triumphantly pulling out a pair of khaki pants. "Take them," he said. "Look, they're almost new; they'll fit perfectly." At that point the door opened and a woman rushed in, breathless, her face stamped by fear that her husband was about to be too generous. When she noticed the "gift," she exclaimed enthusiastically, "A superb pair of pants. Don't be a fool, take them!" For a moment I was torn between laughter and disgust. Then I burst out laughing.

Going down in the elevator, I composed the opening of an article: "Everybody has an uncle in America. And so, alas, do I." The other passengers must have thought I was drunk, I was laughing so hard.

On the other hand, I liked Sam, who was anything but rich. I respected his modest, austere way of life and savored his sharp sarcasm. He adored challenging and even denigrating what he loved. On Friday evenings I would share a Shabbat meal with him, and he often took the opportunity to go over an article of mine, evidently with the sole purpose of demolishing it.

He didn't seem to appreciate my choice of subjects or my style. "Where'd you get that from?" he would ask. I could never figure out why he was so critical. Maybe it was his way of warding off bad luck, or perhaps he was afraid I might take myself too seriously. In any event, I was glad he wasn't my editor, otherwise I would have been looking for work. Nevertheless, I felt genuine affection for him, possibly because he remembered my parents, my house, my town. After he died, years later, I met friends of his from his synagogue. They all told me how proud he was of me.

After feverishly scouring the classifieds for a week and conducting full-fledged searches (accompanied by Israeli colleagues who served as real-estate advisers), I found a room on the ground floor of a five-story building on Seventy-sixth Street between West End Avenue and Riverside Drive. It was a quiet street, a quiet building. I signed a one-year lease without reading it. But if my eyes were closed, my ears were open, and I was awakened the next morning by a feminine voice coming from the floor above. As much as I love music, the relentless scales finally began to annoy me. I responded by pounding my typewriter keys so loudly that my singing neighbor complained. I offered her a deal: If she would stop singing, I would stop typing. Regrettably, she rejected the proposed truce. It seems she was a student at the Juilliard

School of Music and of course she had to practice. She suggested I write my articles longhand. I decided to move, thereby forfeiting my security deposit. I found a cheap room on the eleventh floor of a hotel. The important thing was to be able to work in peace.

Later I moved for a third time, into the Master Hotel on Riverside Drive and 103rd Street, where I lived until my marriage, in 1969. It was a small studio with a breathtaking view of the Hudson and the lights of Manhattan and New Jersey. I spent a lot of time looking out the window. As I wrote, I watched the city shake itself awake at dawn or sink into dusk while the luminous river of cars snaked by on the West Side Highway. More than a few visitors were so entranced by the view that they forgot the purpose of their visit.

It isn't easy to put down roots in a new country. I had done reasonably well in Paris, but I wondered whether I could manage here. How long would it take me to adjust? Why did all those people in Times Square run so fast? Were they trying to gain time? What I wanted was to slow time down. I was going to have to find some milieu in which the refugee in me could feel comfortable.

David Gedailovitch (who became first Gedalya, then Guy in an effort to seem more American) was my constant companion. Born in Slatina, a Czech village across the Tisza River from Sighet, he, too, had been in Buna. I considered him both overly optimistic and devilishly resourceful. He could repair my electric razor and cook his dinner with equal skill. And if there was ever something he didn't know, he always knew someone who did. A perfume merchant and restaurateur, lover of great wines and importer and exporter of all kinds of merchandise, he introduced me to his circle of friends and associates. It was he who helped me overcome the trivial obstacles in my daily life and who found my third studio for me.

I had also run into two or three old friends from Sighet, who lived in Brooklyn and worked in Manhattan. They didn't appreciate my "serious" behavior. They had come to New York not to remake the world but to have a good time, and it was they who introduced me to the American custom of the blind date, by providing me with a list of phone numbers. I spent precious dollars in a thoroughly vain attempt to charm distant beauties.

Jacob Baal-Teshuva, the representative of an Israeli film weekly whom I had met in Paris the year before, showed me how foreign correspondents did their work in New York — a piece of cake. All you had to do was drop in at the editorial offices of *The New York Times* every evening at nine-thirty and pick through "all the news that's fit to print" until one had what one needed for a dispatch. A Western

Union office happened to be nearby. By midnight I was ready to go home.

Richard Yaffe, a correspondent for the leftist Israeli daily published by Mapam, helped me acquire a "desk" in the UN press room. A little older than I, with an open face, horn-rimmed glasses, and a warm smile, he took me under his wing. An excellent reporter and a generous man more interested in truth than in scoops, he passed his tips on to me and taught me to avoid the many pitfalls that lurked for members of the international press corps at UN headquarters. He knew many delegates and had entrée everywhere. He may also have suspected that my financial situation was less than ideal, for he took me to cocktail parties and receptions where I was able to save lunch money by downing petits fours and cheese sandwiches. I loved listening to his analyses and anecdotes. He never talked about himself, and so it was from colleagues that I learned his story. He had been a star reporter for CBS in Eastern Europe in the fifties, but was subpoenaed by the House Committee on Un-American Activities because of his liberal opinions. When he refused to inform on his friends, he was fired from his job. Paranoia was at its height, and his former colleagues shunned him. For several years he was barely able to feed his family. Finally, he was hired by the *Jewish Chronicle* of London and the leftist *Al-Hamishmar* of Tel Aviv. I once asked him why he never spoke of this tragic period of his life. "Why reopen old wounds?" he said. "I felt ashamed. Ashamed of my country and of the people I had worked with and regarded as friends."

Since I have just used the word "ashamed," let me dwell on it for a moment. On the instructions of Dov, who had apparently read a report on the subject in *Time* magazine, I researched an article on organized crime in America: the Mafia, and in particular the hired killers of "Murder Incorporated." As I sifted through the archives of various newspapers and visited the Public Library, I was stunned to come across some Jewish names. In the twenties and thirties there were Jews who offered their services to the criminal underground, murdering men and women who had done them no harm. One of them reportedly boasted of being an observant Jew who wore his kipa to "work" and scrupulously respected the day of rest, the Shabbat. It was also reported that two members of a gang suggested to a Palestinian Zionist leader that they eliminate delegates who planned to vote against the UN partition resolution in 1947. Regrettably, it is also a fact that some Jewish gangsters considered themselves Jewish "patriots." In his memoirs the writer Ben Hecht told of having been "kidnapped" by persons unknown and taken to a garage where, in the presence of various gangsters, he was given a suitcase stuffed with dollars for the Irgun.

These revelations came as a shock to me. I

simply could not imagine a Jew becoming a hired killer. Yes, I had too idealistic a view of Jews, but the fact is that in Eastern Europe my people might have been criticized for just about anything, but not involvement in murders. Jews may have been guilty of lying or cheating, fraud or smuggling, theft or perjury, but murder was unimaginable. Very long ago there had been in my region one case of a Jew who had been arrested, tried, and sentenced to death for murder. His name was Reinitz, and it became common to call criminals "Reinitzes."

I like to think that what accounts for this virtual absence of blood crimes in our communities was perhaps related to the commandment revealed at Sinai: Thou shalt not kill. The voice of God sounds and resounds in our collective memory. But then what accounts for the present reality? The fact is that in modern Israel acts of murder do occur. True, there are few such cases, but even one is too many. It seems we are finally becoming a people like any other, neither better nor worse. Does this mean we are not "the chosen people"? No, we are, but only in the sense that Anglo-Jewish writer Israel Zangwill attributes to the term: "the people that chooses itself, its destiny and mission." And as important, in the sense of teaching all peoples that they, too, must aspire to reach beyond themselves, to lift themselves ever higher, and to see themselves as unique.

★ ★ ★

It was in America in 1956 that I met David Ben-Gurion, when I was assigned to cover his visit with President Eisenhower. The first time I saw him I could not help thinking of the tragic episode of the *Altalena*. Was this the same man, the same ruthless leader, who now spoke of prophetic ethics as often as of world politics, and who said it was Israel's mission to serve as "the light unto the nations"? Despite such thoughts, in the end I fell under his spell.

Working alongside the American and foreign journalists accredited to the White House, I discovered the power of the news media. Indeed, the immense American machinery of state often seemed to function only to mollify them. Today the power of the media is even greater.

Along with the prime minister's advisers (among them Teddy Kollek, future mayor of Jerusalem, and Yitzhak Navon, future president of the Jewish state), the press waited on the White House lawn for Ben-Gurion to emerge from the Oval Office. We amused ourselves by placing bets on how long his meeting with Eisenhower would last. Scheduled for thirty minutes, it had already lasted an hour. Finally they came out. Ben-Gurion was so short that Eisenhower looked gigantic beside him. Seeing them side by side, we felt as though we had been lifted from the realm of politics into that of history.

American current affairs absorbed me day and

506

night, in a way that French affairs had not. To be a foreign correspondent in America is to be ever on the alert. The most extraordinary events occurred at a frenzied pace on this vast and turbulent continent. Barely had I arrived when I began to cover the civil rights struggle. All the world's newspapers spoke of young Autherine Lucy, the first black student admitted to the University of Alabama, and of Martin Luther King, Jr., who was imprisoned for organizing the Montgomery bus boycott. *My Fair Lady* was the big hit on Broadway. Arthur Miller married Marilyn Monroe. That was surely worth an article.

And then there was Jewish life in the United States, more animated and varied than in France, and so highly structured that it was easy to follow. Each organization was headed by a personality influential in the business world. Hence the importance of public relations. As it happened, my newspaper was expanding: its circulation and number of pages were both on the rise. World decisions were increasingly made in Washington rather than London. President Eisenhower was keeping an eye on the Middle East. John Foster Dulles and his team brought back reports and proposals, and drafted accords on which Israel's fate would depend. The slightest border incident brought reactions in Washington and at the United Nations. Secretary-General Dag Hammarskjöld's press conferences were grandiose performances. Eloquent and authoritative, speaking of himself in the third person, he charmed the press. I liked him because he was said to be an admirer of Martin Buber. Might he admire Hasidism as well? His mysticism was fully revealed only after his tragic death in a plane crash in the Congo. He considered the UN's true mission to be theological in nature, and Israel feared him because he saw himself as a kind of messiah or global sovereign. Indeed, Israel, being the only country that belonged to no bloc and had never held a seat on the Security Council, feared anything coming from the United Nations. One political cartoon of the time showed an Israeli delegate at a cocktail party. Standing alone in a corner with no one to toast, he raises his champagne glass and says, "Lehayyim, Lord." Listening to speeches in the Security Council or General Assembly was enough to remind me of what the Bible calls Israel's solitude.

At first I loved the days I spent in the UN's glass palace, center of world diplomacy. In the vast hall of delegates (where free phone service was provided) you might run into India's Krishna Menon or the Soviet Union's Andrei Gromyko or buttonhole a high-powered visitor for a quick interview on the problems of the Middle East. When that happened, I knew my articles would make the front page.

The delegate with whom I spoke most often was Abba Eban, Israel's young ambassador to the UN, known for his keen intelligence and dazzling oratorical skills. His mastery of English was legendary (when Golda Meir named him foreign minister and Henry Kissinger was American secretary of state, she jokingly told President Nixon, "Mine has a better English accent than yours"), and he made fine use of his talents in defending his nation's policies and honor. The Jewish community adored him. I admired him, though I recognized his weaknesses. His opponents in Israel chided him for the elegance of his Hebrew, his pomposity, and his tendency to repeat himself. But it's difficult to be original when you're making three speeches a day. Years later we were to have a distasteful, painful confrontation which I regret to this day, but at this time our relations were correct though infrequent. After all, for him I was but a newly arrived correspondent, the representative of a poor newspaper, and therefore less influential than the other journalists.

To alleviate my financial problems I did freelance work for the Yiddish daily *Morgen Journal*, filling in for its UN correspondent when he was away. The weekly *Der Amerikaner* accepted a few of my articles but would have preferred a serialized novel, which I did not have. "A pity," said David Mekler, its editor in chief and a great lover of fiction, one day when we met. "I have a respectable budget for a novel." I looked at him, a small, nervous man with thick glasses and an ironical expression. Apparently, he was not joking. "In that case," I said, "I think I may have something stuck in a drawer somewhere." I sat at the typewriter that very night, and in a week or two I churned out (under the pseudonym Elisha Carmeli) a romantic spy novel of which I remember only the premise: A man and a woman, both Israeli intelligence agents, are desperately in love, and one or the other is sent on a mission to Egypt. I can't recall if the operation was a success, but I do know that all my characters died at the end, since I wasn't sure what else to do with them. Mekler was as nonplussed as I was, but he published my novel anyway, under the title *Silent Heroes*. I am convinced he never read it all the way through. I didn't read the printed version either, but Simon Weber, news editor of the *Jewish Daily Forward* (popularly known as the *Forverts*), noticed it. He also knew I had written articles for the competition, and he invited me to lunch. A brilliant, cultivated journalist, Weber was proud both of his craft and of belonging to a prestigious team (Leon Crystal, Isaac Bashevis Singer, R. Abramowicz, Hayyim Ehrenreich), headed by Hillel Rogoff. We got along well, and when he offered me a job, I accepted without a second thought. The *Forverts* was, after all, the world's biggest, richest, and most widely read Yiddish daily. I started there as a translator and rewrite man assigned to the general news pages.

I love the Yiddish language, which I speak with the Lithuanian accent I picked up from

Shushani. Before him, in Buchenwald, there was a boy from Kovno who told me of the experiences that had made him an old man. I loved his singsong intonation. It hurts me that I have forgotten his name, but I remember his bony face, creased cheeks, and feverish eyes. And that, too, hurts.

I love speaking that language. There are songs that can be sung only in Yiddish, prayers that only Jewish grandmothers can murmur at dusk, stories whose charm and secret, sadness and nostalgia, can be conveyed in Yiddish alone. I love Yiddish because it has been with me from the cradle. It was in Yiddish that I spoke my first words and expressed my first fears. It is a bridge to my childhood years. As they used to say, God writes in Hebrew and listens in Yiddish.

I need Yiddish to laugh and cry, to celebrate and express regret, to delve into my memories anew. Is there a better language for evoking the past, with all its horror? Without Yiddish the literature of the Holocaust would have no soul. I know that had I not written my first account in Yiddish, I would have written no others. To this day, perhaps more than before, Yiddish fills me with nostalgia.

To my great surprise, my Uncle Sam was suddenly proud of me. It seems some men at the synagogue had mentioned my articles, and their wives had praised my novel. Caught up in his enthusiasm, he blithely advised me to get married, and what's more, he had a bride in mind:

the daughter of a friend of his, a charming girl eagerly seeking a boy like me. "She's a schoolteacher," said Sam, all excited, "an intellectual from a good family. In short, made for you." She often attended Shabbat services. "Why not come along with me on Friday night?" To avoid a long argument, I agreed. "I hope you have a hat," Sam said. I told him I didn't. I wore only berets. "Impossible," he replied indignantly. "You can't come to my synagogue without a hat." He led me straight to a neighborhood shop, and properly fitted me out like a good Orthodox Jew in search of a bride. I presented myself at the synagogue on Friday night. Probably at Sam's instigation, the president of the congregation asked me to officiate. Unfortunately, the audience was sparse, the women's gallery nearly empty. I wondered where "she" was sitting and tried to picture her while chanting Psalms. But the girl of my uncle's dreams either never showed up or left in the middle of the service. Maybe she didn't appreciate my style of prayer. Or maybe she didn't like my hat.

I never went back to Sam's synagogue. For one thing, it was too far. For another, except for the High Holidays and the Yizkor service, I now avoided public prayer, for I was mired in a religious crisis. I had no one to discuss such matters with — Shushani had disappeared, André Neher was far away, and I had not yet met the Lubavitcher Rebbe or my future teacher

512

and friend Saul Lieberman — but the God of my childhood was tormenting me. As I mentioned earlier, it had started during my first visit to Israel, when I "forgot" to put on my tefillin for the first time. And it was in Jerusalem, most sacred and spiritual of cities, that I first felt the need to protest against divine justice and injustice.

In the meantime, I wasn't at all depressed by Sam's failure as a matchmaker. I had not yet forgotten Kathleen, and I had a feminine presence in Aviva, Yehuda Mozes's private secretary. Tall and blond, she was the linchpin of the paper's administrative staff. She could do anything, solve any problem. I had met her during a trip to Tel Aviv, and she was now vacationing in New York. We saw each other often: museums, concerts, walks in Central Park, sandwiches in a neighborhood deli.

One night she joined me for my regular trip to the *Times* office. It was July, in the middle of a stifling heat wave. The scene in Times Square was surrealistic: The usual human anthill of passersby now seemed to walk, laugh, and eat in slow motion. I bought the *Times* and the *Herald Tribune* and flipped through them, certain words and names leaping out at me. In Egypt Nasser was waving nationalist banners before fanatical crowds, while White House spokesman James Hagerty called for calm in the Middle East. There was a speech by Adlai Stevenson, who would be the Democratic candidate in the presidential elections that November of 1956. Hammarskjöld was planning a trip abroad. In short, nothing earthshaking, but I decided to send a cable anyway, if only to say hello to the Old Man. Then Aviva and I would go to the movies. But once again the Yiddish proverb proved correct: Man makes plans, God unmakes them.

I can't recall what film we had decided to see — it may have been *The Brothers Karamazov*. All I know is, we never got there.

As we crossed Seventh Avenue at Forty-fifth Street, I was hit by a taxi. The impact hurled me through the air like a figure in a Chagall painting, all the way to Forty-fourth Street, where I lay for twenty minutes until an ambulance came to take me to the hospital. Aviva later told me that on the way I regained consciousness several times and gave her precise instructions: what to say to Dov, whom to call to replace me, what meetings to cancel, how to tell my sister Bea, whom to borrow rent money from. Then I passed out again. She also told me that the first hospital refused to admit me. Having examined my wallet, an employee found it outrageously, desperately empty. Without money or insurance I was unworthy of treatment. Business is business. Besides, I was considered virtually hopeless, and since there seemed to be no point in keeping me, I was carried back to the ambulance, which took to the streets again, sirens wailing, in search of a more charitable hospital. The orthopedic surgeon on duty at New York Hospital decided to admit me. His name was Dr. Paul Braunstein, and he saved my life.

My entire left side had been shattered. A ten-hour operation was required to reconstruct it, leaving me in a cast from neck to foot. All I could move was my head. Confined to bed and condemned to immobility, one dreams, one thinks about and sees the world in a whole new way. A simple painkiller is worth more than a dozen wondrous poems. I was more grateful to the nurse who came to turn me onto my back or stomach than I would have been to the most ravishing of creatures granting me her all. The most astonishing world news affected me less than the doctor's smile. I later discovered, for example, that Nasser had nationalized the Suez Canal while I was in a coma. Ordinarily, I would have leaped to the telephone, turned on the radio, done something. But now I didn't even care.

After a few days my curiosity revived. Colleagues kept me informed. There were even some funny moments. My battered, imprisoned body ached, and yet all the visitors who came to console me said the same thing: "You're lucky, it could have been worse. You could have lost your sight, your legs, your mind." It reminded me of the old joke about the man reciting a litany of woes to his friend — he has lost his job, his house, his money, his fiancée —

515

and his friend keeps saying, "It could have been worse." Finally the man screams, "How the hell could it be worse?" and his friend mutters, "It could have happened to me."

Haim Isaac, correspondent for the Labor daily *Davar*, replaced me for daily dispatches, but I was afraid my readers would forget me. I therefore decided to resume working, dictating a first-person account of the accident, followed by several commentaries and background pieces. Dictation wasn't easy for me. Dov congratulated me, though he may have been more impressed by my determination than by my writing. (He did say I deserved a Pulitzer Prize, but neither he nor anyone else at the paper ever mentioned the mounting doctor and hospital bills.)

In time my room became a meeting place. Of course, Bea and Aviva visited every day. Nurses came to watch baseball games. Before the television set was hooked up (more for them than for me), it had been impossible to get their attention; now they never left. Colleagues held consultations in my room instead of going to the press club at the UN. They talked politics and exchanged news and gossip. The number one subject was Gamal Abdel Nasser, the young Egyptian colonel who dared to defy Britain and France on Suez. The Security Council was virtually in permanent session. Israel was on the alert. Nasser got bad press in the West, but not in the Third World. The Muslim countries hailed him as a glorious hero destined to reconquer the former empire, a modern-day Saladin. Western reporters wondered whether he would be allowed to violate accords between Egypt and the European powers with impunity. Secretary of State John Foster Dulles counseled moderation and patience, Dag Hammarskjöld preached morality. A new war threatened to erupt. Suddenly the center of gravity for international news had shifted from Washington to the Middle East.

One morning I was visited by a lawyer who said he represented an insurance company. He had a proposition for me: If I signed a certain document, a simple piece of paper, he would hand me a quarter of a million dollars on the spot. I asked him to repeat what he had just said. The vastness of the sum made my head spin.

I was ready to sign that document and any others in his bulging briefcase. But my journalist friend Alexander Zauber screamed, "Are you crazy? Don't sign anything!" I told him to think of the fortune involved. I would never make as much in twenty or a hundred years. He lost his temper: "You really want to let this crook ruin us? Tell him to get the hell out of here! I'll get you a lawyer who defends victims instead of swindling them. You're going to be a millionaire, I guarantee it!" How could I turn down such a treasure?

Zauber showed the insurance company's emissary the door and phoned his lawyer. I was introduced to the supposedly eminent attorney that very afternoon. He seemed serious and professional, and he examined me as if he were a doctor. He also talked to Dr. Braunstein, who confirmed that I was in truly bad shape. The lawyer concluded that this diagnosis was worth at least a million dollars. "At least!" a jubilant Zauber repeated. "See? And you were going to let yourself get fleeced by that insurance bastard! You're lucky I was here to protect you." He was so jubilant that if I hadn't been encased in plaster, he probably would have pulled me out of bed for a dance.

But I was more concerned with the present than the future. The hospital had to be paid. The private room was expensive, and the newspaper, though responsible for its correspondents, would pay me nothing more than my meager salary. Where would I find the funds to pay for my rent and all the other bills? For the moment I was assigned this private room because of the seriousness of my condition and Dr. Braunstein's kindness, but in a few days, when I was feeling better, I would have to share it with one or several other patients. This was a terrifying prospect. Ever since the war the idea of sleeping in the same room with a stranger had panicked me. My sister Bea would help out all she could, but she was almost as poor as I was. None of my friends was rich, and for reasons known only to Himself, God had decreed that none of my colleagues was either.

The insurance lawyer's proposal seemed the only way out. If I accepted, I would get the money right away; otherwise I would have to wait months or even years. Zauber was furious. He insisted I was about to commit the most idiotic act of my life, but I had made my decision. I would ask the first lawyer to come back late that evening, after Zauber had gone. Better a bird in hand than a mirage in the brain.

I had forgotten to allow for the possibility of a miracle. Among my visitors that day was Hillel Kook, who asked Aviva and other friends to leave us alone. He was an unusual man, the archetypal Central European intellectual in demeanor and looks: nearsighted, thin, tense, and curious. I had interviewed him several weeks earlier. He had just founded a political organization to combat Soviet interference in the Middle East. I knew him by reputation only. A member of the Irgun high command under the alias Peter Bergson, he and the writer Ben Hecht had directed the Committee of Hebrew National Liberation during the war. Their main objective was to save European Jews. In fact, no one had done more than Bergson to alert the American public to the tragedy of the Jews under the Nazis. Consequently, he was thoroughly disliked by the American Jewish establishment, which consistently fought and slandered him. During the *Altalena* affair he was even imprisoned by Ben-Gurion. "I heard what happened to you," he said, coming straight to the point. "As you've probably discovered by now, being sick in New York costs money. You don't have any, but I do. So I brought you a few blank checks. Fill them out as the need arises, and let me know when you need more." Hillel's manner was matter-of-fact, as though he made gestures like this every day.

I was so overcome by his generosity that I was unable to utter a word. I gaped at him as though he were a *tzaddik* or an emissary of the Prophet Elijah, most unpredictable of prophets. Finally, I managed to ask him how I would ever repay him. "Don't worry," he replied, as nonchalant as a banker addressing a colleague. "I have plenty to live on. You can pay me back when the insurance company pays you off."

He then reached out as if to shake my hand, thought better of it (since he could have grasped only plaster), said goodbye, and left.

When Aviva and the others came back in, I told them of the miracle. Zauber cried: "It's a sign from God. He wants you to listen to me. Don't be a fool. Now you can stay in your own room and you can hire *my* lawyer." With that, he leaped toward my bed and planted a burning kiss on my forehead. "You're going to be a millionaire," he said. "My friend the millionaire. I warn you, if you sabotage my plans, I'll kill you. And *my* lawyer will defend *me*."

Every week Hillel called to find out if I needed more checks. In the meantime, the lawyer filed the suit that he and Zauber assured me would change my life for good. I made statements, signed documents and depositions. A month, a year went by. I returned to my hotel. Zauber returned to Israel, Bea to Montreal. From time to time I asked the lawyer how things were going. He was a patient man, and he advised me to follow his example. Eighteen months after the accident he accompanied me to court. This was not yet the trial, but a simple procedural matter. Two years after the accident, there was still nothing. One day Hillel called me, and we had coffee together. He asked me about the trial. Wall Street, it seemed, had not been kind to him, and he was short of cash. But not to worry, he would work it out. He would wait. That day I instructed my lawyer to settle the matter within the week. He tried to talk me out of it. That was just what the insurance company was hoping for, he said. If they knew we needed cash, they would offer us peanuts. I replied that I didn't care and that if he stalled I would replace him. The next day he informed me of the result of his negotiations: He would receive 30 percent of my payment and from the rest Hillel would be paid back.

That's how I failed to become a millionaire.

But I did come away from the adventure with some memories. And with a novel that began this way:

"The accident happened one evening in July, in the heart of New York, as Kathleen and I were crossing the street on our way to see *The*

Brothers Karamazov."

My novel *The Accident* was only partly inspired by reality. To begin with, the fictional Kathleen is not the Kathleen with whom I had broken up or, more accurately, who had broken up with me the year before. Second, although the story correctly describes my condition and feelings in the weeks after the accident (I recall that when I came to, I laughed at the irony of having survived the death camps only to be run over in the streets of New York), in the novel the "accident" is a suicide attempt.

Another episode, however, was drawn directly from reality: my encounter with Sarah. I met her on a bus between the Hôtel de Ville and the Place de la République in Paris. I felt her watching me as I read a Yiddish book. Blond and petite, her mouth framed by lines of disillusionment, she seemed lost in her own existence. She invited herself home with me. "Tell me a story," I said, and she replied, "My name is Sarah." My mother's name, I thought to myself. To her I said: "That's not a story." "Yes it is," she said. I sat down at my desk, but she remained standing, leaning against the door as if to prevent an intruder from entering or to stop me from leaving. I sank into an uneasy silence. Was she waiting for questions I never asked? Suddenly her eyes filled with tears and she cried, "Don't you understand? My name is Sarah and I was born in Vilna." I opened my mouth to say that that wasn't a story either, but she now seemed beside herself. In a loud voice she began to tell me of her experiences in a concentration camp, of the torture the Germans inflicted on her, of the solidarity among the other inmates. She was twelve years old at the time. I shouldn't have listened, should have plugged my ears, thought of something else, made love to her — anything to make her stop talking.

For *The Accident*, perhaps in order to transcend the theme of the accident-suicide, I chose as epigraph a quotation from Nikos Kazantzakis's *Zorba the Greek*: "I was once more struck by the truth of the ancient legend: Man's heart is a ditch full of blood. The loved ones who have died throw themselves on the banks of this ditch to drink the blood and thereby come to life again; the dearer they are to you, the more of your blood they drink."

For the camp survivor life is a battle not only for the dead but also against them. Locked in the grip of the dead, he fears that by freeing himself, he is abandoning them. Hence the near-impossibility of loving, or of believing in humanity.

I was released from the hospital in a wheelchair and returned to my hotel room. There were frequent visits from David and daily ones from Aviva. For several days I worked at home, and then, my patience at an end, I returned to the UN on crutches. Colleagues were helpful, among them Shalom Rosenfeld (gifted *Maariv* columnist, who was passing through New York) and Dick Yaffe. These were difficult times at the United Nations. The heroic uprising in Hungary was crushed by Soviet tanks. My Israeli readers were keenly following those events as well as the diplomatic consequences of the Israelis' lightning campaign in Sinai, which was the first of General Moshe Dayan's legendary exploits. Despite my physical discomfort I attended interminable Security Council sessions.

I found these debates absorbing. Most of them concerned Israel, and therefore Jewish history and my people's destiny were at stake. Well-informed sources had no doubt that there was collusion at the highest level between Israel, Britain, and France. Ben-Gurion was reported to have traveled to Paris incognito to meet with top French officials in a well-guarded villa. Other sources denied these rumors. Either way, Abba Eban's speeches were as eloquent as ever, those of the French and British representatives striking in that it was unusual to hear Israel defended so vigorously. The other nations, however, remained faithful to their traditions of hostile neutrality or masked hostility. Indignant, the Soviets and Americans thundered against Israel's alliance with colonialists. President Eisenhower summoned an Israeli diplomat and warned him: "Tell your Jews not to drag the Middle East events into the election campaign." The emissary passed this less-than-diplomatic warning on, and the great majority of Jewish leaders accepted the directive. Few voices were raised in Israel's defense. David Ben-Gurion made no secret of his scorn. Disappointed by the silent acquiescence of American Jewry, he proposed that Baron Guy de Rothschild launch a world association of friends of Israel to replace the Zionist movement.

In retrospect this chapter of Israel's history, once considered glorious, seems problematic. Was it not a tactical and above all a moral error for Israel to fight on the side of the colonialists in a cause that did not concern it directly? On the other hand, this was a perfect opportunity to thwart an enemy who had become dangerously powerful and arrogant. The fact remains that politically the operation ended in a debacle. After receiving a message from the Kremlin threatening the Jewish state with unnamed reprisals, Ben-Gurion ordered Dayan to evacuate the Sinai. In return, Eisenhower offered guarantees which succeeding administrations refused to honor.

Around this time my American visa expired. Equipped with my crutches and wheelchair, I headed for the Immigration office, where an amiable official took a long look at my stateless person's French travel permit and handed it back to me. "Since you have press accreditation at the United Nations, in principle there's no problem. But your travel permit has expired. Where do you want me to put the visa?" He advised me to ask the French consulate to revalidate my permit. At the consulate a less-than-amiable secretary informed me that this was impossible, explaining that according to regulations, this type of document could be validated only in France. Back at Immigration, I spoke to the same official, who gave me a note for the French authorities stating that a U.S. visa would be issued as soon as I presented a suitable document. But French bureaucracy has its own inscrutable ways. When the U.S. Immigration official saw me hobbling in on my crutches for the third time, he asked how long this game would continue. I didn't have enough money to go back to France. Taxis had already cost me a small fortune, and in any case my doctors would have forbidden an Atlantic crossing. As I stood there at a loss, anxiously wondering whether I would be deported or placed on some sort of blacklist, the official leaned toward me, smiled, and said, "For God's sake, why don't you become a U.S. resident? Then later you can apply for citizenship." I stared at him. Could I actually become an American citizen? His smile gave me my answer. I asked if I would receive a real passport eventually, and my new mentor proceeded to lay out the steps that led to my becoming an American citizen.

It is hard to put into words how much I owe that kindly Immigration official, especially when I recall my annual visits to the Préfecture de Police in Paris, with its long lines and humiliating interrogations. When my turn came, the stateless person I was had to try to win over an ill-humored female employee who never even condescended to look straight at me. It was pathetic, even ridiculous, but it was endemic to my condition as a refugee. The refugee's time is measured in visas, his biography in stamps on his documents. Though he has done nothing illegal, he is sure he is being followed. He begs everyone's pardon: Sorry for disturbing you, for bothering you, for breathing. How well I understood Socrates, who preferred death to exile. In the twentieth century there is nothing romantic about the life of the exile, be he a stateless person or a political refugee. I know whereof I speak. I was stateless, and therefore defenseless.

When, five years later, I applied for American citizenship, there were no problems, just simple, rapid formalities. A few days before the ceremony the concierge at my hotel had a message for me: I was to call the FBI; there was a telephone number. The refugee in me was scared. What could I have done to attract the attention of J. Edgar Hoover's omnipotent, omniscient FBI? I called the number. A man answered and told me the agent in charge had just left the office and would not be back until the next day. I prepared for a sleepless night.

That evening the agent called me. "I didn't want you to worry, so I'm calling from home. I must ask you a question. You're going to be an American citizen. Have you thought about registering with your draft board?" I broke into a cold sweat. "No," I stammered. The agent asked why not. "I'm too old," I said. "Besides which, there are medical reasons. I've had a serious accident." The agent was silent. In my mind I saw myself rejected, punished, repudiated — end of naturalization, the American passport forever out of reach. "Well," he said at last, "you'll have to register, as a matter of form. But that should be the end of it."

And it was. A few days later I was handed a brand-new, beautiful American passport.

In 1981, after François Mitterrand was elected president of France, a high official asked whether I would like to acquire French nationality. Though I thanked him — and not without some emotion — I declined the offer. When I had needed a passport, it was America that had given me one.

As promised, Dov and Leah disembarked in New York in 1957. We went to concerts, restaurants. By now I was walking with a cane, which I thought made me look distinguished. But I tired easily. They rented a car and invited me to join them on a six-week cross-country trip, from New York to Los Angeles. Since Dov was my boss I didn't have to worry about work, so I went.

We discovered an America unknown to us, totally different from New York or Washington, which were the only places I knew. Interminable highways disappeared into a blue horizon ringing tall mountains embedded in skies of shifting colors. There were cascading rivers and peaceful brooks, green valleys and yellow hills, violent storms and dramatic sunsets. Never before had I been so close to nature. From the hills of San Francisco we gazed upon small towns floating in the fog as in a dream. In the Rocky Mountains the clouds seemed to wear a crown of snow; to touch it you would have to climb to God's throne. Enchanting mirages, they are so disconcerting you cannot tell which is close and which is far, which is real and which is not. You have a sense of being present at a re-creation of the world.

They say that when Arturo Toscanini visited the Grand Canyon, a companion watched respectfully as the great conductor stood motionless, contemplating the miracle of the Colorado River gorge. Suddenly, after a long and silent meditation, the maestro burst into applause. For him the discovery of deepest America was like attending a concert. For me it was a constantly renewed invitation to learn about my new homeland. In the South I was struck by its citizens' courtesy, and the unforgivable humiliation of its blacks. Looking at the "Whites Only" signs, I felt ashamed of being white.

There was Las Vegas and its slot machines, available even in the rest rooms. Men and women were standing in dazzlingly bright casinos, betting a year's salary or more on a little ball that leaps and dances about indifferently, stupidly, before coming to rest on a number, any number. Wherever you turn, you see frozen faces and trembling hands. The casino in Monte Carlo is the playground of the rich, who seem burdened by their wealth. In Las Vegas one sees ordinary people fed up with not being rich.

At the Sands Hotel we dined with Hank Greenspun, a powerful man in the city who was the owner of the daily *Las Vegas Sun*, who told us of his clandestine activities in support of Israel. In 1948 he was involved in an illegal arms shipment, for which he was indicted and sentenced to several years in prison. Of this he was very proud.

One morning we came upon an enormous sign under the Arizona sun: "Indian Reservation 100 Miles." Instantly we decided to take the detour. None of us had ever met an Indian, our knowledge extending no further than the movie stereotypes of young savages and wise old men. The Indians were always the ones on the attack, shrieking and killing. But why not? In their eyes, the white man was nothing but a rapacious armed invader seeking to drive them from their lands and reduce them to dependency by imposing his language and culture. And all with a revoltingly clear conscience.

The man who greeted us in a tent decorated with feathers and other tribal insignia might have stepped out of a movie. Tall, erect, impassive, and majestic, he had a slow, dignified walk and a weathered, angular face. We hung on his every word as he explained the Indian concept of life and death. He was respectful, and he inspired respect. At one point he asked us to sign his visitors' book. Dov urged me to go first. I don't know why, but I signed in Hebrew, and the Indian rewarded me with a hearty pat on the back. "Sholem aleichem," he said in Yiddish. Dov and Leah nearly collapsed in surprise and laughter.

It turned out our host was Jewish, a camp survivor from Polish Galicia who had first emigrated to Mexico. When things went badly there, he moved to Arizona and made his living as an Indian by day while remaining a Jew by night.

In my diary I wrote: "America is truly a wonderland. Even the Indians speak Yiddish."

It was around that time, in 1957, that I first met Golda Meir, who had succeeded Moshe Sharett, whom Ben-Gurion considered too moderate, as minister of foreign affairs. She had come to the United Nations to negotiate the Israeli withdrawal from Sinai. Initially known only in Jewish circles, she soon became world famous for her impressive strength of character, the depth of her convictions, and an obstinacy unanimously acknowledged by friend and foe. Though she lacked Eban's eloquence, she possessed the gifts of sincerity and simplicity, hence her great power of persuasion. Severe, some-times even cruel toward those she didn't like, she was boundlessly generous toward those she did. I was lucky enough to be among the latter, not because she thought me more talented than other correspondents, but because she took a kind of maternal interest in me. When she saw me on crutches, she evidently decided to take care of me. At first she may have thought I was a wounded veteran with glorious exploits to his credit, for she asked about my military record. I quickly set her straight. Far from being a war hero, not only had I never been in uniform, I wasn't even Israeli. I was just a simple Jewish correspondent working for an Israeli newspaper, my wounds courtesy of an ordinary accident. She was incredulous. "But you speak perfect Hebrew!" I explained that I owed that to my father. "And you're not Israeli?" No. "But why not?" I stammered an awkward reply. Noting my embarrassment, Golda reassured me: "It doesn't matter. You're young, you work for one of my country's newspapers, and you have no one to take care of you. So listen: I don't want to see you hobbling around this place anymore."

She offered me a deal: I would come less often to UN headquarters and she would personally supply me with information. Who could ask for a better source? That very evening I presented myself at the Essex House, where she usually stayed. She greeted me warmly, gave me dinner, and let me look through her papers. The same scene took place again the next day and the day after that. Gideon Rafael, one of her advisers and himself a future UN ambassador, walked in on me one night as I pored over confidential documents. He expressed astonishment, but Golda simply said: "I trust him." As a result, while I was better informed than my colleagues, they were more effective, for I practiced a rigorous self-censorship so as not to betray Golda's trust. My competitor from *Maariv* took advantage of leaks I knew about but kept to myself. Golda appreciated that. I became one of her confidants.

In 1967, while she was out of office (a situation that was commonly referred to as being in "the wilderness"), I was among the few New Yorkers to visit her at her hotel. Even Israeli officials considered her a has-been and were too busy to come and say hello. Pointing to the flowers on the table, she told me to guess who had sent them. The consulate, the UN delegation, the UJA? No, Golda said, laughing — the hotel management. Her humor spared no one, not even herself. Over time our friendship had grown stronger, and that fact was known. When she succeeded Levi Eshkol as prime minister, her entourage of courtiers and flatterers became very friendly to me. As a consequence, during my visits to Israel I noted — not without pride — that all doors were open to me. The honeymoon lasted until 1973.

It was also in 1957 that the Old Man, Yehuda Mozes, died of a heart attack at the age of seventy-five. From now on I would visit the tombs of the Kabalists in Safed alone.

His widow, Manya, told me of his last weeks and days. "He liked you very much," she said. "And because he liked you, so did I." She lowered her voice. "I have to admit that at first it bothered me. My husband was too fond of you and Dov. I was jealous, not for me but for my children. But I always followed him in everything he did." She expressed her desire that his heirs make me a present of a symbolic, founding share of the newspaper: "It's what my husband would have wanted." The heirs refused, but no matter. One share would hardly have made me rich, and in any case I always thought of *Yedioth Ahronoth* as "my" newspaper.

"My" paper was keeping me busy. I covered Ben-Gurion's second quasi-official visit to Boston, Washington, and Ottawa. I attended his historic meeting with Konrad Adenauer. I also covered Ben-Gurion's meeting with the newly elected American president, John F. Kennedy, on the eve of Kennedy's trip to Vienna to meet Nikita Khrushchev. The young leader seemed better prepared than his visitor. It was reported that Kennedy had deliberately raised an unexpected issue. (Too busy to meet with the Israeli leader, Kennedy had been pressured into reconsidering by his Jewish supporters. He reportedly wanted to take revenge.) He demanded that Ben-Gurion give an immediate answer to the question "How many Arab refugees is Israel prepared to take back?" In short, that meeting between the two men was not auspicious.

In Ottawa, Ben-Gurion attended a Shabbat dinner at the home of his ambassador, Yaakov Herzog. The correspondents were invited for coffee with the prime minister. Since he looked tired, I suggested we discuss philosophy rather than more politics. Everyone in Israel knew it was his favorite subject apart from the Bible. He loved to comb bookstores for obscure philosophical works, and read Plato in the original. He seemed pleased by my suggestion. "You know philosophy?" he asked. "I've studied it, that's all." He mentioned Spinoza (whom I revered), I cited Maimonides (with whom he was less familiar), someone else invoked Kafka (with whom he was completely unfamiliar). When someone referred to a Talmudic saying, the conversation became awkward. Ben-Gurion didn't like the Talmud, which he associated with exile.

In my opinion, Ben-Gurion was a better statesman than a philosopher. I can understand why his advisers and assistants were so totally loyal to him. He raised them to his level, inspiring them and teaching them to be sensitive to history. He had a paternal relationship with them for which his enemies unfairly reproached him.

His aide-de-camp, a man called Nehemia, was so completely devoted to him that he had always resisted getting married. When he finally fell in love, the head of the Mossad informed him that the woman was a foreign agent. In his despair, he put a bullet through his head. Ben-Gurion's advisers were afraid the news would upset him too much and they decided to keep it from him. All the Israeli newspapers, including the organ of the Communist Party, agreed to print a special copy of that day's issue, one that made no mention of Nehemia's death, for Ben-Gurion alone.

My daily reporting went on: the ongoing struggle of blacks for civil rights; the first American triumphs in space, the ill-fated Bay of Pigs invasion; Khrushchev's visit to the United Nations, with the unforgettable image of him taking off his shoe and pounding it on the table. There was Jacqueline Kennedy and her children; the scandal of the rigged TV quiz shows; the beginnings of the conquest of space; John Steinbeck's Nobel Prize; Betty Friedan and her feminist prophecy. I did many interviews and almost as many political commentaries.

One interview left a bitter taste. Yaël Dayan, the legendary general's daughter, had just published her first novel and the *Forverts* asked me to interview her. She was in the United States on a speaking tour.

When I arrived at her hotel room, I found her in tears. Critics back home had panned her book. I said what one is expected to say: Pay no attention, reviews come and go, the work endures. I must have managed to console her because she called me several times and briefly I became her confidant. She told me of her troubled childhood and of her stay in Greece, where she had had an unhappy relationship with a famous filmmaker. She wrote me letters that I thought had been lost. An assistant recently found them among my papers. They are embarrassingly personal. She went on to write more books, no better or worse than the first. Why was she always so angry? Fortunately she abandoned literature for politics, where she made many enemies and was not taken seriously. Is that why she wrote so critically about her father and her own family life? She is a woman who wanted to live great passions and wound up letting herself be borne by great hatreds. For some reason in recent years, I, too, have become a frequent target.

In October 1962 there was the Cuban missile crisis. What would the Soviet Union do? Would there be real war or fake peace? Kennedy gave a televised speech. That evening I was blinded by an unusually painful migraine: it was hard to watch and listen to the young president defy Moscow and to ponder and analyze the options and imagine the possibilities. The future of all humanity seemed in peril. Gromyko sat in the Oval Office with Kennedy and dared to deny the presence of Soviet missiles in Cuba. At the UN Adlai Stevenson exhibited aerial photographs that proved the opposite. General de

Gaulle magnanimously aligned himself with the United States. It was a nuclear standoff. One false move by either side, a single imprudent act or an ill-considered decision, would mean a continent in flames. The bombers of the Strategic Air Command were put on alert. The population was on edge; shelters were stockpiled with food and bottled drinking water.

I remember sleepless nights when everyone wondered whether by dawn the planet would be plunged into the ultimate nightmare. I wrote as though every dispatch would be read by the military chiefs in Havana and the Kremlin. The situation relaxed as Kennedy gained the upper hand and Khrushchev backed down. The nuclear peril receded, and the world sighed in relief.

The following year Kennedy was assassinated. It was a Friday, and I had just left the *Forverts* editorial office. As I got into the car, I turned on the radio. "We interrupt this broadcast . . ." By the time I arrived at my apartment, the nation was in mourning, paralyzed by the shock. A new president had been sworn in.

"The gods were jealous. . . ." So began a long article I wrote for the following Sunday's *Yedioth Ahronoth*. I wrote and wrote, feeling as though I were present at history's destruction. Like everyone else, I felt personally affected by the tragedy. Like everyone else, I will not forget John-John at his mother's side saluting his father's coffin. Like everyone else, I got no sleep until after the funeral. That day strong men and women wept.

My last dispatch on the Dallas assassination reported a conversation with Golda Meir, who, with so many other chiefs of state, came to pay homage to the dead president, offering the condolences of the Israeli nation to his young widow. Golda was greatly moved by Jackie Kennedy's dignity and courage, and described to me her impressions of the ceremony at Arlington National Cemetery, the atmosphere in the White House, and the new president, Lyndon Johnson. An excellent observer, she enabled me to report the events as if I had been there myself.

"During the funeral," Golda told me, "I remembered my visit with Kennedy in Palm Beach. . . ." He had been vacationing there. As she told me this story, she was chain-smoking and dropping her cigarette butts into strategically positioned ashtrays. She was visibly agitated, unable to sit still. "I have to tell you about it," she said, flushed with emotion. "Kennedy received me in great secrecy. And something happened. Something I still don't understand. . . ."

It was 1961. America was under the spell of its youthful, eloquent president. Surrounded by liberal intellectuals, he believed in the power of ideas and ideals and was convinced that humanity, fundamentally generous, could devote itself to the quest for "new frontiers." With the lessening of international tensions, disarmament, peace, and goodwill, anything was possible. In his optimism, he couldn't understand why Israel was so insistent on its security needs. At one point he exploded: "All the Jews who plead your cause talk of nothing but weaponry. And you yourself, Mrs. Meir, instead of evoking the timeless message of Biblical morality, the prophets, spiritual or cultural problems, or whatever, the whole time you've been here all you want to talk about is missiles. Isn't there anything else to discuss?" "You're right, Mr. President," Golda replied, "we are obsessed with security. We are an ancient people and twice in our history we have lost our Temple and our sovereignty. Yes, we did survive; we are dispersed but we survived because all Jews, the scholar in Vilna, the merchant in Lodz, the industrialist in Chicago, and the shopkeeper in Salonica were motivated by the same powerful dream: that one day our Temple would be rebuilt. Well, Mr. President, the Temple is not yet rebuilt. We have only just begun. And if this beginning itself is destroyed, we will not even be able to dream anymore." Kennedy stared at her for a long moment and then, without a word, pushed a button and ordered one of his aides to set in motion the administrative process that enabled the Pentagon to supply Israel with its first Hawk missiles.

"What do you think of that?" Golda asked, beaming. "See?" I replied. "A good story can get you anything. Even missiles."

Our relationship grew steadily closer. In Israel

I used to visit her at her office in Jerusalem or at her home near Tel Aviv. Since she was often ill (she told everyone she suffered from migraines, but those closest to her knew she had cancer), I also went to see her in the hospital.

In 1965 Golda's party, now led by Prime Minister Levi Eshkol, was racked by a violent conflict with its founder, David Ben-Gurion. The issue was the repercussions of the lamentable Lavon Affair. Back in 1954 some Israeli secret agents and several Egyptian Jews had been arrested and sentenced in Egypt. The Israeli agents had exploded a bomb in an American movie theater in Cairo in an effort to damage U.S.-Egyptian relations. It was impossible to determine who had given them such a senseless order, which led to the execution of two defendants, Moshe Marzuk and Shlomo Azzar. Several politicians and high-ranking officers, as well as a secretary who was quickly dispatched to the United States, were involved in this politically stupid, professionally inept, and morally inexcusable affair. There was talk of treachery, perjury, and conspiracy. From Sedeh Boker, the kibbutz to which he had prematurely retired, Ben-Gurion demanded a thorough judicial inquiry, which the majority of the Labor Party opposed. The result was internal warfare that led to a split in the party. Golda was appalled. She was loyal to Ben-Gurion, but the Mapai was her whole life. Forced to choose between the two, she opted for the party. "Why is Ben-

Gurion making all this trouble for us?" she complained to me from her hospital bed. "Doesn't he realize that if he keeps it up, we could end up with Begin in the government — and I don't want to live to see that day."

Two years later Begin was part of the government of national unity formed just before the Six-Day War. Ten years after that he was prime minister, and it was he — the hard-liner, the hawk — who made peace with the first Arab country, Egypt.

Why did Golda hate Begin so? She detested the right wing and had fought it since the start of her career in the Zionist movement. In her view, as in Ben-Gurion's, the right could only be fascist. Conditioned by their own propaganda, they were wrong: In domestic policy Begin was no less democratic than they were. But Golda was often stubborn and inflexible; it was not easy to persuade her to change her mind about anything. Sometimes I would plead with her on behalf of this or that person she scorned, but in vain. When I praised Shimon Peres, she replied, "You don't know him." When I mentioned Eban's intelligence, she sneered. A woman like her, so magnificent in her role as mother of Israel, should have been able to rise above petty political quarrels, but Golda, like other great personalities, had strong likes and dislikes. An ambassador who displeased her might easily find himself transferred across the planet overnight. And like most mortals, she was not immune to flattery.

I enjoyed listening to Golda talk about her childhood in Russia, her adolescence in Milwaukee, and her early experiences in Palestine. I was careful not to contradict her in political matters, but was less reticent where history was concerned. As I mentioned earlier, she objected to my position on the Palestinian Jews during the war. I considered them too passive; she thought me too critical. We returned to the subject several times but found ourselves in complete disagreement. Herself a symbol of the political leadership of the Yishuv, the Jewish community in Palestine, in those years, she refused to accept any guilt, while I rejected absolution.

Despite our contrasting views, our relations always remained friendly. After one of her speeches to the UN General Assembly, she had been the guest of honor at a reception in my apartment at the Master Hotel. Now, some four years later, she was prime minister. Once again she came to a reception in her honor at my new home. Knowing that she felt uncomfortable with intellectuals, before escorting her from the Waldorf to my home, I spent an hour describing all of the writers and professors who awaited her. "What can I possibly say to them?" she asked. "I never even set foot in a university." I reassured her. "Don't worry, Golda, they all love you." But she was skeptical. "What am I, compared to all those professors?" she said.

This modesty was uncharacteristic. "Golda," I finally told her, "there are tens of thousands of professors in American universities. But there is only one Golda." Finally, here was an argument she found convincing.

Seated like a queen mother among our guests, she talked about President Nixon, expressing great affection for him. When a professor of political science asked how she could possibly defend his Vietnam policy, she brought all her eloquence to bear in defending her friend in the White House. The humorist Herbert Tarr tried to break the tension by raising his hand. "I have a question," he said. "Mrs. Meir, will you marry me?" Her answer was barely audible amid the outbreak of laughter: "Would *you* be embarrassed if I said yes . . . ?"

My thoughts turned to Golda on September 13, 1993, when, oscillating between hope and fear, I attended the White House signing ceremony for the agreement between Israel and the PLO. "There is no such thing as a Palestinian people," she had confidently asserted. Twenty years after the Yom Kippur war, fifteen years after Golda Meir's death, the whole world recognized with Yitzhak Rabin and Bill Clinton that a Palestinian people does exist and that it has the right to fulfill its destiny.

Rabban Gamliel, son of Rabbi Yehuda the Prince, said: "Be careful in your relations with those in power; they draw you close or allow you to approach them only when they need you. They are your friends when your friendship is useful to them and affords them pleasure, but they forget you when you are in trouble." I have thought of this often. Is it wise for a writer to come too close to power? Is it prudent to be a friend to princes? Naturally, it depends on the writer, on what he values. And what is power? I would later discuss the question with François Mitterrand, and also with my master Saul Lieberman.

In the Jewish tradition there are three powers, or forms of power: those of the king, the prophet, and the priest. In ancient times their election was inspired by God, but none survived the Temple's destruction. Today every leader believes himself king, every member of the clergy takes himself to be the high priest, and "prophets" indulge too much in politics.

During the time Sighet was under Hungarian rule, schoolchildren had to do compulsory service in the Leventes, a kind of scout movement under the supervision of the army and the Ministry of Education. We had to perform various tasks, such as digging trenches at army bases, helping firefighters, or clearing snowbound streets. One day — it was a Friday — I was assigned to head a team. Exempted from the task of wielding a shovel, I was supposed to oversee, command, and shout — very loudly. I took my role seriously, rushing from group to group berating laggards: Hurry up, the snow has to be cleared by nightfall, before Shabbat! Suddenly I found myself face to face with the grandson of the Borsher Rebbe. He was a close friend of mine. We often studied together, and prayed at the same times. He stared at me with an expression not so much of disapproval as of sadness and surprise. Was I going to harangue him too, make him feel my power, my authority? When my eyes met his, I was overcome by remorse. I began to stammer excuses, at which point our commander appeared on the scene. Realizing that I was not cut out for this job, he shook me and screamed, "Next time, you fool, you'll sweat blood like everyone else." Out of the corner of my eye I saw my friend smiling. I would later see men of all ages who, in extreme situations, brutally exercised their power over their fellow inmates. Sometimes I ask myself whether I would have been like them had I been appointed a kapo or *Vorarbeiter*. To this day I feel that no one has the right to judge or draw comparisons. Ultimately, the only power to which man should aspire is that which he exercises over himself.

Over the years I have observed many politicians, who often have disappointed me. Ambition brings them to center stage, where they posture as social reformer or revolutionary ideologue. For too many of them it is theater. They act the part, and the journalist who reports (or even amplifies) their words becomes one of the players, bringing them a broader audience. In the end I came to dislike the game. I feared contamination by the easy cynicism and cheap promises of the holders of power. Besides which, I don't like acting — except when professionals do it. To strive to seem like what one is not, is to insult the Creator Himself, telling Him He made a mistake. To get ahead the priests of power are prepared to disguise themselves as clown or pope. As Saul Lieberman put it: "They would gladly suffer countless humiliations for a sprig of honor." I knew it was not I but the representative of *Yedioth Ahronoth* that Israeli politicians and Jewish dignitaries tried to win over. I was important only inasmuch as I reflected my paper's collective judgment. In some sense, I didn't even exist.

It was in the early 1960s that an old dream, as mad as it was vain, reemerged: to start a Jewish magazine. Michel Salomon, editor in chief of *l'Arche*, and Shuka Tadmor, U.S. correspondent for the Israeli daily *Lamerhav*, were ready to dream along with me.

I had met them at more or less the same time, Shuka in a UN press room, Michel in Stockholm, Pilley at another conference of the World Jewish Congress. Aware of my financial difficulties, Teddy had persuaded me to join his team of interpreters again. Michel was in Stockholm on assignment.

A digression. It was also in Stockholm that I did a series of interviews with a Finnish physiotherapist I met through a Jewish leader, Dr. Hillel Storch. The man's name, Felix Kersten, was familiar to me. I had read somewhere that Heinrich Himmler had been among his patients. Himmler, it seems, suffered from terrible stomach trouble, and Kersten treated him often, sometimes daily. What did the SS Reichsführer talk about as his healer massaged his pain-racked body? According to Kersten, everything, including the Jews. And their extermination? Rarely. But let me quote from our conversation:

"Did Himmler confide in you, Mr. Kersten?"
"Yes."
"Did he sleep during massages?"
"Sometimes."
"So it would have been possible for you to press a little harder on his neck, for instance?"
"Yes, that possibility was open to me. Although . . . the hallway and nearby offices were full of SS men."
"But you could have killed him."
"Yes."
"Why did you spare his life? Because you were afraid to lose yours?"
"No, it wasn't that. I told myself I could have some influence over him. And in fact, I did save human lives. Toward the end of the war I was the one who persuaded him to evacuate the last camp prisoners instead of killing them. I was the one who set up the meeting between Himmler and Dr. Michael Mazur, the delegate

of the World Jewish Congress."

Kersten was a strange man. I felt uncomfortable in his presence, perhaps because he was the only man I knew who had maintained close relations with Himmler. What did he leave unsaid?

Let me go back to my publishing dreams: the weekly magazine that would be the salvation of its founders, if not of all humanity, which, surprisingly, seemed not to care at all.

The project was quite clear in our own minds. A Jewish weekly patterned on *Time*, appearing in three languages: English, French, and Spanish — in full color, if you please. We would solicit the most prestigious bylines: Walter Lippmann for politics, Leonard Bernstein for music, Saul Bellow for literature. We would have vast political and cultural influence. We would discover young talent, encourage original ideas and social initiatives. Jewish life would never be the same. All we needed was the modest sum of one hundred thousand dollars to launch it. I tried to interest the president of the World Jewish Congress, Nahum Goldmann, who advised me to visit the superrich Samuel Bronfman in Montreal. We also decided to try our luck with Philip Klutznick, former president of B'nai B'rith. He advised us to go see Nahum Goldmann.

Then one day Shuka called me with good news: He had found our dream patron. His first name was Oscar, and he was rich and ready. He was prepared to meet with us whenever we wanted. Michel caught the first plane from Paris, and the three of us spent a long night preparing for the decisive meeting. Shuka explained that he had met his superrich friend in London in the 1950s. He was a Jewish immigrant from Czechoslovakia, a Zionist activist, a happy financier, and an unhappy intellectual, because he couldn't seem to get published. He was the ideal candidate. We would help him and vice versa.

Oscar lived in Westchester in a town about an hour's drive from Manhattan. We took my old Chevrolet. It didn't look like much, and Michel made no secret of his apprehension: Oscar wouldn't take us seriously; we couldn't go off to discuss a deal of global import in "that crate." I reassured him: As soon as we got the first hundred thousand, we would buy a respectable vehicle. During the ride up, we had a long discussion about what brand, what year, and what color car we wanted, and whether it should have air-conditioning. However, before we reached these important decisions, we had arrived at Oscar's estate, complete with pool and rose garden.

Our angel — a frail old man with a shock of silver hair and an air of distinction about him — greeted us with the courtesy and respect due future press barons. We went into the paneled library with a fireplace, a chess set on a small table. The room conveyed an aura of success and serenity.

Coffee or tea? The very English Oscar had tea. His trio of visitors preferred coffee. The cups were small, but the coffee was great.

As is God. For Oscar, heaven bless him, was His messenger — messenger of hope, herald of happiness, guardian angel. He was tempted by our project. In fact, he was downright enthusiastic. He had long dreamed of creating a Jewish magazine. Why hadn't we come to see him twenty years ago? But it wasn't too late. God Himself must have brought us to him. Money? That was his business; he would handle it. Our task was to prepare the magazine, to assemble a team, select columnists and critics. We had only just met, and already we soared together to the summit of supreme illusion. "You do your job, I'll do mine," Oscar said. "Draw up a budget, and I'll take care of the financing." We tried, timidly, to clarify a delicate point: what did he expect in return? Praise from the magazine? The opportunity to express himself in it? No, he said. He wanted absolutely nothing. He was doing this for pleasure, out of belief in our mission.

Having downed my fifth cup of coffee and expressed our gratitude to our host, I asked practical questions: What next? When would we meet again? We decided unanimously to get together once a month.

"We forgot the most important thing," Michel remarked, phlegmatic as usual, once we were back in the old Chevy. The most important thing? "Yes, money." That annoyed me. "How can you say that? He asked for a budget, didn't he? Didn't he say he would take care of everything?" Michel smiled. "And in the meantime who's going to pay my plane fares?" He was silent for a moment. "And what about the car? Who's going to pay for the car we have to buy so as not to lose face before this Jewish Rockefeller who could give the real Rockefeller journalism lessons?"

Michel took out a loan to cover his trips and I borrowed money for the car, a used Oldsmobile. We had no magazine yet, but we were already in debt.

Thirty years later I cannot believe how stupid we were — I most of all. Had I forgotten Joseph Givon? How could we be sure Oscar was trustworthy? Did we really think such a project was feasible? How could three unknown, penniless journalists — an Israeli, a Frenchman, and a newly naturalized American — think they were capable of launching a weekly in English, a language none of us was fluent in? But Oscar had an answer for everything, so we dismissed all pessimistic thoughts.

A period of intense activity began. Shuka was to be responsible for the Israeli pages, Michel for the cultural columns, and I for the section on Jewish life. We would sign the editorials on a rotating basis. We proposed to Oscar that he be the fourth editorialist. He deserved that much, didn't he? When we submitted an annual budget of $250,000 to our patron, he was severely critical, finding it too modest. There was no point in even discussing anything less than a million dollars. Where would we get such a sum? He was annoyed by our prudence. Did we dare doubt his word? If he could find a quarter of a million, he could surely come up with four times that amount.

A year after our first meeting we solemnly presented Oscar with a dummy issue. Theoretically, we could now open offices, hire secretaries, and develop an advertising policy. All we needed was a bank account. "Indeed," Oscar said, approving our analysis, "it's feasible." He sank into thought for a moment and then declared: "A million dollars, right?" Right. "Okay," he said. "I'll give it to you in four installments. Is that all right?" That was all right. "But . . ." Suddenly I was on guard. Buts make me nervous. ". . . you must come to London. I'll be there next week. At the Dorchester. I'll give you the first check then." It was somewhat inconvenient, but we took out our appointment books and agreed on a date. I already envisioned us running a vast press empire. Michel, Shuka, and I returned to Manhattan to celebrate. Shuka's wife, Levitta, gently mocked our excessive optimism, but we mocked her no less excessive pessimism.

Michel flew back to Paris. Shuka and I, more broke than ever, decided to economize by sending Michel to London alone. There was no reason all three of us had to be present just to pick up a check. On the designated day Michel flew to London, took a cab to the Dorchester, and asked the receptionist to tell Oscar he was there. The clerk informed Michel that the gentleman was not at the hotel. When Michel asked when he would be back, the clerk replied that he had never checked in. Michel hurried to a phone to tell us. Shuka and I were at a loss. Perhaps Oscar was ill. Shuka called Westchester and got no answer. In the meantime, Michel phoned other luxury hotels, in vain. Our patron was not registered or expected at any of them. I then suggested that Shuka drive the Oldsmobile up to Westchester. Maybe Oscar had had a heart attack. But Shuka found him not only in good health but calm and serene. "You were supposed to be in London," Shuka protested. Oscar didn't even apologize. On the contrary, he chided Shuka for being so naïve. "You really thought I was going to give you a million dollars?" Why had he engaged in this terribly cruel hoax? Well, all alone in his big Westchester estate, he had been bored. And he had found us amusing.

He had robbed us of our time, our energy, and our enthusiasm just for the fun of it. It seems I had learned nothing from my misadventures with Givon.

It took us a long time to pay off our debts. And to sell the Oldsmobile.

Writing

In 1957, during my convalescence, I received good news from François Mauriac: Jérôme Lindon of Éditions de Minuit was going to publish *La Nuit* (Night). The letter of confirmation opened a new chapter in the book of commentaries that is my life.

Lindon didn't like the original title: "And the World Remained Silent." He preferred a biblical phrase, perhaps something from the Book of Jeremiah. But after discussing various suggestions, we settled on *La Nuit*. Lindon also wanted me to tighten the text, given to him by Mauriac, though I had already pruned and abridged it considerably. He proposed new cuts throughout, leading to significant differences in length among the successive versions. I had cut down the original manuscript from 862 pages to the 245 of the published Yiddish edition. Lindon edited *La Nuit* down to 178.

Lindon was unhappy with my probably too abstract manner of introducing the subject. Nor was he enamored of two pages which sought to describe the premises and early phases of the tragedy. Testimony from survivors tends to begin with these sorts of descriptions, evoking loved ones as well as one's hometown before the annihilation, as if breathing life into them one last time. Lindon also preferred to open the story with the portrait of Moishele, the beadle of our synagogue.

The book ended this way (I only quote it for its relevance today):

I looked at myself in the mirror. A skeleton stared back at me.

Nothing but skin and bone.

It was the image of myself after death. It was at that instant that the will to live awakened within me.

Without knowing why, I raised my fist and shattered the glass, along with the image it held. I lost consciousness.

After I got better, I stayed in bed for several days, jotting down notes for the work that you, dear reader, now hold in your hands.

- But . . .

. . . Today, ten years after Buchenwald, I realize that the world forgets. Germany is a sovereign state. The German army has been reborn. Ilse Koch, the sadist of Buchenwald, is a happy wife and mother. War criminals stroll in the streets of Hamburg and Munich. The past has been erased, buried.

Germans and anti-Semites tell the world

that the story of six million Jewish victims is but a myth, and the world, in its naïveté, will believe it, if not today, then tomorrow or the next day.

So it occurred to me that it might be useful to publish in book form these notes taken down in Buchenwald.

I am not so naïve as to believe that this work will change the course of history or shake the conscience of humanity.

Books no longer command the power they once did.

Those who yesterday held their tongues will keep their silence tomorrow.

That is why, ten years after Buchenwald, I ask myself the question, Was I right to break that mirror?

By the time *Night* was published in France, I was at work on another book. One critic, René Lalo, expressed surprise; he was convinced I would write nothing more after *Night*. In one sense, he was right: There was nothing more I could say about Auschwitz, since words that seek to grasp its reality are doomed to fail from the start. But then, what to do with all this acquired knowledge? Is it not imperative to testify if only so as to leave a trace? For whom? For what? Who will decipher it? Understand? And yet . . .

Writing for me is a painful pleasure. The most difficult part is to begin. Once the first sentence

559

appears on paper, the rest follows. The path is clear. "Somewhere a child began to cry." That was *Dawn*. From those few words I knew my characters would live and die in Palestine. "Outside dusk fell upon the city like a vandal's heavy fist." Thus begins *The Town Beyond the Wall*. *The Gates of the Forest* opened with a phrase suggesting encounter and parting, the gulf of forgetfulness and the discovery of sharing: "He had no name, so he gave him his own." In *The Forgotten* it was Elhanan's prayer that served as lure: "God of Abraham, Isaac, and Jacob, forget not their son who calls upon them now."

There are some words I cannot bring myself to use; they paralyze me. I cannot write the words "concentration," "night and fog," "selection," or "transport" without a feeling of sacrilege. Another difficulty, of a different type: I write in French, but I learned the language from books and therefore I am not good at slang.

All my subsequent works are written in the same deliberately spare style as *Night*. It is the style of the chroniclers of the ghettos, where everything had to be said swiftly, in one breath. You never knew when the enemy might kick in the door, sweeping us away into nothingness. Every phrase was a testament. There was no time or reason for anything superfluous. Words must not be imprisoned or harnessed, not even in the silence of the page. And yet, it must be held tightly. If the violin is to sing, its strings must be stretched so tight as to risk breaking;

slack, they are merely threads.

To write is to plumb the unfathomable depths of being. Writing lies within the domain of mystery. The space between any two words is vaster than the distance between heaven and earth. To bridge it you must close your eyes and leap. A Hasidic tradition tells us that in the Torah the white spaces, too, are God-given. Ultimately, to write is an act of faith.

Spring 1958. The war in Algeria was at its height, gaining destructive momentum on both sides. Incredibly, some men invest more passion in killing than in living and bringing new life. At the UN France was on the defensive. Israel was among its few supporters. Yet many American Jewish intellectuals were pro-Algerian. Joseph Golan, a political adviser to Nahum Goldmann and the man who played an important role in the departure of Moroccan Jews for Israel, introduced me and others to prominent Algerians at UN headquarters. The Israeli delegation was displeased, and Golda later punished him for his contacts with Algerians by withdrawing his Israeli passport. Consequently, he left the Jewish arena and moved to Africa, invited by the president of Senegal, Léopold Senghor, to advise on his country's economic problems.

It was around that time that I returned to France to promote *Night*. Mauriac's stirring preface, reprinted on the front page of *Le Figaro Littéraire*, attracted attention, and his praise for the book aroused the reviewers' interest. The work was favorably received, though this kind of literature was not yet fashionable. Neophyte that I was, I read and reread every review and wanted to thank each critic individually. I tried hard not to let the praise go to my head. Mauriac, whom I visited the day I arrived in Paris, had his own way of immunizing me: "One day the critics make us pay for the joy they have given us." Of course, he was right. That day, too, would come. The moment you achieve visibility, you become a target, and often there are more arrows than compliments. I still remember my first negative review: that day, like a child, I wanted to run from newsstand to newsstand to buy up all the copies of the misguided newspaper — and burn them.

I finally met Jérôme Lindon. In his unprepossessing office he explained his opposition to his government's policy. He was fighting for an independent Algeria. To put me at ease he spoke of his family (his father had been a prosecutor at the Nuremberg trials) and his childhood. He made me a present of his lovely translation and commentary on the Book of Jonah. In short, we had a good meeting. It was later, much later, that he adopted political positions that created a rift between us. His preface to the book *Pour les Fédayin* (For the PLO) hurt me and many of his friends, as did his virtually unconditional adherence to the Palestinian cause. But on a personal level, the contact between us was never severed.

I owe him my encounter with Samuel Beckett. One day he said, "He'd like to meet you." I was thrilled at the prospect. We made an appointment at a restaurant, Chez Francis. As is my custom, I arrived half an hour early, taking a seat in the corner without noticing the elegant man seated across the terrace. An hour went by. I wondered if I had been told the wrong day or time. I looked at my watch, and that was when I saw him looking at his. Our eyes met, and we smiled at the same moment. I got up and went over to him. We shook hands. I sat down across from him and waited respectfully for him to initiate the conversation. He waited too. I don't know how long the silence lasted, but I do remember it was he who broke it. Delicately, as if in a whisper, he began to talk — but not about himself or about me. The manuscript of *Molloy* had just been returned to him, and he realized that the epigraph had been omitted from the printed book. "It was a simple phrase: 'in desperation.' " He fell silent again. We sat there for an hour, silent but not mute. We would see each other again, and he would speak to me of the tragic role of the witness.

In the 1960s Lindon sent me a message of friendship through Marguerite Duras, then in New York for a brief visit. She was already known, but not yet famous. I knew nothing about her except her connection to *nouveau roman* circles. I liked her book *Un Barrage contre le pacifique*, but didn't know how to tell her.

We went for a walk in Central Park and along Fifth Avenue. I took her to the UN. She tried to get me to talk about my latest book, my work, and especially the experiences I had described in *Night*. But I was too bashful. We never saw each other again.

For the first time in my life, I was a beneficiary of the luminous boon of television. France's star cultural journalist Pierre Dumayet interviewed me for his program "Lectures pour tous." Israel Adler drove me to the studio on the motorscooter of which he was so proud. His excitement was such that we almost had an accident. "Don't you have stage fright?" he asked. Of course I did. "Try to think about something else." Fair enough. "But be careful of your hands," he added. "On this program they show hands as much as faces."

The next day people recognized me in the street. They didn't know who I was or what I had written, just that I had been interviewed on the small screen by one of its stars. I didn't have the impression that *La Nuit* was selling well, but it was being talked about here and there.

They say Borges insisted on writing personal thank-you notes to everyone who bought his first book. I might well have done the same.

An anecdote for writers just starting out.

Franz Kafka was ill and decided to recuperate in Marienbad. "Your name seems familiar to me," the innkeeper said, glancing at the registration card.

"Impossible," Kafka replied. "I've never been here before."

He took his valise and went up to his room to rest. He had barely dozed off when someone knocked softly at the door. It was the innkeeper. "Excuse me for disturbing you, but I have a question: Are you a writer?"

Astonished, Kafka replied, "Not really. Why do you ask?"

"Because my son says you are."

"Tell him he's made a mistake."

The innkeeper left, and Kafka tried to go back to sleep. He was awakened again. "It's my son," the innkeeper said. "He claims you're a very great writer. He wants to meet you. It's important to him. If you want to get some rest, you'd better say yes and get it over with."

Reluctantly, Kafka agreed, and the innkeeper went to fetch his son. The young man could only stammer, "What an honor, what a pleasure!"

"But why?" Kafka asked.

"Because . . . because . . . you're Kafka."

"So?"

"So? Mr. Kafka, don't you realize who you are? You're a great writer, the writer I admire most in the world."

"Have you read anything of mine?"

"Of course. Your work changed my life."

"Which work?"

"Metamorphosis."

"You read it?"

"Of course I did. I read it and reread it."

"Where did you find it?"

"What do you mean, where did I find it? I bought it."

"So *you're* the one!" Kafka exclaimed.

Despite the praise I received as the author of a first book, I felt a gnawing doubt. I wondered if I had said what needed to be said in the way it needed to be said. The more enthusiastic the reviews, the more anxious I became. In the end I decided that if people liked what I had written they had not understood. Testimony like mine should have aroused anger.

Around the same time, in the spring of 1958, Bea happened to be in London, where an acquaintance of hers was gravely ill. All his friends had gathered at his bedside. Dreaming of a reunion with both my sisters, I invited Bea to Paris, but she phoned to suggest I come to London instead. She was engaged to be married. I assumed she was about to marry the dying man, and exclaimed, "Are you mad?" (I had never stopped urging her — affectionately — to find a husband.) She hastened to reassure me: It was the doctor, not the patient, whom she planned to marry. I caught the first plane to London, where I had dinner with her and her fiancé, Dr. Leonard Jackson. Bea seemed so happy that on a sudden impulse I took off my watch and gave it to my future brother-in-law as an engagement present. Later Bea and her husband settled in Montreal, where they lived happily with their two children, until the day it was discovered that she had lung cancer.

In the United States someone else had come into my life. Georges Borchardt, a New York literary agent whose reputation was on the rise, was desperately seeking an American publisher for my little book. Georges is a former teacher of French origin. He is a man of keen intelligence, deceptively cynical and sincerely skeptical, and, fortunately for his clients, totally discreet and reliable. To have him as an agent is lucky, to have him as a friend a pleasure. Reticent about his past, especially his childhood and adolescence during the war, he falls back on humor when the subject comes up.

When we first met he was living in a small two-room apartment on West Fifty-fifth Street. One of the rooms served as an office. Anne, a young Jewish girl from New Jersey, was his assistant and secretary. One day we were on the way to the airport and Georges offhandedly remarked, "Did I tell you that Anne has decided to change her name?" It was his way of telling me they were getting married.

As for *Night*, despite Mauriac's preface and the favorable reviews in the French, Belgian, and Swiss press, the big publishers hesitated, debated, and ultimately sent their regrets. Some thought the book too slender (American readers seemed to prefer fatter volumes), others too depressing (American readers seemed to prefer optimistic books). Some felt its subject was too little known, others that it was too well known. In short, it was suggested over and over again that we try elsewhere. Refusing to lose heart, Georges kept trying. In the end Hill and Wang agreed to take the risk. Arthur Wang won me over with his lack of concern for things commercial. He still believed in literature as others believe in God. His zest for life deeply impressed me. Sensitive, he listened in depth the way some read in depth. If he didn't like a work, he said so, but gently. "I can't promise you millions," he said, "but I'll do a good job, meaning the best I can." He kept that promise. The American edition sold a couple of thousand copies in its first two years, but it attracted a certain amount of attention. When other houses later offered us better terms for *Dawn* and *The Accident*, Georges and I decided to stay with Hill and Wang.

In Paris Paul Flamand, head of the publishing house Le Seuil, introduced me to George Steiner. Brilliant, incisive, blessed with writing gifts and fluent in several languages, he was the kind of intellectual who enjoys arousing hostility. At ease in both ancient and modern cultures, he upset the Israelis by hailing the Diaspora. "Man is not a tree," he declared; ever in motion, he seeks the roots of knowledge in more than one place.

In Haifa, during a conference on the Holocaust, he managed to alienate the survivors in the audience. The Auschwitz experience, he said, could best be conveyed in German, and gave as example the work of the poet Paul Celan. While reaffirming my affection for him, I pointed out that German was also the language of the killers, and that the great documents on the tragedy had been written in Yiddish and Hebrew. That said, I admired his original way of treating the most complex subjects. George Steiner is a man with a restless soul whose search is never-ending.

Scoops are relatively rare in journalism, and in 1962 fortune smiled upon me, allowing me to outdo my colleagues. The story concerned a boy named Yossele Shuchmacher, whose grandfather, believing the parents were neglecting the boy's religious education, kidnapped him "to save his soul." The event turned Israel upside down. The residences of presumed suspects were searched, extremist sects were closely watched, but with no result. Not only was public opinion aroused, Yossele became a national obsession. Prime Minister Ben-Gurion ordered the Israeli secret services to conduct a worldwide search, exhaustively investigating all Jewish communities and infiltrating ultraorthodox circles. The operation was directed by Issar Harel, legendary chief of the Mossad, the man who supervised the capture of Adolf Eichmann in Buenos Aires. But the most famous boy in Israel had disappeared, swallowed up by the guardians of fanaticism.

Dov phoned me every week. "Anything at your end?" There never was. "Rumor has it he's in Brooklyn," Dov told me. But Brooklyn is a big place. "Use your contacts with the Lubavitch Hasidim. I think they're up to something." My contacts laughed. They were conducting their own inquiry, for they were just as eager as Ben-Gurion to find the boy whose disappearance was an embarrassment to the moderate religious community. Then one Friday afternoon I got a more agitated call from Dov: "We've been told he's definitely somewhere in the New York area. Check it out." I called a friend, Israel Gur-Arye, an Israeli consul and a descendant of the Besht, of whom it was whispered that he was the Mossad's man in New York. "Another false rumor," he said. Was he sure? "Absolutely," he replied. He promised to let me know if anything broke. I called Dov back and told him I trusted Gur-Arye. "If you're not careful," Dov insisted, "you'll let the most sensational item of the last few years slip through your fingers." I agreed to be on guard. In any case, the next day was Shabbat, and ordinarily, nothing out of the ordinary happened in Brooklyn on Shabbat. But I forgot that many extraordinary things can happen at the end of Shabbat.

On Sunday morning Dov's voice on the phone sounded more ironic than annoyed. "So, you still trust that friend of yours?" It took me a moment to figure out what he meant. "You haven't heard?" He seemed surprised. "Mossad agents recovered the boy last night. In Brooklyn." Stunned, I hung up. I had to get hold of Gur-Arye. It was five in the morning, and I hesitated to wake his wife, Shula. But never mind. I would apologize to her, though surely not to her lying husband. It was Shula who answered. "Israel's not here," she said, "but I know he wants to talk to you. Here's the number where you can reach him." I got through on the tenth try. Seething with indignation, I was about to tell my former friend what I thought of him when he cut me off. "Try to understand. The slightest indiscretion could have ruined the operation. The boy was not yet in our hands. We picked him up only two hours ago. We knew where he was hiding, but needed the consent of the American authorities. I was going to call you. . . ." I refused to forgive him. He had tricked me, embarrassed me. He said he was sorry, but I wasn't interested in his excuses. You don't lie to a friend, even if you are a Mossad agent. "Look," he said, "you never know what line might be tapped or by whom." He went on and on, but I rejected his explanations, and finally he grudgingly admitted my anger was justified. "Okay," he said. "I owe you one. Let me find a way to pay you back."

That afternoon he arranged an exclusive interview for me with the boy. The descendant of the Besht could not fail to honor this second promise. "But you have to swear you won't reveal where he is." I swore. "And that you won't ask him about the kidnapping." I swore that too. "And that you won't say I was the one who . . ." I swore that too.

Yossele reminded me of the Jewish boys of my town, with kipa and side curls. He washed his hands before saying his morning and evening prayers, recited a blessing before drinking the glass of water I offered him. I liked his melancholy, innocent smile. I told him that when I was his age, I had been as pious as he. I asked how he had spent his days while hidden in Brooklyn. "I studied the *parsha*," the weekly passage of the Bible. What else? "Rashi." And? "The Talmud." Which tractate? "Berakhot, the Benedictions." There happened to be a complete set of the Babylonian Talmud in the apartment, and the two of us, ignoring the Mossad and FBI agents in the room, pored over the texts that bound us to ancient times.

The interview caused quite a stir, though I didn't reveal anything sensational. I never mentioned that it was an ex–nightclub dancer who had converted to Judaism who had been instrumental in getting Yossele out of the country illegally, nor that Yossele had been disguised as a girl, nor that a fanatical sect had organized the kidnapping. All I did was describe

572

our Talmud lesson.

Dov was pleased, and Gur-Arye and I were friends again. You can't hold a grudge against a descendant of the Besht, even if he is a Mossad agent.

(Some years later I read an article about Yossele in *Yedioth Ahronoth*. He was no longer fanatical; in fact, he had even stopped practicing.)

In France I was compelled to change publishers. Perhaps because he liked *Night* so much, Lindon didn't like *Dawn*. He told me so straight out, adding that he published only works he wished he had written himself. I wasn't at all offended by his directness. I was amused. He also advised me to change the novel's ending.

During one of his trips to Paris, Georges Borchardt happened to spend a morning at Éditions du Seuil, where Monique Nathan told him she had read *Night*. She asked whether I had written anything else, and Georges told her I had. In fact, he just happened to have the manuscript with him. He gave it to Monique, who withdrew to her small office to read it. Fortunately for both of us, it was not a long book. Georges was still talking to Paul Flamand when Monique came out to say she couldn't understand why Jérôme Lindon had rejected it. Still, she refused to steal an author from a rival house, so she phoned Lindon to tell him she thought he was making a mistake. But Jérôme stuck to his decision and Monique kept the manuscript.

Paul Flamand, who ran the house, was not only a wise and daring publisher but also a superbly intelligent and sensitive humanist, a man of vast culture capable of guiding and enlightening an author without offending him. An hour in his office or two hours at a restaurant alone with him was worth a trip to France. He had a way of soothing the heart while arousing the mind. It was impossible not to grow attached to him. The contracts he sent Georges were unusual: he let us fill in the amount of the advance ourselves.

Delivering a manuscript to Paul was a ritual that never changed: He would touch it, caress it, sniff it, put it down and pick it up, flip through it. Finally, he would stuff it into the bulging briefcase he carried home. A day, a week, or six months later, over dinner, he might suddenly refer to the book's theme, construction, and characters, each of which he had thoroughly analyzed. If he failed to understand an episode, he would gently try to show me that I hadn't understood it well enough myself.

I loved our discussions. A devout but enlightened Catholic, he was interested in Jewish tradition and culture as a means of gaining greater insight into his own. I liked the way he asked questions or commented on an author or a text: He would draw you out tactfully, delicately, muttering something like "Well, well," which would force you to go into even greater detail. You could never be superficial with him.

I remember the time we visited the cathedral of Chartres. No one could talk about it or view it as he did. He made the stones tell their stories.

I remember Marguerite Flamand, solemn and contemplative, expressing herself deliberately, covering the essential in just a few words; I remember her as her health declined, as she battled her illness with a stoic strength that accentuated her feminine grace.

I remember Paul, when asked about his wife's health, opening and closing his mouth without uttering a sound.

"What's wrong? You look terrible." I was talking to Saul Friedlander. We had last seen each other at the home of a friend in Manhattan in 1958 or 1959. He was working for Nahum Goldmann. I had never seen him so depressed.

As we sat at an outdoor café on the Boulevard Saint-Germain, he took a Valium and told me his troubles. In the course of preparing his thesis on the diplomacy of the Third Reich, he had come upon sensational documents about Pope Pius XII's policy toward Nazi Germany. He was putting together a book on the subject. I immediately understood what the problem was, for I had lived it: Publishers were no longer interested in that period. I promised I would speak to someone about it.

The next day I brought Saul to Le Seuil and

introduced him to Paul Flamand. It was a turning point for Saul, the beginning of a career.

For ten years, until her premature death, Monique was in charge of my manuscripts. A Jewish convert to Catholicism, peerless reader and talented editor, extraordinarily demanding but never obstinate, she was cultivated, frank, and extremely witty. She was either for or against, all the way. Not for her the golden road of Maimonides. She had an impeccable reputation in the publishing world, and she went over *Dawn* and *The Accident* scalpel in hand. She had me rework a chapter in *The Town Beyond the Wall.* She was right. She had me delete an entire chapter of *The Gates of the Forest.* Here again she was right. We were in perfect harmony. Three successive versions of *A Beggar in Jerusalem* failed to satisfy Monique. Mercifully, the fourth pleased her. She also worked on *Entre deux soleils* (whose American title, *One Generation After,* I preferred).

In her absence (few people knew that she was suffering from cancer), Claude Durand was my editor for *Legends of Our Time.* Then Paul Flamand's son Bruno took over. He became my editor, my ally. Serious, introspective, and meticulous, he could do what many editors cannot: identify with the book rather than its author. I don't know how he managed to understand as well as he did my works on the Bible and its interpretations, the Talmud and its commentaries, Hasidism and its mysterious masters. In the end he assimilated Hebrew texts (in translation, of course) better than certain Jewish thinkers. We were bound by a creative complicity. Even when I felt compelled to leave Le Seuil (temporarily), our relationship endured.

It was the war in Lebanon that brought me into conflict with Le Seuil. Paul Flamand had retired and Michel Chodkiewicz, his successor, published an outrageous letter in *Le Monde* in which he accused Israel of genocide. It was the summer of 1982, early in the war. Since he identified himself as the director of Le Seuil, Chodkiewicz effectively committed the firm to his position, or at least that was my view of the matter. I asked him to issue not a retraction but a correction, one that would explain his thought in more detail, without altering his political or religious philosophy with regard to Israel and the Palestinians (a Catholic by birth, he had converted to Islam). Essentially, I asked for a few lines saying more or less that in the heat of passion he had used a word that offended certain people. Michel categorically refused, saying he believed in freedom of expression. I replied that the word "genocide" must be used with extreme caution. Did he really think that Israel's aim was to exterminate the entire Palestinian people? I was saddened by Michel's obstinacy. Our relations had always been excellent. We shared a love for mysticism, and I admired and respected his knowledge and integrity. Why was he suddenly so inflexible? François Wahl arranged for me to attend a meeting of Seuil's editorial committee. I knew all its members and explained to them that I had been part of the house for more than twenty years and had never asked for anything. But this was a slur on the Jewish people's honor. With the exception of a young woman — Jewish — they all agreed. They tried to persuade Michel, who remained inflexible. After seven months of painful discussions I decided to leave but made no public statements. I was too attached to Le Seuil to wish to harm it.

Antoine Gallimard and Bernard Henri-Lévy (on behalf of Grasset) came to see me in New York in the following weeks. Gallimard's prestige is unequaled, and Antoine and I quickly established a good rapport. I appreciated his dynamism and his devotion to his authors, as well as his vision of the role of literature in society and his concept of friendship. But I was afraid of the size of his firm. On the other hand, Grasset, for me at that time, was Bernard, whom I had known since we met on the Cambodian border, where we both took part in the March Against Hunger. I remembered that when I had shown him the proofs of *Paroles d'étranger*, he told me it was that work that had inspired him to write his first novel. Bernard introduced me to Jean-Claude Fasquelle, whose strong character and discretion I came to admire. He spoke little, but his silences were eloquent. His wife,

Nikki, a magazine publisher, has the keenest sense of humor in the small world of Parisian publishing.

My wife Marion and I spent hours discussing the merits of the two houses with Georges. The Grasset team (Jean-Claude, Bernard, and Yves Berger) worked efficiently and aggressively. When I gave them *The Fifth Son*, Paul Flamand sent me a one-line letter — "I am devastated." Chodkiewicz's word "genocide" stood between Le Seuil and me. But I never considered it a divorce. Le Seuil was still my family, Grasset now became my adoptive family. Bernard visited New York often. (A brilliant philosopher and observer of the social scene, he brought me news of the latest literary intrigues in Paris. No one was better informed about what went on in the circles that concerned us.) I stayed with Grasset until the scientist Claude Cherki succeeded Michel Chodkiewicz at Le Seuil.

I also changed publishers in the United States several times, but, unlike in France, the practice is common here. Few writers publish all their work with a single house. After *The Accident*, Arthur Wang judiciously advised me to take my next novel to a larger house. Paul Flamand put me in touch with Mike and Cornelia Bessie at Atheneum. I gave them *The Town Beyond the Wall*. *The Gates of the Forest*, *Legends of Our Time*, and *The Jews of Silence* were published by Holt, Rinehart and Winston, *A Beggar in Jerusalem* and *Souls on Fire* by Random House,

The Testament and *The Forgotten* by Summit/Simon and Schuster.

These changes upset me, even though they were useful and often necessary. I simply followed my editors. When they changed houses, I went with them.

Peter Mayer was — at the time — the boy wonder of American publishing. He made a success of everything he undertook professionally. As publisher of the paperback editions of my works he got so interested in the landscape of my books that he accompanied me to Sighet and Jerusalem. When he attended a Friday evening service at the Wall, completely unprepared for the experience, he burst into tears. Eventually, his career took him from Avon Books to Penguin. One day he wrote me a long letter. The bottom line was that he was not taking the rights to *The Forgotten*; the hardcover edition was not selling briskly enough. Business is business.

Arthur Kurzweil is a different kind of publisher. As the talented head of Aronson Books, he mainly reprints titles that he considers essential reading. He was my student at City College and at one point wanted to write a book about me. I discouraged him. "Instead," I said, "why don't you write something about yourself?" He did. His book on Jewish genealogy is a "must" for any Jewish home.

Everything went well at Hill and Wang. Its efforts, as a small house, were highly focused, and during the months after *Night* was published, the company promoted it exclusively, with great fervor, and successfully. The literary pages were unanimous in their praise. For the most part the reviewers understood the work well and captured its essential themes. The important newspapers praised the book's austere style and its dimension of truth. My moment of triumph came when *The New York Times Book Review* invited me to write reviews. (In my own Uncle Sam's view, that was at least as good as a Nobel Prize.)

When *La Ville de la Chance* (in the American edition, *The Town Beyond the Wall*) was published in Paris, a reporter from Belgian Radio asked me — and I quote — "How much longer are you going to wallow in suffering?" In France, as in the United States, some critics began to suggest that the time had come to let go of the subject. Their objections were less literary than personal. Had they said that my characters were too transparent or too opaque, that my words or images were unsatisfactory, I could have learned to live with it. But most framed the discussion in other terms, questioning the theme and my own experience. In other words, either overtly or obliquely, they expressed annoyance with me for having lived a past different from theirs and for being the Jewish witness that I am. Even when my theme was the Bible, the Talmud, the Middle Ages, or Hasidism, there were those who linked the works to the Holocaust.

In France my novels now met with silence, or smug politeness. I was awarded the Prix Médicis for *A Beggar in Jerusalem*, even though only three or four newspapers reviewed it. Only after the Médicis was announced did critics allow that it had merit.

In France and the United States the Jews were not yet being accused of "collecting the dividends of Auschwitz," but in interviews I was often asked: "Are you ever going to stop writing about the Jewish tragedy? Don't you think other, more recent tragedies are equally worthy of attention?" (In the 1980s one Goncourt juror commented, "We'll give him the prize when he brings us a novel on some other theme.")

I responded only rarely, with a phrase borrowed from the writer Manès Sperber, who in turn had paraphrased a Talmudic saying. Even if I wrote on nothing else, it would never be enough; even if all the survivors did nothing but write about their experiences, it would still not be enough. After a while I ceased to react, especially since nasty rumors had begun to circulate. It seemed my colleagues and I were making a fortune off the Holocaust. Sperber, whose advice I sought when it all started in the mid-sixties, was enraged. But he didn't know how to stop the slanderous rumors, and neither did I. All this criticism leveled at writers on the Holocaust was outrageous and unworthy of reply. Just as it is humiliating to have to combat the Holocaust deniers by reiterating that the tragedy did indeed occur, that our parents and grandparents were in fact murdered. At some point in their lives, every writer who has written about the Holocaust has had to defend himself against this sort of accusation, which leaves one feeling smeared and powerless. Yet it is crucial to denounce such malevolence, whose most dangerous and perverse effect would be to make people shrink from speaking of the Holocaust.

In my essay "A Plea for the Survivors" I wrote: "You who have not experienced their anguish, who do not speak their language and do not mourn their dead, think before you offend them, before you betray them. . . . Wait until the last survivor, the last witness, has joined the long procession of silent shadows whose judgment one day will resound and shake the earth and its Creator."

Yes, who will tell the censors, so determined to attribute their own baseness to us, to have the decency to be quiet? Who will tell them that we have nothing to learn from them?

But I am ashamed to admit that the charge of being mercenary did hurt me at first, as it did many of my fellow writers. Probably in response to it, I decided to share the prize money from my two French awards with the French Jewish writers Piotr Rawicz and Arnold Mandel. In 1970, in an epilogue to *One Generation After*, I announced my intention to bring this chapter to a close: "And now, teller of tales, turn the page. Speak to us of other things. Let your mad prophets, your old men drunk with nostalgia, your possessed, return to their nocturnal den. They have survived their deaths for more than a quarter century now. That should suffice. And if they refuse to be gone, at least make them keep quiet. At all costs. By any means necessary. Tell them that silence, more than speech, remains the sign and substance of what was once their world and that it, like speech, demands to be recognized and transmitted." This passage earned me an "open letter" from the Jewish historian Joseph Wulf (who committed suicide several years later in Berlin). He urged me not to give up. He spoke of the duty of testifying. In truth, how can anyone fail to see that a witness rendered mute betrays the living as much as the dead?

One French Jewish critic, a judge by profession, was particularly virulent in his personal attacks on me. Having heaped praise on my first writings, he now began to express an antipathy that grieved my friends in Paris. Living in New York, I was unaware of this, but with obvious pleasure he informed me of it in person.

He came to see me at my hotel in Paris in 1966. I had just returned from Moscow, where I had barely escaped arrest for having written *The Jews of Silence*. When the judge telephoned, I assumed he wanted to question me about the tragedy of the Soviet Jews. In fact, he wished to tell me why his attitude toward me had changed. "You're too attached to God and Israel," he said. "I find that disappointing." No doubt he did, but those who knew him felt there was something else at issue as well. He was annoyed by what he considered my "celebrity." And not only mine. Three leading French Jewish intellectuals, André Neher, Emmanuel Levinas, and Léon Ashkenazy, also drew his ire. His articles denouncing our influence were violent and irrational.

My only response was silence. Once again I recalled Mauriac's warning: first they build statues to you, then they dismantle them. Of course, literary envy is hardly new. Even the Talmud refers to *kin'at sofrim,* or writers' jealousy. Tolstoy called Shakespeare a scribbler, Strindberg accused Tolstoy of plagiarism.

At the end of the daily Amidah prayer, we ask the Lord to spare us envy: "May I not feel it toward others, may others not feel it toward me." I understood this prayer far better once I began to write. Too mystical for some, I was not mystical enough for others; too Jewish or not Jewish enough, too much or not enough the believer, too accessible or too obscure. They think you have power, and they insist they have claims on you. Since you have attained "success," it is incumbent upon you to help all those who demand your assistance. How many writers are angry with other writers because they did not praise their work, because they refused to supply a blurb for the jacket or failed to place their manuscript with his or her publisher?

I realize I ought not to linger on this unpleasant subject. But I have not yet spoken of Alfred Kazin. This critic remains one of my great disappointments. I forget who it was who said, "The writer the gods wish to destroy, they make Kazin's friend." He is among the few people whose paths I regret ever having crossed. When I was unknown, his praise of *Night* in an intellectual weekly called *The Reporter* helped me get noticed. When, at last, several of my books had found readers, he did what he could to turn them away. Why? I have been told he has acted similarly with other writers. His generosity is often short-lived. In 1994 he caused a furor when he accused his former friend Saul Bellow of racism.

In his most recent outburst of venom, he wrote the following ghoulish and mean-spirited lines about a writer who left us a remarkable body of work: "Jerzy Kosinski committed suicide — in sensational fashion, of course — sitting in the bathtub, his head in a plastic bag." According to Kazin, it was just another publicity stunt. "I never managed to believe a word he said," Kazin wrote in *The New Yorker*. "He always manufactured himself in public. Probably it was all tied to the fact that he was a Holocaust survivor." Once again he let the mask slip: he distrusted Kosinski, repudiated and condemned him in large measure because he was a survivor.

There was a time when we saw each other

or spoke on the phone regularly. He was a member of a literary panel founded by survivors of Bergen-Belsen, headed by Yossel Rosensaft. Kazin accompanied the group to Belsen and then to Jerusalem. Rosensaft took good care of him, providing a luxurious hotel room, pocket money, gifts for him and his wife. Back in Manhattan he even invited him to his home. But all Mr. Kazin found to say about his hosts in a smug magazine article was that Yossel's wife was the owner not only of a luxurious apartment but also of an inordinately large number tattooed on her arm. As though she had ordered it from Cardin. As for me, he was annoyed with me for having too sad a face and too frail a body. But worst of all, in a text in which he recalled "what he owed" to Primo Levi and me, he wrote that he would not be surprised to find that the episode in *Night* describing three inmates who were hanged together had been invented. How dare he? There were thousands of witnesses, some of them still alive, among them Yaakov Hendeli, who now lives in Jerusalem, and Freddy Diamond of Los Angeles, whose brother Leo Yehuda was the youngest of the three victims. (The two others were Nathan Weisman and Yanek Grossfeld.) Of all the vile things this bitter man who has aged so badly has written in his life, this is the most intolerable.

The witness has nothing but his memory. If that is impugned, what does he have left? In the last analysis, a man like Kazin is lending credence to those who deny the Holocaust. If *he* refuses to believe me, why should others, more removed, believe any survivor? For some people it is easier and more convenient to say that the event never happened, that it is merely an abstraction, a delusion, a Hollywood production. How to explain to them that it was an experience that can neither be imagined nor shared?

Let me be clear: I don't blame the critics. They are just doing their job, some in good faith, others not. No author should expect only praise. But he has the right to condemn abuse and personal insult. I place my trust in readers, hoping I will be understood. They must know that the truth I present is unvarnished; I cannot do otherwise. Sing or die, said Heine. Write or disappear. Kazin's concept of writing and mine are not the same, nor are our motives. For him literature is an end in itself. Not for me. I don't believe in art for art's sake. For me literature must have an ethical dimension. The aim of the literature I call testimony is to disturb. I disturb the believer because I dare to put questions to God, the source of all faith. I disturb the miscreant because, despite my doubts and questions, I refuse to break with the religious and mystical universe that has shaped my own. Most of all, I disturb those who are comfortably settled within a system — be it political, psychological, or theological. If I have learned anything in my life, it is to distrust intellectual comfort.

I therefore understand why survivors irritate certain writers who see them not as individuals who have suffered, but as symbols, guardians of the flame. The Talmud tells us that in the days of the Temple the original parchments of the Holy Book were exhibited so that scribes might readily consult them and correct possible errors. Survivors are a bit like these parchments. So long as they exist, so long as some of them are still alive, the others know — even if they don't always admit it — that they cannot trespass certain boundaries. I have violently criticized films, plays, and television programs that trivialize Jewish memory. William Styron has not forgiven me for having publicly decried the film made of his novel *Sophie's Choice* as deplorable and indecent. If only I had kept silent, or at least uttered a few kind words about fantasies born of good intentions.

Then there are the political critics on the left of the political spectrum who refuse to forgive my love for Israel and the people of Israel. Of course, that is their right and their choice. I will return to this subject as well.

For the moment let me say that I consider myself lucky. I work, I do what I like to do. There are moments of anger, others of gratitude, but never of bitterness. I have made friends, and they are my true recompense. They are there for me in moments of doubt. But what has moved me the most are the letters I receive from young people. Hundreds of schoolchildren write to me each year, among them children of survivors who tell me of their parents or grandparents. And then there are the strangers who speak to me in public places. An old woman approaches me: "Thank you for having survived." A younger woman, waiting on line at La Guardia Airport, comments on a televised discussion among scholars and experts on the nuclear peril: "I watched the program, you spoke for me." Messages from survivors: "Thank you for our children." Or: "Thank you for my parents." I appreciate these messages from all kinds of people, Jews and Christians. They help me rally at times of weariness and disappointment, counterbalancing the insults and death threats that pile ever higher on my desk.

In the middle of the 1960s, an Israeli consul introduced me to a young Franco-American couple who in turn introduced me to a friend of theirs, a young mother of Austrian descent in the process of getting divorced.

"My friends told me about you," she said. "They've been trying to introduce us for a long time. But I said no."

I wasn't sure what I found most striking about her: the delicacy of her features, the brilliance of her words, or the breadth of her knowledge of art, music, and the theater.

The following week I invited her to lunch

at an Italian restaurant across the street from UN headquarters. I ordered an omelette but never touched it. I only listened.

She, too, had spent the war years in Europe. There were stories about her childhood in Vienna, her visits to her grandfather's house in Lvov, and her family's flight to Belgium, France, and Switzerland. For the moment, concealing my fear of falling in love on the spot, I simply listened and looked at her, timidly.

We saw each other again, exchanged confidences, and became friends. I advised her to read Robert Musil, Elio Vittorini, Cesare Pavese. She knew Thomas Mann better than I did. Likewise the theater: she had studied acting with one of the most famous drama coaches in New York. From time to time we went to concerts. There was David Oistrakh at Carnegie Hall, and a particularly lovely evening at the Metropolitan Museum of Art listening to Rudolf Barshai and his Moscow Chamber Orchestra. Fluent in at least five languages, she was about to cofound an association of professional translators. We didn't know it yet, but she was to become my wife.

Her name is Marion. Her little girl, Jennifer, was the best and most beautiful little girl in all the world.

For the moment I was leading a bachelor's life in my tower overlooking the Hudson and Riverside Drive. It was a disciplined, nearly ascetic existence devoted to journalism and writing. I was up at six in the morning and worked on the current book until ten. Then came meetings, visits to the UN, press conferences, and the typing of my dispatches. Then back to my apartment, where I wrote while listening to chamber or choral music or at times Hasidic songs. Records were my one big luxury. Sometimes, when it wasn't too cold, I would go for a walk on Riverside Drive, alone or with a colleague. (In those days it was not yet dangerous to walk the streets of Manhattan alone.)

My journalist's job gave me a plausible excuse to decline unwanted social invitations and to leave dinners on the pretext of having to send cables. My own preference was to grab a sandwich (when I could afford it) at the kosher deli on the corner of 100th Street and Broadway.

I had been trying, since *One Generation After*, to discover a new language, to forge a style of narration consisting only of dialogue and disembodied, anonymous words. I knew I was taking a chance. Perhaps only the survivors, those who escaped, would understand, and perhaps their children.

In truth, my major concern has always been the survivors. It was for them that my first works were meant. Did I strive to speak for them, in their name? I strove to make them speak.

For they have lived in isolation for a long

time, locked away, remaining aloof so as not to wound those close to them. Whenever there was talk of the war years, they would clench their teeth and change the subject. It was impossible to get them to let go, to touch wounds that would never heal. They had reasons to be suspicious, to think that no one was interested in what they had to say, and that in any case they would not be understood. With my books and articles I tried to convince them of the need to testify: "Do as I do," I told them. "Tell your stories, even if you have to invent a language. Communicate your memories, your doubts, even if no one wants to hear them." I shared with them my conviction that it is incumbent upon the survivors not only to remember every detail but to record it, even the silence. I urged them to celebrate the memory of silence, but to reject the silence of memory.

At first it was difficult, but eventually my efforts met with success. I began to receive manuscripts: memoirs, narratives, private diaries. I wrote countless prefaces and commentaries, mobilized acquaintances and relations, yet I probably didn't do enough.

For me survivors constitute a family like no other, an endangered species. We understand one another intuitively. We are haunted by the same past, the same problems concern us, the same mission moves us. We often have the same friends and always the same enemies. There are all kinds of survivors, sages and whiners, optimists and pessimists, generous ones and bitter ones. Some decided to celebrate their survival by making money. Having lost everything, they re-created a family, a life, preferably a comfortable one. Wealthy, often very wealthy, it took some of them years to become aware of the importance of joining the battle against forgetfulness. As they get older, they are catching up.

Night and my articles in the Yiddish press were at the root of my friendship with Yossel Rosensaft and his Bergen-Belsen group.

Brimming with vitality, Yossel was short and stocky, shrewd and imaginative, a man who loved telling off-color jokes and irreverent anecdotes. Though rough, his language was brilliant and his lifestyle was princely. Yossel first impressed me as a study in contrasts. He lived in a luxurious apartment filled with canvases of Impressionist masters. Originally from Poland, a former inmate of Auschwitz and Belsen, he talked about the camps endlessly and without the slightest inhibition. I confess that at first I was taken aback. I thought he was trivializing our common experience and I couldn't understand what motivated him. Yet he radiated a charm that was difficult to resist. He was a self-made man who respected writers and intellectuals and liked to surround himself with them. He had a sure taste — and was a good adviser — in art, as demonstrated by the quality of his Picassos, Chagalls, Renoirs, and Manets. He loved to laugh and make you laugh. He enjoyed life and was always ready to have a good time. Yet he was easily moved to tears. His friends adored him.

When I came to interview him for *Yedioth Ahronoth*, he told me about the transformation of Belsen just after war's end. As president of the camp, which had become a center for displaced persons, he managed to establish a kind of temporary, autonomous Jewish town, with its own security, courts, hospitals, schools, and synagogues, even its own theaters, newspapers, clubs, and political parties. He must have liked my article, for he invited me back, but when I stepped off the elevator into his apartment, he wasn't there. I waited five minutes, ten minutes. I scribbled a few harsh words — "Money gives you certain rights, but not the right to waste my time" — and walked out.

He phoned immediately to apologize. There had been a misunderstanding, a mistake, a message that somehow went astray. Would I please come back? He would send his driver for me. I told him I was too busy — and I stayed busy for another few years.

His best friend, Sam Bloch, a former partisan and born conciliator, was the Bergen-Belsen Association's most likable and dynamic member. Like the high priest Aaron, he found quarrels intolerable. I know few people who invest so much time and energy in fostering harmony

595

among his fellows. However, with me he failed: I refused to see his friend again, at least until 1965.

Once again Yossel called and asked to see me. His group was organizing a pilgrimage to Belsen and he wanted to invite me. Something in what he said made me relent. I agreed to join the "Belseners," as they called one another. After that we saw each other often. No matter what part of the world he happened to be in, he was always surrounded by his Belsen buddies, always rehashing funny or pathetic memories with them. "Remember the guy who showed up with his cow? And the British officer who came to harass us because of the way we were aiding illegal immigration to Palestine? And the stir our delegation made at the Zionist Congress in Basel?" He loved making speeches in Yiddish (his English was anything but polished). "When we look back on it . . ." they began.

At his home I met Jewish and non-Jewish notables, among them Israeli politicians and Yiddish writers. It was a varied group: Nahum Goldmann; Meyer Weisgal, one of the founders of the Weizmann Institute of Science; Levi Eshkol, a prime minister of Israel; and, for contrast, the actress Angie Dickinson. Some came to ask for money (I saw him hand an emissary of the Rabbi of Guer a thousand dollars in cash), others (among them collectors and art historians) to admire his pictures.

Like everyone else, he had enemies who expressed many reasons for their hostility (especially his wealth, which I suppose he flaunted) and friends who found as many reasons to defend him, including his commitment to the memory of the Holocaust.

Attached as he was to the Belseners, for whom he functioned as banker, lawyer, and a Jewish variety of father confessor, he was even more devoted to his wife and their son, Menahem. He admitted to spoiling him. After all, "he's a Jewish child of Belsen," he often said, perhaps too often. "You must help him to . . ." For me it was an irresistible argument. For obvious reasons, the children of survivors are particularly precious to me.

Nobody seems to have known it, but one day Yossel found himself ruined. Shortly thereafter he collapsed in the lobby of Claridges in London, and died. It probably was a heart attack, but there were rumors that he had killed himself. I never believed it. It wasn't his style.

The funeral took place in the synagogue of our mutual friend, Rabbi Joseph Lookstein. It was the eve of Yom Kippur. In my eulogy I took leave of him in Yiddish: "When your soul rises to heaven, six million of our brothers and sisters will come to greet you. . . ."

I stayed in close contact with many survivors, among them Manes Schwarz, Berl Laufer, Max Zilbernik, Itzik Guterman, Mendel and Dora Butnik. Gena and Yossele Tenenbaum, Sam

Bresler from Toronto. Also, the Halperins, the Pantirers, the Bukiets, the Wilfs and Siggi Wilzig from New Jersey, as well as Felix Lasky and Dr. Hillel Seidman . . . every one of them active for Israel and the cause of remembrance in their communities. There was also a couple, Vladka and Ben Meed. Vladka had been a liaison agent for the (Bundist) Jewish Resistance in occupied Warsaw. In her autobiography (for which I wrote a preface) she recounts the socialist dreams of her adolescence. In 1944, living clandestinely in the crushed Polish capital, she celebrated May Day with a group of comrades by sending a message of solidarity to the "workers and pro-letarians" of the free world. A significant detail that is often overlooked: It was the hunted men and women, the humiliated and oppressed Jews, who encouraged their free, armed comrades, and not the other way around.

But of all the survivors it was Sigmund Strochlitz who became my closest friend and confidant. With his wife Rose, also a survivor, he lives in New London, Connecticut, where he is the *éminence grise* of local political life, and the owner of a Ford dealership. Nothing has ever divided us since we first met in 1965. Whether defending a Jewish cause or protesting against Israel's enemies, we rarely act without consulting one another. Sigmund possesses both common sense and loyalty to the highest degree. His kindness and generosity are legendary. A valuable associate, he came to play a central role in many of my future projects.

During the eventful years of the 1960s I spent much time in the editorial offices of the *Jewish Daily Forward*. Like *Yedioth*, it was a place where people lived in the past. Once, headed by the legendary Abe Cahan, the paper had boasted a circulation in the hundreds of thousands.

My work consisted of editing agency dispatches and translating news items from the *Times*. Sometimes I wrote unsigned editorials.

In those days the paper was still the world's most influential Yiddish daily, a gathering place for poets and actors, Zionist militants and Bundist activists, all of them angling for a review. A Yiddishist in poet's garb would corner you in the elevator and make you listen to his latest masterpiece, declaimed with great spirit. In the very same elevator an actress well into middle age would tell you of her having just been cast as an ingenue. A nihilist-anarchist would insist that his (unpublished) essay was essential to the survival of the Jewish people. A humorist would desperately try to make you laugh, out loud if possible, before you got to the ninth floor.

The editor in chief, Hillel Rogoff, was a kind, talented man who was capable of passionate involvement in causes. Curiously, he preferred to address his collaborators in English rather than Yiddish. His assistant, Lazar Fogelman, a dreamer with a penchant for sudden outbursts of humor, had common sense only in his dreams. The number-three man was my friend Simon Weber. When I worked in the news bureau he was my supervisor, although it was to Rogoff and Fogelman that I submitted my articles for editing and approval.

Weber was a man of culture, thoroughly involved in both Jewish and American politics, an excellent journalist with great ironic wit. He had begun his career on the staff of the Communist Party's Yiddish daily newspaper, but had quit the party as soon as he grasped the extent of its lies and horrors. He could tolerate anything from his colleagues except lack of talent.

The Yiddish literary and cultural world was dwindling, living its final hours of glory. One by one its lights were extinguished. If the language wasn't dying, its speakers were barely hanging on. Like everything else, including nostalgia itself, the Second Avenue Jewish theater in Manhattan was not what it used to be. Nor was the Jewish press. Yet prestigious bylines still appeared in *Der Morgen Journal*, *Der Tog*, and the *Forverts*. I admired Jacob Glatstein, whose poem "It was in Sinai the Torah was given to us, it was in Lublin that it was taken back" moved a whole generation of readers. I loved the Judeo-Romanian reminiscences of Shlomo Bickel and the religious polemics of Chaim Lieberman. I soaked up knowledge and wisdom: S. Margoshes and his political editorials; Chaim Grade and his essays on the world of the Mussar; A. Leyeles and his lyrical verses; Almi and his pessimist philosophy; the poems of Itzik Manger, as beautiful and enchanting as a minstrel's songs. I thirsted for learning and, God knows, I had a lot to learn. At first I wrote articles in Yiddish without any real knowledge of the giants of its literature. In my ignorance, I made a regrettable mistake. Writing about Isaac Bashevis Singer (whom we called, simply, Bashevis), I struck a tone of unforgivable condescension as I compared other Yiddish writers to him. Not only was I wrong to cause them grief, I was wrong in my assessment.

Yiddish novelists, essayists, thinkers, ideologues, theorists: they knew one another and were jealous of one another. Since I was younger and completely unknown, and therefore no threat to them, I was the exception. I loved listening to them talk about their past.

Zalman Shneur was a great Yiddish and Hebrew novelist whose conversation both unnerved and amused me. Today his poems are studied in every Israeli high school. Like Bialik and Tchernichowsky, he is considered a classic author. He had a carefully trimmed beard, drooping moustache, bow tie — the appearance and the substance of a nineteenth-century writer. He would speak French to his wife in front of me until he realized I understood. Fiercely intelligent, he was especially adept at deflating celebrities. I spent an entire afternoon listening to him mock Ben-Gurion, who, regrettably, had shown him a lack of respect.

I spent a weekend in Montreal, where my sister's rabbi, David Hartman, had organized a colloquium on the principle of tolerance in the Jewish religion. The guests included rabbis, professors, and intellectuals of the Orthodox, Conservative, and Reform branches of the community. The aim of the meeting was to bring them together in an atmosphere of tolerance and camaraderie by emphasizing Judaism's pluralist aspect. There I made the acquaintance of the young theologian Yitz Greenberg, the philosopher Emil Fackenheim, and Maurice Friedman, the Buber specialist. For three days and nights I listened to discussions on subjects like our relationships to the Laws of Sinai, attitudes toward the non-Jewish world, and the limits of the interpretation of tradition. Not a single word was uttered about the Holocaust.

Since then, that has changed. For some time now the event has been central to the reflections of all three branches of Judaism.

Armed with a precious green card and later an American passport, I traveled a lot during the sixties. In 1960, two Israeli colleagues and I were invited to Cuba by Fidel Castro. At the time he simply referred to himself as a revolutionary, nothing more. Hence the popularity of his message. We were greeted by young men, barely more than teenagers, all of them high officials: department heads, ambassadors, and even cabinet ministers. We spent three weeks

meeting with the charming young revolution-
aries who had overthrown President Fulgencio
Batista and his corrupt regime. Factory workers
greeted us with the cry *"Venceremos!"* (We shall
win!). The same promise was voiced in Fidel's
speeches, which could last all night, while the
excited, mesmerized crowd periodically chanted
"Venceremos!" Magnificent young machine-gun-
toting militiawomen repeated the phrase with
a smile as they guarded the entrances to government offices and the big hotels, stopping all
who entered and searching (though none too
seriously) those they found suspicious. We wondered how to arouse their suspicion in order
to be searched by one of them, for some of
Castro's militiawomen were lovely indeed. Still,
we all have priorities and I yearned to get back
to New York for Rosh Hashana. Unfortunately,
the official in charge of us at the Ministry of
Foreign Affairs informed us that all flights were
fully booked — for at least two or three weeks.
I protested, shouted, begged. Even the Israeli
embassy could do nothing. I was eventually offered a seat on a flight from Havana to Prague.
That was when I almost panicked. The situation
awoke my old anxieties. In the end I got back
to New York in time to celebrate Rosh Hashana
in my *shtibel* among the Hasidim of Guer.

I felt as though I were back in Sighet when
I went to that *shtibel*. All the congregants were
survivors. They prayed with a fervor I have
encountered nowhere else. It was as though they

were trying to persuade the Lord to once more become a Father to His people instead of their Judge.

I remember Shimon Zucker and his tales of the Lodz ghetto: the raids, the hunt for Jewish children, the cries of their parents. He fought to hold back his tears when he told of his own little boy who wanted so much to live.

And then there was Reb Avraham Zemba, the gentle, reticent nephew of the chief rabbi of Warsaw. He was quite old and would regularly take me aside and ask whether I knew the Talmudic saying according to which we are not alone when we bring sacrifices to God. Just as regularly, he would answer himself that the angel Michael, who is in heaven, is also bringing sacrifices to God, though his souls are those of the Righteous. "So it continues even on high!" Reb Avraham Zemba would exclaim.

Having tracked down Menashe Klein, my old friend from Buchenwald, Ambloy, and Taverny, I now saw him regularly. He looked older, but I could have picked him out in a crowd of a hundred rabbis. I could not have forgotten his determined glance, his stately bearing, the way he leaned over a tractate of the Talmud.

Never give in, never give up: that had been his motto. He repeated over and over that our people had seen other ordeals. Granted, this one was unique, but it was incumbent upon us to surmount it, as our ancestors had surmounted theirs. They rebuilt their sanctuaries, reopened their schools, helped one another resist the wicked. May we be worthy of their strength and their faith; otherwise the enemy will be victorious.

To this day I see Menashe at least once a month, sometimes more often. We share a project: to build a Beit Hamidrash (House of Study) in Jerusalem in my father's name.

Here is how I sometimes speak to the God of my childhood: "Why, then, did You create man? Is it because You have need of him? But what can he do for You? How can his meager triumphs and absurd defeats have any meaning for You?" I have looked in the books Menashe urged me to study and in others as well, but I have not found the answer.

I made several trips to Europe and Israel. In London my publisher was concerned about *Night*: It was not selling well — in fact, it was not selling. In Paris I attended the summit conference at which de Gaulle brought Eisenhower, Macmillan, and Khrushchev together. The latter was enraged by the U-2 spy plane's flight over Soviet territory.

Friends told me of a novel that had created quite a stir: André Schwarz-Bart's masterpiece, *The Last of the Just*. Schwarz-Bart and I first met in a corridor at Le Seuil. When we eventually lunched together, I at last discovered a

605

novelist more timid than I. An immediate alliance was forged. I admired his writer's talent and his poet's intuition. There was a curious mixture of fervor and reticence in the way he spoke of himself. Jealous colleagues had falsely accused him of plagiarism and ignorance. It hurt him, and I tried to soothe him by telling him what friends would later tell me when bad reviews of my books appeared: "Pay no attention, the book will survive its critics." André smiled skeptically. I asked him what he would work on next, and he said he wasn't sure. He felt he needed to study Jewish texts, but he lacked access to sources. I suggested he either come to New York or go to Jerusalem. I gave him the names of several teachers who would be delighted to take him under their wing. He was tempted by the idea, but between two appointments with me he met Simone, a beautiful young woman from Guadeloupe, who later became a novelist in her own right. Eventually, he followed her to her island.

In Israel I covered the Eichmann trial, writing reports for the *Jewish Daily Forward*. I also wrote an essay for *Commentary* and *l'Arche*. Day after day I went to the Beit Haam, the "People's House," to listen to survivors' depositions. The prosecutor, Gideon Hausner, and his colleagues evoked the Crime and the Tragedy with a chilling intensity that sent shivers through the audience. Some sobbed, others merely seemed dazed. The three judges were living embodiments of moderation and dignity. They listened well.

I could not take my eyes off the defendant, who sat in his glass cage impassively taking notes. He seemed utterly unmoved by the recitation of the crimes against humanity and the Jewish people of which he was accused. He looked like an ordinary man. I was told he ate heartily and slept normally. Considering the crushing pressures of the trial, he seemed to bear up well. Neither the prosecutors nor the judges were able to break him.

I thought I remembered him. I knew that he had been in Sighet to supervise the deportation, and I wondered whether he was the man I had seen at the station, visibly saddened because there were no more convoys to send out of this town now emptied of its Jews.

I spent my evenings with Israeli correspondents covering the trial: Haim Guri (lyric poet of the Palmach, who later translated *Night* and *The Jews of Silence* into Hebrew); Shmuel Almog (future television boss), and my friend Eliyahu Amiqam (for *Yedioth*). Their reports were classics of their kind. I talked with them about Israel's destiny, upheavals, and dramatic turnabouts. Who could have dreamed in the years from 1941 to 1945 that Eichmann would one day stand trial in an independent Jewish state? For the Jews, their rediscovered sovereignty imposed the ethical duty of shaping history rather than enduring it. Justice and truth, power and understanding, needed to be reconciled. And what of the Eichmann trial in all that?

Hannah Arendt was surrounded by her coterie. Many Israeli journalists avoided her, finding her arrogant and condescending. She knew everything before and better than everyone else. I met her only later, at her home, where we discussed her theories of "the banality of evil," which some survivors found simplistic and offensive and which I was invited to refute in print. She greeted me amiably, telling me she had read and liked my work. Was she being sincere or merely courteous? I found her disconcerting and chillingly aloof. How could one delve into the tragedy and still retain that hardness in one's eyes? The question I asked her was simple: "I was there, and I don't know. How can you possibly know when you were elsewhere?" Her reply: "You're a novelist; you can cling to questions. I deal with human and political sciences. I have no right not to find answers." My essay "A Plea for the Dead" was an attempt to refute her accusations against Israel and to respond to the disdain she exhibited for the dead. In a famous letter Gershom Scholem scolded her for her lack of love for the Jewish people.

After court sessions I often joined a group of intellectuals who gathered around their uncrowned king, Joseph Kessel, on the terrace of the King David Hotel. The best French reporters were part of this circle. Kessel talked about other trials, other adventures. I liked him and admired his blend of strength and tenderness, and his stunning sensitivity and humanity. For him, as for us, Eichmann was an enigma and a challenge.

I remained obsessed by the same old questions. How to explain the power of evil and the complicity of the "neutral" countries? What about the passivity of American Judaism and the Palestinian Jewish community? If only the defendant could be declared irrevocably inhuman, expelled from the human species. It irritated me to think of Eichmann as human. I would have preferred him to have a monstrous countenance, like a Picasso portrait with three ears and four eyes.

I stared at him for hours on end, and he frightened me. Yet in his present state, locked in a bulletproof glass cage, he presented no danger. Why did he inspire such fear in me? Is there an ontological evil unrelated to action?

Jurists had long technical debates about the necessity of the trial, its conduct, and its probable outcome. Some said it would have been better for Israel to have turned Eichmann over to an international tribunal. Another debate: Could there be any punishment for crimes of this magnitude? Cain, after all, exterminated half the human race when he killed his brother, Abel, yet his only punishment was to bear the mark of his crime on his forehead. He remained alive, even untouchable. No one had the right to harm him. Martin Buber declared himself against the death penalty for Eichmann. He was not alone. As for me, I trusted in Israeli justice.

Years later, during a March of the Living, a pilgrimage of some five thousand youths to Birkenau, I stood near a retired Israeli police officer originally from my region. He was a camp survivor, a quiet but intense man. We said Kaddish together. He had been one of Eichmann's executioners.

The Town Beyond the Wall appeared in 1962. I used a disquieting quotation from Dostoevsky as an epigraph: "I have a plan — to go mad." But my plan was to combat madness. By which I mean that the only way to escape being contaminated by another person's madness is by attempting to cure it. It was a lyrical, mystical adventure novel recounting one survivor's itinerary — religious childhood, deportation, arrival in France; faith, rage, and friendship. His dreams of returning to his native town land him in a Communist prison cell, in the company of a mute madman. This book, my fourth, was favorably received and won the Prix Rivarol, awarded annually to a foreign novelist writing in French. One judge hesitated to grant the prize to the stateless person I still was.

During the reception in my honor I met Anna and Piotr Rawicz. Anna, blond and dynamic, was a film producer. Piotr, a writer of Polish origin, had won the same prize the year before for his masterly novel *Le Sang du ciel*, later published in the United States under the title *Blood from the Sky*. Today, as I write these words, I see Piotr in front of me: tall, his wiry frame slightly stooped, his gaze a mixture of irony and desperation. I will speak of him, and of his death, later.

Increasingly absorbed in my own writing, I gradually reduced my commitments to *Yedioth*. But I continued to write about political and Jewish current events for the *Forverts*. Sometimes I replaced the permanent UN correspondent, Shlomo Ben Israel, the author of remarkable detective novels. In time Rogoff and Fogelman allowed me to do more book reviews. I wrote about the work of Albert Camus and Nikos Kazantzakis, Ernest Hemingway and André Schwarz-Bart, Shmuel-Yosef Agnon and Nelly Sachs. I also wrote reviews of works by minor authors I regrettably believed it judicious to pan. I should have been more disciplined, more circumspect. But I was young, and enjoyed flaunting my power over talented but unfortunate (or vice versa) writers who thought they had "made it" in the Yiddish world. Indeed, every nasty review earned me winks and compliments from my colleagues, whereas praise brought pleasure only to the recipients. Even the angels in heaven are afflicted by jealousy, the Midrash tells us.

The star of the show was Bashevis Singer, several of whose stories had been translated into

English, notably by Saul Bellow (who to this day likes to chat with me in Yiddish). Singer was not liked by his colleagues. They complained of his greed, egocentricity, and vanity. As might be expected, he was envied, and as a result people made fun of him behind his back. His introduction of sensuality and eroticism into the Jewish experience shocked puritans but was well received by most. One critic in particular wrote an essay about him that, though it was never published, was widely circulated. In it he argued that Singer's Jewish characters reflected classic anti-Semitic stereotypes: men and women obsessed with money and sex. His conclusion, purely rhetorical of course, was that if Polish Jews had been as Bashevis Singer portrayed them, did not their enemies have every reason to hate and persecute them?

My relations with Bashevis were for a time correct, even cordial. Sometimes we took the subway uptown together. Occasionally we were invited to the Webers' at the same time. Bashevis considered me a slightly misguided, inoffensive beginner, of little interest to him since I didn't write my novels in Yiddish. In fact, it is unlikely that he ever read them. I did read his, however, but also never referred to them in our conversations. A crisis erupted when Rogoff asked me to review one of Singer's works. The article not only earned me unpleasant remarks from his enemies, who thought it too favorable; he, too, manifested his discontent. He had been expecting a rave, and subsequently took his revenge by writing a lukewarm review of my book *The Jews of Silence*. My reply was a satirical sketch of "the second son of the Haggadah," in which I was careful not to name him. The second son is the wicked son, the *rasha*, who arrogantly questions the meaning of the Pesach festival. The text is hostile to him. In our tradition no one likes the *rasha* because he doesn't like anyone.

When I read my article to Weber over the phone, he burst out laughing. "That's him, exactly," he said. "Give this article to Fogelman, let's see what he says." I was sure he would recognize Bashevis, but Weber felt it was worth a try. With a show of innocence, I handed my text to Fogelman, as though it were an ordinary news article. I don't know if he read it, but it was published the following week. Singer's enemies were jubilant. I expected to be scolded by Fogelman, but I had underestimated him — he congratulated me. For once, Singer must have read my article, because from that moment on contact between us became increasingly rare and finally stopped. No more polite smiles in the elevator. When I praised his foremost rival, Chaim Grade, in *The New York Times*, calling him (sincerely and with conviction) "the greatest contemporary Yiddish writer," the rift was sealed.

The day my satirical article appeared, I was the most popular man in Yiddish circles. I noted with a mixture of amusement and sadness how unappreciated Bashevis was by the Jewish "man in the street." Other Yiddish writers sulked at every honor he received. The day his Nobel Prize was announced was a day of mourning for many of them.

Yet his fortnightly articles were stunning successes, especially among female readers. He was fond of recounting his amorous exploits and did so with great exuberance and talent. What his colleagues reproached him for most of all was his lack of solidarity. They accused him of maneuvering to prevent their own writings from being translated, and of posing as "the last writer in this dead language." That kind of attitude enraged Yiddish writers: "He's trying to bury us alive." Many felt, as I do, that among living Yiddish novelists Chaim Grade surpassed him; others whispered that any one of them surpassed him (I disagree).

He aroused such animosity inside the Yiddish world because he appeared to be distorting and caricaturing the image of the Eastern European Jew. Without denying or minimizing Singer's talent, the purists among Yiddish writers complained that his protagonists were frequently ugly and morally deficient, charming but unbalanced, clever but perverse. He painted a picture of Polish Jews as sex maniacs, of pious rabbis who dreamed of nothing but adultery on Yom Kippur eve. Yes, I know it is fiction, but still . . .

The more the general public admired him, the more Yiddish authors rejected him. He was well aware of this. One evening, at a dinner at the home of a well-known rabbi, he said, "Jews are never satisfied. Whatever I write, they say it wasn't what they expected of me. I've never seen such ungrateful readers." He laughed about it, but it annoyed him. In fact, he was easily annoyed. Yet his admirers are legion, and they remain faithful to him.

As for myself, I like his short stories most of all. He was a superb storyteller; his strength lay in his compression. I appreciate his imagination and taste for the occult. His world was inhabited by sprites and demons, in whom he truly believed. He invited a rabbi friend to his Nobel Prize ceremony in order, he said, to ward off the evil eye: with so many mischievous spirits everywhere, a rabbi's presence couldn't hurt, which nobody could dispute.

His funeral was pathetic. There were few mourners, the Yiddish literary world was virtually unrepresented. A rabbi delivered a eulogy in English with a phrase or two of Yiddish thrown in.

Though I was not among his admirers, I felt sad. It should have been different.

The Yiddish (and Hebrew) author to whom I felt closest was Aharon Zeitlin, a childhood friend of Singer's. I loved him as a man and as a writer. His father, Reb Hillel Zeitlin, produced a literary and philosophical corpus I re-read with ever-renewed emotion and amazement. They say he left the Warsaw Ghetto in 1942 wrapped in his talit, the Zohar under his arm, along with several thousand other Jews who were taken to the Umschlagplatz, where sealed cattle cars were waiting to carry them to Treblinka.

Once a month I visited Aharon, the last survivor of a long line of sages and scholars. Bald, with a thin, almost transparent face and blue limpid eyes, he spoke rapidly in a voice of great clarity. I loved listening to his memories of literary Warsaw, sayings of his father's, reflections on his contemporaries. Singer publicly acknowledged how much he owed him, but refused to help him find an American publisher. Zeitlin was not bitter.

Reb Aharon died of a heart attack. At his funeral this is what I wrote in my notebook.

Aharon Zeitlin believed that the Angel of Death has no grip on man, who is in essence immortal. Two of his works sought to demonstrate this. The dead, according to him, live on in the other world, maintaining contact with ours. They speak to us and warn us, but the living are too busy with their own terrestrial concerns to understand the language of the world of truth. The science of parapsychology, Zeitlin maintained, is proof of this. He believed that God did not create man in order to kill him. Death is but a transition: another world awaits on the other side, a world where all is truth, all is holy, all is eternity.

There was no talent richer and more varied in all of Yiddish and Hebrew literature [than his]. A master of foreign cultures as well as his own, he wrote epic poems and historical plays, litanies and literary essays citing Talmudic laws and Midrashic thought, sayings of Rabbi Nahman and reflections of Socrates. But his knowledge never weighed upon his style. On the contrary, his writing was stamped with the simplicity that remains the essence of art.

Some writers are angry, others are forgiving. Reb Aharon belonged to the latter category. He was literally incapable of saying anything pejorative about anyone. He shunned slander as one would an obscene spectacle. . . . When he recounted his experiences as a new immigrant, or when he spoke of the solitude, anguish, and distress of the war years, his every phrase was accompanied by a little laugh, as though he were begging pardon for his inability to judge others. I can still hear his voice: "How can I condemn another when I have not yet resolved the problems I have with myself? I am still trying to penetrate the secret of my survival. . . . Why did the hangman

617

spare me rather than my brothers and sisters?"

I made friends with another Yiddish poet and thinker from Warsaw, Abraham Joshua Heschel, the great-grandson of the Rebbe of Apt, whose name he bore. Heschel was profoundly Jewish, a deep believer and a sincere pacifist who wrote lyric poems in Yiddish (one of which I recited at his funeral). He also produced a magnificent work on Rebbe Mendel of Kotz, and two volumes of Talmudic studies in Hebrew as well as theological works in English. He was generous with his advice when I was writing on Hasidic masters.

We spent hours together, sometimes strolling up and down Riverside Drive discussing God, prayers, Polish Hasidism compared to Hungarian Hasidism, Lithuanian Yiddish folklore, and Polish Yiddish literature. He loved to reminisce about Frankfurt, where in the thirties he succeeded Martin Buber at the Institute of Jewish Studies. Heschel was a man motivated by humanism and civic virtue as well as Hasidic fervor. Nor did he conduct his quest for knowledge from an ivory tower. He was an active opponent of the war in Vietnam. One Shabbat afternoon he confided to me that Israeli friends had asked him — possibly on the initiative of American officials — to keep a lower profile in his struggle against Lyndon Johnson's policy in Southeast Asia. "What can I do?" Heschel asked. "How can I keep silent when week after week thousands of Vietnamese civilians are being killed by our bombs? How can I forget the Jewish concept of *ra'hmanut*, of pity, of charity? How can I proclaim my Jewishness if I remain insensitive to the pain and mourning of men, women, and children who have been deprived of sleep by years of nighttime bombing?" He was genuinely distressed and since he was asking my opinion, I gave it to him. Press on, I told him, even at the cost of annoying the administration.

Heschel was the major spokesman for Jewish ecumenism, a Jewish friend of all the oppressed. He was among the first to fight for Russian Jews and — it should be noted — for American blacks. It was he who introduced me to Martin Luther King, Jr., whom he revered. In the civil rights movement they called him Father Abraham, as a result of which certain Orthodox circles kept their distance from him, which grieved him. "He's too close to the Christians," they said. Nonsense, I replied when I heard such criticism. What is wrong with a Jew teaching Judaism to non-Jews while defending the honor and tradition of his people? When he went to see Pope Paul VI in Rome, it was to discuss the Catholic Church's anti-Semitism. He believed that a Jew must not lock himself into a kind of spiritual ghetto, forever separated from the society that envelops or opposes him. It is not human, it is not Jewish, to ignore everything that is not Jewish. Scripture teaches us the value of human life — all human life, whether Jewish or not. Our sages insist on the obligation of *pikua'h nefesh,* of coming to the aid of any endangered person whatever his ethnic origin, social standing, or religious faith. That is why the Talmud offers us two versions of the same precept: One says that to save a human life is to save humanity, the other that to save a *Jewish* life is to save humanity, thus tempering a universalism and particularism either of which could easily be exaggerated. In other words: one can be a good Jew and work with those who are not Jews to create a better world. Heschel expressed and lived that wish in his way, I in mine.

There is an anecdote about Martin Buber. Addressing an audience of priests, he said something like this: "What is the difference between Jews and Christians? We all await the Messiah. You believe He has already come and gone, while we do not. I therefore propose that we await Him together. And when He appears, we can ask Him: were You here before?" Then he paused and added: "And I hope that at that moment I will be close enough to whisper in his ear, 'For the love of heaven, don't answer.' " In matters ecumenical Heschel was even more direct and engaged than Buber.

At Stanford University in California a group of professors was dining with the Reverend William Sloane Coffin, the highly renowned "liberation theologian" from New York. The conversation turned to Heschel, and everyone had an amusing anecdote or touching episode to relate. Coffin offered his contribution. "One day, during an ecumenical meeting in which the ever-present subject of anti-Semitism came up, Heschel turned to me and said, 'Do you really think God wants His blessed people to be shamed, persecuted, and perhaps even wiped off the face of the earth? Do you think God would be pleased with a world without Jews?' To which I replied: 'Do you think it was God's desire to see His son persecuted, humiliated, and repudiated by the very people He had come to save? Do you think the Father was happy to see His son rejected by His brothers?' Heschel smiled: 'Here I admit your questions pose a problem. . . .' " Everyone else at the table seemed to enjoy the anecdote, but I didn't. I said to Coffin: "I don't believe Heschel could have said that. Jesus would have posed no problem for a faithful Jew like Heschel."

As in Buber's case, the more Christians admired Heschel, the more certain Jewish circles distanced themselves from him and his teaching. He spoke of disappointments at the Hebrew Union College in Cincinnati, which had welcomed him during the war, and the Jewish Theological Seminary, where until his death he held a chair on mysticism and ethics. He also taught human rights — by example.

In Paris I discovered Manès Sperber. It was inevitable that one day our paths would cross, though Manès did not believe in fate. A free-thinker, his credo was liberty, a subject I loved to hear him talk about. In fact, I loved to hear him talk about anything. A peerless dialectician armed with Socratic irony and encyclopedic knowledge, he could move from Pushkin to the Besht to Adler almost without transition. *Like a Tear in the Ocean* is a dazzling work. Not even Itzhak Leibush Peretz, his hero and mine, could have written it. I remember with pleasure the hours I spent with him: they were always serene and soothing. We were never complacent.

Manès was important in my life. His intellectual rigor, literary talent, humanist vision — rarely have I found these qualities united in a single individual. Yet outwardly we were worlds apart. He had been a Communist, I had not; he was drawn to psychology, I to mysticism; he rejected religion, I had returned to it. But what bound us to each other was profound. I treasured his counsel. I was constantly asking for his views. After his death Jenka, his wife, told me he thought of me as a kind of younger brother. He was always critical, especially of those he loved, and never sentimental. I emerged from every encounter with him more lucid. I would not have written *The Testament* had I not read and heard his accounts of the years he spent working for the Comintern in Yugoslavia. I heeded his advice and warnings: not to go after success, not to let myself be swayed by honors. He never flattered anyone, never uttered an insincere phrase, never wavered in his analyses. He instinctively rejected facile popularity.

It was through him that I came to know the writer Jean Blot and the German Jewish novelist Eric Kästen. It was Manès who introduced me to Paul Celan, ever subdued, turned inward, as though listening to his magnificent *Todesfuge* (Fugue of Death).

I devoured Manès's works: *The Burned Bramble*, *The Abyss*, his essays on Communist betrayal and on the Holocaust. They are masterpieces that will endure.

Of course, we had our differences. He did not share my unconditional loyalty to Israel; he wished I could be more critical. One day he chided me privately, for having publicly stated that the destiny of the Jewish people depended on that of the state of Israel. In his view the national catastrophes that had befallen our people, though causing much bloodshed and filling many a cemetery, did not truly endanger its existence.

My friend Manès was an excellent professor and an eloquent speaker. He was a close friend of André Malraux, Ignazio Silone, and Arthur Koestler (whom he published in France). But few know that it was thanks in part to him that French readers discovered Anne Frank's

623

Diary. His observations about contemporary literature will stay with me always, as will his comments on the moral and philosophical richness of shtetl humor. He loved the places and people of his childhood as I love mine.

His trilogy will endure, as indispensable testimony to the ideological and political turmoil of our century. It contains it all: a yearning for justice, a passion for humanity, a deep love for the Jewish people. There is not a wasted word or unrealized scene. Drawn to characters whose destiny appears gloomy, he chose a style that is pure and spare. They are painfully intense, strikingly exemplary. They seem to be drawn from life, from Communists and devout Jews alike. He wrote only of what he knew, of what he had lived.

I loved to hear him recount the mysterious stories and legends of his shtetl of Zablotov. He wandered easily among its lightless cottages and through the Houses of Study where, morning and night and especially on Shabbat and during holidays, the faithful chanted their prayers. Other Jewish writers have tried to portray the myriad colors of the shtetl, but none has ever written with such authority, or such tenderness.

In 1964 I decided the time had come to visit Sighet once again. I set out for Sighet by way of Budapest, Bucharest, and Baia-Mare. In Budapest I visited the Jewish quarter, seeking traces

624

of its past. I wondered what I would do if I ran into one of those gendarmes who had added an extra measure of sadistic brutality to the deportation of the Hungarian Jews in 1944, using the tragedy to unleash their own ancestral anti-Semitism. I wanted to consult official archives, to determine who was present, where, in which office, when the decision was made to deport the Jews of Sighet and the surrounding villages. I wanted to see the ghetto, the houses protected by Raoul Wallenberg and the Swiss consul. I wanted to know why humanitarian aid from the so-called free world was so late in coming. On the Lánczhid, the suspension bridge guarded by fierce stone lions, I looked for a worried-looking woman taking her frail young son to the Jewish hospital to be examined by a great specialist. Why did he suffer from so many headaches? The boy had grown up, and the headaches had not left him. I went to the synagogue and spoke to the faithful. One of them wanted to know if I was married. Not yet, I told him. Why do you ask? There was a girl he was trying to get out of the country, and a pro forma marriage would do the trick. In Bucharest the former general Zvi Ayalon, now Israel's ambassador, issued empty statements. I was wrong to condemn and ridicule him in my articles. (At the time, inexperienced in dealing with totalitarian regimes, I had trouble understanding his caution and distrust.) I went to the Yiddish theater. There was a large audience. Not all the actors were Jewish. Some were Romanians who spoke perfect Yiddish. No surprise there. Our Maria, too, had been fluent in Yiddish.

Maria, the kitchen, the yard, Shabbat, *heder*, the landscape of my childhood — dream long enough and the dream becomes obsession. I related my return to Sighet in *The Town Beyond the Wall*. Except for the chapter on the childhood of Michael, the protagonist, this was a fictional work. When he goes home, he finds no one there. He opens the door of his father's store and a stranger asks him what he wants. Candles, Michael replies, taken aback. Why candles? He doesn't know. When the Communist police arrest him, they are intrigued by these candles. Inspectors slice them into pieces, certain they will find coded messages and microfilm inside. Disappointed, they torment the suspect. What did he mean to do with these candles? Why had he bought them? Michael has no idea what to say — for I didn't know myself. I had made him buy candles without thinking about it, simply because he had to account for his presence in the store. I could have had him ask for buttons or scissors. And yet . . .

When I finally did return to Sighet, the cemetery was the first place I wanted to visit, to meditate at my grandfather's grave. As is customary, I would have to light candles. I found a store and bought two candles. So it was that I had the feeling I was following a scenario written by someone who existed only in my imagination. Michael was my precursor, my scout. I followed his every step. I saw through his eyes, felt what he felt as I wandered the streets among passersby who didn't recognize me or even glance at me, and as I entered my home, a stranger in my own house.

Though it hadn't changed, I found it hard to orient myself in the little town. It seemed not to have endured a war. The streets were teeming with people. The park was as it had been, the trees and benches still in place. Everything was there. As before. Everything except the Jews. I looked all over for them, looked for the children whose joyous laughter once filtered through from the garden near my home, looked for the Talmudic students whose melodious chanting had always filled me with happiness and nostalgia. I looked for a sign of the exhausted porters who leaned against the wall at dusk to recite the minha prayer, and for the princes disguised as madmen. And I looked, too, for my comrades possessed of the messianic dream. But all were gone, swallowed by the night. Yes, they do live on — for a time — in the survivors' memory. And then? Primo Levi may have been right: Perhaps they go on living in the memories of the dead.

I roamed the streets, stopped at the movie house, went to the hospital. No one paid attention to the prodigal returning home from afar. It was not only as though I didn't exist, but as though I had never existed. Had there really been a time when Jews lived here?

Friends had given me the phone number of Leibi Bruckstein, a Communist Yiddish writer who lived on what used to be "my" street. I called him. He was afraid to see me alone. It was 1964, and the walls had ears. But we did manage to walk together for an hour or two. "I'm going to have to file a report," he warned me. I understood his concern. My visit threatened to cause him trouble with the Securitate. He would have to be careful.

We walked around. Here was the house where my friend Dovid'l had lived, and there was Itzu's, and further on Yiddele's, whose grandfather I remembered well. He had been the *dayan*, or rabbinical judge, always elegant and pleasant. Across the street was a former House of Study. "Can I go in?" I asked. My companion hesitated, then nodded: "Yes, but it will be in my report." I asked him, very softly, "How can you live like this?" He looked over his shoulder. No one was following us. "I would love to leave for Israel," he whispered, "but it's complicated. Asking for an exit visa makes you suspect. You instantly become isolated and targeted. And then, what would I do there? I'm too old to start from scratch." I shuddered. My father had spoken almost exactly those words. "Don't stay here," I begged this Jewish Communist writer who, though not religious, was more Jewish than Communist. "Don't let this regime crush you." I offered to help him get an exit visa. I would speak to Dr. Moshe Rosen, the chief rabbi of Romania, and to Israeli friends who dealt with questions concerning Eastern European Jewry.

Eighteen years later I found myself at the Wall in Jerusalem. And there was Leibi Bruckstein. What was the atheistic Communist doing in the midst of this praying throng, stuffing a piece of paper into the interstices of the Wall? What could he be requesting? Only later did I understand: Both he and his wife were gravely ill.

I continued my rediscovery of Sighet. Walking down the Street of Jews — almost every town in Eastern Europe had one — I saw nothing but sealed shutters and doors nailed closed. All those apartments, with their tiny, gloomy, poorly ventilated rooms, now stood empty. How could my friends and their families have lived that way? It struck me how poor they had been, those Jews of Sighet so dear to me. That was true of all of us, though as a child I had been unaware of the poverty that prevailed in the Jewish neighborhoods. Fragments of memories resurfaced: a widow coming to the store on a Friday begging for more credit; an old man accosting me at the entrance to the synagogue on the morning of Tisha b'Av, a day of commemoration, saying, "You're fasting today? Well, think of it. I fast every day." I saw my father looking gaunt and anxious; and my mother, tenderness personified, her face lined by long days and evenings at the shop. There they were, late one winter night, huddled in a corner, whispering about a debt that had come due. From whom could they borrow? A wave of pity engulfed me. As for everything else, it was too late.

I set out to see the synagogues again. Most were closed. In one I found hundreds of holy books covered with dust. The authorities had taken them from abandoned homes and stored them here. In a frenzy, I began to look through them. I was rewarded when I discovered a few that had belonged to me. I even found some yellowed, withered sheets of paper in a book of Bible commentaries: a commentary on the commentaries I had written at the age of thirteen or fourteen. The handwriting was clumsy, the thoughts confused. I rushed out into the street, and in my madness I saw a scene of unkempt beggars — men with dazed expressions, ageless women with their hair hidden under black scarves, cripples leaning on crutches. They were all there, waiting for me, palms extended. Were they the last, the very last Jewish remnant of what had been the flourishing community of Sighet? Had they felt the presence of the writer whose every page welcomes them? Surely I was hallucinating. I gave them everything I had with me: cigarettes, candy, money. They murmured words I could not comprehend. Suddenly I felt in danger again. I began to run, like a fugitive.

★ ★ ★

The Holiday table is set. Is it Rosh Hashana? Probably, since my grandfather presides. I ask him to sing, but he seems not to hear. I ask my father to speak; absorbed in his thoughts, he refuses to listen. My little sister turns to me and says, "Go ahead, you sing." I say: "Yes, I will sing for you." But I realize with dread that I have forgotten all the songs I have ever learned. My little sister says: "Since you don't want to sing, tell me a story." I say: "Okay, I'll tell you a story." But I have forgotten the stories too. I want to shout: "Grandfather, help me, help me find my memory!" Did I shout? My grandfather looks at me, astonished: "But you're not a child anymore. Look at yourself! You're almost as old as I am." I nearly choke. Me, old? I look for a mirror but there isn't one. That's only natural: When a house is in mourning, the mirrors are covered with black cloth or taken down. But who died? I glance questioningly at my family. Their eyes seem filled with pity.

Several years later I returned to Sighet with an NBC television crew. Leibi, the Yiddish writer, was still there, not yet delivered from his political "friends." The authorities ordered him to serve as our official guide. The cameraman was filming in the courtyard of my house, the cemetery, the railroad station. The main sequence would be my interview with Moshe. . . . But first I must tell you more about that strange gentleman.

The day before I had left New York, I had received a cryptic telegram from the NBC director, Martin Hoade, who was already in Sighet with his crew: "We've been lucky enough to find your Moshe. He will participate in the broadcast." Marion and I read and reread that telegram, telling ourselves that surely Martin had lost his mind. Didn't he know that "my" Moshe — the man I speak of in my writings, Moshe the beadle, also known as Moshe the madman, who returned from "there" to warn us of disasters to come — couldn't possibly be alive? I had seen him depart with the first convoy. Was it possible he had survived and returned to Sighet? I rushed to the phone. Of course, it was impossible to get through to Sighet, but suddenly I could think of nothing but Moshe, the first of the Sighet Jews to have seen death at work in Kolomyya and Kamenets-Podolski.

When we landed at the Baia-Mare airport, I grabbed Martin before even saying hello. "What about Moshe? Is it true he's still alive?" Martin's reply was reassuring: "I guarantee it. I saw him just yesterday." As we were driven to Sighet over terrible mountain roads, I bombarded Martin with questions: Where did you find him? Where is he now? What does he look like? In what language did he speak to you? Martin was evasive and I presumed that he was trying to maintain the suspense to make our reunion as dramatic as possible. My disappointment was all the greater. The man had the same first name and the same past — common to all of us — but he was not "my" Moshe. No matter, I liked him anyway. Like all my favorite characters, he seemed out of place. Dressed in the manner of Hasidim of long ago, he was the very last Hasid of Sighet and its environs. He had a white beard, deep blue eyes, a wonderfully kind face, a childlike smile. Rembrandt would gladly have painted his portrait. After we had shaken hands, I asked him what he was doing in this godforsaken town, and he replied that he was the region's *shokhet,* or ritual slaughterer. Martin was not disappointed. But he postponed the shoot until the following day. He wanted to film us in the context of two survivors from the same town exchanging memories and impressions. In the meantime, I chatted with Moshe. He lived alone, in a tiny, airless hut he had to crawl into on all fours. "Like a dog," he told me, never having heard of Kafka and unaware that he was echoing one Joseph K. But he did not complain, for he felt he had a mission. There were still Jews in Sighet and its surroundings who kept kosher and therefore needed him. How many were there? A few in Sighet, two or three in this village, three or four in that village. "How many doesn't matter," Moshe said. "Without me they wouldn't be able to eat meat on Shabbat." Late that evening, before returning to my hotel, I asked him if he needed anything. He smiled. "Me? I don't need anything. But there is something. . . . The community is suffering. We have only one synagogue still open here. Maybe you could help us repair the roof. . . . It leaks. . . ." I offered him money, but he refused. It was illegal to take money from a foreigner. Then I had another idea. On camera, during our filmed conversation, I would ask him to tell me his greatest wish, and he would reply that the synagogue roof badly needed repairs. I felt confident that after such public exposure the authorities would take care of the problem. Moshe agreed. We rehearsed my question and his reply, and he asked me, incredulously, "Do you really think . . . ?" I told him I could guarantee it. The roof would soon be repaired.

I slept fitfully, assailed by my usual entourage of ghosts, who dragged me to the cemetery, where we gathered at the grave of my grandfather whose name I bear. But that's another story.

The next day Moshe and I met for the filming. There was an atmosphere of tension on the "set," namely the community "offices." Martin gave his instructions, setting camera angles and positioning the lights and adjusting the sound. Then came the final commands: Quiet on the set, lights, camera, action! Moshe turned out to be a natural, as if he had studied dramatic arts somewhere. We talked about the Rebbe of

Wizhnitz, who used to be our rebbe. I asked him about his childhood in the mountains, and his religious studies. Then about the war years, the deportation, the camps; the return to an empty town, and, despite it all, his faith. How had he managed it? Moshe smiled. There was no point in asking him that, he said, the question should be addressed to the Holy One, blessed be His name. He quoted a Talmudic saying that love of God comes from God, but fear of God is the domain of man. He, Moshe, loved God and feared Him too. What was so hard to understand about that? Though they grasped not a word of our Yiddish, the entire crew had tears in their eyes. There was something surrealistic in our exchange. Fully at ease in his role, Moshe went on speaking, and I let him. Finally, after a silence heavy with meaning, I asked *the* question: "Do you have a special wish?" He waited a long time before replying softly, "Yes, I do." Then he fell silent. I wanted to remind him of our plan for the new roof, but he seemed lost in thought. The silence dragged on, gathering weight. I pointed discreetly — I hoped — at the ceiling. Moshe didn't react. Poor Martin, also at a loss, seemed frozen. Suddenly Moshe stared straight at me and sighed. "Yes," he said, "I have a wish." He paused. "I would like the Messiah to come. But please let Him hurry, for we can't take it anymore. That is my deepest wish." I was stunned. Had he forgotten our plan? Or was he the reincarnation of the other Moshe, my Moshe? I collected my thoughts. "Moshe," I said, "dear Moshe. Might you perhaps be content with a little less?" No, he replied, he would accept no less. It was the Messiah or nothing.

I later learned that our first conversation had been bugged. A Jewish official who understood Yiddish had awakened Moshe and threatened him: Didn't he know that it was forbidden to complain? Didn't he know that complaints were tantamount to defamation of the socialist state? To say that the Communist roof of the only Communist synagogue in Sighet was in disrepair constituted anti-Communist agitation and therefore treason. Moshe had been unable to warn me before the filming.

Thereafter I found it hard to continue our dialogue. "You're waiting for the Messiah, and so am I. You await Him here, I await Him in New York. We can wait for Him anywhere. What matters is to wait. But you are old and alone. Why not leave and await the Messiah in Israel?" His reply was poignantly pragmatic: "Israel needs young soldiers. I sent my three sons there. They need a mother, so I sent my wife. But me? They don't need an old man like me. Here at least I can be of use to some Jews. . . ."

The interview lasted an hour. When it was over, I said: "Reb Moshe, don't be angry, but I still don't understand why you never went to Israel, if only as a tourist. You could have gone and come back. Aren't you curious to see Jerusalem, to wander through the Old City, to pray at the Wall?" Suddenly his smile was gone. "Curious?" he said faintly. "You ask if I'm curious? The word isn't strong enough. I dream of going, ache to be there even for an instant, just long enough to utter a single 'Amen.'. . ." Perhaps it was wrong of me to press on, but I did: "In that case, Reb Moshe, what stops you? Tell me." He seemed to be gasping for breath as he searched for an answer, perhaps a justification. "It's a question that troubles me," he murmured. "I think about it all the time. I don't understand it myself. Perhaps I'm unworthy of going. . . ." He tried to go on but could not. It was then that all of us — the crew, Marion, and I — broke down. This *tzaddik* of the Carpathians, as I call him in my journal, doubted that he was "worthy" of treading on Jerusalem's soil. Once again I found myself thinking of "my" Moshe, the madman, the beadle, the beggar, he who never returned.

And yet. . . .

Danny Stern had read the account of my "Return to Sighet" in a magazine. He phoned and asked to meet me. "I've published some novels," he said as he shyly handed me a manuscript, "but they really don't count. I think this may be my first true literary effort." This very anxious, gentle man had a passion for literature, particularly contemporary literature. "Do you teach?" I asked. No, he worked in advertising and played the cello. Fine, I would read his manuscript. I felt flattered. It was the first time an American writer had sought my advice.

The title of his novel, *Who Shall Live, Who Shall Die*, was taken from the liturgy of the High Holidays. Its action took place in the camps, where the main character holds a post important enough to influence the inmates' fate.

I tend to be suspicious of fiction whose theme is Auschwitz. Talent is not enough. Something else is needed. Danny knew it. There was a hesitancy in his writing, as though he were unsure, phrase by phrase, of how to continue.

Danny had never written on the subject before. A profoundly and authentically Jewish writer, he explores in his book the Jewish past through characters firmly anchored in the present. His publisher asked me for a few lines to help his novel. I was happy to do it.

Israeli authors were beginning to solicit my support in getting their works translated in America. I was suddenly feeling myself becoming "influential." I recommended several of them to publishers and editors. There were a few acceptances, more rejections. Still, Hanokh Bartov published his novel on the Jewish Brigade, Haim Guri his news articles on the Eichmann trial. Several magazines requested my collaboration. I met Philip Roth, who had recently written a harsh critique of *Exodus*, contrasting it to *Dawn*. I savored the philosophical humor of his short stories, admired the lucidity of his novels. Arnold Foster, who led the major battles against anti-Semitism as head of the Anti-Defamation League, spoke to me of his nephew Harold Flender, author of a Hemingwayesque novel called *Paris Blues*. We met and became friends. Harold later wrote a vivid account of the rescue of the Danish Jews, and never abandoned the theme of the camps. (When he died a suicide a few years later, I was devastated.)

I continued to ask myself harrowing questions. Had I finally made something of my life? Had I made something of my survival?

In 1964, twenty years after leaving my town and the mountains that surrounded it, I published *The Gates of the Forest*. It was an elegy to friendship, a hymn to solitude, a flight from myself into myself, and a song of remembrance for Maria. I developed various themes already touched on in *The Town Beyond the Wall*: the call of God, the provocation of His intervention in human history, the interrogation of silence by silence. *Gates* examines the implications of faith, *The Town* the rush toward madness. The two novels are of a piece but bear little resemblance to each other.

In 1965 an unexpected journey to the Soviet Union became a turning point in my life. Meir Rosenne and Ephraim Tari, two of the most effective and devoted young diplomats in the

Israeli Ministry of Foreign Affairs, prepared me. Both spoke French, were interested in literature, and, as it turned out, belonged to a semiofficial government office reporting directly to the prime minister. Meir in New York and Ephraim in Paris oversaw clandestine activities on behalf of Soviet Jews. It was an arduous task, more dangerous than it appeared. Arduous because even the largest and most influential Jewish communities refused to become actively involved. They were delighted to aid Israel, but the desperate Jews behind the Iron Curtain were both distant and invisible. Nobody seemed to know what concrete action Soviet Jews really wanted Jews in the West to take for them. The fact was that it was far more comfortable to express solidarity with our heroic Israeli brothers than with our unfortunate Soviet cousins. Also, as Israel could not afford to openly arouse the Kremlin's ire, American and European public opinion followed suit. In any case, American and French Jews had other priorities. But Meir and Ephraim refused to give up. They tirelessly appealed to senators, congressmen, journalists, and clergymen. They organized seminars, colloquia, and petitions. At stake were countless human beings whose only claim was their right to dignity and hope. How many were they? There was talk of millions, but that figure seemed implausibly high. "You ought to go and see," both Israelis told me. "You have been a witness before, now you must go and find out the Soviet Jews' true situation and testify for them." Gershon Jacobson, a Yiddish journalist originally from Soviet Georgia, helped prepare my itinerary. I was briefed by experts. There were strict warnings: Watch out for beautiful women who turn up naked in your hotel room or railroad compartment. They will be there not because you're so handsome, but because they are KGB. Unfortunately, the warnings proved baseless. No female members of the secret police were dispatched to entrap me.

I left for Moscow in time for the High Holidays, then went on to Leningrad, Kiev, and Tbilisi. I returned transformed. I who have striven to give testimony for the dead now found myself a messenger of the living. I immediately felt close to these forgotten, tenacious Jews. I admired their capacity to resist oppression and their fidelity to their people. Having survived the massacres of the Nazi era and the Stalinist persecutions, they proclaimed their Jewishness even in the heart of the Gulag and the cellars of the NKVD and KGB. And these were not religious men and women like the Hasidim or, before them, the Marranos, who practiced and taught the Torah and its Laws in secret, risking their freedom and their lives. No, these were people who had received a secular education, and who had been part of the Communist dream.

In *The Jews of Silence* I described my experience and presented as best I could the point of view of the courageous Jews whose struggle

I now shared:

Their eyes — I must start by telling you about their eyes, for their eyes precede all else, and everything is comprehended within them. The rest can wait. It will only confirm what you already know. But their eyes — their eyes flame with a kind of irreducible truth which burns and is not consumed. Shamed into silence before them, you can only bow your head and accept the judgment. Your only wish is to see the world as they do. . . . Their eyes, all shades and ages. Wide and narrow, lambent and piercing, somber, harassed, Jewish eyes, reflecting a strange, unmediated real pity, beyond the bounds of time and farther than the farthest distance. . . .

If only they could speak . . . but they do speak. They cry out in a language of their own that compels understanding. . . . They all speak the same language, and the story they tell echoes in your mind like a horrible folktale from days gone by.

My response was to tell the world of the clandestine gatherings — usually at the cemetery — where young Soviet Jews studied Hebrew and learned Israeli songs. I told of samizdat publications, those secretly printed, worn sheets one read with a virtually religious respect. I described the terror of old people in Kiev, Hasidic joy in Leningrad, the celebration of the Torah in Moscow, the jubilant crowd near the central synagogue on Arkhipova Street. If one day I appear before the celestial tribunal and am asked, "What did you do that was worthy of benevolence?" I will reply, "I was present at the dance of Jewish history in Moscow."

On Simchat Torah, the celebration of the Torah, I stumbled like a sleepwalker through a huge crowd of young people singing and dancing. I moved from one group to another, taking in the beauty of their voices and the urgency of their appeals.

I wrote:

Where did they all come from? Who sent them here? How did they know it was to be tonight, tonight on Arkhipova Street near the great synagogue? Who told them that tens of thousands of boys and girls would gather here to sing and dance and rejoice in the joy of the Torah? They who barely know each other and know even less of Judaism — how did they know that?

I spent hours among them, dazed and excited, agitated by an ancient dream. I forgot the depression that had been building up over the past weeks. I forgot everything except the present and the future. I have seldom felt so proud, so happy, so optimistic. The purest light is born in darkness. Here there is darkness; here there will be light. . . . I wanted to laugh, to laugh as I have never done before. To hell with the fears of yesterday, to hell with the dread of tomorrow. We have already triumphed.

My attention was drawn to a lovely young woman who seemed to dominate the crowd. She was shouting, "Who are we?" and they all responded, "*Evrei*, Jews, we are Jews!" And she called out again, "Who were we yesterday?" and again they all responded, their faces flushed "*Evrei*, Jews, we were Jews, and Jews we want to be!" It was a delirious dialogue in which all the Jews of all exiles and all times seemed to participate. At one point I found myself next to the young woman. I asked her what she knew of Judaism. "Not much," she said. "Only what my grandparents told me." Then why was she so determined to be Jewish? She shrugged and did not reply. But when I turned to leave her for another group, she caught me by the sleeve of my raincoat. "You asked an important question," she said, "and I owe you an honest answer. Why do I so want to remain Jewish? Well, it's because I love to sing." Her answer dazzled me and I felt like embracing her. Yes, a Jew is someone who sings. He even sings a few steps from the Lyubianka Prison. And he sings when he is joyful and when he is not. A Jew is someone who turns his suffering into a song, his solitude into a chanted prayer. I thanked the young woman: "I will not forget the lesson you have just taught me."

Years later, during extended stays in Israel in 1971 and 1972, I would go as often as possible to a remote section of Lod Airport to witness the arrival of the first Soviet Jewish immigrants. They came in on predawn flights from Vienna. I would watch the stirring reunion of the young and the old, the religious and the freethinkers. They would kneel to kiss or just touch the ancestral soil. There was weeping and laughter, hugging and silent embracing. Their joy was contagious. One morning a handsome young woman came down the passageway. She looked vaguely familiar. Then I realized who she was, but she didn't recognize me. Probably mistaking me for an official of the Jewish Agency, she said something to me in Russian. I was about to remind her of Moscow, 1965, when suddenly a broad, lovely smile lit her face. "Oh," she exclaimed, "imagine how much singing I'll do now!" And for the second time I felt like taking her in my arms to thank her.

It is through song that the Jewish soul expresses itself best; it is melody that keeps it alive when there is every reason for sadness. I am told that during the funeral of the great Yiddish theater director Solomon Mikhoels, in the middle of a Moscow winter, a violinist appeared on the roof of a nearby building and began to play Kol Nidre.

Meir Rosenne, Ephraim Tari, and Izso Rager

were among the earliest and most effective advocates for Soviet Jewry and all three became my close friends. All three have had interesting careers. Meir and Ephraim were appointed ambassadors, Izso was elected mayor of Beersheba. Sometimes we meet in Paris, New York, or Jerusalem, and sooner or later the conversation always turns to the days when we were young and enthusiastic and ready for anything. We were determined to help the Jews left behind the Iron Curtain, even if we had to defy the Kremlin and all its police. We had been privileged to make the surprising discovery that with a number of notorious exceptions, even Communist Jews had remained Jewish.

A journalist friend told me that Zinoviev — Lenin's companion and ill-fated admirer/adversary of Stalin — faced execution with the Shma Yisrael on his lips. All his life he had clung to his atheism. For a Jew to be a Communist meant repudiating his or her Jewish faith, Jewish tradition, Jewish history. And so many became resigned to integration, assimilation, and mixed marriages — anything to ensure that their children would no longer be tied to the Jewish people or to Jewish destiny. And yet . . .

Ilya Ehrenburg was an example. During the last years of the war, along with Vasily Grossman (author of the brilliant *Life and Fate*), he scoured cities and villages, gathering chronicles and testimony from survivors of the ghettos and the camps. Together they compiled an anthology of human cruelty and Jewish suffering reaching from Vilna to Minsk, Berdichev to Kiev, Kharkov to Odessa. This "black book" contained accounts one cannot read without feeling despair. It was not published because by 1945 Stalin had changed his policy toward both Germany and the Jews. The Kremlin's spokesmen and propagandists received orders to no longer emphasize German atrocities or the calvary of their Jewish victims. Ehrenburg had to relinquish the original manuscript, and it was thought that the secret police had destroyed it, an assumption that proved not entirely correct: A single copy had been preserved and covertly transmitted to Yad Vashem in Jerusalem. Only twenty years after Ehrenburg's death was it revealed that the writer himself had taken steps to protect this work of Jewish memory. It was he who had entrusted a copy of the manuscript to a reliable friend who was to convey it to Jerusalem when the chance arose. Novelist, pamphleteer, propagandist, and Communist, if not Stalinist, Ehrenburg nevertheless had remained a Jew at heart.

My stay in the Soviet Union had brought encounter upon encounter, adventure upon adventure. I had promised everyone I spoke to that I would not forget them, that I would transmit their greetings to their uncles and cousins in Tel Aviv and Brooklyn, and most of all that I would try to be their spokesman. Though I did try my best, I was later to acknowledge that I had failed in America and France. Yes, my testimony did cause a stir, but despite the publication of excerpts of my book in *L'Express* in France and *The Saturday Evening Post* in America, the movement to support Soviet Jews remained largely lethargic. Because Arthur Cohen wanted the book to be published as soon as possible, he asked Neal Kozodoy to translate it from my *Yedioth* articles written in Hebrew.

I decided to return to the USSR about a year later. Thinking that it would be safer not to go alone, I asked my friend, the physician and poet Michel Salomon, to go with me. The KGB, it seems, was more brazen when dealing with lone travelers. Michel was doubtful: "Do you really think they'll give you a visa after what you've written?" I explained that I had submitted my application before my book was published. He agreed to come along. We left from Paris, determined to keep a low profile. The first thing I saw when we deplaned was that the Israeli chargé d'affaires, David Bartov, and his wife, Esther, had come to greet us. I called out to them, and David answered in Hebrew. Michel nudged me to remind me that we were supposed to be inconspicuous. We sped through the city in David's diplomatic vehicle. Two spacious rooms had been reserved for us at the National Hotel. That very evening the Bartovs took us to a performance by a traveling Yiddish troupe. It was an enthusiastic audience, with many young people. Everyone seemed to know everyone else. There were standing ovations for the actors. After the performance people gathered around us, asking questions about what was happening "outside" and especially in Israel. I remembered some of them from the year before. When they asked if they would see me at the synagogue, I told them nothing could keep me away, but the next day David said it was "out of the question" for me to go to services. "You're not going anywhere except to the airport," he said. "It's imperative you get on the first plane for any Western capital." He had learned from a reliable source that the KGB had just realized that the author of *The Jews of Silence* was on Soviet soil and that I was about to be arrested. But I never like to take action based on rumors. David insisted. Childishly, I refused to listen. "It's the eve of Yom Kippur," I said. "Where shall I go to listen to the Kol Nidre prayer? And, anyway, how can I let down the rabbi and his congregation?" David tried in vain to reason with me. But I was stubborn: "To be in Moscow and not be at the young people's demonstration is inconceivable."

For security reasons, we held our discussion outdoors, in the street, and at one point David told me to look behind us. "See those two thugs pretending to be looking for an address? We know them. They're watching you. We know that orders have been issued to arrest you on the slightest provocation. Do me a favor and get out of here." I refused. "Well, don't say I didn't warn you," my friend finally said.

I went to the synagogue on Arkhipova Street. The entire embassy staff was there, and Michel went with me. At first he felt ill at ease. All those people praying, all those old women weeping, all those informers spying on foreigners. But soon he too, was drawn into the atmosphere, and the poet in him began to sing the soft evening prayers with us, celebrating the Kippur with us, in his fashion. Then came the festival of the Torah, and he was transformed. He glanced sidelong at me as I danced among the faithful with the sacred scrolls. And finally he overcame his reluctance and joined us. Michel claims to be the ultimate cynic, but I could see how moved he was as he clutched the Torah tight to his chest. He who considered himself "far from all that" was not so far after all.

My memory of that festival is as powerful as mine of the previous year's celebration. The crowds in the street carrying torches, the collective defiance, the dances of the brave young dissidents and refuseniks — their eloquence and simplicity had their effect. "Now I understand why you love them so" was his only comment. He dedicated several elegant, bitterly lyrical poems to them.

We returned to the hotel shortly before dawn, escorted by an "adviser" to the Israeli embassy. Interestingly, though Michel was a French citizen and I an American, it was Israeli officials who saw to our security. I teased them and David, calling them paranoids who saw KGB agents everywhere. As if the secret police had nothing better to do.

I returned for morning services without Michel, who was exhausted from the night before. I felt the same soaring excitement at seeing the familiar faces again. As before, slips of paper were stuffed into my pockets: "I have an aunt in Chicago. . . . A relative of mine lives in Rishon Le-Zion. . . ." People whispered in my ear. "For the love of heaven, don't forget us." Or: "Tell the American Jews, the European Jews what you are seeing here." Knowing that I was being watched, I would answer barely moving my lips, promising that I would do all they asked of me, promising to keep the faith, to come back as soon as possible, surely for next year's High Holidays. An old man kissed my hand as though I were a rabbi. I wept.

When I got back to the hotel, my room had been searched. I wasn't surprised. The year before I had walked in on a KGB agent rummaging through my things. He had shrugged without the slightest embarrassment, as if to say, Sorry, just doing my job. I opened the closet, checked my suitcase, the drawers, the bathroom — everything was in its place. But my notebooks had been opened, my shirts moved. Suddenly I remembered the book. I ran back to the closet, reached into the inside pocket of my raincoat — it was gone, the copy of *The Jews of Silence*

I had foolishly brought along to give to a Soviet Jewish intellectual so he could let as many Jews as possible know that I had kept my promises, that I was speaking of them, for them. And now the volume was in the hands of the KGB. When I phoned David, he told me to wait there for him. I knocked on Michel's door. After he had let me in, he whispered that his room had been searched that morning while he was at breakfast.

David arrived within minutes and we went into the street to talk. "Watch out for our guardian angels," he murmured. "There are six of them today." I gave him a brief report. He thought for a moment, then announced: "Michel has nothing to fear, but you do. I'll see what we can do." He knew we were scheduled to leave Moscow the next day on separate flights to Paris. I was taking the morning Aeroflot flight, Michel the afternoon Air France flight. "Tomorrow is a long way off," David said. He made a call from a phone booth, issued brief instructions, and came back to my room with me. We chatted about this and that: the magnificence of Moscow's theater, museums, even the subway. A quarter of an hour later there was a knock on the door. Michel and I started, but David was calm. He opened it, and two men walked in. I had seen them before — probably Israeli security agents. "Get your things ready," David whispered. "You'll spend the night at the embassy and tomorrow morning

652

we'll take you to the airport. It'll be safer that way." I was ready in three minutes. I said goodbye to Michel: "If anything happens to me . . ." He told me not to be a fool, but I could see that he, too, was worried. I could tell from the way he sucked at his pipe. My room had been paid for in advance through Intourist, so we left without stopping at the desk. Two KGB vehicles followed us to the embassy quarter. "Stepped-up surveillance," David commented. By then it was four or five o'clock in the afternoon.

I was angry with myself for having brought the book. But it had just been published, and the temptation had been too strong. Now I would have to pay for it. On David's advice I phoned several friends abroad to let those monitoring the lines know that my arrest would not pass unnoticed. "If you don't see me tomorrow, call *Le Monde* and Mauriac," I told Ephraim. "You might have to get in touch with the *Times* tomorrow," I told Meir, "and with Senator Javits." I called Marion but chose not to worry her. "I might have to extend my stay," I said.

David's two men showed up at seven in the morning. "Something's going on outside," they told us. I gulped down a cup of scalding coffee, and David gave his people instructions: "Don't let him out of your sight until he boards." He corrected himself: "No, until the plane takes off."

Outside, the street seemed quiet and there

was no suspicious activity. Still, there were the same KGB vehicles as the day before. I told myself it was going to be all right. Maybe the secret police had simply decided to tighten surveillance of foreigners this week. The trip to the airport was uneventful. A clerk at the Intourist counter even smiled at me. When I checked my suitcase with Aeroflot, a friendly young woman stamped my ticket, issued me a seat number, and wished me bon voyage. But my nerves were on edge as I lined up at passport control. It was a long, slow-moving queue. A Frenchman behind me was reading *L'Humanité* the Communist paper. In an effort to relax, I spoke to him. He was an engineer, a Communist Party member on his way home from North Korea. He was annoyed because he had lost his new raincoat, but what the hell, some North Korean comrade would find it, and we had to help those gallant fighters for peace in North Korea, didn't we? I couldn't tell if he was serious. Finally, I reached passport control. The official took his time, consulted documents, looked me over, stared. I expected him to pick up the phone or push a button to inform his superiors that they could come and get the enemy of the people. But to my surprise, he closed my passport and handed it back to me. Turning to the two Israelis standing near me, I said, "See? No problem. You can go now." One of them phoned David and came back shaking his head. "We will stay with you until the plane takes off," he said.

They had special permits letting them through the checkpoints. Once we reached the waiting room, I felt safe; surely they weren't going to arrest me in front of all these foreigners. Besides which, boarding was about to begin. The Aeroflot crew had arrived. There were two final checks at the end of the ramp: An Intourist stewardess on the right took my boarding card, an officer on the left examined my passport. The young woman motioned to me to board, but at the same instant the officer shouted something. Suddenly things moved quickly. Before I realized what was happening, the two Israelis were at my side. One of them took my ticket while the other snatched my passport out of the officer's hand. I felt myself being lifted like a package. They ran, and so did I, amid whistles and shouted orders. I don't know how we managed to jostle our way through all the gates and barriers, but we jumped into the embassy car and took off. Why the police didn't stop us, I don't know. I was too stunned to try to understand, too dazed to think about it. The Israeli behind the wheel drove as if he were back home in Tel Aviv. I would worry about that later. In a moment we were on embassy grounds. "Do you believe me now?" David said as he opened the car door for me. Walking up to his office I suddenly remembered my suitcase, which must have left for Paris. How was I going to get it back? David shook his head in disbelief:

"Is that what you're worried about? Don't you understand what trouble you're in?" Then he reassured me: I would be all right here. He emphasized the "here." By then I was in a cold sweat. How long did he think they would keep me, I asked, remembering Cardinal Mindszenty, who lived in the American embassy in Budapest for years.

David went into an adjoining room and returned some fifteen minutes later. He had contacted his "sources," and things looked bad. "They" were determined to arrest me. I already saw myself in a cell in the Lyubianka Prison, but David seemed calm. "As long as you don't fall into their hands, my boy, there's hope." He advised me to be patient and let him handle the situation. I was happy enough to let him handle it, but being patient was a different story. I couldn't sit still. I became obsessed with the idea that I would be stuck here for a week, a month, or — who knows? — all my life.

To make things worse, there was a pompous young diplomat named Yoram staying at the embassy who was determined to give us the "benefit" of his "ideas" and advice. I had to get back to Paris, if only to be rid of him. I sent frantic appeals to Meir and Ephraim. Mauriac was informed. I was later told that he had interceded with General de Gaulle. David mobilized his American and European colleagues and called in IOUs with some of his contacts within the Communist bureaucracy. But the hours dragged on, the clock refusing to budge.

I spent three days and nights at the embassy before getting the signal to leave. David never told me how he managed it, and I made no real effort to find out, though the journalist in me would have loved to know. The important thing was to get out of Moscow, to find freedom again.

Accompanied by my two Israeli bodyguards, I returned to the airport. Everything went smoothly. The Intourist and Aeroflot employees greeted me amiably. I was told my suitcase was waiting for me in Paris. There was no problem at passport control. The other passengers were already on board. I shook hands with my guardian angels. The young Intourist hostess invited me to go aboard, the officer wished me a pleasant flight.

The plane was half empty. I had the whole first-class section to myself. Suddenly I noticed the Communist engineer returning from North Korea. He had been close to boarding — why hadn't he left three days ago? When I said hello, he looked at me with hostility and snapped, "Go away! Go away or I'll call the captain!" Perplexed and offended, I went back to my seat, wondering what I had done to make him so angry. He gave me the answer at our stopover in Copenhagen. He came up to me in the waiting room, his face a deep red, and said: "I don't know who you are, and I don't care to know, but on account of you I spent three most unpleasant days and nights in the police station being interrogated. Even my party card didn't help. They wanted to know where and when I first met you, whether I was your accomplice, and whether a certain Michel Salomon was a friend of mine. They released me only this morning." I apologized profusely and offered to buy him a drink. He glared at me. "I don't drink with people who slander the Soviet Union," he said.

I arrived in Paris just in time for the annual conference of French Jewish intellectuals organized by Jean Halpérin and André Neher under the auspices of the World Jewish Congress. Rather than speak on that year's designated topic (God and . . .), I recounted my experiences and impressions while in Moscow: the clandestine meetings, the celebration of Simchat Torah, the desperate calls for help from these Jews I found so admirable in their defiance.

The next day I returned to the subject during the popular television program "Lectures pour tous." Its normally unflappable host, Pierre Dumayet, seemed shaken and incredulous. He didn't say so, but I sensed it in his questions, and I could understand why. He could not believe that fifty years after the Communist revolution there were still Jews in the Soviet Union devoted to their Jewishness. I tried to explain it, but confronted, as I was, by a man of secular, rationalist logic, especially of the French type,

I found it a difficult task.

As I walked into my hotel later, the phone rang. It was Yaakov Herzog, secretary to Levi Eshkol, in Paris on an official visit. "The prime minister would like to see you," he said. What about? "He'll tell you himself." We made an appointment for Saturday afternoon, at the Bristol. As usual, I arrived early. "He's in a meeting," Herzog told me, "and he'll be late. He asks you to excuse him." But the prime minister wasn't late. At the appointed hour I was ushered into the suite that served as his office.

Years later my friend, the former ambassador of Israel Emile Najar, recalled: "Eshkol was more Jewish than Israeli. Imagine: In 1966 he summoned all his European ambassadors to Paris. The meeting had a full agenda, but in the middle of the discussion he stood and asked to be excused. He had a meeting with 'some Jew' who had come to talk about the fate of Soviet Jews." At that time Emile didn't know I was that Jew.

Eshkol bombarded me with questions: How badly were the Jews suffering? Did they still live in fear? Did they have hope? Was it true they wanted to remain Jewish? I reported in detail. He interrupted frequently. Was I absolutely sure there were many young Jews who wanted to return to Judaism? Had I really seen them dancing on the night of Simchat Torah? Was it true thousands of people had come out into the streets? As I answered his questions, he stood from time to time and paced back and forth, hands behind his back, punctuating his march with exclamations: "Incredible! After fifty years of Communist oppression . . ." After nearly two hours, a secretary came in and whispered something to him. "Let them wait," the prime minister replied, before launching into more questions. It was nearly dinnertime when he escorted me to the door. "One last thing," Eshkol said. "Tell me, what do you think we can do for them, apart from what we're already doing?" I was about to suggest a more determined political campaign, a push for greater press coverage, more critical speeches at the UN. But I knew there were limits to what he could do, and to ask for too much made no sense. So I decided to be realistic. "While I was there," I said, "I often listened to Israeli radio broadcasts aimed at Soviet Jews. These broadcasts are listened to religiously." I told him I thought the content and tone of these programs needed to be changed. They picture Israel as too perfect, as though there were no difficulties in adapting, as though everyone were always happy. What if the gates were someday opened and masses of Soviet Jews immigrated to Israel? They would most certainly be disappointed. Eshkol listened intently. "What do you think we should do?" he asked. "Tell the truth," I replied, "even if it's unpleasant." He looked at me sadly and said, "You and I both know that the gates will not open anytime soon. The Soviet Jews will stay where they are. Why sadden them? At least let them dream."

Levi Eshkol died before he could see the realization of the dream. He was a generous and good man. Golda Meir succeeded him as the first waves of Soviet Jews began arriving in Israel.

Upon returning to the United States I threw myself into the struggle for Soviet Jews. Both here and in France my testimony at last brought some reaction, especially among young people, but little action, official or otherwise. Abraham Joshua Heschel and I pleaded with audiences in the United States and Canada. Disappointed by the sparse attendance of adults, I often began by asking high school students, "Where are your parents? Why didn't they come with you? Next time make them come too!"

Wherever we went, we found that only the young responded. How could we awaken the powerful Jewish communities? I wrote article after article in the *Forverts*, *Yedioth*, and *Hadassah* magazine, circulated appeals and petitions, rushed from demonstration to demonstration and convention to convention: rabbinical associations in Toronto, Miami, and New Jersey, institutes and conferences of philanthropic groups. I accepted all radio, television, and press interviews on the subject. But nothing happened, and like Meir and Ephraim, I felt frustrated. We had to do something else, we had to do more.

Gershon Swet, of Russian origin and dean of correspondents for Israeli newspapers, proposed that I meet with several influential Jewish intellectuals at his home. I told them of the complacency and silence of the old people and the courage and defiance of the young. I told them how miraculous it seemed to discover so many Jews defying the most feared regime on earth in order to remain Jewish. Imagine, I said, a course in Talmud in Moscow.

They asked questions, and I replied as best I could. One man in particular stood out. I was struck by the combination of irony and kindness in his blue eyes. He asked for details about the Talmud course in Moscow: the number of participants, their ages, the length of the session, the treatise they studied, the commentaries they used. Fortunately, I recalled every detail of my visit to the Moscow synagogue.

When the host offered us tea, I took the opportunity to inquire about the man who had posed all those questions. "Don't you know him?" he asked, surprised. "That's Dr. Saul Lieberman." So this was the man whose landmark work on the Jerusalem Talmud I had studied and so admired. Just then the master came over to where we were standing, hand extended. He asked more questions. "Tell me the truth," he said in a low voice so that no one else could hear. "Is it true you studied the tractate of Sanhedrin in what you call the Moscow yeshiva?" I told him it was true, except it wasn't really a yeshiva. "Are you certain it was really the Talmud?" I was. "You're interested in the Talmud, then?" Yes. "Since when?" Since childhood. Gershon Swet intervened: "You ought to come to one of his lectures at the 92nd Street Y." Lieberman smiled: "Oh, you teach?" Intimidated, wishing to drop the subject, I replied: "Yes, but it's not important." But Lieberman would not let it go. "What do you teach?" A little of everything, I said, but really, it's not important. "Still, what are you going to talk about in your next session?" I swallowed hard and murmured that I would deal with, well, a Talmudic subject. "Really! In that case, I'll be there." He called his wife, Judith, over, introduced us, and asked her to make a note of the date of my lecture. Judith took me aside and politely told me not to count on their showing up. Her husband would probably discover he was otherwise engaged that evening.

She was wrong. Though I had prepared as well as possible, I got stage fright when I saw the couple in the audience. Was I now to talk about the Talmud in the presence of my generation's greatest Talmudist? I began by citing the maxim that a disciple who dares teach the Halachah (the Law) in his master's presence is guilty of a capital crime. As it happened, Dr. Lieberman was not (yet) my master, and I proposed to treat not the Halachah but the Aggadah, the Talmud's legendary aspect. I don't know how I managed to concentrate, but I do know that Dr. Lieberman waited for me outside after the lecture. Friends who heard him couldn't believe their ears. A compliment from Lieberman was not only the most prestigious of honors, but also extremely rare. "Do come and see me tomorrow," he added.

Anxiously, I knocked at the door of his office at the Jewish Theological Seminary. He himself answered and invited me to follow him in. It was my first visit to this room, which looked ready to burst if just one more volume were added to it. I was to return to that room twice and sometimes three times a week for seventeen years, literally until the day he died.

He began by questioning me about my past and present life. As I answered, I wondered what he had really thought of my lecture, whether I had not in fact made many mistakes. I was eager to hear his commentary and criticism, but he hadn't yet finished his introductory queries. He had read my articles on Russia, in Yiddish in the *Forverts* and in Hebrew in *Yedioth Ahronoth*. He was pleased that I spoke Hebrew. He spoke of Motele, his hometown near Pinsk, and asked me about Sighet. I mentioned that a childhood friend, David Weiss-Halivni, had been a pupil of his at the seminary. Finally, almost in passing, he came to the subject I yearned to speak of. "Toward the end of the first half of your lecture," he said, "you explained an apparent conflict concerning a text of the Mekhilta. Was that explanation your own find?" "I think so," I stammered. "I see," he said. "You think so." He stood up, took a dusty volume from the very top of a bookshelf and flipped through it, until he found a certain page. "Look," he said. "Your finding dates back . . . six centuries." I told him I was pleased to walk in such footsteps, but the impish look on his face suggested he only half believed me. He returned to the attack: "A little before the conclusion you presented a solution to the problem raised by Maimonides with regard to Aristotle. Did you also think this solution was your own finding?" I nodded. "All right," he said. "Let's see." This time he opened an even older and dustier volume and pointed to an annotated page: "Here it is." Disappointed? On the contrary. I repeated my defense, adding that for me study meant not discovery but rediscovery. My purpose was not to answer questions but to know them, and if possible to invent them. My mother never asked me whether I had given the melamed good answers, but whether I had asked a good question. As I answered him, I was staring at my feet, speaking hoarsely in a tone I hoped was convincing. Lieberman was silent at first, then he said, "Is twice a week all right with you?" All right? Joy flooded through me. I wanted to shout and dance.

What I learned from him is what, of all my knowledge, I value most. He made me aware that to be a Jew is to place the greatest store in knowledge and loyalty, that it is because he recognizes divine justice that he speaks out against human injustice. That it is because a Jew remains attached to his God that he is permitted to question Him. It is because the prophets loved the people of Israel that they admonished them and reprimanded their kings. Everything depends on where you stand, my master used to say. With God anything can be said. Without God nothing is heard. Without God what is said is not said.

Le Chant des morts was published in 1966. In English the collection was entitled *Legends of Our Time.* "For our time" would have been more accurate. How to prevent the past from receding too rapidly into the distance? How to keep alive the dead who, beyond time and speech, beckon us, not to torment us but to reassure us that they reproach us not for clinging to life but for living in forgetfulness? And yet, I don't know what a son can do or say to commemorate a father who died in the camps. I pray, light candles, say Kaddish, try to see his face as I meditate, but I know it is not enough. It can never be enough.

How to evoke a childhood buried in ashes? How to speak of masters whose eyes are veiled forever and yet whose glance still burns into ours? What to make of the silence wrenched from the blackness that covered heaven and earth in those days?

To forget nothing, to efface nothing: that is

the obsession of survivors; to plead for the dead, to defend their memory and honor. So much has been said about them. They have been subjected to countless analyses, dissected, exhibited, and made "presentable" for theological, scientific, political, and commercial purposes. Treated like objects, they have been insulted, belittled, and betrayed. To resist this tide survivors — and they are becoming ever fewer — have only words, poor, ineffectual words, with which to defend the dead. So some of us weave these words into tales, stories, and pleas for memory and decency. It is all we can do, for the living, and for the dead.

Jerusalem

In 1967 the Six-Day War stamped a whole generation of Jews with its halo of glory. I remember every phase and aspect of the war as if it were yesterday, as if I had fought in it myself. I remember the three somber, tension-laden weeks that preceded it. I remember the outrageous words, the overt, brutal threats of our enemies, and the silence of our friends and allies. And I remember Israel's solitude.

It started one spring day in 1967. Israel was celebrating the nineteenth anniversary of its independence. During the military parade in Jerusalem, Prime Minister Eshkol received a brief military report that something was afoot with the Egyptians in the south. The next day there was talk of troop movements. The gravity of the situation quickly became clear. Cairo announced the beginning of its policy of aggression: the blockade of the Strait of Tiran, the revocation of the demilitarization of the Sinai Peninsula. To facilitate the massing of his armies there, Colonel Gamal Abdel Nasser demanded the evacuation of the UN units. Secretary-General U Thant's hasty submission to Nasser's

671

demand surprised the international community. There was no longer any doubt about Egypt's offensive aims. The situation deteriorated daily. When would war break out? In fact, it had already begun with the blockade, a *casus belli* under international law.

Israeli correspondents and all those sympathetic to Israel reported on the debates in the UN Security Council with mounting unease. Ahmed Shukairy, Yasir Arafat's predecessor as head of the PLO, made no secret of his dream of witnessing the demise of the state of Israel. Soon, he declared, there would be no further Jewish problem in Palestine: The Jews would be driven into the sea. No one silenced him. No one protested. Gideon Rafael, Israel's permanent ambassador to the UN, a seasoned diplomat, exposed the Arab countries' objectives. His words fell on deaf ears. Most delegates tended to mind their own business, perhaps vaguely pleased that the Middle East was once again relieving their boredom. There was, however, one exception: Arthur Goldberg, the former Supreme Court justice who had been named U.S. ambassador to the UN by President Johnson. He fought day and night for Israel's security and survival.

The Eshkol government undertook intense diplomatic activity in Western capitals, exhausting all its resources in an effort to forestall armed conflict. Eshkol abhorred war, and he believed that if the great powers did their duty, it could be averted. He sent Abba Eban, his minister of foreign affairs, to Washington, London, and Paris. His was a tough assignment, though some top-level meetings were less discouraging than others; a few were even cordial. But no one was prepared to intervene. The so-called great powers suddenly seemed very small. Leading officers of the Israeli general staff urged Eshkol to unleash a preventive war: Every day's delay threatened to carry a greater price in human lives. One young general burst into the prime minister's office, tore the epaulets from his uniform, and threw them on the table, lecturing the head of the government, who was also the minister of defense: Failure to order an immediate attack would mean the destruction of the Third Temple and the end of the Jewish state. But the cautious Eshkol temporized, especially since the war option did not have the unanimous support of his cabinet. General Yitzhak Rabin, chief of the general staff, put on civilian dress and journeyed to a kibbutz in the Negev to solicit the view of David Ben-Gurion. Ben-Gurion counseled patience, urging that war be avoided as long as possible. He recommended a strategy of retrenchment, using the term *titkhapru*, meaning "dig defensive trenches." He felt that a war at that moment could lead to national disaster. "The chief we once worshipped had lost confidence in the army," Rabin later told me. His intense disappointment drove him into a depression that, fortunately, lasted only twenty-four hours.

Saul Lieberman was more confident. His argument was based not on military science but on theology — and economics. "The Lord," he said, "is also a banker. He has invested so much in our people's history that He can no longer turn away from them without forfeiting His capital."

On Sunday, June 4, 1967, I felt anxious but content as I went to the graduation ceremony of the Jewish Theological Seminary. The chancellor, Louis Finkelstein, had invited me to deliver the commencement address. In a sense, I was one of the graduates, for I was to receive my first honorary doctorate. The Israeli ambassador, Gideon Rafael, was among the invited guests.

My address was later published in *One Generation After*, under the title "To a Young Jew of Today." In it I spoke of commitments and obligations to our own community and to the human community at large, of our common memories and hopes. In the printed text I deleted a brief exhortation, a call to the students to stand by Israel, now threatened by so many enemies. "Should war break out tomorrow," I told them, "we must come to Israel's aid." I was speaking, of course, only of a hypothetical tomorrow.

Very early the next morning I was awakened by Rafael, who asked me how I knew. "Knew what?" I asked sleepily. "That there would be war today," the ambassador replied. In other circumstances I would have laughed, but I didn't feel like laughing on that day, one of the worst since 1945. The news was depressing, Jerusalem's silence ominous. We didn't know that the new minister of defense, Moshe Dayan, had ordered a strict blackout on news from the front. The only available information came from Arab capitals. Radio Cairo, Damascus, and Amman were jubilant: The Israeli front had collapsed, Beersheba was about to fall, the army was disintegrating, Tel Aviv would soon be in flames.

In fact, the Egyptian air force having been annihilated in the first three hours of battle, Egypt had already lost the war. As yet, the Arabs didn't know it. Neither did the American public.

In Brooklyn (with the exception of the anti-Zionist Hasidim of Satmàr and the Neturei Karta, who hailed the supposed Israeli defeat), Jews gathered in the Houses of Study to recite psalms. Forty-seventh Street, the heart of the Manhattan diamond industry, came to a virtual standstill as groups formed to discuss the situation. Emergency funds were collected everywhere, from rich and poor alike. Senators and representatives were besieged with requests to intervene. Doctors volunteered to fly to Israel to help their overwhelmed colleagues.

The entire Jewish population now offered its unconditional support to Israel. The Diaspora communities, as if lifted by a tidal wave of solidarity, rose to the occasion. Even intellectuals who had suffered their Jewishness as an embarrassing contradiction now openly proclaimed it. Assimilated Jews forgot their complexes, sectarians their fanaticism. There was a sense of responsibility for the survival of Israel. American Jews called Israeli relatives and friends offering to take care of their small children as long as necessary. Isaac Stern canceled his concerts and flew to Tel Aviv, declaring: "Our enemies say they will exterminate two and a half million Jews. Well, let them add one more to the list."

I knew I had to leave for Israel. I made the decision in the first hours of the crisis, even though I had no illusions: Israel did not need men like me. I had no experience with weapons, and would probably even be a burden as a soldier. But I had to go anyway, determined to stay to the very end, which I feared would be bitter. Deep within myself, I was convinced this war would mark the end of the Jewish state, the death of a dream. I should have had more faith in the Israeli army, I know. But at the time I was terrified. As I listened to Arab speeches and observed the passivity of Western governments, I told myself it was happening all over again. Clearly the Jews would fight courageously, as they had in the Warsaw ghetto, but they would be outnumbered, as before. The well-equipped Arab armies would crush Israel in the end. Then the so-called civilized world would shed crocodile tears and deliver grandiloquent funeral orations on our death. I say "our" death because, like so many of my contemporaries, I associated mine with Israel's. For me it was inconceivable to wish to live in a world that had no place for a sovereign Jewish state.

My pessimism was ill-founded. The war turned in favor of the Israel Defense Force shortly after it began. I told my friends I was going even though I had no idea how I would cover the travel costs. *Yedioth* certainly would not, and Simon Weber at the *Forverts* announced that he would be delighted finally to have a war correspondent, though he would have to be unpaid. This trip would deplete my savings account. But that was not my only problem: getting there was not easy. Most airlines had suspended their flights to Lod, and seats on El Al were at a premium. It was, however, the only company where I had some connections, and on the afternoon of June 6 luck was on my side and I obtained passage on a flight from Paris to Lod. I jumped in a cab, rushed to Kennedy Airport, and caught a TWA flight to Paris. I changed planes in Orly and was the last passenger to board the El Al flight, which took off just as I boarded. Exhausted, I closed my eyes. A short nap would do me good. Everyone already knew that Israel was out of danger, but my own anguish was not so easy to quell. Sure, I was no longer afraid of Israel's demise and my own with it. Instead, my fear was of the kind that comes over us at the approach of the unknown, the anxiety that comes with the certainty of reaching a turning point, a shift in life's pace and intensity. I knew I was about to live a new chapter in Jewish history.

A pretty stewardess lifted my morale. She brought me coffee and whispered in confidence that she knew who I was. A little later she mentioned that she had read and liked my book. In the singular. I knew that if I asked her, "Which one?" she would be embarrassed, so I merely thanked her again. I tried to doze off, but the young stewardess had other ideas. Since regulations did not permit her to nap, she decided to keep me company. She told me she read a lot, "especially between Paris and New York, when the passengers are asleep and the cabin is quiet." Usually, she said, she read quickly, "but I liked your book so much I forced myself to slow down. In fact, there was something in the fourth chapter I didn't understand, Mr. Schwarz-Bart."

My humility back in place, I told her she was making a mistake. "I'm not André Schwarz-Bart." She waved away my denial: "I know you're traveling incognito. I promise I won't tell anyone." I repeated that I was not Schwarz-Bart. She smiled knowingly and went to bring me another coffee, a snack, and some fruit. Loath to usurp a great writer's identity and fame, I resolved to press on. "Listen," I told her, "your mistake is understandable. André and I have a lot in common. To start with, we're both writers. And some of my works are concerned with the same subject as his. We even have the same publisher. In fact, we're friends, and some even say we look a little alike. So it's only natural for you to confuse us." She didn't believe a word of what I said, and by now her admiration had turned into affection. "I thought I knew all about you and your work, Mr. Schwarz-Bart, but I never realized you had such a good sense of humor."

Twenty minutes before we landed, the stewardess was back, as pretty as before but less affable. Earlier she had leaned toward me and spoken softly. Now she stood up straight and raised her voice so the whole cabin could hear her accuse me of lying to her: "I don't know who you are, sir —" "It's about time," I interjected, but she went on triumphantly, "— but I know you're not André Schwarz-Bart." I said: "Prove it." Savoring the moment, she paused dramatically before delivering the final blow: "You're not André Schwarz-Bart, because André Schwarz-Bart is sitting right there!" I looked over to where she was pointing, and there was my friend André in a seat three rows behind me. I unbuckled my seat belt, made my way past the stewardess, and hurried over to him. We fell into each other's arms. "André, what are you doing here?" He asked me the same question. Even as the pilot announced that we were about to land, we were still standing and talking in the aisle, not hearing the stewardess, who was asking us to sit down. What were we doing here? We knew we had come for the same reason and with the same aim: to be there and to testify.

My people's quest was mine, its memory my country. Everything that happens to it affects me. I have lived its anguish and been scorched by the fire of its dreams. I belonged to the community of night, the kingdom of the dead, and henceforth I would also belong to the wondrous, exhilarating community of the eternal city of David. It is incumbent upon the Jewish writer to be witness to all that has haunted the people of Israel from its beginnings. That is his role — not to judge but to testify. And in our tradition the responsibilities of the witness are greater than those of the judge; if the testimony is true, the verdict will be just.

The next day, before the reconquered Wall in the Old City, I began writing *A Beggar in Jerusalem*.

It was an unforgettable day. War was still raging in the Sinai and had not yet broken out in the Golan, but everyone's imagination was fired by the long-awaited liberation of Jerusalem. "The Temple Mount is ours!" shouted Colonel Motta Gur, commander of the parachutists. His cry was heard on every radio in every tank and vehicle. Soldiers and officers burst into tears. People wept throughout the Holy Land. Suddenly the war seemed suspended. Isolated Jordanians were still firing from rooftops, but thousands of Jews rushed to the Old City. No force could deter them.

Rabbis and merchants, Talmudic students and farmers, officers and schoolchildren, artists and scholars — all left whatever they were doing and converged on the Wall, and, when they reached it, kissed the stones and shouted ancient prayers and requests. On this day everybody was running.

I did too. Never did I run so fast, never did I say "Amen" with so much fervor as when I heard the parachutists reciting the minha prayer. On that day, more than ever, I grasped the true meaning of *ahavat Israel,* devotion to the people of Israel.

An old man, who looked as if he were stepping out of a novel I was to write later, murmured as if to himself, "Do you know how we managed to defeat the enemy? Six million Jewish souls prayed for us." I touched his arm. "Who are you?" I asked. He looked at me gently: "I am one who prays."

Entries from my (Yiddish) diary of the time:

. . . Before telling the story, it is incumbent on us to recall its genesis: the first miracle, the first prayer, the first spark of the fire that lit its path. We must tell everything, but I don't know where to begin. Doesn't the Bible itself begin with a *beth* and not an *aleph?* So be it. But this I know: Now, more than ever, we must begin with Jerusalem, city of a thousand generations of men who dreamed of deliverance and paved the way for today's heroes, Jerusalem, ancient and renewed city bridging the beginning of beginnings and the end of time.

To be sure, young warriors have died to sanctify His name on other fronts, shedding their blood for their people. Young men and women who only yesterday spent their evenings in the nightclubs of Tel Aviv have suddenly taken their places in the ranks of the Righteous. They are bearing Jewish history on their shoulders. And some have fallen under its weight.

But Jerusalem comes first. Jerusalem is the absolute priority. All roads lead to it. It is in Jerusalem that our people have been initiated into what our mystics call *aliyah neshama,* or ascension of the collective soul. Our ancestors have helped them lift themselves ever higher. Hence the question: Where and with whom to begin? With King David, who with his strength and his Psalms built this city dedicated to peace and eternity? With the Zealots who fought for it? With Rabbi Akiba and his fellow martyrs, who by going to their deaths sanctified the Jewish people's faith in their mission?

When did I first come to love Jerusalem? I cannot say. The poet Rabbi Yehuda Halevy expressed the Jew's nostalgia in his song: The Jewish heart lies forever in the

East, though we may find ourselves far away, in this or that region, in this or that continent.

The Jew in me loves Jerusalem with a different, unique love. A lullaby my mother sang to me before I was old enough to speak told of the widow Zion who awaited her beloved alone on the grounds of the Temple in Jerusalem. Like her — with her — I awaited the legendary little she-goat and her offerings, awaited her so that she might lead me to this city which breathes Jewish life and where the stones themselves tell tales of Jewish kings and princes of our often glorious, often sad, but always exhilarating past.

I remember: At *heder* my friends and I would let our imagination soar and allow it to lead us through secret tunnels buried in the Carpathians, to the land of Israel. It would be enough to pronounce a "name," and invisible gates would open before us. And then, at once, persecution, hatred, and fear would end. Master of the Universe, we asked, please send us an emissary to reveal this holy, all-powerful "name" to us. But, sadly, no emissary ever appeared to enlighten us.

And here I am in Jerusalem. It took me a long time to get here, but here I am. I dream that I'm dreaming. I dream that words become jumbled on my lips and that they burn my tongue.

And yes, it is both a privilege and a duty to speak of Jerusalem.

Of the heart that is full, so full that if it doesn't open it will burst. Of the alleyways of the Old City, which have made me want to sing like a madman, to sob like a child. To paraphrase Rabbi Nahman of Bratslav, I will have to make words of my tears.

Nothing must be omitted from this chronicle of the events of June 1967. All must be retained, transmitted, shared. From beginning to end, though the story began before the beginning and the end is far from being the end. This is a story that reaches beyond the individual and transcends the moment, just as Jerusalem is something more than the houses and shadows that inhabit it. . . .

Mid-June 1967, Sharm al-Sheikh. A sandstorm moves over this area that was the technical and legal pretext for the recent hostilities. The base commander welcomes us and we wait for the storm to pass. The officers make no secret of their frustration: This site was taken without a struggle, Egyptian artillery failing to fire a single shot.

We notice the wedding preparations of a groom who is stationed here, the bride in the

Sinai. A military chaplain will perform the ceremony. A tent is used as synagogue. I feel like laughing. The whole world has been in jeopardy because of this island, and now all that matters is the impending wedding.

All over the country they sing the praises of the valiant fighters who saved the nation: *"Kol hakavod le-Tsahal"* (All honor to Tsahal, the Israel Defense Force) is the slogan on all the walls, the headline in all the newspapers. But knowledgeable observers also speak of the victors' melancholy.

In the speech General Yitzhak Rabin delivered at the end of June on Mount Scopus, I find the same moving restraint as in another address he delivered twenty-six years later in Washington, in the presence of President Bill Clinton and Yasir Arafat:

It is strange to note to what extent Israel's fighters do not feel joy. They seem to be closed to joy. Some try to show gaiety, but their heart is not in it. Others do not even feel like trying, for they have seen not only glory but the suffering that goes with it. They have seen their closest comrades fall bloodied and maimed. . . . But that isn't all. The price paid by the enemy also weighs upon our soldiers. Conditioned by its past, the Jewish people has never been able to feel a conqueror's pride or

685

victor's exaltation. . . .

In *A Beggar in Jerusalem* I echo Rabin's reflections on the sadness felt by the Israelis in the face of the vanquished Arabs, especially the children who saw them as victors and therefore as capable of doing them harm. I saw such children in the Old City, encountered them in Hebron, Ramallah, and Nablus. They were afraid of us, of me. For the first time in my life, children were afraid of me.

From my travel diary:

The war is over, and in the turmoil I seek joy but do not find it. I encounter only beings with grave faces and wounded eyes. Shaken by the experience they have just lived, they seem unable to grasp its implications. It seems the stuff of legend rather than history. The accumulated anguish and anger before the fury, the reversal of roles: it all happened too fast, too suddenly. Victors and vanquished will need time to catch their breath and absorb the meaning of the event. David has vanquished Goliath and now wonders how he did it. No one knows, he less than anyone else. His astonishment, more than his victory, should arouse admiration and hope alike. . . .

. . . The victors, in fact, would have preferred to forgo battle. Saddened, they returned to their homes without hate or pride, disconcerted and withdrawn. The world has never seen such victors as these.

. . . This event has had a moral and perhaps a mystical dimension. I understood that the day I found myself in the Old City of Jerusalem and saw thousands of men and women parading before the Wall, sole vestige of the Temple. I was struck by how awed and contemplative they looked. Suddenly I thought I saw, intermingled with the living, the dead converge from the four corners of exile, from all the cemeteries and all memories. Some seemed to emerge from my childhood, others from my imagination. Mute madmen and dreaming beggars, masters and their disciples, cantors and their allies, the Righteous and their enemies, drunks and storytellers, children dead and immortal, all the characters of all my books — yes, they had followed me here to manifest their presence and to testify like me, through me! Then they left, and I had to summon them back.

The war was over, and I went home via Paris, where I took part in a highly popular television program called "Dossiers de l'écran." Every week the program featured a film followed by a debate. That week the film *Exodus* was shown and the debate was devoted to the Six-Day War. The moderator, Armand Jammot, had invited four Arabs (not yet called Palestinians) and four Jews (three of them Israeli), to take part in a dialogue. To our surprise, the Arabs refused to sit at the same table with us, insisting instead on speaking from a neighboring studio. We decided to withdraw from the program in protest, but before leaving, I made a statement which went something like this:

I came to this broadcast without hatred, hoping to reach out. But now I find myself treated like an object.

Tonight my existence as a man is being denied. My Arab fellow guests on this program refuse to talk or listen to me. I find this humiliating and unacceptable, for as a Jew and a writer, I still believe in the power of words.

Tonight I had hoped that human beings on both sides, setting aside feelings of bitterness and injustice, would look at one another and rise above what separates them. I was wrong. And that saddens me.

It saddens me because it reminds me of a time when our enemy turned us into statistics. Even in death, he did not consider us human.

I am prepared to have my opinions challenged, to be accused, or even to be cursed. But I will not tolerate being treated as if I did not exist.

I feel no hatred for the Arabs. I don't

even feel hatred for the Germans. The time has come to put an end to the war in the Middle East. I came here tonight in the hope that we might begin a common struggle against war. That we might take our first steps together, that I might shake hands with men who, like myself, would say "No!" to death and evil. That even though I might look into his eyes with pain and discomfort, together we might denounce the forces that stifle hope. That I might weep with him — why not? — over all the evils and all the punishments we have inflicted on one another.

I am a man alone, alone as are my people. As my people were a month ago, facing threats of annihilation, while no nation came to their aid. Never again will I accept such solitude. If the Arabs agree to see me as a man, I will stay. Otherwise I will leave, for I will not play the game by their rules.

The war in Israel was not over, not really. It simply took other forms: the infiltration of saboteurs and terrorists from Syria and Lebanon; Egyptian artillery fire against the Bar-Lev Line along the Suez Canal; airplane hijackings. Then, six years later, came the Yom Kippur War, followed by Anwar Sadat's visit to Jerusalem, his speech to the Knesset, and the signing of the Camp David Accord. At the White House I shook the hands of Begin, Sadat, and Carter to convince myself I wasn't dreaming. Later, much later, Yitzhak Rabin and Yasir Arafat, in the presence of three thousand guests and millions of television viewers, exchanged handshakes. "Enough war," declared the man who had won the Six-Day War. "Enough tears and funerals!"

In 1968 Paul Flamand brought me to Paris because, as he put it, "There is a chance that you may receive the Prix Médicis" (for *A Beggar in Jerusalem*, the first of my novels dedicated to Marion). As we sat in his office waiting for the jury's decision, we spoke of politics, literature, Israel, America. Paul was impatient. I had never seen him so agitated. He stood up, sat down, telephoned his office. Still nothing. I was tired and jet-lagged, but calm. Unable to contain himself, he exclaimed, "How can you be so calm? Doesn't this prize mean anything to you?" Of course it did. "It would be great to win the Médicis," I told him "but whenever something good happens to me, I remember where I was — now it is twenty-five years ago — and suddenly what seemed so good really isn't anymore. And then again, when something bad happens to me, I also remember the past, and what seemed so painful really isn't." It all depends on your vantage point.

This doesn't mean that I cannot be hurt by

the wickedness of some people or that the respect of others affords me no pleasure. On the contrary, the survivor in me is at once vulnerable and strong. I am stung by the slightest offense, moved by the slightest act of generosity. But looking back on my life is enough to sustain me and keep me true to myself.

The Prix Médicis earned me two important encounters. One was with Marguerite Yourcenar, who had just been awarded the Prix Femina for her *Oeuvre au noir* (published in English as *The Abyss*) and the other with Albert Cohen, whose *Belle du Seigneur* won the French Academy's Grand Prix for fiction.

Marguerite Yourcenar and I met at a booksigning. Sitting side by side, we exchanged memories and observations while writing "best wishes" to definite buyers and possible readers. She spoke little, contemplating as she did the world around her with a skeptically compassionate eye.

This woman whose smile seemed to contain its own secret is a writer whom one cannot read without entering her universe. Her historical novel *Memoirs of Hadrian* is a literary masterpiece that one reads and rereads with both an anticipation and a joy that never cease to renew themselves. It is not a coincidence that she became the first woman to be inducted into the Académie française.

Several times she invited Marion and me to her home in Maine. Out of respect for her privacy, I kept postponing the trip. Then it was too late.

I met Albert Cohen at his apartment in Geneva. Frail, gracious, wrapped in a silk robe, he transported his enchanted visitors to sun-soaked isles peopled with brave characters. I loved listening to his vision of the Prophet Ezekiel, even though I prefer Jeremiah. He was interested in my Hasidic masters and enjoyed talking about them. I remember the mysterious light that shone in his eyes.

I discovered Cohen while reading *Solal*, a grandiose work of fiction with a philosophical sense of humor in which Cohen's imagination carries the reader along toward faraway and mysterious horizons, those of the soul as well as those of destiny. Later on, I devoured *Mangeclous* and *Le Livre de ma mère*. A Sephardic Jew, a romantic and an adventurer searching for absolute love as others chase after absolute truth, Cohen keeps us under his spell to the point that endless readers identify with him.

During this period my relations with Professor Saul Lieberman grew closer and more intense by the week. I studied with him as I had never studied before. The only subject of contention between us was Hasidism. As a good Lithuanian of the school of the Gaon of Vilna, he had remained a Mitnagged, a man of the Establishment and therefore an opponent of Hasidism and its leader, Rabbi Israel Baal Shem Tov, also known as the Besht. He knew little about it except what its original adversaries had said: that Hasidism, founded by ignorant men (beginning with the Besht himself), glorified ignorance. It took me many months to even start to sow seeds of doubt in his mind. First I urged him to read the scholarly works of the Besht's companions, who were great masters. Would they have followed a man who was utterly unknown at the time if he, too, had not been versed in study? Indeed, all of them were Mitnagdim who had "converted" to Hasidism. (There were few instances of Hasidim converting to the opposition.)

Little by little my master accepted the idea that Hasidism and study were not incompatible, that Hasidic tales possessed not only a certain charm but also genuine depth.

He began to attend my 92nd Street Y lectures in which I explored Hasidic teachings through a series of portraits of the movement's founders. He was intrigued by Rabbi Menahem Mendel of Kotzk and liked Rabbi Nahman of Bratslav whose knowledge and original discoveries he admired. A precursor of Franz Kafka, this great master and descendant of masters (he was the Besht's great-grandson) was in my view the greatest storyteller of Hasidic literature. "He was also a scholar, an erudite man, a true *talmid 'hakham,*" said Lieberman. Coming from him, this was a rare compliment.

In his office the day after the Bratslav lecture, when Lieberman treated me to a lecture on my lecture, I realized that he understood the Bratslaver Rebbe better than I did.

As I said, we met at least twice a week. Almost without preliminaries, we would sit down on opposite sides of his desk, the Babylonian and Palestinian Talmuds open before us, along with the corresponding books of commentary. Each session lasted three hours. Some subjects were familiar to me, for I had already studied them, though badly and hastily. That was true even of my studies with Shushani. Shushani was an *ilui,* a genius of immense knowledge, but not a methodical teacher. Only at the end of his presentation would his perspective become clear to his students. Lieberman was an *ilui* too, but also a *harif* and a *baki,* a man whose brain encompasses everything and dissects it before your eyes. He would lead you and excite your imagination, but at every step you knew where he was taking you; at each turn you understood his intent. Where Shushani's teaching was intense but disjointed, Lieberman's was highly structured. With Shushani it was his erudition that fascinated you, while with Lieberman there was that and much more, including the beauty of his reasoning. He showed how everything is linked, how Greek culture and Latin culture are integral to the Talmud, that you could not appreciate the sages of Tzippori if you were ignorant of the ancients of Athens. (He had mastered ancient Greek and Latin and was fluent in French.) Thus, he could read my writings in the original French. He often returned what

I gave him annotated and corrected. Everything I write about the Bible and the Talmud, and even about Hasidism, bears his stamp, including the novels.

When a Hebrew weekly proposed to pay tribute to him, he asked me to introduce him. Naturally, I agreed. I described at some length the impact of his work on the entire field of contemporary Jewish studies and concluded with these words: "I don't know how Professor Lieberman would like to be introduced, but I do know how I would like others to introduce me: as his disciple."

I have always cherished his influence on me. I have only to open a treatise of the Talmud to see his smile and even hear the telephone messages he would sometimes leave for me: "Reb Eliezer, Reb Eliezer, *ve-Torah ma tehe aleha?*" — What shall become of the Torah if we forget to study it?

One Thursday night at the "Y" he saw me with Marion after a lecture. "I'll officiate at your wedding ceremony," he said to me the next day. At the time I didn't know we would marry. He had already understood.

From that moment on he began to discuss practical matters with me. He proposed to confer *smiha* upon me — in other words, to anoint me a rabbi. "That way if your books don't sell, you'll have a job and a source of income." It was the only time I ever said no to him. I refused, telling him I wasn't cut out for a career as a rabbi. "Neither am I," he replied with the sly little laugh I knew so well.

It was thanks to him that I met, often at his home, the great Israeli and American Talmudic scholars. Many of them possessed such vast learning that I felt intimidated by them and I rarely participated in their discussions, choosing rather to listen.

Gershom Scholem, founding father of modern mystical studies, was among his close friends. They were bound by complex relations. It was said that Scholem feared Lieberman, as did much of the Jewish academic world. Perhaps he only showed him special respect.

Scholem was tall and thin, a tense man with restless eyes, immense ears, and flaring nostrils. He looked like a warrior ready for battle, prepared to repel evil, be it Satan, a false Messiah, or a false prophet. He was deeply involved in the eternal struggle between the forces of Good and Evil, the Sons of Light and of Darkness. I admired the breadth of his knowledge and his boundless curiosity. He was eager to integrate every newly acquired piece of knowledge into a system whose key was Jewish mysticism. His works go beyond commentary, for he was a discoverer and an innovator. Today it is impossible to broach the mysterious, enchanting world of the Kabala without reading Scholem. His masterly book on the false Messiah Shabbatai Tzevi reads like a thriller as does his monograph on Jacob Frank, another false Messiah. Despite their complexity, his essays on the origins of Lurianic mysticism and of the Gerona school are so illuminating that they make these texts not only accessible but absorbing.

At our very first meeting, at the home of Norman Podhoretz, editor in chief of *Commentary*, he talked to me about my native town as though it had been his own. He knew every street and every house. When he saw how astonished I was, he explained, "No, I've never set foot in your Sighet. But I know things about it you're probably not even aware of. Did you know there was a strong Frankist sect there?" I didn't. Frankists were disciples of Jacob Frank, who flouted the fundamental laws of Judaism in an effort to hasten ultimate deliverance. They were men and women who led a secret life of debauchery. Adultery and incest in Sighet? I knew he savored my disarray, but he didn't show it. "Frankist writings were found in the walls of a collapsed building," he explained, looking mischievous. "Collective confessions and litanies."

On the first day of Passover, which was also the day after our wedding, Marion and I visited him in his apartment in Jerusalem. I loved asking him questions about the forbidden memories of my city. Fania, who had been his pupil and now was his wife, took part in the conversation. You could sense the strong bond between them. We spoke of Martin Buber, and I asked Scholem why he had waited until the philosopher was very old before demolishing his ideas in a stunning essay. "Should I have waited till after his death?" he asked, clearly taken aback. He hadn't understood that I meant why hadn't he published his critique when Buber was still young and capable of responding to the attack.

Lieberman didn't hesitate to discuss his complicated relations with Scholem. How could a rationalist and a scholar of mysticism get along so well? I had heard the following anecdote, whose authenticity Lieberman confirmed. Invited to deliver a lecture at the Jewish Theological Seminary, Scholem was introduced to an audience composed of New York's intellectual elite by the seminary's prestigious rector, Professor Lieberman. "Ladies and gentlemen, you surely know of Professor Gershom Scholem, who holds the chair of mysticism at the Hebrew University of Jerusalem. What, then, is mysticism?" He paused, then added gravely, "Mysticism is . . . nonsense." The audience was stunned. People looked at one another. Lieberman waited for the shock to subside, then he went on. "Ladies and gentlemen, nonsense is nonsense, but the history of nonsense is scholarship."

Lieberman attracted students even while imposing distance and respect. Everyone had to stand when he came in. They say his students feared him, and it's true. In class he was fierce and demanding. Though he lightened the atmosphere with his humor, his students, most of them future rabbis, trembled before him, wondering how they would get through the reading of the daily passage from the Torah. He never raised his voice, never lost his temper. He could be charming, even soothing, but he had his intractable side. One evening one of the future rabbis ran into him in the elevator. He had an appointment for a final exam. (Lieberman's exams usually took place late at night.) On the elevator they chatted about this and that, then walked to the door of Lieberman's office, where the professor said, "Good night."

"But what about the exam?" the student stammered.

"Knowledge may take a long time to measure," Lieberman replied, "but ignorance does not." Usually he was more merciful. Could it be that he was not aware of the terror he inspired? I believe he was, though we talked about it only once, on a flight to Israel.

When Lieberman lost his wife, we became even closer. He asked me to speak at her funeral service at the Jewish Theological Seminary, and of course I agreed. When I asked where the *shiva,* the week-long mourning period, would be observed, he told me he was taking Judith to Jerusalem for burial. I then asked who from the Seminary faculty would be going with him, and he said he was going alone. "In that case, I'm coming with you," I said. At that he burst into tears. It was a tragic moment that clarified the relations between us: he was my master, but I was not only his disciple but his friend.

I will never forget that flight, which lasted fourteen hours. He told me of his childhood in Motele, his adolescence spent in the yeshiva of Slobodka, the center of the Musar movement, his experiences in Palestine, and his encounters with modern masters. Throughout the journey he mingled anecdotes, Talmudic findings, and intimate thoughts.

I was silent about my friendship with his Seminary colleague Dr. Abraham Joshua Heschel, the distinguished descendant of the Rebbe of Apt, a leader in Hasidism. Heschel and I fought for many of the same social causes. But he and Lieberman did not get along. In fact, they were not even on speaking terms. Was it still the old quarrel between the Mitnagdim and Hasidim? Or was there another explanation? I was told they had once been inseparable. What had changed? I never found out.

Which leads me to a funny story from before my marriage:

After the Simchat Torah festival Lieberman asked me where I planned to celebrate Purim. I told him it was too early to make such plans. Still, he invited me to spend Purim at his home. The winter passed, and one day Heschel phoned to invite me to the Purim meal. "Sorry," I stammered, "but that won't be possible. . . ." I couldn't tell him why. Heschel insisted, but finally said: "In that case, I'll go to my cousin's, the Kapitsinitser Rebbe in Brooklyn." That suited me fine. Lieberman and

Heschel lived in the same building on Riverside Drive, and if Heschel spent the evening in Brooklyn, I wouldn't have to worry about accidentally running into him. On the night of Purim, a bottle of vodka in hand, I pushed the elevator button, and when the door opened, out came Heschel and his wife, Sylvia. "What are you doing here?" he asked in what I took to be sincere astonishment. I replied without hesitation: "I came to bring you a Purim gift." I handed him the bottle. He asked how I knew he was home. "I didn't," I said. "I was going to leave it at your door." Why not with the super? "Well, I didn't trust him. This vodka is too good."

"Oh," said Heschel, "then let's go up and have a drink." Since I couldn't confess that I was expected at Lieberman's, I made something up. (On Purim you're allowed to tell a lie.) "Sorry," I said. "I am late for my appointment and I must go home first." Heschel insisted that since I was already there, we might as well raise a glass in honor of the holiday. Rather than argue, I went upstairs with them. He opened the bottle, and we had a drink; I was on pins and needles, but Heschel took his time — and mine — sitting in his armchair talking about memories of Purim back in Poland and chanting half-forgotten Hasidic tunes. I kept stealing glances at my watch; I was already late. Finally, we left and Heschel offered me a ride home. I told him I preferred to walk. "Out of the question," he said. So he drove me home. I waited three long minutes and went back out, looking for an open liquor store. I bought a second bottle of vodka, hailed a cab, and hurried back to the same building, the same elevator.

Lieberman was too polite to ask why I was late. I took my place at the table. Among the guests were the great names of the city's Talmudic and cultural community. The conversation was brilliant and lively. I listened in silence. The meal ended at about four in the morning, which is not unusual on Purim, and when I got to the elevator I hesitated, wondering if I ought to take the stairs. But the elevator was on its way up; the door was about to open. I prayed to God to spare me fresh embarrassment, and my prayer was answered. It was empty. Another prayer was answered downstairs. There was no one in the street. God is great. Now all I had to do was hail a cab, and here was one now. It slowed, came to a stop, and a smiling Heschel got out. "See?" he said. "I knew you were waiting for a taxi."

A week before Passover, 1983, my old friend Rabbi Wolfe Kelman phoned me. I could tell by his voice that he had bad news. I was stunned, but somehow not surprised. "Blessed be the Judge of Truth," I murmured. "It happened on the plane to Israel," Wolfe said. I felt lost. A moment later the historian Yosef Yerushalmi called. "I have sad —" he began, but I told him I knew. "He died in his sleep," Yerushalmi added. "The funeral will take place in a few hours. It will be impossible for you to get there in time."

As I said, I wasn't surprised. Lieberman had acted strangely when I saw him last. At the end of our lesson he had stood up and embraced me. He was to leave that afternoon for Jerusalem, to celebrate Passover with his older brother. I was in a hurry. I was giving a lecture at Yale that afternoon. He walked me to the door, but suddenly exclaimed, "Would you like to come back, Reb Eliezer?" We went back and reimmersed ourselves in study. I remember the passage: It was the one about an anonymous corpse discovered in a public place. The Law demands that the community elders expiate with a sacrifice. My master's commentary on assigning the blame: They allowed a lone visitor to depart without protection. Never was Lieberman more brilliant than on that day. He was inspired by Palestinian sages, and by his adored Radak, the Gaon of Vilna.

An hour went by. Once again he accompanied me to the hallway, we embraced, and I got into the elevator, but my friend and master took me by the arm and said, "We still have time, Reb Eliezer, don't we still have time?" We went back to his desk, took our places, and opened the Talmud for another hour. It was by then one o'clock in the afternoon. This time no delay was possible. I left with a heavy heart, for during the lesson I had noticed that his desk, always

703

strewn with books, magazines, and papers, was entirely clear. This unprecedented fact brought another image to my mind.

One morning, years before, Heschel had phoned me. He needed me urgently. I jumped in a cab and rushed to the Seminary. Heschel opened his door and, without saying a word, leaned his head on my shoulder and began to sob like a child. Rarely have I seen an adult cry like that. Still standing in the doorway, I noticed that his ordinarily messy table was neatly arranged. We parted without exchanging a word. Heschel died the next day. Now Lieberman's table was clear too.

The Talmud tells us that the Righteous are warned of their impending death, to allow them to put their affairs in order. Heschel and Lieberman, each in his own way, surely were among the Righteous.

I miss Lieberman. I miss my master. And I have come to fully understand the Talmudic law that says a man must mourn his master as he mourns his parents. When a master departs, his disciples are orphans.

Curiously, Lieberman and I never discussed faith. He never lectured me on the subject, never demanded a stricter observance of the Halachah, the Law. He understood my problems in this domain. It was with Menahem-Mendel Schneerson, the Lubavitcher Rebbe, that I discussed them.

I speak of this in *The Gates of the Forest,*

as I describe a Hasidic celebration in Brooklyn. It was his celebration. The songs, vows, and fervor of the faithful were such that I felt as if I were with my own rebbe, back in my hometown.

The spiritual power emanating from the person of Rebbe Menahem-Mendel Schneersohn of Lubavitch was impressive. He was like a sovereign who made it possible for his subjects to live and work in peace. When he spoke, the crowd held its breath; when he sang, all their souls sang with him. Whatever he asked for, he obtained. Few contemporary Hasidic masters have had such authority. His disciples can be found on all five continents. Sometimes he would summon a young rabbinical student and tell him he was about to be sent here or there to help a Jewish community. And without the slightest discussion or consideration of any practical matter, the student would take his family and go.

The Rebbe's faithful constantly paid tribute to his erudition. They gloried in his holiness, in his powers, and in his organizational and educational talents. It was said that he had studied science at the Sorbonne and philosophy at Heidelberg, and that he spoke six languages fluently. Some followers even believed he possessed supernatural gifts.

My first visit to his court lasted almost an entire night. I had informed him at the outset that I was a Hasid of Wizhnitz, not Lubavitch, and that I had no intention of switching allegiance. "The important thing is to be a Hasid," he replied. "It matters little whose." We then changed the subject. The Rebbe had read some of my works in French and asked me to explain why I was angry at God. "Because I loved Him too much," I replied. "And now?" he asked. "Now too. And because I love Him, I am angry at Him." The Rebbe disagreed: "To love God is to accept that you do not understand Him." I asked whether one could love God without having faith. He told me faith had to precede all the rest. "Rebbe," I asked, "how can you believe in God after Auschwitz?" He looked at me in silence for a long moment, his hands resting on the table. Then he replied, in a soft, barely audible voice, "How can you not believe in God after Auschwitz?" Whom else could one believe in? Hadn't man abdicated his privileges and duties? Didn't Auschwitz represent the defeat of humanity? Apart from God, what was there in a world darkened by Auschwitz? The Rebbe stared at me, awaiting my response. I hesitated before answering, "Rebbe, if what you say is meant as an answer to my question, I reject it. But if it is a question — one more question — I accept it." I tried to smile, but failed.

Our dialogue continued for years. After the publication of each of my books, he would write to me with his commentaries. He wanted me to write about the life and teachings of the first Rebbe of Lubavitch, Rabbi Shneur Zalman of

Ladi, author of the *Tanya*. I am still working on it.

One year, during Simchat Torah, I visited Lubavitch, as was my custom. The Rebbe, seated in his place at the head of a T-shaped table, presided over the celebration with fervor. He was surrounded by dignitaries, but as a sign of respect the chairs to his immediate left and right had been left vacant. I stood at the entrance, in my raincoat and Basque beret, plagued by a terrible migraine. Had anyone paid any attention to me, they would have thought I was an observer from the outside, possibly a spy, an intruder, unable to comprehend the nature of Hasidic joy. But, luckily, everyone was looking at the Rabbi.

Suddenly the Rebbe saw me and beckoned me to approach. I pretended not to notice. The Rebbe motioned to me again. I didn't budge. Then he called me by name. When I still didn't move, powerful arms grabbed me and carried me over the heads of the crowd to the central table, depositing me like a package in front of the Rebbe. I wanted to die then and there if only I could do so without disturbing the celebration. The Rebbe was smiling. Would he tease me instead of coming to my aid?

"Welcome," he said. "It's nice of a Hasid of Wizhnitz to come and greet us in Lubavitch. But is this how they celebrate Simchat Torah in Wizhnitz?"

"Rebbe," I said faintly, "we are not in

Wizhnitz but in Lubavitch."

"Then do as we do in Lubavitch," he said.

"And what do you do in Lubavitch?"

"In Lubavitch we drink and say *lehayim,* to life."

"In Wizhnitz too."

"Very well. Then say *lehayim.*"

He handed me a glass filled to the brim with vodka.

"Rebbe," I said, "in Wizhnitz a Hasid does not drink alone."

"Nor in Lubavitch," the Rebbe replied. He emptied his glass in one gulp. I followed suit.

"Is one enough in Wizhnitz?" the Rebbe asked.

"In Wizhnitz," I said bravely, "one is but a drop in the sea."

"In Lubavitch as well."

He handed me a second glass and refilled his own. He said *lehayim,* I replied *lehayim,* and we emptied our glasses. After all, I had to uphold the honor of Wizhnitz. But as I was unaccustomed to drink, I felt my head begin to spin. I was not sure where or who I was, nor why I had come to this place, why I had been drawn into this strange scene. My brain was on fire.

"In Lubavitch we do not stop midway," the Rebbe said. "We continue. And in Wizhnitz?"

"In Wizhnitz too," I said, "we go all the way."

The Rebbe struck a solemn pose. He handed me a third glass and refilled his own. My hand trembled; his did not. "You deserve a blessing," he said, his face beaming with happiness. "Name it!"

I wasn't sure what to say. I was, in fact, in a stupor.

"Would you like me to bless you so you can begin again?"

Drunk as I was, I appreciated his wisdom. To begin again could mean many things: begin again to drink, to pray, to believe, to live. And then it was Simchat Torah, which is also my birthday.

"Yes, Rebbe," I said. "Give me your blessing."

He blessed me and downed his vodka. I swallowed mine — and passed out. I awoke outside, stretched out on the grass, where I had been carried, again, by the same arms, above the heads of the crowd. Several paces away a young Hasid was offering a dozen or so men an eloquent explanation of the "profound" aspect, the mystical significance, of my exchange with the Rebbe.

One day the Rebbe sent me a long letter about my attitude toward God. It concluded: "But now let us leave theology and speak of a personal matter. Why aren't you married yet?"

On the day of our wedding Marion and I received a superb bouquet with a card bearing his signature and his blessings. He sent us an even more beautiful bouquet the day of our son's circumcision ceremony.

After my trip to the USSR I visited the Rebbe

regularly to discuss with him the situation of Soviet Jews. I shared with him my frustration at the passivity and silence of the Jewish community. To my surprise, he justified that approach. He preferred silent diplomacy — a pity.

Also regrettable were the excesses to which their love and admiration for him drove his followers. They believed that he was capable of modifying laws of nature, that he had cured some of cancer, saved others from ruin. The same had been said before, about earlier masters, many of whom were famous for their miracles. If their followers felt the need to believe in their gifts, that was their business. But among the faithful of the Lubavitcher Rebbe were some who saw him as the Messiah. In February 1993 they even crowned him "King and Savior." I found their attitude dangerous. Had they forgotten Shabbatai Tzevi, the false messiah of the seventeenth century? Whenever a community raises a man to the rank of messiah, it inevitably condemns itself to shattered hopes. I begged influential followers of the movement to halt this campaign because it was harming the Rebbe, who was too ill to defend himself.

On the rainy afternoon of June 12, 1994, I stood in the crowd of mourners surrounding his casket on Eastern Parkway in Brooklyn. Tens of thousands of men and women, some of whom had come from Europe and Israel, recited psalms as they accompanied him for the last time. Weeping children and adolescents lined the avenue. I thought of my encounters with the Rebbe, his solemn smile, his piercing blue eyes, the way he sang and made others sing. The last time I saw him he had asked me why I still hadn't written a book on the founder of his movement. And he had given me a blessing for Marion and for our son Elisha. There had been huge signs on the walls of neighboring houses: "Long live our Master and Teacher and King, the Messiah."

In 1968, preoccupied with the tragedy and courage of Soviet Jews, I looked for ways to aid them more effectively. I discussed the matter with a filmmaker friend, Hy Kalus, an American who had become Israeli, a redhead who radiated creative energy. To my question — What else can I do? — he replied without hesitation: "What about the theater? Why don't you write a play?" I protested that I had never written for the stage, that I had no idea how to go about it. But Hy insisted: "Try it. What do you have to lose?"

So I tried, in secret. My subject was the solitude of Soviet Jews; my main character, the chief rabbi of Moscow, Reb Yehuda-Leib Levin.

The rabbi was a tall, robust man with a graying beard and moustache and eyes that mirrored a boundless weariness bordering on resignation. During our first encounter — on the night of Kippur in 1965 — I sat at his left on the *bima* (dais) with Israeli and foreign diplomats. I didn't dare speak to him. At that time it would have been dangerous for him. There were undoubtedly many informers in the assembly. But I couldn't take my eyes off him. The following year I saw him again, once more on the *bima,* for the solemn Kol Nidre ceremony. He recognized me and smiled as he shook my hand. Perhaps it was his way of thanking me for not having forgotten him, for having come back.

As I looked at him, I suddenly realized that he had an obligation to break the silence that had stifled his community for decades. He had to break free, to let his rage explode. In the presence of this community of thousands of Jews, he had to reveal what had secretly tormented him, the price that the oppressor had extorted from our battered people. I stared at him intently, silently imploring him: "Have courage, Rebbe! Lift your head! Stand up, stop being a martyr! Raise your fist and bang it on the pulpit, interrupt the service and cry out, shout that the Jewish faith is threatened here, that it is scorned and imprisoned. Do it, Rebbe, and you will become a living legend, a hero of Israel."

Unfortunately, the chief rabbi of Moscow was exhausted. Having lived — excuse me, survived — so long under Communist rule, he no longer had the strength to raise his voice in protest. At the time and in the weeks that followed, I felt sorry for him, and for his community. I pitied him for being unable to fulfill the mission no one else but he could have undertaken: to

712

overcome submission and fear.

As I pondered the play I now wanted to write, the tormented, resigned countenance of the chief rabbi came to mind. Malraux argued that it is literature's task to redress injustice. Well, in my play I would seek to correct the injustice done to Rabbi Levin: on stage I would allow him to do what he never dared do. That would be my theme.

Since I always need a madman to enliven my fictional landscape, I confronted the rabbi with a madman, whom I called Zalmen. (In the buried chronicles of the Sonderkommandos I later learned about two astonishing men, both named Zalmen.) His role was to act as a catalyst to the rabbi, urging and inciting him to go mad on the evening of Kippur, to hurl the truth of his suffering into the face of an indifferent, complacent, and complicitous world.

I needed a female presence in the play, and so I gave the rabbi a daughter, Nina, thirty or forty years old. She needed a husband, and I chose for her Alexei, a Communist Jew, more Communist than Jew, who would be the rabbi's counterpoint. The couple had to have a child, so I gave them a son, Misha, twelve years old. When his grandfather asks whether he is preparing for his bar mitzvah, Misha replies, "What's a bar mitzvah?" That would be Zalmen's moment of triumph: "You see, Rabbi?" he would shout. "Your line is disappearing. Go mad, I tell you! Turn your truth into a cry! It's your only chance — and mine, and your little grandson's too! Your future and our people's depend on you and you alone!"

Other themes involved the mystery of Jewish survival, the role of memory, the metaphysical aspect of laughter, the limits of coexistence and collaboration, and the potential impact of one solitary act. What price resistance? How far may one bend? In the end the rabbi does go mad. He cries out his truth, but it is all for naught.

I worked on the play full-time, thrilled at having discovered a new medium. Hy Kalus's assistance was valuable. I also received help from Marion, who had studied drama and knew instantly when a line of dialogue seemed contrived or rang false.

After a few false starts René Jentet, a producer and talented director, accepted the manuscript for France-Culture radio. A private reading that included our friend the actor Joseph Wiseman was organized in New York at the apartment of Lily and Nathan Edelman near Columbia University. Wiseman showed *Zalmen* to his American producer and director friends. It was fortunate that Alan Schneider, director of plays by Beckett and Albee, found it to his liking. He spoke to Zelda Fichandler of the prestigious Arena Stage in Washington, who accepted it. Aided by Marion, who by now was my wife, Alan staged a polished, moving production whose reception was all we could have hoped for. Mel Gussow, after mentioning in *The New*

York Times my having said I would not write for the stage again, commented that he hoped I would change my mind. PBS, the Public Broadcasting System, decided to film the play for prime-time television. Irving Bernstein, who was at that time executive director of the UJA, decided to preview the production at his organization's annual congress — at Carnegie Hall.

Bernstein insisted I introduce the program. My brief presentation was entitled "A Song of Songs for Russian Jewry." After the film I hurried home for Shabbat. On my desk I found a letter from a woman in Brooklyn: "My name is Rivka, and I am the daughter of the chief rabbi of Moscow." She said she wanted to meet me. I was amazed, for I had no idea Rabbi Levin had a daughter. I reread the letter several times, then picked up the phone to call her, but it was too late. It seems Shabbat comes to Brooklyn earlier than to Manhattan. I would have to wait more than twenty-four hours. Pious Jews would not answer their telephone until Saturday evening.

When the requisite three stars appeared in the frigid, gray-white sky that Saturday night, I called Brooklyn immediately. The phone rang and rang. No answer. I tried again. No luck. I dialed the number five times in succession. At last a human voice responded, a man. "Yes?" "May I speak to Rivka?" I blurted out. He asked who I was, and I told him. He voice hesitated briefly. "Are you sure she wants to talk to you?" "Yes, I have a letter from her right here in front of me. . . ." Finally, the voice said, "Okay, take it easy." I heard the man shout her name — and at last the chief rabbi's daughter was on the line. She confirmed her wish to meet me, and I told her it was mutual. "How about this evening?" I suggested. Impossible. Tomorrow afternoon was the earliest.

She turns out to be about forty — like my Nina. She was dark, with a sad face — like my Nina. She was accompanied by a relative; a pious Jewish woman must not be alone with a man. We chatted. I tried not to show it, but my impatience got the better of me: "Tell me," I asked, "have you seen my play?" She then gave me a lesson in humility. "Play?" Rivka asked, her eyes wide. "What play? I don't know what you're talking about." I was stunned. "You didn't know I wrote a play about you, a play that has been staged in Washington and is going to be on television?" Looking somewhat annoyed, she shook her head as if to reprimand me. "Last Friday you didn't know I existed, and now you say you've written a play about me?" "Then why did you want to see me?" I asked. She answered without hesitation: "I read some of your works in samizdat, including the one about Russian Jews in which you mention my father. Do you remember him? Well, one day, when he was already quite old and sick, he called me in Odessa, where I worked as a dentist. He asked me to come to Moscow, said he needed me urgently. I left my husband and children and hurried to him. My poor father was very pale. He knew he was dying, and he wanted to tell me his last wish: 'Rivka,' he said, 'promise me you'll make sure your children grow up Jewish. I know you can't do that here, so I want you to go to Israel. If that's not possible, then go to New York, to Brooklyn.' Naturally, I promised. He insisted I swear it. Those were his last words: 'Swear it!' Of course, I want to keep my promise. But it isn't easy. My husband . . . you see . . . he's Jewish . . . of course . . . but to be Jewish annoys him . . . being Jewish bothers him . . ."

I felt like shouting: "Just like my Alexei, like Alexei in the play." But I didn't. I just listened.

". . . and he refused to raise our children in the Jewish tradition. It was impossible to convince him, he just wouldn't bend. Our children would be Communists like him, he said. Nonbelievers, atheists . . . I argued, wept, reminded him of my oath. In vain. We grew farther and farther apart until we fought day and night. The endless disputes finally wore me down, and I decided to get a divorce and to go to Israel with my children. Only my husband wouldn't let me take my son. My two daughters, yes. They left with me. One married in Israel, the other will soon marry a Lubavitch Hasid in Brooklyn."

Guessing what was coming next, I felt a lump

in my throat. "And your son?" She lowered her voice. "My son stayed with my husband."

Disturbed by the resemblance between this boy's fate and young Misha's in *Zalmen*, I remembered that when I had created the character, I couldn't decide on his future. Should I give him to his Communist father? I didn't have the heart to take him away from our people. Give him to his grandfather, the chief rabbi? I don't like sentimental endings. As I was uncertain, I left the conclusion vague, ambiguous. Let the audience decide Misha's fate. But now I had heard it from his own mother's mouth: Misha would not be a Jew. Softly, I asked Rivka: "How old is your son?" She seemed taken aback by the intensity or my voice. "Today? He was thirteen a few months ago." Perhaps she guessed my next question, for she told me: "To my great sorrow, he was not bar-mitzvahed. You see, his father was violently opposed."

A special bond developed between us, as if I had somehow become a member of her fractured family, perhaps because we shared a nostalgia for our lost past. Or perhaps she was grateful to me for having guessed the secrets of her life. In January, after seeing *Zalmen* on television, she sent me a warm letter: "I wept throughout the broadcast, telling myself over and over that's exactly how it was, exactly how it happened." Then she returned to Israel.

Many months later I got a call from a rabbi in the New York metropolitan area. "I know you like stories," he said, "especially stories about Russian Jews, and I've got one I'm sure you'll appreciate." I invited him over that same day. "You won't believe what just happened to me," he began. "Last week I was in Israel," he went on, very excited. "First in Tel Aviv and then Jerusalem, where I have family . . ." Sensing my impatience, he quickly came to the point. A friend of his who worked for the government took him to Masada, the fortress where, according to Flavius Josephus, Judea's last surviving insurgents decided to kill themselves rather than surrender to the Romans. "That day," the rabbi said, "I had the privilege of attending a remarkable ceremony there. About thirty war orphans were bar-mitzvahed under the direction of a military chaplain. When I was introduced to the chaplain, I expressed my astonishment that there were so many children whose fathers had fallen in combat. Yes, he said, the cruel consequences of human folly were indeed hard to bear. Then his face brightened. He pointed to a boy in the front row. 'But take a good look at him,' he said. 'That boy is not a war orphan but the grandson of the late chief rabbi of Moscow.' I thought I should tell you. . . ." I must have turned pale because the rabbi asked if I was all right. I felt like showering him with gifts and screaming at him at the same time. He had just shown me, once again, that a Jewish writer works under a handicap: He cannot invent anything.

Zalmen was performed in many theaters in Europe and the United States. The play contains two particularly painful monologues. In one the old rabbi, having gone "mad," pleads with Western Jews not to forget their Russian brothers:

"I say and I proclaim that it is more than we can bear! You, our brothers who see us now, hear the last cries of a shattered community! To you I say: The sparks are dying and our heritage and our very destiny are covered with dust. Broken are the wings of the eagle, the lion is ill. . . . And know this, brothers . . . that so much silence is breaking my heart, that hope has deserted me. Know it is more than I can bear, it is more than I can bear."

In the other the inspector (a KGB commissar) informs the shattered old man that his daring, mad revolt was in vain, that his sacrifice has been rejected:

"Poor hero, poor dreamer. You have lost, and I feel sorry for you; you have fought for nothing. Your offering was not accepted. Worse — it wasn't even noticed. How could you have been so naïve? Did you really — really — believe that your gesture would shake the earth? . . . In your imagination you saw Jews marching in the streets of Paris, London, New York, and Jerusalem, shouting that you here are not alone? You thought their anger would explode and shatter human conscience? Well, it's too bad. Your Jews have their own concerns. . . ."

The inspector's speech is hard and cruel. He reminds the rabbi that even during the war, when

". . . day after day, night after night, hundreds of thousands were disappearing into mass graves or burning to cinders . . . holidays were celebrated; charity balls and dinners were organized; people went to concerts, to the theater. . . . Everything went on as if nothing were happening. And today? Life goes on. And those who don't suffer refuse to hear about suffering — and particularly about Jewish suffering."

I often think about that speech when participating in demonstrations in support of persecuted Jews anywhere, and I tell myself the inspector was wrong. In the play the aged rabbi's cry is heard. All the characters undergo a metamorphosis in the second act; even his adversaries rally to him. And yes, a man's desperate cry is never lost. The sacrifices of the Soviet Jews were not in vain. As I write these lines, thousands of them are landing at Lod Airport. If they were released, it was thanks in part to people like Rivka's father, who, before he died, shared with his daughter his conviction that a Jew's honor is linked to his Jewishness.

Of all the productions of *Zalmen*, it was the one in Tel Aviv that proved most disappointing, nearly causing a break between my old friend Dov and me. It also marked a turning point in my relations with certain Israelis.

Until then I had been quite kindly regarded. I had friends in the establishment and the opposition alike. I tried not to take sides in the political quarrels that have always divided the Israeli nation and the Jewish people at large. My news reports and articles on cultural affairs were greeted positively, my books favorably reviewed in the press. At *Yedioth Ahronoth* my colleagues wondered whether I had any enemies at all. In time this would change, and the first sign of that change came with the production of *Zalmen*.

It all began with a proposal from the director of Habimah, the National Theater, who came up to our table in the restaurant at the King David Hotel in Jerusalem, introduced himself, and shared with us his indignation. "I just got back from Germany, where I saw a performance of *Zalmen*. An outrage." I asked him politely what exactly he was talking about. "Your play should have had its world premiere here in Israel and nowhere else," he declared. Then he pulled up a chair, but seemed even more unhappy sitting down. Marion and I listened in silence, wondering whether we should tell him we didn't even know the play had been staged in Germany. I waited for him to come up for air and then told him how sorry I was to see him so unhappy on my account. "I would like to buy the rights to your play," he said. I replied that the rights belonged to my French publisher, Le Seuil, and that he should get in touch with them. He made a note of the name, address, and phone number. "It is high time," he then solemnly announced, "for *Zalmen* to come home to live among his own people."

Back in New York we thought no more about it. The world of the theater is full of promises and illusions, and I knew enough not to take this kind of commitment seriously. That was my first mistake. Some six or eight months later Le Seuil informed me that Habimah was interested in the rights to *Zalmen*. In fact, the letter said, it seemed I had already agreed. I immediately corrected that impression: I had agreed to nothing. Next came a phone call from Tel Aviv. The director of the National Theater appealed to my kind Jewish heart and to my love of Israel: it was absolutely essential that *Zalmen* open the season. After all, the play was about Soviet Jews, and was there any cause more sacred to me than the struggle for their freedom? In fact, the director remarked, rehearsals were about to begin. I protested that he had no right to stage the play before a contract was signed, that Le Seuil could sue him. Not to worry, he said, agents and lawyers would take care of the contract. The purpose of his call was simply to assure me that he intended to use only the best talents and that the play's integrity would be scrupulously respected: Not a word would be added, not a word deleted. His passion and energy persuaded me to yield, especially since he promised to invite me to Tel Aviv in a few weeks to attend the initial rehearsals and correct any small, if unlikely, mistakes. A week went by, then a month, then two months, and we heard nothing more from him. Then, one day, there was another phone call from the director, inviting me to the premiere. This time I lost my temper. "What premiere?" I asked.

"The premiere of your play, of course."

"When is it scheduled for?"

"A week from now."

"In other words, you held rehearsals and plan to open without a signed contract?"

He was unflappable. The contract, he said, had been duly signed; his agent had convinced Le Seuil that I had agreed. "You're wrong to react like this," he said. "It's going to be a huge success." I should come, and see for myself that I had not been betrayed. Yes, a few changes had been made, but they were minor. "What changes?" I asked, sensing catastrophe. He repeated that they were minor. Now I was getting annoyed. "Such as?" Well, Joseph Milo, the great director, had been replaced. What else? The starring role would be played not by Aharon

Meskin, at that time Israel's greatest actor, but by someone less well known. Was that it? Well, he said, the title had been changed; he preferred *The Jews of Silence*. Here I blew up: "That's the title of another book!" If he had dared change the title, I feared the worst. And indeed, he had also cut a few passages here and added a few there. "As I told you, aside from these details, we've made no changes in your play." I told him that I forbade him to stage the play and that if he did anyway, I would see him in court. And I hung up.

I alerted Le Seuil. The person in charge of foreign rights was dumbfounded. "What signed contract? Signed where? By whom? We never signed anything." I was furious. "We must stop this production *before* the premiere," I said. A threatening telegram was dispatched immediately, and the reaction was swift. The director was on the line again, informing me that I could not do "such things" in Israel: What would the Israelis say, what would the Soviets say, and what about the anti-Semites? Had I thought about that? My reply was brief. He had lied to me, and I don't like dealing with liars. Now he started whining. What was he supposed to do? The premiere was scheduled for this week. Prime Minister Golda Meir had announced she would attend; diplomats, members of the academy, politicians, and journalists would be there too. It would be a scandal for the state of Israel, for the people of Israel. I refused to budge. Another call soon came in from Jerusalem: a famous writer pleading Habimah's cause. "He shouldn't have lied to me," I replied. The next call was from the poet Haim Guri. I gave him the same reply. Then a Labor member of the Knesset called, followed by a colleague. You would think the state of Israel had nothing more important to worry about. Then someone called on behalf of Golda. At that point I gave up. They had worn me down, and yes, I had to concede: to file a lawsuit against the National Theater of Israel would not be pleasant.

With the exception of Dr. Haim Gamzu, the critic of the largest morning daily, *Haaretz*, nearly everyone panned the performance. They were right. And I was wrong to quarrel with Dov, whom I chided for publishing a review by the *Yedioth* critic that did not mention my disagreement with the director and the whole sad saga of the production. But, to my great surprise, the play was a commercial success, a sellout. One month later, when I decided to see the show incognito, a friend of mine had to pull strings to get me a (paid) seat in the second balcony. The performance that evening was held in the presence of the minister of foreign affairs, Abba Eban.

But what I saw on that stage went beyond my worst fears. My play had become an incoherent, sentimental mess, complete with ethnic dances, the sounding of the shofar, and a

Kaddish. It was pure kitsch.

But the audience loved it. They applauded and wept. I found that intolerable. I paid a visit to Golda, who failed to understand my indignation. The play was doing well, what was I complaining about? Besides which, she thought I should be delighted to have succeeded. It was a public relations coup: Everyone was talking about Soviet Jews. "Sit back and enjoy it," she advised me. Determined at least to explain my position, I went on television and asked, among other questions, whether those in charge of Habimah would have acted in such a cavalier way had I not been a Jew devoted to, and an unconditional defender of, Israel? I said that I considered the production a betrayal, and I appealed to the public to boycott it. The play was withdrawn a few weeks later.

The entire incident left me troubled and sad, especially since it had an unpleasant sequel. While *Zalmen* was being performed in Tel Aviv, a man who claimed to have been an aide to the late prime minister Eshkol asked me to support an Israeli committee for Russian Jewish intellectuals. He wanted me to introduce him to rich people. I replied, politely, that I did not do fund-raising, not even for Russian Jews or Israel. But he was so insistent that in the end I made him an offer: Just as the proceeds from the American production had been donated to the New York Conference on Soviet Jews, so all the proceeds from the Israeli production would go to his committee. I told him I would so instruct Le Seuil that very day. For months thereafter he called me from Jerusalem two or three times a week: "Le Seuil's check still hasn't arrived. It's outrageous!" Though it did take time, he eventually collected quite a hefty sum. I expected a word of thanks, which never came. The same was true of a certain New York organization: it received the royalties and forgot to say thank you.

Let me backtrack a little, for I have not yet spoken of the events that marked the 1960s: the war in Vietnam, the beginnings of ecumenicism, the Prague Spring, the May '68 riots in France. All these events brought about changes in our sensibilities, in our way of looking at the world and at our responsibility for it.

The Chicago Seven in the United States, with Abbie Hoffman and Jerry Rubin; Daniel Cohn-Bendit and his slogan "We are all German Jews" in France; the occupation of the Sorbonne; Columbia University students clashing with the police, demanding change. There were those who viewed the revolt of youth as signifying a thirst for transcendent truth and justice. I happened to be in France in May of 1968, and I loved the students' mixture of combativeness and generosity. Some of the slogans were wonderful: "Power to the imagination," "It is forbidden to forbid," *"Changer la vie."* I was less appreciative of slogans such as "CRS = SS?" (the

CRS is the French state police). To compare the French police to the SS was not only historically inaccurate and politically outrageous, but in thoroughly bad taste. It was not entirely the students' fault. The philosophy of '68 was linked to the Occupation and the Resistance. Listening to or reading this new generation of French intellectuals made you think you were back in 1944, when life was a struggle against received ideas and oppressive laws, a fight for freedom, for the right to say and write whatever you pleased. But so much had been said and written since the Liberation.

I speak of these times in *The Fifth Son*:

America, Europe, and Asia underwent deep, gripping convulsions on a global scale, shaking the youth of my generation. . . .

Ideas and ideals, slogans and principles, rigid old systems and theories, anything linked to yesterday and yesteryear's supposed earthly paradise was rejected with rage and scorn. Suddenly children struck fear in their parents, students in their teachers. In the movies it was the criminal and not the police who won our sympathy, the malefactor and not the lawman who had the starring role. In philosophy there was a flight to simplicity, in literature a negation of style. In ethics humanism stirred laughter. . . . Universities no longer taught literature or sociology but revolution and counterrevolution, or even counter-counterrevolution of the right, the left, or somewhere in between. Students could no longer write a sentence or formulate a coherent thought, and they were proud of it. If a professor happened to voice his displeasure, he was boycotted, called a reactionary, told to go back to his university titles, scholarly works, and archaic concepts. Next time let him be born into another society, another era.

These insurgents, with their fiery dreams, accomplished the ouster of General de Gaulle. It was patricide.

The Czechoslovak insurgents and fighters suffered a more tragic fate: Their spring was extinguished. The Soviet tanks smothered the fervor of Alexander Dubček's supporters, and the world did not take action. Yes, I know, tender souls cried out, speeches were made. But Moscow didn't care. Its tanks crushed Prague. And Lenin did not awake to tell his disciples they had all gone mad.

In the United States the Democratic Party fell victim to the student rioting. Hubert Humphrey lost the election, fulfilling Richard Nixon's dream of living in the White House. A star appeared in the international political firmament: Henry Kissinger, a refugee from Germany and a respected political scientist from Harvard. I shall write more about this soon.

On April 2, 1969, in the Old City of Jerusalem, an ancient synagogue, the Ramban, that had been destroyed by Jordan in 1948, was opened for a wedding. Officiating was Saul Lieberman, who insisted that a local rabbi also be present. (After all, rabbis have to make a living too.) Time was of the essence, for it was the eve of Passover, and guests would have to hurry home to prepare for the holiday.

Bea and Hilda were there with their families. There were a few cousins, many friends. The groom's mind wandered, seeking others who were absent. For this was a day he had in some ways dreaded, and now he feared being unable to contain his emotions. He should have been happy at the thought that his parents would have approved of his getting married. But he wasn't happy.

As Lieberman recited the seven customary prayers blessing the couple, the groom, overwhelmed by sadness, saw neither his two older sisters, nor his nephews, nor his cousins, nor even his wife-to-be. He saw himself, as a child and then as an adolescent, at home, far away. He saw his father, his head slightly bent, and his mother, biting her lip. The night before, he thought that he must go and invite them to the wedding. Custom dictates that before his wedding an orphan go to meditate at the grave of his parents, respectfully requesting the honor of their presence. But this groom's parents, like millions of others, had no grave of their own. All Creation was their cemetery.

The people shouted *mazel tov*, wishing the newlyweds joy, happiness, and peace, showering them with all the good wishes in the lexicon of the living. People shook hands and kissed. Cousin Eli Hollander wanted to sing a wedding song, but the groom dissuaded him. Jubilation might offend those who weren't there.

Back in New York the Shabbat before — known as *Shabbat Hagadol,* or the Great Shabbat — an *aufruf* had been improvised in his honor at the small Hasidic *shtibel* he attended with his friend Heschel. In the congregation there were many survivors of the ghettos of Warsaw and Lodz, and of Treblinka.

Heschel had organized it all with Reb Leibel Cywiak. When the groom was called to the Torah to recite the appropriate blessings, almonds, raisins, and candy began raining down upon him.

After the service there was a Kiddush where wine, liqueurs, and cakes were served. Seated at the table, Reb Leibel and Heschel followed tradition by praising the groom. Joyous tunes were sung. There was dancing, frenetic Hasidic dancing of great fervor.

And the groom could no longer hold back his tears. He who since his liberation had always managed to control himself let go. The more his friends urged him to sing, to dance, the more he sobbed. The Hasidim pretended not to notice.

On the wedding day, in accordance with rabbinical law, two witnesses accompanied the newlyweds to the door of their room, on the sixth floor of the King David Hotel. The window overlooking the Old City was open.

Of what does a man dream when he is forty years old and has made the decision, consecrated by the Law of Moses, to make a home with the woman he loves?

He sees himself as a child, clinging to his mother. She murmurs something. Was it something about the Messiah? He feels like telling her, "You died, and He didn't come. And even if He does, it will be too late." He walks with his father to Shabbat services, and suddenly finds himself in the ranks of a procession toward death. He wishes he could reassure his father, console him: "Don't worry, your son will try to be a good Jew." But he says nothing. He soundlessly calls to a gravely smiling, beautiful little girl and caresses her golden hair. His thoughts scale mountains and hurtle down steep pathways, wander through invisible cemeteries, both seeking and fleeing solitude and receiving stories already told and those he has yet to tell.

Glossary

Aggadah   Traditional Jewish literature, especially commentaries, aphorisms, legends of the Talmud

ahavat Israel   Love for, attachment to, the Jewish people

aliyah   "Ascent" to Jerusalem; by extension, immigration of Jews to Israel

Amidah   The major daily prayer

bar mitzvah   The ceremony marking the assumption of adult religious responsibilities, at age thirteen

Beit Hamidrash (or Beit Midrash)   A House of Study and Prayer

Betar   An organization of Jewish Zionist youth

Bund   The European Jewish socialist movement preaching development of Jewish communities in their countries of exile

Eretz Israel   The land of Israel

Haganah   A Jewish paramilitary self-defense organization in Palestine

Halachah   The body of rabbinical Law

734

Hasid (pl.: Hasidim) Literally, "pious man." A disciple of the movement founded by the Baal Shem Tov and influenced by the Kabala

havdalah The separation ceremony marking the end of Shabbat

heder A religious elementary school; Hebrew school

Irgun A Jewish nationalist organization fighting against the British occupation in Palestine

Kabala The study (or practice) of Jewish mystical sciences

Kaddish The prayer for the dead

kavanah Concentration of the mind on prayer or other religious acts

kiddush The evening prayer before meals on Shabbat or holidays

kipa The skullcap, or yarmulka, worn by Jewish males

kosher Ritually pure, in accordance with the dietary laws

Kol Nidre The prayer opening the Yom Kippur evening service

Lehi An underground Jewish organization opposed to the British presence in Palestine; also known as the Stern Gang

Maariv The evening service

maggid A preacher

Makhzor The prayer book for Jewish holidays

Mapai The Labor Party in Israel

melamed A teacher who gives elementary religious instruction

Midrash Commentary and exegesis on the Scriptures

Minha The afternoon service

minyan The quorum of ten men required for a communal religious service

Mishna The collection of rabbinical laws and decisions

mitzvah A divine commandment

Musaf The additional service following the main morning service on the Shabbat and holidays

Musar A movement founded in Lithuania to foster the teaching of traditional Jewish values and ethics

niggun A song or melody

Nyilas The Hungarian anti-Semitic, fascist party

Palmach The elite Haganah troops recruited from kibbutzim

Pesach Passover, the Jewish holiday celebrating the Exodus from Egypt

phylacteries See **tefillin**

Purim The holiday (marked by games, exchanges of gifts, and skits) commemorating the victory of Persian Jews over their enemy Haman

Reb A title of respect accorded any man versed in study

Rebbe The title accorded a Hasidic master

Rosh Hashana The Jewish New Year

rosh yeshiva The director of a rabbinical academy

Shavuot The holiday commemorating the revelation of the Law on Mount Sinai

Shekina The presence of God among His people

Shma The fundamental Jewish prayer, Shma Israel: Hear, O Israel, the Lord is our God, the Lord is One

shofar A trumpet made of a ram's horn used on Rosh Hashana and Yom Kippur

shtetl A Jewish village in Eastern Europe

shtibel A Hasidic place of prayer

shtreimel A wide-brimmed fur hat traditionally worn by Hasidim

sidra A passage of the Bible read at synagogue on Shabbat

siddur Prayer book

talit Ritual prayer shawl

Talmud The collection of rabbinical teachings and commentaries

tefillin Phylacteries — two small leather boxes containing four excerpts from the Bible, one strapped to the left forearm and one to the forehead during weekday morning prayers

Tetragrammaton The four-letter representation of the ineffable name of God

Tisha b'Av A day of fasting in memory of the destruction of the Temple

Torah The body of Mosaic Laws given in the Pentateuch and by extension in the whole Bible

Tsahal The Israeli army

tzaddik One of the Righteous, who seeks social, moral, and religious perfection

yeshiva A Talmudic school

Yishuv The Jewish community in Palestine before the establishment of the state of Israel

Yizkor The service in memory of the dead

zemirot The canticles sung during Shabbat meals

Zohar The Book of Splendor, which is the major work of the Kabala, esoteric commentary on the Pentateuch

A Note about the Author

Elie Wiesel is the author of more than thirty books, including his unforgettable international best-sellers Night *and* A Beggar in Jerusalem, *winner of the Prix Médicis. He has been awarded the Presidential Medal of Freedom, the United States Congressional Gold Medal, and the French Legion of Honor with the rank of Grand Officer. In 1986, he received the Nobel Peace Prize. He is Andrew W. Mellon Professor in the Humanities and University Professor at Boston University. He lives with his wife, Marion, and their son, Elisha, in New York City.*